WAR, STRATEGY & HISTORY

ESSAYS IN HONOUR OF PROFESSOR ROBERT O'NEILL

WAR, STRATEGY & HISTORY

ESSAYS IN HONOUR OF
PROFESSOR ROBERT O'NEILL

EDITED BY DANIEL MARSTON
AND TAMARA LEAHY

PRESS

Published by ANU Press
The Australian National University
Acton ACT 2601, Australia
Email: anupress@anu.edu.au
This title is also available online at press.anu.edu.au

National Library of Australia Cataloguing-in-Publication entry

Title:	War, strategy and history : essays in honour of professor Robert O'Neill / editors: Daniel Marston, Tamara Leahy.
ISBN:	9781760460235 (paperback) 9781760460242 (ebook)
Subjects:	O'Neill, Robert J. (Robert John), 1936-
	Strategy.
	War.
	Military history.
	Festschriften--Australia.
Other Creators/Contributors:	
	Marston, Daniel, editor.
	Leahy, Tamara, editor.
Dewey Number:	355.02

All rights reserved. No part of this publication may be reproduced, stored in a retrieval system or transmitted in any form or by any means, electronic, mechanical, photocopying or otherwise, without the prior permission of the publisher.

Cover design and layout by ANU Press.

Cover photograph: THE XUYEN MOC BATON. This hand-carved baton was presented to Captain Bob O'Neill by the commander of Xuyen Moc District, Phuoc Tuy Province, Vietnam, Captain Duc, on 4 October 1966. O'Neill made the first visit to this isolated outpost by allied personnel after the arrival of the 1st Australian Task Force in the province. Bob, his interpreter and assistant, and RAAF helicopter pilot and co-pilot, had no confirmation that they were flying into and landing in a secure area. All went well and Captain Duc showed his gratitude by presenting O'Neill with this baton just before departure. Photograph: Stuart Hay.

This edition © 2016 ANU Press

Contents

List of Acronyms and Abbreviations vii

Foreword ix
Michael Howard

1. Exploring Political–Military Relations: Nazi Germany 1
Gaines Post

2. Vietnam: A Winnable War? 15
Ashley Ekins

3. The Vietnam Chapter 31
Tony White

4. A Strategic Career 39
Desmond Ball

5. Robert O'Neill and Australian Security Policy 47
Paul Dibb

6. Robert O'Neill and the Australian Official War Histories:
Policy and Diplomacy 61
Peter Edwards

7. The Evolution of Australian Official War Histories 73
David Horner

8. The Postwar Evolution of the Field of Strategic Studies:
Robert O'Neill in Context 91
Catherine McArdle Kelleher

9. Strategic Studies in Britain and the Cold War's Last Decade . . . 107
Lawrence Freedman

10. The Uncomfortable Wars of the 1990s 127
John Nagl and Octavian Manea

11. A Mission Too Far? NATO and Afghanistan, 2001–2014 155
Mats Berdal

12. Theory and Practice, Art and Science in Warfare:
    An Etymological Note 179
    Beatrice Heuser

13. A Pivotal Moment for Global Nuclear Arms
    Control and Disarmament Policies: The Contribution
    of Robert O'Neill. 197
    Marianne Hanson

14. Robert O'Neill's Institutional Leadership: The End of the
    Cold War and the Re-emergence of a Global World Order 217
    John Hillen

15. Lessons for Iraq and Afghanistan 235
    Carter Malkasian and Daniel Marston

16. Robert O'Neill and the Birth of ASPI 251
    Hugh White

17. The Rumble of Think Tanks: National Security and Public
    Policy Contestability in Australia 265
    Allan Gyngell

18. Australian Thinking About Asia 285
    Michael Wesley

Contributors 301

Index 309

List of Acronyms and Abbreviations

1ATF	1st Australian Task Force
1RAR	1st Battalion, Royal Australian Regiment
2IC	Second-in-Command
AAA	American Australian Association
ACRI	Australia–China Relations Institute
ADF	Australian Defence Force
AIIA	Australian Institute of International Affairs
ANSF	Afghan National Security Forces
APEC	Asia-Pacific Economic Cooperation
ARF	ASEAN Regional Forum
ASEAN	Association of Southeast Asian Nations
ASPI	Australian Strategic Policy Institute
AUMF	Authorization for Use of Military Force
CEE	Central and Eastern Europe
CFE	Conventional Forces in Europe
COIN	Counter-insurgency
EU	European Union
FCO	Foreign and Commonwealth Office
ICNND	International Commission on Nuclear Non-proliferation and Disarmament
IISS	International Institute for Strategic Studies
INF	Intermediate-Range Nuclear Forces
ISAF	International Security Assistance Force
JIO	Joint Intelligence Organisation

KLA	Kosovo Liberation Army
LSE	London School of Economics and Political Science
MOOTW	Military Operations Other Than War
NATO	North Atlantic Treaty Organization
NFZ	No Fly Zone
NGO	Non-Government Organisation
NLF	National Liberation Front (National Front for the Liberation of South Vietnam)
NPT	Non-Proliferation Treaty
OEF	Operation Enduring Freedom
OSCE	Organization for Security and Co-operation in Europe
PGM	Precision Guided Munition
PRT	Provincial Reconstruction Team
QIP	Quick Impact Project
R2P	Responsibility to Protect
RMC	Royal Military College
RUSI	Royal United Services Institute
SA	*Sturmabteilung*
SDI	Strategic Defense Initiative
SDSC	Strategic and Defence Studies Centre
SIPRI	Stockholm International Peace Research Institute
SS	*Schutzstaffeln*
START	Strategic Arms Reduction Talks

Foreword

Michael Howard

Fifty years ago, I compiled a Festschrift for Sir Basil Liddell Hart. Naturally, a key contribution had to be something about his influence on German military doctrine, which I had lined up a distinguished German scholar to provide. At the critical moment, he fell ill. I desperately asked Basil's advice about a replacement, and he made rather a surprising suggestion. There was a very able young Australian Rhodes scholar, he said, who had been consulting him about the thesis he was writing on the German Army and the Nazi Party. Why not try him? I did, and Captain Robert O'Neill produced, bang on time, a superb contribution that more than held its own in the company of those by, among others, Andre Beaufre, Henry Kissinger, Yigal Allon, and Alastair Buchan.

A few months later I found myself acting as an examiner for Bob's PhD thesis. In order to write it Bob had taught himself German well enough not only to read the relevant documents, but to seek out and interview many of the German officers and their relations who figured in his pages. It was a path-breaking piece of scholarship that could have led him straight into a distinguished academic career, had he not decided to remain in the Australian Army for long enough to serve in Vietnam and gain some first-hand experience of war. Had he remained in the army, he would certainly have gone straight to the top of his profession. As it was, after publishing another path-breaking work on General Giap, he reverted to academic life, where he was rapidly snapped up to undertake the thankless but essential task of writing the official history of Australia's role in the Korean War, a work that remains an indispensable — and highly readable — source for historians.

Military history remained a major interest for Bob, but it was rapidly overtaken — as it was for many other historians of his generation — by the broader field of strategic studies. He had been in England in the 1960s when we were getting the International Institute for Strategic Studies (IISS) under way, and he became one of our earliest members. After he joined the staff of The Australian National University, we kept closely in touch with his activities, and he with ours. When we were seeking a new director in 1982, the experience Bob had gained and the contacts he had made while running the Strategic and Defence Studies Centre in Canberra made him the obvious choice. All his predecessors had been European and their interests focused on the Cold War. Bob's Antipodean background and contacts enabled him to make the institute truly global at a moment when the Atlantic was ceasing to be the storm-centre of the world, and Japan, Korea, India, Pakistan, and Southeast Asia were becoming major actors on the strategic stage.

The five years that Bob spent at the institute gave him an international reputation. When the Oxford Chair of the History of War fell vacant in 1987, he chose to don the gown again and returned to the parochial world of academe. As his predecessor in that chair, I had eased his path by instituting the Gallipoli campaign of 1915 as a special subject for undergraduates, which he taught with all the enthusiasm and expertise to be expected from his background. He strengthened the strategic elements in the international relations courses already established by his fellow countryman Hedley Bull in the previous decade, and he brought new vigour to the extension of postgraduate studies throughout the university. At the same time, his extra-mural activities established him as a national figure. He became a member of the Commonwealth War Graves Commission, Governor of the Ditchley Foundation, a Rhodes Trustee, a trustee and later Chairman of the Imperial War Museum, and — not least — Chairman of the Council of the IISS, in which capacity he steered the institute through a constitutional crisis that had threatened to wreck it, and laid the foundations for the enormous expansion it has undergone over the past two decades. Then, at the dawn of the new millennium, he returned to Australia to pick up the threads that he had temporarily dropped 19 years before, and to begin a further, but by no means final, stage in a remarkable career.

How did Bob do it? There have been, of course, costs. After his return to academic life he wrote little. But his record of publication already spoke for itself, and he inspired plenty of his pupils to take up the challenge. But basically the key to his success has been his personality. He has an air of easy authority that immediately inspires confidence and marks him out as the obvious person to take charge of any enterprise to which he has set his hand. I have watched Bob's career for over half a century, and have seen how in every field in which he has been involved, he has won not only the respect of his colleagues, but their deep affection. He is a chairman made in heaven.

It is impossible not to like Bob. He is not just exceptionally able, but is an extraordinarily nice man. And he has had one supreme advantage: he has been blessed, in Sally, with an extraordinarily nice wife. God bless them both!

1

Exploring Political–Military Relations: Nazi Germany

Gaines Post

I met Bob O'Neill at Oxford University in October 1961. We were lieutenants. He was on temporary leave from what he presumed would be a career in the Australian Army. I had just finished my tour of active duty in Germany with the US Army, delighted to return to civilian life shortly after the Berlin Crisis had threatened to ignite the Cold War and extend my service for at least another year. We were Rhodes scholars: he at Brasenose College, I at New College. And we were oarsmen, members of our colleges' first eights, mine bumping his during Eights Week in June 1962, the only bump in our long friendship.

For our generation, 'the war' meant the Second World War. We had memories of that war, and mentors who had fought in it, among them the Warden of Rhodes House, E. T. (Bill) Williams, Field Marshal Montgomery's Chief of Intelligence in North Africa and Europe. In my conversations with Bob about military history, the Second World War was usually the central reference point, and soon our scholarly interests converged on Germany before and during the conflict.

In the English-speaking world, anti-German sentiment had waned since Germany joined NATO in 1955, six years after the establishment of the German Federal Republic, 10 years after American occupation forces posted signs in their sector of Germany saying, '*Ihr seid schuldig*' ('You are guilty'). In 1946, while the Nuremberg trials were under way, philosopher Karl Jaspers had written compellingly about individual and collective guilt (*Die Schuldfrage* — translated into English as *The Question of German Guilt*),[1] but more than a decade passed before West Germans began earnestly confronting their Nazi past. Two indicting novels published in 1959 were widely read: Heinrich Böll's *Billard um halbzehn* (*Billiards at Half-Past Nine*), and Günter Grass's *Die Blechtrommel* (*The Tin Drum*).[2] When the trial of Adolph Eichmann opened in Jerusalem in April 1961, West German television followed it, and the city of Frankfurt published a booklet refuting claims that most Germans knew nothing about Nazi brutality against the Jews. Later that year, large audiences watched the appallingly explicit television series *Das Dritte Reich*.

At the same time, postwar historiography had been shaped in part by authors who found the origins of Nazism in German autocracy, militarism, and anti-Semitism dating back to the Middle Ages and Reformation. William Shirer's *The Rise and Fall of the Third Reich*[3] was a bestselling example of this 'Luther to Hitler' thesis, in which long distances of German history are marked by signposts of continuity and inevitability. This was a far cry from Alan Bullock's measured biography of Hitler as opportunist, *Hitler: A Study in Tyranny*.[4] Many academic historians criticized Shirer, but even some of these applied inevitability to the fall of the Weimar Republic: it was doomed to fail by inherent flaws, irreparably wounded by the civil unrest and devastating inflation of the early 1920s, and (never mind the relatively stable years of 1924–1929) knocked off by Nazis and their sympathisers during the Great Depression.

For recent German military history, Oxford students in the early 1960s read B. H. Liddell Hart's *The German Generals Talk*, John Wheeler-Bennett's *The Nemesis of Power: The German Army in Politics, 1918–1945*, Gordon Craig's *The Politics of the Prussian Army, 1640–1945*, and, among the few German works in translation, Walter Görlitz's

---

1   Jaspers, Karl (1947) *Die Schuldfrag* [*The Question of German Guilt*], Munchen: Verlag.
2   Böll, Heinrich (1959) *Billard um halbzehn* [*Billiards at Half-Past Nine*], Munchen: Verlag; Grass, Günter (1959) *Die Blechtrommel* [*The Tin Drum*], Munchen: Verlag.
3   Shirer, William L. (1960) *The Rise and Fall of the Third Reich*, New York: Simon and Schuster.
4   Bullock, Alan (1952) *Hitler: A Study in Tyranny*, London: Harper & Row.

History of the German General Staff.[5] Liddell Hart had interviewed captured generals, among whom he found three types: old style Prussians, younger 'blustering and boorish' officers favoured by the regime, and, in the majority, 'essentially technicians, intent on their professional job, and with little idea of things outside it'. There was broad consensus among Anglo-American historians on several themes regarding the army in the 1930s: the continuity of Prussian influence on the values of the officer corps (obedience, loyalty, duty, bravery); the broad support among officers for reviving Germany's military power and regaining territories lost in the Treaty of Versailles; the overlapping jurisdictions of military and Nazi organisations; the High Command's readiness for the armed forces to swear allegiance to Hitler (instead of the constitution) after the death of President von Hindenburg in August 1934; and the major changes in the High Command's leadership and organisation in early 1938 that strengthened Hitler's authority over military planning.

When I left Oxford in the summer of 1963 to begin graduate studies under Gordon Craig at Stanford, Bob had received permission from the Australian Army to stay on for an advanced degree. Having observed his keen and resolute mind at work, I was certain he would find his own way. He did so, albeit with guidance from Williams, Liddell Hart, Wheeler-Bennett, and, above all, Norman Gibbs, who supervised the doctoral thesis that became *The German Army and the Nazi Party, 1933–1939*.[6] In his acknowledgments, Bob also thanked Michael Howard, Professor of War Studies (and founder of that department) at King's College London. No one would have guessed the continuity imbedded in that roster: Howard succeeded Gibbs as Oxford's Chichele Professor of the History of War in 1977, and O'Neill followed Howard in 1987.

Bob's book was the first on this subject to be written by a member of our generation. It offered a fresh approach in several ways — sources, judgments, ambiguities. It remains a fine example of how skilled apprentices can equal or surpass distinguished masters. In this case, I'm certain that generation was decisive. Bob was old enough to

---

5   Hart, B. H. Liddell (1948) *The German Generals Talk*, New York: William Morrow; Wheeler-Bennett, John (1953) *The Nemesis of Power: The German Army in Politics, 1918–1945*, London: Macmillan; Craig, Gordon (1956) *The Politics of the Prussian Army, 1640–1945*, Oxford: Clarendon Press; Görlitz, Walter (1953) *History of the German General Staff*, London: Hollis and Carter.
6   O'Neill, Robert J. (1966) *The German Army and the Nazi Party, 1933–1939*, London: Cassell.

remember the Second World War, and to have chosen a military career before the Vietnam conflict eroded the ideals of patriotism and service that the 'last good war' had inspired. He was a young enough military professional, with enough self-confidence and ambition, to wonder how seasoned generals of any country (US intervention in South Vietnam had begun to escalate) could get themselves into a war they were likely to lose. Nazi Germany provided a test case, and Oxford preferred history to political science. Bob set out not to condemn or exonerate anyone, but to see whether new material would help him answer the question as objectively as possible.

He found a lot of new material, and he had good command of German after studying the language for six years in school. He relied heavily on documents, most of which had been seized by the Allies after the war and were later returned to West German authorities, housed at the Bundesarchiv in Koblenz, the Militärgeschichtliches Forschungsamt in Freiburg, the Institut für Zeitgeschichte in Munich, and the Bibliothek für Zeitgeschichte in Stuttgart. He read published diaries and memoirs, and his list of secondary sources remains one of the best in the field.

A 'major piece of good fortune', as he now puts it, was his discovery in the Bundesarchiv of an account written after the war by General Freiherr Maximilian von Weichs. The Weichs paper, based on detailed notes he took at the meeting, documented Hitler's meeting with leaders of the armed forces and SA (*Sturmabteilung*) in late February 1934. It is one of several unpublished documents whose broader significance Bob was the first to reveal (more on this below). What made Bob's research unique, however, were his interviews with nearly 20 former generals and admirals of the Wehrmacht. These included Field-Marshal Erich von Manstein, Generals Franz Halder and Gotthard Heinrici, and Grand Admiral Karl Dönitz. Much less famous but far more instructive was General Hermann Flörke, to whom I introduced Bob by letter as he prepared to leave for Germany.

It was my good fortune to meet Flörke early in 1961 while I was stationed in Giessen, a small university city of little historical interest about 40 miles north of Frankfurt. Born in 1893 in Hanover, he served as a junior officer on the Western Front in the First World War and remained in the Reichswehr during the Weimar Republic. He fought on western and eastern fronts in the next war, rising to the rank of lieutenant general and in command of a corps that resisted the American First Army as it pressed north eastward from the Remagen bridgehead in April 1945. Flörke considered himself 'lucky to have surrendered to an American and a nice one too'. Released from detention in 1947, he soon became head of an organisation of German civilians who were employed by the American supply depot on the north east side of town. He had retired by the time I arrived in Giessen, but remained active in German–American organisations and was head of the local chapter of the *Verband deutscher Soldaten* (Association of German Soldiers).

In time, Flörke, his wife and step-daughter invited me to their apartment on Sundays, and conversation easily turned to history, usually with Schubert in the background and Mosel in the glass. The general always wore a bow tie and prefaced many of his remarks with 'one must consider' and 'one should not forget'. There was nothing militaristic about the man, whose modesty understated the distinguished record that I gradually pieced together with help from his family, from men who had fought under his command, and, during my own research a few years later, from German archives. He had received one of Germany's highest decorations, the *Ritterkreuz mit Eichenlaub* (Knight's Cross with Oak Leaves), awarded to him personally by Hitler in August 1944 for exceptional valour during the unrelenting Soviet offensive of that summer. He had allowed his officers and men more initiative in combat than was the norm, and had shown them more respect as individuals. Among superiors and subordinates, he was known as a fine commander who cared for his men, and they remembered him with affection.

Widely read in military history, Flörke could sketch Lee's gamble at Gettysburg and Grant's subsequent strategy of attrition. He reminded me that Germany and Europe had much longer histories with powerful symbols. 'One should not forget', he said about Germany's strategic position in the centre of Europe, that the Romans configured their line of fortifications (*Limes Germanicus*) so as to guard against a 'barbarian' invasion of their empire through the 'Fulda Gap' (where my artillery battalion would try to block the most likely route of a Warsaw Pact offensive into West Germany), or that Louis XIV burned Heidelberg.

We talked about the Weimar Republic, anti-Semitism, Hitler's popularity, genocide, and resistance. Flörke defined *Freiheit* (freedom) and *Geltung* (worth) as political assets that Germany lacked during the Weimar period. He justified Nazi foreign policy up to the invasion of Poland, which, he warned his battalion officers, marked the beginning of a long war that Germany would surely lose. We began disagreeing over topics that we would debate until his death in 1979. He emphasised a nation's freedom from international pressures, claimed that his units in Poland and Russia had no connection with the Final Solution, blamed Hitler for bad military decisions, and reproached the opposition movement for betraying the state while it was at war. I dwelt on personal freedoms, indirect connections, military advisers, and higher moral laws of insubordination.

Compassionate, cultivated, principled, and a gentleman in every sense of the word, General Flörke led me to reconsider the German Army as if I were serving under him. I would have respected and trusted him as my commander. In him I saw an example of loyalty and courage that did not suggest arrogance, blind obedience, or apolitical indifference. I could not have learned this from books.

Flörke had much the same effect on Bob. Bill Williams had told Bob that his wartime experience in intelligence taught him to be sceptical toward generalisations about the Wehrmacht. Flörke reinforced the point in his own way. In doing so, and in lending stature to Bob's inquiries, the German general enabled the Australian lieutenant to maximise the usefulness of his interviews.

While preparing to write this chapter, I interviewed Bob. He recalled being determined not to appear naïve or hostile, as had many Anglo-American interrogators since the war. 'Being a German-speaking Australian — not British — army officer helped a great deal', he added. He carefully prepared for each interview and began the conversation by putting the subject at ease. For example, he asked Manstein how he had managed to persuade Hitler to replace the High Command's plan for invading France and the Low Countries in 1940 (Operation Yellow) with his own 'sickle-slice' strategy of pushing through the Ardennes. Manstein happily obliged, Bob soon manoeuvred to the 1930s, and the interview lasted three hours.

Thanks to meeting Flörke shortly after arriving in Germany, Bob knew there must have been other 'relatively liberal and sensible' men who defied the stereotype of the German general. In the course of his interviews, he found some of them and evidence of others who, in the 1930s, were in the 'mid-level military class' — colonels and (brigadier) generals who had served in the Great War, many of them later hand-picked for the small officer corps of the Weimar Republic. Among these were sons of educated families in the middle or upper-middle class. Bob and I agreed that such officers fit none of Liddell Hart's three types, but constituted a fourth that Liddell Hart had either not found or wrongly included among 'essentially technicians'. Bob's interviews helped him augment documentary material while sharpening his eye for signs of this fourth type.

In *The German Army and the Nazi Party*, Bob describes three stages in which the small Reichswehr, which could hardly defend the Weimar Republic, was transformed into a large modernised force intended for conquest by the Third Reich: Hitler's immediate and positive impression on the entire army; the Nazi Party's skilful intervention in military affairs to increase the army's obedience to Hitler; and the High Command's eventual willingness to wage a war of aggression. Bob's research increased our understanding of these stages.

On 28 February 1934, 13 months after the Nazis seized power, Hitler called a conference of leaders of the army, SA, and SS (*Schutzstaffeln*). Everyone there knew that Hitler would address the conflict between army and SA over control of the 'people's army' that he would raise for national defence. To the relief of the officers, he announced that the army would exercise command, that the militia proposed by Ernst Röhm would be insufficient, that the Wehrmacht was the sole bearer of arms for national policy, and that the SA would be restricted to 'internal political tasks', although it could be used for pre-military training and protecting borders during the rearmament period. According to the account of General von Weichs, however, and corroborated by Manstein and Heinrici in interviews, Hitler unexpectedly 'set forth his complete foreign policy programme and … intimated the probability of aggressive war'. In about eight years, in order to counteract economic recession, Germany would need to create additional living space, 'the Western Powers would not let us do this', and thus 'short, decisive blows to the West and then to the East could be necessary'. Looking back after the war, Weichs regretted that the army's representatives 'did not take at face value these warlike prophecies ... The soldier was accustomed never to take the words of politicians too seriously.'

As Bob points out, Hitler had alluded to *Mein Kampf* and the need for living space when he met with army leaders only a few days after taking power. Since then, however, Hitler's successes had given the High Command more reason to take him at his word. Indeed, they did so when he said the SA would be limited to political tasks. In Bob's view, this would have been an opportune time for the generals to ask Hitler hard questions about long-term aims. Instead, they remained silent, thus postponing a reckoning over the mission of the armed forces. At that moment, they were gratified by Hitler's determination to rearm, and confident they had achieved victory against the SA. If any of them thought they could ward off Nazi ideology, they were deluding themselves.

Bob was one of the first historians (another was Wolfgang Sauer) to examine German Army–Nazi Party relations at the local level. He sifted the records of military districts (*Wehrkreise*) into which Germany was divided, and again interviews provided anecdotal substantiation. Nazi propaganda spread steadily into military commands and communities, from top down and bottom up. At the highest level were pro-Nazi generals such as Werner von Blomberg (Defence Minister 1933–1935, War Minister 1935–1938), Walther von Brauchitsch, and Wilhelm Keitel. Speeches and directives from the High Command to military districts contained this sort of language: since the 'Seizure of Power', it is clear that 'the change concerns not only [a new] political arrangement, but a fundamental transformation of the mind and will of the entire people, and the realization of a new philosophy';[7] National Socialism 'embraces the idea of the fellowship of blood ... and anyone today who does not completely adopt the idea of national partnership, excludes himself';[8] 'I make it the urgent duty of all Commanders to ensure, by example and by education, that the conduct of every single officer, in every case becomes positively National-Socialist'.[9]

---

7 Werner von Blomberg, September 1933.
8 Werner von Blomberg, May 1934.
9 General Friedrich Dollmann, Commander of the Ninth Military District, January 1936.

Political indoctrination steadily increased through officer training and unit instruction. Moreover, the High Command accepted the encroachment of Nazism at all levels of military life, affecting families and social relations through ideological materials in post reading rooms; prohibitions against shopping in stores owned by Jews; warnings to Christian churches not to appear disloyal to the state or the Nazi Party; requirements to invite local party leaders to dances and other social functions; and affirmations of the government's dividing Germany into 'Blocks' in which party officials could spread doctrine and ensure loyalty among neighbourhoods and households.

By 1938, the army had become enmeshed in the Nazi state, adapting to its structure, ideology, and rearmament for war. The SS had gained enormous political clout, expanding the Gestapo and political police, and forming its own volunteer fighting units, a threat to the army's role as sole bearer of arms. In February 1938, Hitler ordered major changes in the High Command, arrogating to himself the duties of War Minister and Commander-in-Chief of the Wehrmacht, establishing the Armed Forces High Command or OKW (*Oberkommando der Wehrmacht*) as his own staff for military planning, and appointing as its chief the pliable and sycophantic General Keitel. Any faint remaining chance of limiting or postponing war until Germany had completely rearmed was lost when General Ludwig Beck resigned as Chief of the General Staff in August 1938. Beck argued that using force against Czechoslovakia would lead to a European war that Germany was not strong enough to win. He also had this to say about the responsibilities of the army's leaders (taken from his notes for talks with Brauchitsch, Army Commander-in-Chief since February):

> Their military obedience has a limit where their knowledge, their conscience and their sense of responsibility forbid the execution of a command. If their warnings and counsel receive no hearing in such a situation, then they have the right and the duty to resign from their offices. If they all act with resolution, the execution of a policy of war is impossible.

They did not so act, as Beck had hoped some would when he resigned. Why not? For any historian, especially one who has served in uniform, that question lies at the heart of political–military relations. Friction is inevitable between professional soldiers, who have their particular goals, and politicians, who have theirs. Both camps must decide where and when to compromise. Bob recounts the accelerating preponderance of the political over the military in a particular case: during peacetime, in a one-party dictatorial state whose leader and ideology envisaged an offensive war of expansion. The German Army was neither totally subservient nor willing to stop the momentum. In the High Command and military district commands, old-school and largely apolitical conservatives welcomed the end of Germany's instability and military weakness, yet they also resented the increasing sway of pro-Nazi generals at the very top. We shall never know how many of these officers, or divisional and regimental commanders, actually skirted directives from Blomberg, nor how many might have been heartened by stronger examples of professional leadership when Hitler repeatedly defied the army's advice on the pace and purpose of rearmament. There were certainly more than Wheeler-Bennett or Craig surmised, perhaps more than Bob might have estimated from his interviews. On the other hand, military expansion brought in large numbers of junior officers and enlisted men whose views had been shaped by the Hitler Youth and Nazi propaganda. In February 1934, before the still small army had sworn allegiance to Hitler, its leaders were impressed by Hitler's resolve to rearm. In August 1938, with rearmament in full swing, the army acquiescent to Nazi propaganda, and war on the horizon, it was too late for all but Beck to act with resolution of their own before Hitler's stunning triumph at the Munich Conference in September.

Bob's book is still praised for its thorough research, detailed appendices, cogent personality sketches, and fair judgments of competing theses about the German Army. Although he did not overturn the established interpretation of a conservative military elite, he complicated it by finding a prudent and thoughtful type of officer, especially at the middle professional level, that Wheeler-Bennett and others had missed. Bob's work weathered the *Historikerstreit* (historians' quarrel) of the 1980s between those German scholars who believed the Third Reich was uniquely German and incomparably evil, and those who considered it but one — perhaps not even the worst — example of a dictatorship that committed mass murder. He is cited in both intentionalist and structuralist explanations of Hitler's preparations for war and genocide. *The German Army and the Nazi Party* remains an exemplar in the field, and its analytical framework of political–military friction, compromise, and imbalance provides a model for both history and political science. I would expand Bob's notion of 'political–military' so as to include career civil servants and heads of government departments, who can affect the balance of national policy one way or another, even in a dictatorship. Still, his general model certainly applies, with eerie echoes, to the 'revolt of the generals' in the spring of 2006, when six retired American generals publicly criticised Secretary of Defense Donald Rumsfeld for mishandling the Iraq War. A few of the six held that the war was unnecessary in the first place, and that the Joint Chiefs of Staff should have warned forcefully against undertaking it.

One can claim that studying the German Army in peacetime spared Bob's having to grapple with military complicity in the Final Solution, which later scholarship has shown to have been more widespread than he or I guessed, or with how wartime virtually sanctifies the soldier's duty to obey orders. I would argue that there is much to be gained by concentrating on what, in retrospect, are considered interludes or calms before storms. Such periods give us a chance to suspend our knowledge of their futures, to recognise anomalies, admit ambiguities, and consider alternative outcomes. They enable us to ask 'what if?' right up to the brink of what historians later mark as both an end and a beginning.

That is one reason why I became interested in the Weimar Republic. Certain that it was not doomed to fail, I devoted one book[10] and countless lectures to showing why, always subconsciously hoping that this time it would not collapse. I argued that, in its calmest years, 1924–1929, Weimar Germany combined democracy with authoritarian tendencies that might have endured even without the Great Depression and the rise of Hitler. The republic also mixed international cooperation with the pursuit of national objectives — particularly rearmament and recovery of territories lost to Poland and Czechoslovakia at Versailles — that would have shaken the European status quo, through war if peaceful means failed, as soon as the government deemed the strategic situation favourable. This was a Germany poised somewhere between the inevitability of Nazism and the likelihood of democracy and peace over the long term.

---

10   Post, Gaines (1973) *The Civil-Military Fabric of Weimar Foreign Policy*, Princeton: Princeton University Press

I described to my students the thrill of archival treasure hunts, on one of which I had found military documents that had neither been confiscated by the Allies nor cited by other historians. I told them about General Flörke, and about my correspondence and interviews — inspired by Bob's interviews that took place two years earlier — with other Wehrmacht generals and admirals who had served in the Reichswehr during the Weimar Republic. I had used chronological and factual filters to determine the accuracy of oral testimony. Although I trusted documents more than memories, I soon found the latter valuable for recapturing attitudes and weighing possibilities. I encouraged students to put themselves in other shoes: how could members of the Reichswehr, Defence Ministry, Foreign Office, Reichstag, and president's staff have collaborated so as to save the republic, with all of its ambiguities? In the conclusion to his book, Bob implicitly raises a similar counterfactual question: how could officers such as Flörke and Beck have restrained their superiors? Bob and I can imagine what we might have done in their place. But imagination can lead anywhere, and interviews can shock.

The reminiscences I heard sometimes drifted from Weimar into the Third Reich, testing my diplomatic skills. Heinrich Hausser, who joined the Waffen-SS in the 1930s and commanded one of its divisions during the war tested me the most. Toward the end of our conversation in his drab apartment in Ludwigsburg in May 1966, Hausser denied that the Waffen-SS was a racial elite: 'If you take the cream of the volunteers, you are bound to get many tall, fair men.' I held my tongue. Even taller than the men in his division, he continued as we stood up before I took my leave, were those in General Josef ('Sepp') Dietrich's *Leibstandarte Adolf Hitler*. (This unit had begun as a small bodyguard for the Führer in 1933, and during the war it became the most decorated division — and Dietrich the most popular commander — in the Waffen-SS. Dietrich died in Ludwigsburg a few weeks before my interview with Hausser, and around 7,000 Waffen-SS veterans attended the funeral.) Looking me up and down and nodding approvingly, Hausser said, 'Herr Post, you could have been in Sepp Dietrich's division'. That casual recruitment so rattled my nerves that, on the way back to my lodgings in Stuttgart, I stopped my VW and took a long walk.

I still look at German history through subjective and subjunctive lenses. So does Bob, although he left the field for a varied career that required detachment and pragmatism. As combat officer, scholar, teacher, and policy wonk, Bob has been at home in the expanding realm of university departments, research institutes, think tanks, and media panels dealing with political–military relations and strategy. Grounded in history, he can wrestle with causes and consequences. He can visualise Flörke and other generals at work. He can recognise a brink when he sees one. *The German Army and the Nazi Party* was a prelude.

2

Vietnam: A Winnable War?

Ashley Ekins[1]

In late 1966, Australia's military intervention in the Vietnam War reached a watershed. As soldiers of the 1st Australian Task Force (1ATF) completed the first six months of their deployment to South Vietnam, their commanders took stock. During a brief lull in the tempo of operations, Captain Robert O'Neill, intelligence officer with the 5th Battalion, Royal Australian Regiment (5RAR), prepared a paper at the request of his commanding officer. He examined the operational experiences of the battalion during the previous six months in Phuoc Tuy province and assessed the likely effectiveness of alternative approaches to operations in the future.[2]

In his rigorous analysis, Captain O'Neill made a number of observations, forecasts, and conclusions, many of which would prove prescient. 'The final outcome of this war', he wrote, 'will be determined by the feelings of the Vietnamese people. No purely military victory, however overwhelming, can provide a permanent solution unless the victory is won by the side whom the people favour.' Time was also a crucial factor, he noted, and clearly was on the side of the communist forces, not the

---

1   On behalf of my late colleague, Dr Ian McNeill, joint author of the volumes of official history of Australian Army ground operations in Vietnam, I acknowledge our debt to the scholarship, counsel, and inspiration of Professor Robert J. O'Neill, whose outstanding work has illuminated understanding of the Vietnam War and its complexities for a generation of historians.
2   O'Neill, Robert J. (1968) *Vietnam Task: The 5th Battalion, Royal Australian Regiment, 1966–67*, Sydney: Cassell, chapter 13.

United States and its allies. In a protracted war with little indication of a conclusive outcome, mounting casualties would inevitably erode domestic political support, and lead to war weariness and dissent among home front populations. Above all, O'Neill concluded: 'Control over the villages is the key to the war.' He conceded the necessity of conventional operations aimed at eliminating Viet Cong main force units, or at least restricting them to areas far from the centres of population. But the Vietnamese village, he maintained, 'is the closest equivalent to a front line in this war', and 'without victory in the villages the war can drag on'.[3]

These were mature and astute assessments by the 30-year-old army captain. They were based on his personal observations and experiences on operations, and informed by his military and academic training. In one of his first appointments after graduating from the Royal Military College, Duntroon, in 1958, O'Neill worked as assistant to Colonel F. P. Serong, then Chief of Staff at Southern Command Headquarters in Melbourne. 'Ted' Serong had acquired a legendary reputation as an authority on counter-insurgency, and his ideas made an impression on the young officer, who would continue to develop his own thinking on approaches to the war as his career developed and the conflict in Vietnam evolved. After completing an engineering degree at the University of Melbourne, O'Neill continued his studies at Oxford University as a Rhodes Scholar in 1961. He returned to Australia in 1965 with a doctorate in modern history for his thesis on the changing relationship between the German Army and the Nazi Party prior to the Second World War.[4]

In May 1966, he commenced a 12-month tour of duty in Vietnam. Serving initially as second-in-command of a rifle company of 5RAR, in August he was appointed intelligence officer and took over the intelligence section on battalion headquarters. This role involved him in the planning and command of operations. It also demanded, in addition to his knowledge and experience as a soldier, the application of his scholarly skills of research in gathering information from multiple sources, and analysis and interpretation to compile

---

3   O'Neill, Captain R. J. (1967) Memorandum: 'An analysis of the operational experience of 5RAR in Vietnam, May–Dec 1966', 5RAR, Ap An Phu, South Vietnam, 4 January 1967, paragraphs 2, 6–9, 11, 25, 26, personal papers of Robert J. O'Neill, OW90/4, Box 2, Australian War Memorial (hereafter AWM); copy in Official Historian's Collection, E/2/18, AWM 257.
4   O'Neill, Robert (1966) *The German Army and the Nazi Party, 1933–1939,* London: Cassell.

authoritative dossiers on the composition, activities, command structures, and probable plans and movements of the communist forces in the task force area of responsibility. The enemy formations present at that time comprised two strong Viet Cong main force regiments, a mobile Viet Cong provincial battalion, and local district guerrilla units, totalling over 5,000 troops and outnumbering the Australian Task Force of some 4,000 men. O'Neill's work was vital for the success of operations and required a deep understanding of the local situation. He became a keen observer with genuine empathy for the problems of the local South Vietnamese people, and an interest in their social and political structures, culture and economy, and military and civilian leaders. Most importantly for posterity, he recorded and published his impressions.

In early 1967, as he delivered his formal army memorandum analysing battalion operations, O'Neill also published — apparently without censorship or reproach by senior military authorities — a frank and enlightening article in the Australian journal *Quadrant*. He recounted the pattern of Australian military interactions with the local people of three typical Vietnamese villages over the previous six months, as the task force strove to force the Viet Cong away from the populated areas and assisted in the restoration of security and government control. He vividly described the dilemmas of the villagers, caught in a web of their own apathy and distrust, and stranded between the harsh realities of intimidation and the brutal exercise of terror by Viet Cong guerrillas, the anti-government propaganda and activism of local cadres, and forced recruitment, taxation, and persuasion through 're-education' by hard-core communist sympathisers. Amid this constant turbulence, Australian clashes with enemy units — including 6RAR's publicised victory in August at the battle of Long Tan — and the limited successes of various civil aid projects offered little more to the people than the promises of the remote government regime in Saigon. In his guardedly optimistic evaluation of the impact of the task force presence on the local population and the continuing war in Phuoc Tuy, O'Neill maintained that support for the people should be the primary focus of military intervention: 'the essence of victory in Vietnam', he wrote, 'is the battle for the hearts and minds of the millions of peasants who make up the country'.[5]

---

5   O'Neill, Robert (1967) 'Three Villages of Phuoc Tuy', *Quadrant* 11(1), pp. 4–10.

While on active service in Vietnam, O'Neill also compiled a comprehensive chronicle and commentary on the war. As a battalion intelligence officer, he was daily engaged in arduous and sometimes dangerous work. He was mentioned in despatches for 'his skill and industry in collecting and interpreting' intelligence sources while displaying 'high personal courage in seeking out and confirming information both by ground and air reconnaissance'.[6] Yet he somehow found the time and energy, often working from late at night into the early hours of the following day, to write regular, detailed accounts of the daily activities on operations of his infantry battalion and its 800 soldiers. These informal despatches he mailed home every few days to his wife, Sally, who typed and filed copies. During his leave on return from Vietnam, O'Neill wove them into an invaluable record of an Australian battalion at war. It was published in 1968 as *Vietnam Task*, a book that remains a seminal work as one of the first Australian unit histories from Vietnam and for its unique perspective as a soldier's personal account. In this and subsequent writings on Vietnam, Robert O'Neill was to pave the way for a generation of Vietnam War scholars by providing valuable observations, insights, and inspiration for later researchers.[7]

The war Captain O'Neill encountered on his arrival in South Vietnam in May 1966 had already become a focus of world attention. The conflict had increased in intensity since 1961, when the communist National Front for the Liberation of South Vietnam (NLF), supported and directed by the Democratic Republic of (North) Vietnam, began an armed insurrection aimed at destabilising and overthrowing the shaky government of the Republic of (South) Vietnam.

As Cold War tensions increased during the 1960s, the conflict in Vietnam assumed a disproportionate strategic significance. Vietnam became the focal point for a supreme struggle between the communist

---

6   Citation for Captain R. J. O'Neill, recommendation for Mention in Despatches (MID), 10 January 1967, Governor-General's file 5/5/29, CRS A2880, National Archives of Australia (NAA).
7   See numerous index references to Robert O'Neill in the three volumes on army operations of the nine-volume series, *The Official History of Australia's Involvement in Southeast Asian Conflicts 1948–1975*: McNeill, Ian (1993) *To Long Tan: The Australian Army and the Vietnam War 1950–1966*, Sydney, Allen & Unwin in association with the Australian War Memorial; McNeill, Ian and Ashley Ekins (2003) *On the Offensive: The Australian Army in the Vietnam War 1967–1968*, Sydney, Allen & Unwin in association with the Australian War Memorial; Ekins, Ashley with Ian McNeill (2012) *Fighting to the Finish: The Australian Army and the Vietnam War, 1968–1975*, Sydney Allen & Unwin in association with the Australian War Memorial.

bloc, and the United States and allied nations. The Hanoi leadership and their communist allies proclaimed their struggle to unify Vietnam under communist rule as part of an inevitable global transition from capitalism to communism, and a test case for the international solidarity of 'true communism'. Leaders in Washington promoted the war as a test case in the 'Free World's' struggle against communist wars of national liberation and as part of America's wider mission of containment of communism.

The commitment of Australian military forces to Vietnam was a process of gradual escalation against the backdrop of Cold War concerns over regional security and communist expansion. The Australian Government's rationale for the commitment embraced two objectives. Firstly, the government claimed, it sent forces to help support the emergence of an independent state in South Vietnam as a barrier to communist expansion in Southeast Asia. Versions of the domino theory were invoked, although the tenet that the survival of an independent Vietnam was crucial to Australia's strategic security was widely challenged. A second objective, arising from the first, was to remove the threat of oppression and terror which was believed to be the destiny of the 15 million people of South Vietnam if they fell under communist domination from the North. These aims were consistent with the strategy of forward defence, the cornerstone of Australian defence planning in the 1960s and a concept which meshed with the American strategy of containment of communism in Southeast Asia.

By supporting the United States in Vietnam, Australia also sought both to maintain an American presence in Asia and to secure a guarantee of American assistance in the event of Australia's own security being in jeopardy. A Defence Committee Report of the time considered it 'vital to Australia's strategic interests to have a strong United States military presence in South East Asia [and] to show a willingness to assist the United States to achieve her aims in South Vietnam'.[8]

In 1962, Australia made its first military commitment to Vietnam by deploying a team of 30 military advisers to assist in training South Vietnamese forces. By 1965, this team had expanded to 100 soldiers, working within a huge American advisory structure of some 16,000

---

8   Defence Committee Report, 'Further military assistance to South Vietnam', 6 April 1965, p. 4, para. 10, attached to DCA No. 13/1965, 6 April 1965, DMO&P file 161/A/3, AWM 121.

advisers. But it was becoming apparent that the communist insurgency in South Vietnam could not be stemmed solely with advisory and training assistance. The Viet Cong were continuing to grow in support and strength, and the tide of the war was turning against the South. In March 1965, the US began to escalate American military involvement through the first commitment of combat troops and the commencement of a massive aerial bombing campaign of North Vietnam. In late April, following America's lead, the Australian Government committed the first Australian combat troops to South Vietnam.

At each stage of involvement in the war, Australia's military commitment to Vietnam shadowed that of the United States. The first battalion of Australian ground combat forces entered the war in tandem with American forces and was integrated within an American brigade. Australian combat forces were progressively built up to maintain pace with the massive increase in American forces; both reached their peak in 1969. By late 1970 a wind-down and withdrawal of American forces was underway, with Australia awkwardly attempting to keep pace through a parallel wind-down, and the withdrawal of all forces was finally completed by mid-1973.

Australia's commitment, although substantial in terms of its military capabilities, was minuscule in comparison with the military contribution of the United States. Over three million Americans served in the war and the total number of American personnel in Vietnam reached a peak of over 542,000. Some 60,000 Australians served in the war, and at its peak strength of over 8,300 personnel in mid-1969, the Australian force in Vietnam comprised elements from all three services: an army task force of three infantry battalions with combat and logistic support, along with a separate army advisory team; air force helicopters, medium bombers, and transport aircraft; and navy support vessels, guided missile destroyers, and helicopters. For Australia, however, Vietnam was predominantly a ground war. The Australian Army conducted 85 per cent of operations and did most of the fighting — and most of the dying: soldiers suffered 96 per cent of Australian fatal casualties in Vietnam. Moreover, the nature and intensity of operations in Vietnam placed Australian soldiers into longer periods of contact, or imminent risk of contact, with the enemy than perhaps any time since the Gallipoli campaign of 1915.

As a minor partner in a large coalition force, Australia could exert little influence over the higher strategic direction of the war or the strategy employed in Vietnam. As in previous major conflicts, Australian ground forces came under operational control of an allied field commander. In making what amounted to an unqualified and open-ended commitment of combat forces in 1965, the Australian Government and its advisers forfeited their opportunity to negotiate wider war aims with those in the United States directing the war effort. They failed to evaluate the risks inherent in military involvement, and to assess the likelihood of victory or defeat. As historian Ian McNeill later wrote: 'The lack of a defined, clear aim at the highest level, or an agreed notion of what constituted success, prevented the adoption of a coherent strategy and bedevilled the whole conduct of the war.'[9]

Over time, it would become clear that the Americans too had not adequately considered and resolved many of these issues. Former US Secretary of Defense Robert McNamara later admitted that he and other defence advisers failed to ask the 'most basic questions' before deciding to commit troops. Would the fall of South Vietnam trigger the fall of all Southeast Asia? Would that constitute a grave threat to the West's security? What kind of war — conventional or guerrilla — was likely to develop, and could US troops win it, fighting alongside the South Vietnamese?[10] The latter unresolved questions, in particular, were to prove crucial to the tactical approaches adopted by Australian forces and their joint involvement in operations with American forces.

In May 1965, the 1st Battalion, Royal Australian Regiment (1RAR) and support forces, totalling 1,100 men, arrived in Vietnam and were placed under American operational command, joining the elite US 173rd Airborne Brigade as its third battalion. Initially confined to protecting the large American air base at Bien Hoa, 25 kilometres north east of Saigon, the battalion's role was later extended to include offensive operations in nearby regions dominated by the Viet Cong. The Australian unit performed outstandingly with the American brigade, notably during Operation Crimp in the Iron Triangle,

---

9   McNeill, Ian (1993) *To Long Tan: The Australian Army and the Vietnam War 1950–1966*, Sydney, Allen & Unwin in association with the Australian War Memorial, pp. 64–5; Ekins, Ashley with Ian McNeill (2012) *Fighting to the Finish: The Australian Army and the Vietnam War, 1968–1975*, Sydney Allen & Unwin in association with the Australian War Memorial, p. 691.
10   McNamara, Robert S. (1996) *In Retrospect: The Tragedy and Lessons of Vietnam*, New York: Vintage Books, p. 39.

breaching the vast Cu Chi tunnel network and discovering an important Viet Cong headquarters complex. However, Australian soldiers soon found themselves at odds with the very different American doctrine and tactical principles.

The Australians had come to Vietnam through their experience of counter-insurgency warfare in Malaya and Borneo, and training in low level, counter-insurgency warfare techniques. Their methods involved pacification, the restoration of government control, separating insurgents from the population, searching, patrolling, and ambushing, all concepts emphasising patience and stealth.

The Americans intended to fight a very different war. They had come to Vietnam through North Atlantic Treaty Organization (NATO) preparations for land warfare in Europe, and their experience in Korea. They favoured the direct approach, in which they could bring their numbers, mobility, and firepower to bear in order to kill large numbers of the enemy. The search and destroy operation evolved as the principal tactic of American ground forces, and body counts became the measure of success. In 1965, this strategy was probably the only way in which an impending communist victory could be thwarted in Vietnam. But the American attrition warfare approach often randomly destroyed Vietnamese lives and property, giving rise to the new military euphemism — 'collateral damage' — and alienating Vietnamese support. This approach also involved US willingness to risk high casualties to their own forces. Australian senior commanders firmly resisted American overtures to deploy the single Australian battalion on hazardous operations with an American mobile reserve force.

In mid-1966, as 1RAR's tour ended, the Australian commitment was expanded to an independent task force of two battalions with combat and logistic support. The increase in Australian ground forces was made primarily for diplomatic and strategic reasons, to meet American expectations, but it also had a sound military basis. Although the task force was still under American operational control, this arrangement enabled the Australians to operate more independently and to practise their own doctrine of counter-insurgency operations. The 1ATF established its base at Nui Dat, in the heart of the southern province of Phuoc Tuy, and quickly made impressive gains. By the end of 1966, as Robert O'Neill observed, the Australians were expanding their area of operations and consolidating government control over areas of the province.[11]

Throughout 1967, however, the limitations of the two-battalion task force became increasingly apparent. Despite the pressing need for tanks and a third infantry battalion, it took over 15 months before the government decided to commit the required forces — and then the decision was made, not on the basis of military necessity, but with a view to its impact upon the American alliance. It took a further three to five months before the third battalion and tanks finally arrived in Vietnam and joined the task force.

In the meantime, the under-strength Australian force struggled, with its limited manpower and combat resources, to pursue the elusive and aggressive Viet Cong forces which outnumbered the Australians in Phuoc Tuy province. For the want of tanks, in particular, numbers of Australian soldiers were killed and wounded during assaults against enemy bunkers and on operations around the Viet Cong stronghold in the Long Hai hills.

The lack of a third manoeuvre battalion and tanks mirrored wider weaknesses in the Australian force structure in Vietnam. This was to be a recurring problem throughout the Australian commitment. After years of neglect, the Australian Army was depleted in numbers and plagued by shortages of weapons and equipment; it lacked flexibility and was over-stretched in meeting its obligations under the government's strategic policy of forward defence. To compensate for manpower shortages, the task force included soldiers conscripted under the National Service Scheme introduced in late 1964. Over the course of the war, almost 64,000 20-year-old males were called up by a selective ballot system and enlisted in the army; over 15,000 of them served in Vietnam. The issue of conscription for Vietnam would become a principal source of dissent and opposition to the war, and a political millstone for the government, particularly as Australian casualties mounted.

---

11 O'Neill, Robert J. (1968) *Vietnam Task: The 5th Battalion, Royal Australian Regiment, 1966–67*, Sydney: Cassell, chapters 13 and 17.

To compensate for the limitations of his under-strength force, one task force commander attempted an innovative approach. In mid-1967, the task force laid a 12-kilometre-long barrier minefield to deny the Viet Cong access to the populated area in the southeast of the province, and to separate the guerrillas from their popular bases in the villages. The minefield contained some 21,000 anti-personnel mines; but it was not adequately secured by both Australian and South Vietnamese forces. Before long, the Viet Cong learned to remove large numbers of the mines and re-laid them, with disastrous effects on Australian patrols.

By mid-1969, the enemy mine campaign had produced the heaviest Australian casualties of the war, and the barrier minefield was widely viewed as the biggest blunder of the war. The enemy-laid mines inflicted an average of six Australian casualties per mine, with peaks of up to 18 casualties from a single mine incident. Occasionally, so many soldiers of a platoon were killed or wounded that the entire platoon became ineffective, forcing the curtailing of operations.

In early 1968, the task force increased in size and effectiveness with the addition of a third manoeuvre battalion and a tank squadron, becoming in the process a more balanced, brigade-sized force with enhanced flexibility and firepower. These additions were timely, coming just prior to the communist Tet Offensive. The tanks proved to be the decisive factor in several heavy enemy engagements. But the continuing limitations of the task force, even at its peak with three infantry battalions, armour, and other support elements, made it extremely difficult for commanders to mount protracted operations in depth into remote, enemy-held base areas without substantial US Army armour, artillery, air, and logistical support.

In response to the continuously changing nature and intensity of the war, successive task force commanders evolved their own concepts of operations and approaches to the war. But all faced the same operational dilemma: the requirement to simultaneously conduct conventional operations in depth to destroy the enemy's main forces, while also conducting pacification operations around the populated centres. The former involved the task force in operations in the remote, enemy-dominated areas of the province. Several commanders took the view that this was the most effective use of the task force. On the counter side, by keeping the enemy main forces at bay and on the move through operations in depth, the task force risked falling into an enemy strategic trap, as the communists could effectively use their main forces to keep the Australian troops occupied and far away from the unprotected villages, which were the real target for both sides.

The task force was required to conduct pacification and reconstruction operations to eliminate the influence of communist local forces, cadres, and infrastructure in the towns and villages. But it lacked the manpower, resources, and time to maintain a continuous presence in the pacified areas. Once it moved on, the Viet Cong quickly returned, and the communist infrastructure remained intact.

Many nevertheless believed the war in the villages was the main role for the task force and was of much greater importance than operations to pursue the enemy main forces. O'Neill was one such advocate. The 12-month experience of his battalion, he wrote in April 1969, had reinforced many of the lessons for conducting counter-insurgency warfare. He and many of his fellow officers were convinced that 'the solution to the Vietnam crisis lay in the villages rather than in the jungles', although there remained a need for Australian forces to pursue and defeat the communist main forces who were the enforcing arm of the North Vietnamese government in subjugating the South.

'But these actions will not win the war for either side', O'Neill wrote, 'they will simply help to prevent the winner from losing'.[12] With these words, he echoed the much quoted statement by US National Security Adviser Henry Kissinger: 'the guerrilla wins if he does not lose. The conventional army loses if it does not win.' Kissinger's full statement gives the aphorism its context:

> We fought a military war; our opponents fought a political one. We sought physical attrition; our opponents aimed for our psychological exhaustion. In the process we lost sight of one of the cardinal maxims of guerrilla war: the guerrilla wins if he does not lose. The conventional army loses if it does not win. The North Vietnamese used their armed forces the way a bull-fighter uses his cape — to keep us lunging in areas of marginal political importance.[13]

---

12   O'Neill, Robert (1969) 'Australian Military Problems in Vietnam', *Australian Outlook* 23(1), pp. 46–57; O'Neill, Robert J. (1968) *Vietnam Task*, p. 247.
13   Kissinger, Henry (1969) 'The Vietnam Negotiations', *Foreign Affairs* 48(2), p. 214.

By mid-1970, the influence of the communist forces was waning. Main roads had been opened, markets and trade were flourishing, local government in villages was more effective, and civic action had produced improved local roads, schools, market places, water supplies, and medical services. The task force had kept the enemy main force units from the populated areas and reduced Viet Cong influence over the population. As the Australians began a phased withdrawal from Phuoc Tuy, government control had been restored to large areas. But continuing success was dependent on the presence of the task force. The Viet Cong had the ability to withdraw into sanctuary and base areas, reform and recruit, and their infrastructure in the villages was not eradicated. After the task force withdrew in late 1971, the Viet Cong influence was expected to increase and erode government control.

After visiting Phuoc Tuy province and the task force headquarters in June 1971, Robert O'Neill, now a strategic analyst and head of the Strategic and Defence Studies Centre at The Australian National University, concluded that the outcome of the war in Indochina still lay in the balance. The main role of the Australian Task Force was now to secure the northern part of Phuoc Tuy province where there were an estimated 600 Viet Cong and North Vietnamese Army troops. If South Vietnamese territorial forces, numbering 6,000 in Phuoc Tuy, were unable to cope with that number of enemy forces once the Australians withdrew, 'then their whole situation is hopeless', O'Neill concluded. The South Vietnamese would need to develop experience in operating in the remote regions against the enemy, and they would lack the air support and mobility available to 1ATF. The quality of some of the local South Vietnamese forces was 'indifferent', but they were better equipped and armed than the communists. Security in the province would slip backwards once the local forces took over, but by how much remained unknown.[14]

Two months later, O'Neill again cautioned that although the task force had worn down the communist main force regiments and provincial force units over the past five years, the Viet Cong infrastructure had 'survived the Australian presence largely intact', and was able to

---

14 O'Neill, R. J. (1971) 'The War in Indo-China: A Conflict Still in the Balance', *Canberra Times*, 12 July. O'Neill visited 1ATF in June 1971 during a tour of Indochina. HQ 1ATF, message SD0988, 30 May 1971, 1ATF Commander's Diary, June 1971, [1/4/224], AWM 95.

observe, plan, and report on Australian movements. While the enemy was unable to eject the task force from Phuoc Tuy, he believed they 'can still do us a powerful amount of damage in a few short encounters, as recent events have shown'. The withdrawal could offer tempting opportunity targets to the enemy, and 'one must not forget D445 Battalion which must be ready for the fray again'.[15]

As the task force prepared to come home in November 1971, Creighton Burns, Assistant Editor of the Melbourne *Age*, assessed the Australian military effort in Phuoc Tuy. Burns noted that the Australians had kept substantial Viet Cong forces off balance, disrupted their supply systems, and occasionally inflicted heavy casualties on them; but they were never able to make Phuoc Tuy 'the model of counter-insurgency security' that the government maintained had been achieved. They were never properly equipped for that, and lacked the strength in numbers and supporting arms; any security provided by the task force instantly evaporated after the Australians moved on. After the Australians left Vietnam, Burns believed, the province would 'slowly revert to apathetic acceptance of Viet Cong control'.[16] In fact, the collapse came much quicker and more violently than he anticipated. Four months later, the communist Easter Offensive of March/April 1972 swept over Phuoc Tuy like a tsunami. An Australian officer who observed the security situation deteriorate to the levels he had experienced at the start of the commitment in 1966, observed in some amazement that it seemed 'as if we had never really been there'.[17]

In what would become a familiar pattern in later conflicts, there was a gulf between the claims made by politicians and diplomats vaunting the successful completion of the mission, and the more realistic assessments of soldiers with experience on the ground.

The United States had entered the war with laudable ambitions: to resist communist aggression and subversion, and to secure the independence of an emergent, democratic Republic of South Vietnam.

---

15   O'Neill, Robert (1971) 'Vietnam Departure Risks: While Packing Up — A Sitting Duck?', *Financial Review*, 27 September.
16   Burns, Creighton (1971) 'The War we Didn't Win', *The Age*, 15 November; Ekins, Ashley with Ian McNeill (2012) *Fighting to the Finish: The Australian Army and the Vietnam War, 1968–1975*, Sydney Allen & Unwin in association with the Australian War Memorial, p. 632.
17   Major F. A. Roberts, AATTV, 1971–1972, *Interview*, Canberra 2, 3, 10 February 1978, Part II, p 75, Canberra, AHQ file 707/R2/39 folder 11, AWM 107.

But frustration ensued as the war dragged on into a stalemate, followed by disillusionment and despair as it became a costly quagmire from which the US could neither withdraw honourably nor achieve a decisive victory.

When Saigon fell to a massive assault by conventional communist forces in April 1975, the damage to US prestige was profound. It was widely claimed that the world's greatest superpower had been defeated by a barefoot army of peasant guerrillas. This was a fallacy, but the failure of US military intervention in Vietnam continued to linger in American popular memory.

Military strategists and historians have long argued over the mistakes and lessons of the Vietnam War. Many of these arguments mirror the debates that took place during the war: how the conflict arose and developed, and the origin of American involvement; whether Vietnam was a civil war between nationalist and imperialist factions, or the focal point of a wider struggle between expansionist forces of communism and their containment by democratic capitalism; whether an enormous American military commitment to a geographically remote conflict was justified on the grounds of morality or national security; and whether the United States might have won the war through a different application of its military power.

The key to the American and allied defeat in Vietnam, however, lay in the failure of the political aims of the war, rather than the military struggle. From March 1965, when the first American combat forces arrived in Vietnam and the collapse of South Vietnam seemed imminent, the South Vietnamese Government could claim little real legitimacy to rule Vietnam. As former North Vietnamese Army Colonel Bui Tin argued, American military involvement managed to delay the communist defeat of South Vietnam, but the Americans and their allies were never able to establish the national consensus they had hoped to create: 'Rather they eroded it.'

Australia came out of the Vietnam War as awkwardly as it went in — still striving to gain access to American intentions and policy decisions, and vainly trying to influence the US to retain a strong military presence in the region.

By the most optimistic estimates, the intervention in Vietnam might be viewed merely as a holding action which may have bought time for neighbouring, emergent nations in Southeast Asia, allowing them to achieve political stability and economic security. For the nations of Indochina, however — Cambodia, Laos, and Vietnam — the war resulted in enormous human loss, ecological devastation, and economic ruin.

Australia's senior military leaders later drew definite lessons from the Vietnam War. Lieutenant General Sir Thomas Daly, Chief of the General Staff, and the senior soldier responsible for the Australian Army during the Vietnam conflict, argued: 'The major lesson is that we should never allow ourselves to become involved in a war that we don't intend to win. Holding campaigns are fruitless. They result in a loss of life which is incommensurate with the results achieved.'

Daly's judgments were echoed by the former Chairman, Chiefs of Staff Committee, General Sir John Wilton. The principal lesson of the war, said Wilton, was, 'don't go into a war unless you are prepared to win'. With that understanding, he said, 'you've got to employ all the resources at your disposal or which can be made at your disposal' in order to win. Combat operations against enemy forces are 'not something that you can just put one foot in and feel the temperature', Wilton argued, 'you've got to jump right in'. He believed the Americans 'greatly underestimated what the war would involve, right from the start. They came into it piecemeal and didn't fully appreciate the nature of the war in which they had become involved.'[18]

Debate continues over the reasons for failure, and whether different approaches and applications of military force may have succeeded. Proponents of conventional warfare claim that military force offered a rapid solution, while others maintain only an unconventional, counterinsurgency strategy could have been effective. Some argue that the war exposed the limits of American military power; others that the US misapplied its military power or failed to use it decisively and without limit. Some believe the US exaggerated the strategic significance of Vietnam, others that it misjudged the issues at stake.

---

18   Daly and Wilton quoted in Ekins, Ashley with Ian McNeill (2012) *Fighting to the Finish: The Australian Army and the Vietnam War, 1968–1975*, Sydney Allen & Unwin in association with the Australian War Memorial, pp. 705–6.

But many of these may even be the wrong lessons to draw. Most analysts agree that a more decisive use of conventional military force in Vietnam may have been counter-productive, or even have led to disastrous global escalation.

For Australia, the Vietnam War stands as a reminder that open-ended military commitments carry unforeseeable risks, even when based on perceived national self-interest and strategic advantages, or conducted for altruistic or humanitarian reasons. The costs can never be accurately foreseen, and the end result is rarely what was intended.

In what has become a timeless, pessimistic observation, the nineteenth century German philosopher Hegel said experience and history teach us that 'nations and governments have never learned anything from history, or acted upon any lessons they might have drawn from it'.[19]

The lessons from Vietnam are clear for those who will read them, as Robert O'Neill has amply demonstrated in his writings. He has also drawn insights from the parallels between Britain's enthusiastic commitment to the ill-considered Gallipoli campaign in 1915 and the more recent rush to war by the Bush Administration in the invasion of Iraq in 2003. He wrote in 2013:

> The lessons from history's page are obvious, but do we have politicians who are prepared to take the time necessary, and do the hard studying, to develop real expertise in the management of international security policy? The experience of the past decade suggests that we are as far away from that goal as were the national leaders of 1914–15.[20]

If political leaders fail to grasp the lessons then, hopefully, historians, strategic analysts, and veterans will perceive them and prove more persuasive. The experience of Vietnam shows that the costs can be too great to ignore the lessons of history.

---

19 Hegel, Georg Wilhelm Friedrich (1975 [1830]) *Lectures on the Philosophy of World History: Introduction*, Cambridge: Cambridge University Press, p. 21.
20 O'Neill, Robert (2015) 'Gallipoli: Foreshadowing Future Conflicts' in Ashley Ekins (ed.), *Gallipoli: A Ridge too Far*, Wollombi: Exisle Publishing, p. 302.

3

The Vietnam Chapter

Tony White

Between 1966 and 1967, Bob O'Neill saw 12 months of combat duty with an Australian army infantry battalion in Vietnam. It is not widely known that Australia was one of a number of countries — including Thailand, the Philippines, the Republics of China (Taiwan) and Korea, Spain, and New Zealand — which, alongside the US, constituted the so-called Free World Military Forces in the Second Indochina War (1961–1975). These allies supported the Government of the Republic of (South) Vietnam against insurgents of the National Liberation Front (NLF), which, in turn, was sustained by the communist regime of North Vietnam. As in the United States, in Australia there would later be bitter opposition to involvement in the Vietnam War. However, what is less well known is that, at the outset, the war had widespread popular support. The domino theory, whereby Southeast Asian countries would — one after another — fall to the southern thrust of communism, was entirely credible in this era of Cold War.

In 1962, Australia made a modest contribution to the Saigon-based anti-communist alliance by dispatching 30 military advisers to bolster South Vietnamese army units in the field. In a major escalation, combat troops from the US and Australia arrived in 1965, with an Australian battalion under US command. The following year, the Australian Government decided to send an expanded and autonomous task force under Australian command and operating in its own area.

In January 1966, Captain Robert J. O'Neill of the Royal Australian Corps of Signals joined the 5th Battalion, Royal Australian Regiment (5RAR) at its Holsworthy base on the outskirts of Sydney. 5RAR and a second battalion and supporting arms (artillery, armour, etc.) would constitute the task force. Bob's initial posting was as regimental signals officer commanding the signals platoon, but he was almost immediately transferred to the infantry corps and appointed second-in-command (2IC) in the battalion's B Company. Here his immediate superior was Major Bruce McQualter. Bruce had been a year ahead of Bob at the Royal Military College, Duntroon, and they knew each other well. Bruce was delighted to know that Bob would be joining the battalion, particularly as his 2IC. The job of a company 2IC is to understudy his commander. He is to be fully prepared to step into the role should the situation demand it, whether this be due to the absence, death, or disablement of his commander. In the meantime, the 2IC relieves his commander of many of the routine administrative and house-keeping chores associated with the lives of the 100 or so troops under their control.

The rationale behind the posting of a high-flying academic into such a prosaic job was undoubtedly to bring him down to earth and reacquaint him with the nuts and bolts of soldiering. Bob was soon to be seen involved in such tasks as overseeing the pouring of concrete slabs, and discussing soldiers' equipment and rations.

5RAR was a brand new battalion, founded on 1 March 1965, only 14 months before its deployment to Vietnam. Preparing a military unit for war is a considerable undertaking, involving prolonged, arduous training, and the development of leadership and teamwork at all levels to produce an effective fighting force. This preparation was complicated by the fact the battalion was the first to be made up of both conscripts and career soldiers — roughly 50 per cent of each. There was a degree of apprehension as to how the conscripts would adjust to the constraints of army life, but this soon proved groundless. Although there was always a widespread assumption that — sooner or later — the battalion would be sent to Vietnam, a formal order was not issued until less than three months before its departure to the war zone. This lack of certainty was something of an additional encumbrance to the preparations. Fresh reinforcements were still arriving in the final weeks and there was an atmosphere of haste and improvisation just short of chaos.

Bob did not slip into the battalion unnoticed. Here was a newcomer not only with an engineering degree from Melbourne University, but a Rhodes Scholarship and an Oxford doctorate. It was known that his doctoral thesis was shortly to be published as *The German Army and the Nazi Party, 1933–1939*. Such a stellar academic record certainly attracted widespread and intense interest in the battalion. Within military culture, however, deeds are generally valued more highly than words, and such a background could well have invited comments about ivory towers and detachment from reality. It was soon evident that Bob had his feet well and truly on the ground, and would be readily and warmly accepted by all ranks. He was, from the start, friendly and approachable. In conversation, it was apparent that he had an unfeigned interest in the other person's views. Bob's affability and early identification with the battalion contributed in no small way to the development of *esprit de corps* in this new unit. It also stood him in good stead when, a few months later, he was appointed to the post of the battalion's intelligence officer, where informal contacts are invaluable. Time was found for Bob to deliver a series of pre-departure presentations to the troops on the history and culture of Vietnam as well as the strategic situation, a task for which he was well equipped.

The battalion left Sydney for Vietnam in late May 1966. Vehicles and equipment sailed together with one company to the Vietnam port of Vung Tau aboard an aircraft carrier converted to a troopship. The rest of the troops flew into Saigon in a series of civilian flights.

Their first home in Vietnam was in tents on sand dunes above a beach on the South China Sea, close to Vung Tau and some 130 kilometres from Saigon. Here, in the relentless sweltering heat, the battalion sorted itself out, preparing for its first operation.

The Australian Task Force, of which 5RAR formed a part, had been allocated its own area of operations, the province of Phuoc Tuy, which lay on the coast to the east of Saigon. With a population of 103,000, the main industries of Phuoc Tuy were rice-growing, fishing, and charcoal burning. There were also extensive French owned and operated plantations of rubber trees. These had been established by the French colonists after World War I, and were still operating to a limited extent despite their situation in the midst of the communist insurgency. It was understood that there was a mutually beneficial financial arrangement in place between the French owners and the

NLF that enabled production to continue despite the war. Another main feature of Phuoc Tuy Province was the port of Vung Tau, through which passed a considerable volume of supplies for Saigon and beyond, thereby taking the pressure off Saigon's river port. With the exception of the port, the province capital (Baria) and scattered outposts, Phuoc Tuy was entirely in enemy hands at the time of the Australian Task Force's arrival in 1966. Road traffic, even in convoys, was subject to attack, road blocks, and NLF tax collectors. Movement at night was impossible.

On 24 May 1966, the battalion left the temporary beach camp and set forth on its first operation. Bob was one of 800 soldiers aboard an armada of four flights of 30 helicopters, clattering 30 kilometres inland over jungle and rice paddies, to land close to an abandoned rubber plantation. Their mission was to establish a permanent base (Nui Dat) from which the task force would operate. This would be their home for the next 12 months. No time was lost in erecting defences. Noise was minimised and no lights were to be seen after sundown. A program of active patrolling and ambushing commenced immediately.

The wet season in South Vietnam runs from May to October. The heat and humidity were oppressive and the common daily pattern was for torrential rain to fall for an hour or two each afternoon. Clothing and equipment would be saturated. The rich red soil soon turned to deep mud. Latrines in the early weeks were simply shallow trenches which would be progressively covered up by successive users. Anyone who has experienced camping in the rain would understand the practical difficulties of daily life, quite apart from the threat of enemy attack. Mosquitos, scorpions and snakes abounded, and chomper ants could eat their way through the soldiers' webbing and nylon ground sheets. For the first two months, the troops slept on the ground in bivouacs. Later, tents were erected, with a floor of sand trucked up from the beach, and life in the base area improved.

It was on day one of this first operation that Bob O'Neill began writing a journal. He used a small, loose leaf pocket book, and every few days for the next 12 months would mail the completed, often mud-stained pages to his wife, Sally, back in Sydney. Sally — herself a historian — typed up and edited these notes, which provided the material that Bob would use on his return to Australia to write an account of 5RAR's experience in Vietnam. This was published as *Vietnam Task* in 1968, and constitutes the battalion's official history. Being the first such account in Australia's 10 year involvement in the Vietnam War, the book attracted considerable attention and has remained a valuable reference.

During the year, 5RAR carried out a total of 17 operations in the province. Each lasted between two days and two weeks, after which the troops — tired, ragged, and filthy — would return to the Nui Dat base for a week or two to debrief, re-equip, and prepare for the next excursion. Many of the tasks consisted of cordon and search operations. Under cover of darkness, the battalion would creep up on a village overnight, to have it surrounded by first light, thus preventing the escape of potential enemy. During the following day, South Vietnamese army personnel would search the village and interrogate the inhabitants. While this was proceeding, the battalion conducted a medical clinic, food was distributed, and, on occasion, the battalion band entertained the villagers. These operations proved to be very cost effective at recovering weapons and documents, as well as apprehending Viet Cong suspects.

Bob was tasked with conducting the reconnaissance of the village of Duc My as preparation for the battalion's first such cordon and search operation. Moving hundreds of troops at night through enemy territory, silently and without lights, was highly hazardous, and a sound knowledge of the terrain on the approaches was essential to lessen the chance of disaster. Bob led his patrol of 30 men out of the base in the late afternoon. Monsoonal downpours and the need to skirt impenetrable clumps of bamboo and swampy terrain made navigation extremely difficult. His plan to use a creek leading to the village as a reliable guide proved impracticable — even for this small patrol — owing to the tangled undergrowth. To attempt to move the whole battalion along this route could have been calamitous. The patrol was nevertheless able to probe the perimeter of the village closely, to the extent of being able to hear a snoring sleeper, and returned safely to the base by sunrise. The information gained from this night reconnaissance was invaluable. The approach route was changed and the operation was carried out successfully shortly afterwards.

Illness resulted in the loss of 5RAR's Intelligence Officer and led to Bob's appointment to this position three months into his Vietnam tour of duty. This involved a move to battalion headquarters and brought him into close association with the senior officers, in particular Lieutenant Colonel John Warr, the Commanding Officer. Warr had seen service as a platoon commander in Korea and had been wounded. He was a perceptive leader who had a sound grasp of the nature of counter-insurgency warfare. This understanding was shared by the battalion's company commanders, most of whom had seen service in the Malayan Emergency in the 1950s, combatting communist guerrillas. The principles of this type of warfare were to separate the insurgents from the support of the civilian population, and to win the hearts and minds of the latter. This 'softly, softly' approach was backed by a program of quiet but relentless patrolling and ambush. This strategy was at variance with the US military higher command, who favoured search and destroy sweeps conducted by large forces, set-piece battles, and who attached greater importance to body counts. Bob was firmly in the Warr camp.

He immediately took to his intelligence officer duties with relish. To quote Major Max Carroll, 5RAR's Chief Staff Officer and Battle Second-in-Command:

> [H]e assumed the position the day before we commenced a major operation, the cordon and search of Binh Ba on 7/8 August 1966, for which all of the planning and orders had been completed. On his first day, on his own initiative, he produced an operational contingency plan, from the enemy Viet Cong viewpoint, to counter our actions against Binh Ba. His assessment was so accurate that it was taken to be a captured plan, which initially caused considerable alarm amongst some of our US allies! There is no doubt in my mind that as Intelligence Officer Bob found his true military metier. With his keen, analytical mind he was a natural; and his assessments were always well found, accurate and invariably accepted.[1]

Xuyen Moc, an isolated government outpost and district headquarters in the east of the province, attracted Bob's attention. The village had been cut off for five years. Farmers wanting to sell their produce in the province capital had to travel on a road dominated by the Viet Cong, who extorted a heavy burden of tax. Bob devised a risky plan to drop in on the village compound by helicopter to meet the district commander and gain an appreciation of the tactical situation. Communications were poor, and there was no way of knowing how secure the landing

---

1   O.M. Carroll, 5RAR S3 (Battle Second-in-Command), personal communication.

zone was. Accompanied only by his Vietnamese interpreter and his batman (a commissioned officer's personal assistant/bodyguard/general gopher), Bob was dropped into the compound by a helicopter which immediately departed to avoid presenting an attractive target to the enemy. It was a fruitful visit, and Bob was able to pass on valuable intelligence to the Australian Task Force commander, resulting in an expansion of government control in this part of the province and a reopening of the road.

On several occasions, Bob managed to inveigle his way into the US headquarters known as HQ 2 Field Force Vietnam at Long Binh to find out what was in the big picture. This was an act involving a high level of chutzpah. As a rule, these mid-level American staff officers would never have allowed a humble captain from one of their own battalions to walk into their headquarters asking all kinds of probing questions about what they knew about Viet Cong strengths and intentions. As it happened, they were intrigued by the irregular approach from this representative of their unfamiliar ally, and they opened up and gave him serious answers. Bob was able to pass the gist of it to the Australian Task Force intelligence people, which kept them tolerant of his unusual initiatives.

Bob was a strong supporter of the battalion's civil action program. This included the provision — whenever practicable — of medical care to Vietnamese civilians by the battalion doctor, performances by the brass band, and football matches and combined church services attended by villagers and soldiers. He would always make an effort to engage the locals in friendly conversation. A pleasant break from army rations — accompanied by the commanding officer and medical officer — was an occasional lunch in the colonial splendour of the residence of the French manager of the nearby rubber plantation.

Throughout the year, Bob continued to re-evaluate strategy in the light of the battalion's experience and intelligence gathered. He paid particular attention to the views of junior commanders and ordinary soldiers. Michael von Berg, who was decorated for his actions as commander of the reconnaissance platoon (the brainchild of the commanding officer and Bob), observed that Bob's debriefing sessions were always searching and thorough, but also helpful and encouraging: 'Bob's knowledge of the enemy and potential movements was pretty accurate and this helped me enormously as to what type of enemy you were likely to engage … When talking to Bob it's like you are the only person in the world because he is giving you his total attention.'[2]

Twelve months of dangerous living in spartan conditions in the oppressive tropical climate of Vietnam placed huge demands on everyone's mental and physical resources. However, Bob never seemed to flag, and maintained his cheerful and professional demeanour throughout. It was not unknown for him to be seen up on a table in the officers' mess, singing German beer-hall songs. In the half century since that year, he has continued to keep up with his former comrades in arms and participate fully in the 5RAR Association. He made a return visit to Vietnam in 1971 — which included visits to Laos and Cambodia — towards the end of Australia's military involvement, in order to compile a survey of the war as a whole and collect material as a first step towards the writing of the eventual official history of Australia's part in the war in Vietnam.

For his services in Vietnam, Bob received the award of a mention in despatches. The citation for this award reads as follows:

> Captain R. J. O'Neill was the Intelligence Officer of the 5th Battalion, The Royal Australian Regiment during the greater part of the tour of duty of the unit in South Vietnam. His skill and industry in collecting and interpreting available information regarding the enemy enabled the Battalion to undertake operations with the greatest possible knowledge of the Viet Cong. On numerous occasions Captain O'Neill displayed high personal courage in seeking out and confirming information both by ground and air reconnaissance. His conduct was at all times an inspiration to those who worked with him and the leadership displayed by him was of the highest possible order.

---

2   Michael von Berg, 5RAR Reconnaissance Platoon Commander, personal communication.

4
A Strategic Career[1]

Desmond Ball

Bob O'Neill rose to the pinnacle of his chosen profession — the academic study of arguably the most critical subject of public policy, that of war and peace, strategy and defence policy. His route took him to be Director of the International Institute for Strategic Studies (IISS) in London from 1982–1987, Chairman of the Council of IISS from 1986–2001, and the Chichele Professor of the History of War at All Souls College at Oxford University from 1987 until his retirement in 2001. These posts were fiercely competitive and required navigating the complex shoals at the confluence of the academic and policy worlds. He needed to be internationally recognised for his scholarship, but he also needed to demonstrate extraordinary project management and fund-raising propensities, to have a dedication to institution-building and a steadfast commitment to the strategic studies profession, and ultimately to be comfortable in the corridors of power to which he enjoyed access in many places around the world. But he did it in his stride — as purposefully as he strides out in front in his walks with family and friends in the Australian bush or the English countryside.

---

1   This chapter was previously published as Ball, Desmond (2006) 'Robert O'Neill: A Strategic Career, *Australian Journal of International Affairs* 60(1), pp. 7–11, and is reproduced here with the support of the Australian Institute of International Affairs. Minor edits have been made to update the concluding paragraphs.

I worked most closely with Bob from 1974, when I joined the Strategic and Defence Studies Centre (SDSC) at The Australian National University as a research fellow, to 1982, when he moved to London, eventually becoming his deputy head and often serving during his absences as acting head of the centre. We continued to consult frequently after he moved to the IISS and I became Head of SDSC, and we worked together when he was Chairman of the Council of the IISS, of which I was then a member. I saw him functioning at close quarters in his many different capacities.

I first met Bob around 1970. He had come to ANU as a Senior Fellow in the Department of International Relations, where I was a PhD student, in 1969. He became Head of SDSC in 1971, although he remained in International Relations. The centre had been set up by Dr T. B. Millar, another former army officer, in 1966, when he was also a Senior Fellow in International Relations, to 'advance the study of Australian, regional, and global strategic and defence issues'. It was initially funded by a grant from the Ford Foundation, and was organisationally an independent offshoot of International Relations. Bob presided over the centre's expansion and rise to international recognition through the 1970s and early 1980s.

He was a former Australian Army officer who had served in Vietnam as an infantry captain from 1966–1967 and had been mentioned in dispatches; he had been a lecturer in military history at the Royal Military College, Duntroon, from 1967–1969; and he was already the author of three books. His first was *The German Army and the Nazi Party, 1933–1939*,[2] the classic text on civil–military relations in Nazi Germany, based on the thesis he wrote as a Rhodes Scholar at Oxford in the early 1960s. It had an introduction by Sir Basil Liddell Hart, who had befriended the young Australian soldier-scholar, and who had the greatest intellectual influence on Bob's approach to military history and strategic thinking. His second book, *Vietnam Task*,[3] was based on his experiences in Vietnam. His third book was *General Giap: Politician and Strategist*,[4] a biography of the North Vietnamese military leader, the architect of the Viet Minh victory at Dien Bien

---

2   O'Neill, Robert (1966) *The German Army and the Nazi Party, 1933–1939*, London: Cassell.
3   O'Neill, Robert J. (1968) *Vietnam Task: The 5th Battalion, Royal Australian Regiment, 1966–67*, Sydney: Cassell
4   O'Neill, Robert J. (1969) *General Giap: Politician and Strategist*, London: Cassell.

Phu in 1954 and, two decades later, of the defeat of the US in South Vietnam. He was, by 1971, regarded as Australia's leading soldier-historian and one of its best military historians ever.

Bob's major research project during his 11 years at SDSC was his two-volume, 1,300-page official history of *Australia in the Korean War 1950–53* — *Volume I: Strategy and Diplomacy* was published by the Australian War Memorial and the Australian Government Publishing Service in 1981, and *Volume II: Combat Operations* followed in 1985.[5] Reviewers said that the twin works 'will always be the indispensable reference' on Australia's role in the Korean War, that they had 'enhanced existing standards of research, authenticity and unremitting attention to detail', and that they revealed 'enormous energy'. The basic politico-strategic assessment that underlay the history, that Australia's deployment of troops to Korea was 'primarily in the interests of Australian-American diplomacy', an exercise in alliance politics, was more telling than might have been expected from other official historians.

By 1974, Bob's talents were already turning to institution-building and project leadership. His first task was to build a critical mass of research posts in SDSC, based on a core staff of longer-term appointments. He promoted the centre through regular public conferences and by developing contacts with the media. The conferences were usually products of extensive research projects, and usually addressed the subjects for the first time in Australia.

Through the mid-1970s he obtained financial support for several core posts. In 1974, when Lance Barnard was Defence Minister in the Labor Government, he secured funding from the Department of Defence for two academic posts, and was later able to obtain two to three University-funded posts. He also forged a strong relationship with the Ford Foundation and, later, the McArthur Foundation.

He recognised that viable institutions require continuous regeneration. He encouraged promising honours and masters graduates from around the country to undertake PhDs in international relations at ANU, and

---

5   O'Neill, Robert J. (1981) *Australia in the Korean War 1950–53*, Volume I: Strategy and Diplomacy, Canberra: Australian War Memorial and Australian Government Publishing Service; O'Neill, Robert J. (1985) *Australia in the Korean War 1950–53*, Volume II: Combat Operations, Canberra: Australian War Memorial and Australian Government Publishing Service.

he closely attended their subsequent progress. His former students invariably recall the prompt and meticulous comments they received on their drafts. Some of them, including David Horner, Ross Babbage, and later Ron Huisken, took up senior positions in SDSC after Bob's departure. Tim Huxley is the Senior Fellow in charge of Asia-Pacific security matters at IISS.

Bob was the editor or co-editor of seven books from 1975–1982. The first of these was *The Strategic Nuclear Balance: An Australian Perspective*,[6] consisting of papers prepared for a conference held in July 1974. It was the first serious examination of US, Soviet, and Chinese strategic nuclear policies and capabilities, nuclear arms control and non-proliferation, in this country. Later volumes covered *The Strategic Environment in the 1980s*,[7] weapons proliferation in the Indian Ocean and Western Pacific regions, and *New Directions in Strategic Thinking*[8] (1981), as well as aspects of Australian defence policy.

The edited books were products of his collegiate style of leadership, whereby small and fairly loose teams worked on large issues with himself as the team leader and resource diviner. The largest proportion of the centre's work under Bob's tenure concerned the defence of Australia. The centre was at the forefront of the conceptual revolution in Australian defence policy, from 'dependence on great and powerful friends' to 'greater self-reliance', and from 'forward defence' to 'defence of Australia', which occurred during this period. The core people involved in this work on Australian defence were Bob, myself, Ross Babbage, then a PhD student, and J. O. Langtry, who was the SDSC Executive Officer from August 1976 to December 1988. Langtry was a former army officer who had worked in the Joint Intelligence Organisation and army combat development areas, and whose ability to think of novel strategic and operational concepts was inspirational.

---

6   O'Neill, Robert J. (ed.) (1975) *The Strategic Nuclear Balance: An Australian Perspective*, Canberra: Strategic and Defence Studies Centre, The Australian National University.
7   O'Neill, Robert J. (ed.) (1980) *The Strategic Environment in the 1980s*, Canberra: Strategic and Defence Studies Centre, The Australian National University.
8   O'Neill, Robert J. and D. M. Horner (eds) (1981) *New Directions in Strategic Thinking*, Sydney: Allen & Unwin.

Bob's second edited book was on *The Defence of Australia: Fundamental New Aspects*.[9] It consisted of papers from a conference in October 1976, and was designed to assist policy-makers struggling with the transformation of Australia's defence posture. It included papers by leading overseas experts on the concept of 'total defence', and on the strategic and tactical implications of new conventional weapons technologies, by a recent defence minister (Bill Morrison) on the role of the minister in policy-making since the reorganisation of the Defence Department from 1973–1975, on force structure and equipment acquisition matters, and Bob's own paper on the development of operational doctrine for the Australian Defence Force (ADF).

Bob produced the formative studies of the requisite command and control structure for a joint ADF in defence of Australia contingencies, including the establishment of functional command arrangements. His Dyason House Paper on 'Structural Changes for a More Self-Reliant National Defence',[10] was the first coherent statement of the need for functional commands, adopted a decade later. He also contributed to the development of new ideas concerning the reorganisation of the defence portfolio; greater utilisation of the civilian infrastructure, especially in defence of Australia contingencies; greater appreciation of the challenges of lower-level contingencies in northern Australia; regular officer education and training; and particular force structure issues. Members of the centre were credited with an influential role in the government's decision in 1981 to acquire the F/A-18 as RAAF's tactical fighter aircraft. Costing $4 billion, this was the largest capital program in Australia's history.

The second large area of work in the centre under Bob's tenure, which brought it to international attention, concerned the strategic nuclear balance between the United States and the Soviet Union, and related issues of nuclear proliferation. This had been the subject of the first centre conference he had organised in 1974, and he returned to it frequently over the next couple of decades. From 1995–1996 he served as a member of the Canberra Commission on the Elimination

---

9   O'Neill, Robert J. (ed.) (1977) *The Defence of Australia: Fundamental New Aspects*, Canberra: Strategic and Defence Studies Centre, The Australian National University.
10 O'Neill, Robert J. (1976) 'Structural Changes for a More Self-reliant National Defence', Dyason House Working Paper 3, Canberra: Research School of Pacific and Asian Studies, The Australian National University.

of Nuclear Weapons, which recommended the complete elimination of these weapons. He was a very active player in the commission, and worked energetically on the final drafts of the report.

The third broad area of centre research during this period concerned security issues in the Asia-Pacific region. Bob organised a succession of two- to three-year appointments on various aspects of regional security, funded variously by the Department of Defence, ANU, and the Ford Foundation. The appointments included Peter Hastings, the pungent, waggish and quarrelsome journalist, who worked on political and security issues concerning Indonesia and Papua New Guinea; Lee Ngok and Don McMillan who worked on China; Paul Keal on Japan; and R. Subramanian, S. D. Muni, Sreedhara Rao, and Pervaiz Iqbal Cheema on South Asia. Their names are associated with standard reference works in their respective areas.

I saw Bob display not only superb diplomatic skills, but also an immense personal integrity and a commitment to academic values. Some of the centre's work was intensely controversial, as befitting path-breaking scholarship on major national and international issues. Some senior defence and intelligence officials regarded my own work on US installations in Australia, such as Pine Gap, with great suspicion. While I argued that in a democracy it was necessary for the public to know the purposes and implications of these facilities, a proposition now taken for granted, Sir Arthur Tange complained that I was dangerous and irresponsible, opening up matters which 'successive American and Australian governments have deemed it a national interest' to keep secret. He was especially upset since my post was then funded by the Department of Defence. Bob defended the right of academics to pursue unfettered research. Only when I later became Head of SDSC and inherited the files of correspondence between Bob and Sir Arthur did I fully appreciate the extent of his discourse and the solidity of his refusal to countenance any hint of infringement on the principle of academic independence.

When Bob moved to London to head the IISS in 1982, he took his leadership qualities and adeptness at collegiate and foundation politics to a higher plane. He initiated the planning for the fund-raising campaign to acquire new and much larger premises for the institute, consummated by John Chipman, his successor as director and by then his closest working colleague, with the purchase of Arundel House in

1997. He greatly expanded the number of young research associates in the institute. He broadened the work of the institute to cover Asia as well as Africa and Latin America, making it a really international institute rather than an Atlanticist organisation with some regional appendages. His magisterial summings-up of IISS conferences on such broad, complex, and different themes as 'The Conduct of East–West Relations in the 1980s' in Ottawa in 1983, 'New Technology and Western Security Policy' in Avignon in 1984, and 'East Asia and International Security' in Kyoto in 1986, evinced his complete intellectual mastery of the ever-changing strategic landscape.

The Chichele Professorship at Oxford allowed him to return to thinking as much about military history, always his first love, as about current strategic developments. But he did not resile from a myriad of boards and councils which allowed him continued oversight of his domain. In addition to the demanding position of Chairman of the Council of the IISS, he was Chairman of the Trustees of the Imperial War Museum in London from 1998–2001; Chairman of the Council of the Centre for Defence Studies at King's College, London, from 1991–1996; Chairman of the Sir Robert Menzies Centre for Australian Studies in the University of London from 1990–1996; and a Governor of the International Peace Academy in New York and of the Ditchley Foundation in Oxfordshire. He also served as the Armed Services Editor of the Australian Dictionary of Biography until his retirement in 2001.

At the same time, he relished fostering and encouraging good, young PhD students at Oxford. Many of his stable are already widely recognised, including Daniel Marston, the war historian of the eighteenth, nineteenth and twentieth centuries, and strategic analyst of counter-insurgency today; Carter Malkasian, who has published on the strategy of attrition, and after spending several years on the ground in the Iraq and Afghanistan conflicts, has published *War Comes to Garmser*;[11] John Hillen, the author of a critically acclaimed book on UN military operations and former Assistant Secretary of State for Political Military Affairs, Washington DC; the late Paul Collier, who has published on the North African and Mediterranean theatres during the Second World War; Elsina Wainwright, known for her

---

11   Malkasian, Carter (2013) *War Comes to Garmser: Thirty Years of Conflict on the Afghan Frontier*, Oxford: Oxford University Press.

work on post-conflict governance issues and, more specifically, for her Australian Strategic Policy Institute paper on 'Our Failing Neighbour',[12] commonly regarded as the blueprint for the multinational intervention in Solomon Islands soon after; and John Nagl, a retired US Army officer who served in the First Gulf War and the Iraq conflict, who has published a comparative study on the Vietnam War and the Malayan Insurgency, and *Knife Fights*,[13] on the Iraq and Afghanistan conflicts.

As Bob has supervised over 50 doctoral students, I shall not go on further through the list. It is sufficient to say that he has developed a multinational group of critical thinkers on strategy who are now hard at work on the world's current security problems. They share an unabashed loyalty to him. They effectively comprise a personal regiment, deployed around the globe, committed by profession to the promotion of the intellectual institution he valued most, the independent and rigorous study of military history, strategy, and security policy.

---

12 Wainwright, Elsina (2003) *Our Failing Neighbour: Australia and the Future of Solomon Islands*, Canberra: Australian Strategic Policy Institute.
13 Nagl, John A. (2014) *Knife Fights: A Memoir of Modern War in Theory and Practice*, New York: Penguin.

5
Robert O'Neill and Australian Security Policy

Paul Dibb

I have known Bob O'Neill for over 40 years and, as is well known, he is a highly distinguished scholar both nationally and internationally. He is also a man of many parts, as a former army officer, official war historian, the Head of SDSC for almost 12 years, the Director of the highly prestigious International Institute for Strategic Studies (IISS) in London, and Chichele Professor of the History of War at Oxford. This is truly a stellar career that very few Australian academics have been able to match, and much of this book will examine his academic achievements. My contribution will be to focus on his interest in the broader issues of Australia's national security policy and, in particular, our cooperative endeavours in seeking to understand the policies of the Soviet Union in the Cold War, the roles of China and Japan in regional security policy in the 1970s, and his early work on Australian defence policy and how it assisted my own endeavours in coming to grips with working for the Minister for Defence Kim Beazley in the late 1980s. I will also address the challenges I faced as head of SDSC for almost 13 years, from 1991 to 2004, and how much I owed to the strong basis he had established for its intellectual reputation, both in Australia and internationally. However, the most important part of this chapter is to record the huge debt I owe to Bob O'Neill for supporting and publishing my controversial views on the Soviet Union.

Intelligence and National Security Issues

I first met Bob O'Neill in the mid-1970s when I was a newly minted Head of the National Assessments Staff, which prepared draft intelligence assessments for the consideration of the National Intelligence Committee. It was a considerable challenge for me, because my previous career had been primarily as an economist dealing with Australia's overseas trade, analysing Soviet agriculture, and writing a book whilst at ANU in the late 1960s with the obscure title, *Siberia and the Pacific: A Study of Economic Development and Trade Prospects*.[1] The world of strategy, military capabilities, and technical issues to do with the central nuclear balance between the US and the USSR were completely foreign to me. It was a very steep learning curve at the age of 34, and I owe a great deal to the guidance and generous mentoring Bob gave me. His background in the Australian Army in the Vietnam War, the fact that he was writing the official history of the Korean War, and his headship of SDSC gave me unique insights into the arcane world (or so it then seemed) of strategic and defence studies. He was able to direct me to others at ANU, such as Harry Rigby, Geoffrey Jukes, and Bob Miller, who were deeply knowledgeable about the USSR's political leadership, military capabilities, and economy, as well as scholars such as Amin Saikal, who was invaluable to me when the Soviets invaded Afghanistan in 1979 — a country I knew absolutely nothing about.

Through Bob O'Neill, I also got to know Hedley Bull, Tom Millar, J. D. B. Miller and Des Ball. They were a formidable intellectual asset for me to consult as I struggled with formulating multidisciplinary and long-range intelligence national assessments. It is hard to imagine a more fortuitous and helpful set of individuals who were so prominent not only in strategic studies but also international relations practice.

I was also extremely fortunate because Bob — unlike many scholars — clearly understood that intelligence analysis is quite different from academic work. Intelligence analysis as a profession does not afford the time to focus on international relations theory and footnoting sources; rather, it must conform to national intelligence priorities, be relevant

---

1   Dibb, Paul (1972) *Siberia and the Pacific: A Study of Economic Development and Trade Prospects*, New York: Praeger.

to policy, and is rarely the product of an individual as distinct from a team. I was able to share these different approaches intellectually with Bob, and obtain guidance about how to present them in formal intelligence committee meetings — which, for example, rejected my attempts to introduce ideas such as Robert Jervis's 'perceptions and misperceptions in international relations' in my analysis of foreign countries.

In return, I was able to offer Bob some modest assistance regarding the problems of an academic research unit working in the sensitive area of defence policy. SDSC's relations with the Department of Defence bureaucracy and its suspicious attitude toward academics needed to be handled with great diplomacy, which Bob had no problem demonstrating. On several occasions, there were particular issues to do with Des Ball and the focus of his research on the highly sensitive issue of the purpose and operations of the joint US–Australia facility at Pine Gap. Extremely few Australian intelligence or defence policy officers were briefed on the highly classified compartment dealing with Pine Gap. (I retained that clearance for 30 years, including 13 years as professor at ANU.) I was O'Neill's closest contact in the Department of Defence in the 1970s and early 1980s. We kept in close touch during those years, and Bob says I gave him valuable guidance on how to handle problems when they arose — such as the formidable Secretary of the Department of Defence, Sir Arthur Tange, bearing down on SDSC over Des Ball's Pine Gap revelations. I was also able to introduce Bob to people I worked with in the Joint Intelligence Organisation (JIO), including its Director and Chairman of the National Intelligence Committee, Gordon Jockel, and Bob Mathams, the Director of Scientific and Technical Intelligence who, with the CIA's Carl Duckett, chose the site for Pine Gap. Mathams was the resident technical and scientific expert regarding the role of the joint facilities in monitoring the USSR's strategic nuclear capabilities and evidence about whether it was conforming to strategic nuclear arms control agreements. The other key person that I facilitated contact with for Bob was the Deputy Secretary for Defence, Bill Pritchett, who became Secretary in 1979 after Tange retired. These were all people who essentially wanted to be helpful to SDSC, but sometimes faced difficulties because of SDSC's need to address salient, and therefore sensitive, issues in public comment.

The Soviet Union, China, and Japan

I had a particular interest in the Soviet Union and China, but for different reasons: I was the resident defence intelligence expert on the Soviet Union, which in the 1970s was seen as posing a fundamental military challenge to America. Our intelligence interest was in China's growing opposition to the USSR and its opening up of relations with the US and Australia. Sir Arthur Tange instructed me to go to Moscow in 1976 and hold detailed discussions with the USSR about their naval operations in the Indian Ocean, which were of particular concern to the then Prime Minister Malcolm Fraser. In 1978, Tange also agreed to an invitation by the Chinese Embassy, and I was the first Australian senior defence intelligence officer to visit China. I was invited to inspect the Chinese submarine building yards in Shanghai and go on board a Chinese Romeo class submarine.

I was able to assist Bob in developing his knowledge of these important countries. Bob made a few visits to Moscow in the 1970s, and I was able to give him a list of very valuable contacts in the think tanks and the foreign ministry. From that experience, he was able to invite some well-suited specialists to Canberra, especially those from Soviet think tanks specialising in our region. I also helped Bob to open up a workable and sensible relationship with key people in the Soviet Embassy in Canberra, including the Deputy Chief of Mission Yuri Pavlov and the Counsellor Igor Saprykin. These were both highly intelligent and active Soviet diplomats who enjoyed a vast array of contacts in Canberra and ASIO had concerns about their real intelligence functions. Pavlov and Saprykin were accomplished public speakers and were quite comfortable participating in vigorous ANU public conferences about such subjects as nuclear arms control, Soviet naval activities in the Indian Ocean, and the US–USSR strategic relationship. I tried to do my bit for SDSC as a discreet participant in opening up a less hostile relationship with the Soviet diplomats in Canberra. Bob has told me that I made a big difference indirectly to the expertise of SDSC's output and understanding of the USSR, even while I was in the Department of Defence.

I was also able to assist Bob in developing relations with government departments and research institutes in China. When he first visited China, shortly after my 1978 visit, I was able to give him a long list of contacts across the defence and foreign ministries and think tanks, from which he was able to make contacts which he tells me were still useful to him 20 years later. He says they were especially valuable when he was at the IISS, trying to broaden its outreach with Asia, which had not traditionally been a key interest of the institute, which was heavily focused on Europe and North America. Bob has told me that as he was travelling around in China on that first visit, he became used to hearing my name spoken in discussion groups that he attended. Certainly, Bob had my strong support in visiting China, because we were keenly interested in developing a relationship and opening up Beijing to a more transparent exchange of views on strategic and military matters.

Bob and I were also interested in the issue of developing our strategic relationships with Japan. The first Japanese official to attend the IISS was the Foreign Ministry's experienced Asianist Yukio Sato who later organised — with Bob's strong support — the first IISS Annual Conference in Asia in 1986 in the Japanese city of Kyoto. It was a resounding success due to Bob's imaginative management. Later, in 1990 when I was Deputy Secretary for Defence, Sato and I held Japan's first strategic bilateral discussions with any country other than the US. Sato went on to be Japan's Ambassador in Canberra in the mid-1990s, and I maintained a close relationship with him. The IISS established progressively deeper relationships with Japan and was responsible for nurturing an entire generation of Japanese strategic thinkers.

Managing the IISS

Bob O'Neill was the Director of the IISS from 1982 to 1987, and these were crucial years in the formulation of my own career, which would not have occurred without his generous support. When I was in intelligence during the 1970s, I began to formulate ideas about the USSR that I knew would become controversial. Toeing the party line on the Soviet Union in Canberra was *de rigueur* and there was an unspoken requirement to conform, which was a reflection of the belief that the views of the US intelligence community should not be challenged. As already mentioned, in 1976 Sir Arthur Tange sent me to Moscow, stating that he wanted an Australian — not a US or UK — point of view. I stopped at London on my way to Moscow and talked in detail with the Cabinet Office Assessments Staff, which I found to be much more nuanced than the CIA. By 1979, an idea was beginning to formulate in my mind that the Soviet Union had real weaknesses and problems, and I began to think of it as the incomplete superpower. I discussed this with O'Neill, who suggested that I join him at ANU, which I did in 1981. This involved resigning from my position in defence, and I left with the warning of the then Secretary for Defence, Bill Pritchett, ringing in my ears: 'You'll be working down the corridor from that Desmond Ball and we'll be watching you, Dibb.'

I worked in the Department of International Relations in 1982 and then transferred to the Strategic and Defence Studies Centre. By this time, Bob had gone to run the IISS in London. He quickly arranged for me to agree to write a book about the USSR for the institute, which became *The Soviet Union: The Incomplete Superpower*.[2] Bob strongly encouraged me in the writing task over the next three years and I made several visits to Moscow and Washington. The book was published in 1986 by the IISS, reprinted in 1987, and a second edition in 1988. In America, it was published by the University of Illinois Press. It caused quite a stir, particularly in the United States, and most especially in the American intelligence community. In 1987, I had returned to defence and was Director of the JIO. In that role, I had a meeting in Washington with Robert Gates, who was then Deputy Director of the CIA. I well remember him giving me a little lecture about how the agency disagreed with my book and that the CIA's view was that 'the USSR was poised to outstrip the US in military power'.

I well understood that, without Bob O'Neill's continuing encouragement, my book would never have been published, and I owe him an enormous debt for having stuck his neck out on such a controversial subject. This was especially the case in those days when the institute very much relied on its transatlantic connections with America. I strongly believe to this day that, without Bob's support for this project, it may never have seen the light of day. Most academics these days have no idea of the harsh pressure that existed in the 1980s to conform to the US official views about the Soviet threat. All this was deeply seared into my mind when I was called over to the office of the new Secretary for Defence, Sir William Cole, who told me that

---

2   Dibb, Paul (1986) *The Soviet Union: The Incomplete Superpower*, Champaign: University of Illinois Press.

he could not give me the job of Director JIO because of my views on the Soviet Union. My retaliation came a few months later when I was made ministerial consultant to Minister for Defence Kim Beazley to write the *Review of Australia's Defence Capabilities*.[3] I remember Sir William saying to me, in the same office where he had rejected my appointment as Director JIO just a few months earlier: 'Well, Paul, this is a turn up for the books.' It was, and I made sure that Cole's performance as secretary was scrutinised by the Dibb Review. I don't think Bob ever realised these threats to my career were going on at the time, but I have never forgotten his unwavering support for the publication of *The Incomplete Superpower*.

While I am addressing the issue of Bob's leadership of the institute, I would be remiss if I didn't record that he was an outstanding manager of that body, and the only Australian to have ever done so. I watched him at the institute's annual conferences, masterfully undertaking a role that was completely beyond me. Over two full days of a large international conference, he would be busy listening and analysing what the key points were, and at the end of the conference he would make the final address, which would draw together what invariably were very complex and competing ideas. That is a role that very few people can do, but Bob O'Neill did it with great aplomb.

Australia's Defence Policy

As the Head of SDSC, Bob O'Neill took important steps to bolster the centre's academic research into Australian defence policy. His predecessor, Tom Millar, had pioneered university work in Australia on defence policy issues, including his book *Australia's Defence*, which observed that '[s]uccessive governments have not been especially interested in defence as a subject'[4] and his 1967 ANU booklet *Australia's Defence Policies 1945–65*.[5] O'Neill himself had edited another early publication called *The Defence of Australia:*

---

3   Dibb, Paul (1986) *Review of Australia's Defence Capabilities*, Canberra: Commonwealth of Australia.
4   Millar, T.B. (1965) *Australia's Defence*, Melbourne: Melbourne University Press, p. 163.
5   Millar, T.B. (1967) *Australia's Defence Policies 1945–65*, Canberra: The Australian National University.

Fundamental New Aspects, which was published by SDSC in 1977 and ranks among the centre's first publications on detailed Australian defence policy matters. [6]

In the foreword to that publication, O'Neill observes that he had long wanted to organise a conference on the defence of Australia, but had been deterred by it being such an ambitious undertaking:

> [It] would be a pioneering effort in terms of the assembly of expertise and the availability of relevant scholarly literature. It would also involve public entry into a field in which the numbers of those in Government service with real expertise must inevitably outweigh heavily the numbers of academic participants, thereby raising the very real question of by what right was the Strategic and Defence Studies Centre venturing to hold such a conference.[7]

Bob went on to state that, 'until approximately 1975, the Centre lacked the people around whom such a conference could be built'.[8] He went on to note that, in 1974, with the establishment by Mr Lance Barnard, then Minister for Defence, of the two posts in the centre occupied by Mr Peter Hastings and Dr Desmond Ball, and Mr Ross Babbage's arrival to work for a PhD on Australian defence policy, 'the Centre now had a team around which a conference on the Defence of Australia could be built'.[9] Bob proceeded to build on that remarkable team, and later recruited Jol Langtry as executive officer. Under Bob's guidance until he left the centre in 1982 to go to London, this team was responsible for producing a substantial output of publications concerning defence policy in Australia, particularly pioneering academic work on the north of Australia and its central relevance to the defence of Australia concept. This included such books as:

- *The Future of Tactical Air Power in the Defence of Australia*[10]
- *Australia's Defence Resources: a Compendium of Data*[11]

---

6   O'Neill, Robert J. (ed.) (1977) *The Defence of Australia: Fundamental New Aspects*, Canberra: Strategic and Defence Studies Centre, The Australian National University.
7   Ibid., p. v.
8   Ibid.
9   Ibid., pp. v–vi.
10   Ball, Desmond (ed.) (1977) *The Future of Tactical Air Power in the Defence of Australia*, Canberra: The Australian National University.
11   O'Neill, Robert, J. O. Langtry and Jolika Tie (eds) (1978) *Australia's Defence Resources: A Compendium of Data*, Canberra: The Australian National University.

- *Controlling Australia's Threat Environment: a Methodology for Planning Australia's Defence Force Development*[12]
- *Problems of Mobilisation in Defence of Australia*[13]
- *Options for an Australian Defence Technological Strategy*[14]
- *Rethinking Australia's Defence*[15]
- *New Directions in Strategic Thinking*[16]
- *Strategy and Defence: Australian Essays.*[17]

In addition to his administrative and conference management responsibilities and writing forewords and conclusions to various books, Bob O'Neill had time to write SDSC Working Papers with titles such as: *The Defence of Continental Australia*, *Structural Changes for a More Self-reliant National Defence*, and *The Structure of Australia's Defence Force.*[18] I mention this because many of the publications I cite above, as well as later centre publications, became important to me when I was writing the Dibb Review for Minister for Defence Kim Beazley. I probably never got around to mentioning that to Bob, but I do so here. When I combined the output of the centre, together with over a decade's worth of hard work on defence of Australia concepts in the Department of Defence, they made my task immeasurably easier in 1985.

---

12 Langtry, J. O. and Desmond Ball (eds) (1979) *Controlling Australia's Threat Environment: a Methodology for Planning Australia's Defence Force Development*, Canberra: The Australian National University.
13 Ball, Desmond and J. O. Langtry (eds) (1980) *Problems of Mobilisation in Defence of Australia*, Canberra: Phoenix Defence Publications.
14 Gower, S. N. (1982) *Options for an Australian Defence Technological Strategy*, Canberra: Strategic and Defence Studies Centre, The Australian National University.
15 Babbage, Ross (1980) *Rethinking Australia's Defence*, St Lucia: University of Queensland Press.
16 O'Neill, Robert J. and D. M. Horner (eds) (1981) *New Directions in Strategic Thinking*, London: Allen & Unwin.
17 Ball, Desmond (ed.) (1982) *Strategy and Defence: Australian Essays*, Sydney: Allen & Unwin.
18 O'Neill, Robert J. (1978) *The Defence of Continental Australia*, SDSC Working Paper, Canberra: Strategic and Defence Studies Centre, The Australian National University; O'Neill, Robert J. (1978) *Structural Changes for a More Self-reliant National Defence*, SDSC Working Paper, Canberra: Strategic and Defence Studies Centre, The Australian National University; O'Neill, Robert J. (1979) *The Structure of Australia's Defence Force*, SDSC Working Paper, Canberra: Strategic and Defence Studies Centre, The Australian National University.

Bob had the strategic perspicacity to observe in the final chapter of *The Defence of Australia: Fundamental New Aspects*:

> The acceptance by recent Australian Governments that Australia's defence policy should be concerned primarily with the defence of Australian territory rather than that of non-communist South-east Asian states is perhaps the change of greatest significance. It means that we must conceive policies for the defence of the nation at large and accept prime responsibility for conducting military functions to carry those policies into effect ... The change in posture requires that the services develop techniques for operating in and around Australia, rather than Southeast Asia — obviously creating a major task for the Army in particular.[19]

With great foresight, he argued: 'Primacy must be given to our operational doctrines to the defence of Australia.'[20] He strongly supported 'a nationwide, functional joint service command structure', which he believed would 'be the ultimate answer to our requirements'.[21] In this seminal work, he concluded that

> military history suggests that we have little experience on which to draw in the area of shaping nationwide response capacities and strategies. It is in this area principally that our attempt to develop doctrines will be most crucial. It promises to be many years before the intellectual challenge has gone out of the field of Australian defence studies.[22]

As I tussled with the Dibb Review, I constantly kept this key intellectual guidance in my mind.

Managing SDSC: From O'Neill to Dibb

Bob O'Neill and I were the two longest serving heads of the Strategic and Defence Studies Centre: together, we managed the centre for almost a quarter of a century. We both experienced the problems of running a small centre with inadequate finances, and we were discriminated against in The Australian National University's allocation of funds

---

19   O'Neill, Robert J. (ed.) (1977) *The Defence of Australia: Fundamental New Aspects,* Canberra: Strategic and Defence Studies Centre, The Australian National University, p. 126.
20   Ibid., p. 131.
21   Ibid., p. 134.
22   Ibid., p. 143.

because we were a centre and not a department. However, we managed the centre in entirely different geopolitical circumstances. Bob's reign was effectively after Australia's commitment to the Vietnam War had ended, but at the height of the Cold War and the USSR's military strength. My management of the centre from 1991 coincided with the end of the Cold War, Fukuyama's end of world history thesis, and the need to retool traditional strategic studies to our own region. As I said in the book commemorating the 40th anniversary of the centre, the reorientation of the centre after the Cold War was a difficult transition.[23] Both Bob O'Neill and his successor, Des Ball, grew the centre to international repute during the 1970s and 1980s. But with the sudden end of the Cold War and the collapse of the Soviet Union in 1991, the centre had to adjust rapidly to an altered international strategic environment and to new subjects for strategic analysis. In the mid-1990s, the government changed and there was a move away from defence ideas which the centre had played a key role in developing from the early 1970s. The policy focus shifted away from the defence of Australia to Australian expeditionary forces in the Middle East — which remains the case to this day.

During my tenure, ANU also experienced significant financial difficulties, which had a serious impact on the centre's budget and its ability to fund research on important issues.[24] By the late 1990s, we were barely a critical mass, with only five academic staff, and the future did not look all that promising. I say that noting Bob has expressed a view that, 'I think it has been many years since any head of the Centre has needed to worry about whether it would be in existence in one or two years' time'.[25] Of course, he was right, and we did indeed turn the corner as SDSC entered the new century and its finances improved once again. Right now we have by far the largest academic staff numbers the centre has ever enjoyed in its 50 year history (and in the Hedley Bull Centre we have by far the best accommodation we have ever had). Moreover, we have also built on the legacy that Bob O'Neill left us in such areas as media appearances, giving evidence before

---

23 Dibb, Paul (2006) 'SDSC in the Nineties: A Difficult Transition', in Meredith Thatcher and Desmond Ball (eds), *A National Asset: Essays Commemorating the 40th Anniversary of the Strategic and Defence Studies Centre*, Canberra: The Australian National University, p. 83.
24 Ibid.
25 O'Neill, Robert (2006) 'From Childhood to Maturity: The SDSC, 1972–1982', in Meredith Thatcher and Desmond Ball (eds), *A National Asset: Essays Commemorating the 40th Anniversary of the Strategic and Defence Studies Centre*, Canberra: The Australian National University, p. 55.

parliamentary committees, massively developing our postgraduate and undergraduate programmes, and our teaching commitments at the Australian Command and Staff College at Weston Creek under the very competent direction of Professor Dan Marston.

Thanks to Bob's groundbreaking work in establishing the centre's domestic and international reputation, we are the leading academic authority in Australia on strategic and defence problems, and we are a well-recognised entity within the regional and international network of research institutions in the field of strategic studies, as Bob has pointed out.[26] The centre was indeed fortunate that Bob devoted more than 11 years of his career to establishing SDSC's reputation from such slim resources. And I am fortunate that as Director of IISS he was so willing to undertake the gamble of publishing my work on the USSR — for which I remain greatly indebted.

Concluding Thoughts

In conclusion, Bob would be more than pleased to read the words of the then Secretary for Defence, Tony Ayers, in 1996 to the ANU Chancellor when I was head of the centre:

> The Centre brings much credit to the University for its contribution to the understanding of defence matters in the Australian community and in our region ... The Centre's excellent reputation in the region has ensured continuing participation in its programs by officers and civilian defence planners from regional countries. This helps to promote a rational and disciplined approach to defence policy-making in neighbouring countries. From the perspective of Australian Defence personnel development, the Centre's courses, programs and publications have directly benefited Australian Defence Force officers and civilian staff.[27]

This does not mean that SDSC should only focus on practical defence policy issues. As I noted in the essays commemorating the 40th anniversary of the centre, we must continue to be well-grounded in academic scholarship on the security of our region and the contending

---

26   Ibid., p. 58.
27   Research School of Pacific and Asian Studies (1996) *Annual Report*, Canberra: The Australian National University, pp. 77–8.

theories of strategic studies.[28] These are thoughts I know Bob O'Neill would thoroughly endorse. But, unlike in his day and mine, the centre faces more competition from a proliferation of well-funded new research organisations in Australia, including the Australian Strategic Policy Institute, the Lowy Institute for International Policy, and the Institute for Regional Security (formerly the Kokoda Foundation). The centre does not receive such lavish private sector or government funding, but one of our comparative advantages continues to be that we operate within the university system, where there are no financial strings attached; we can be frank in what we say on any subject without fear of angering our sources of funding. And, for good reasons, we do not accept any funding from defence companies — except for some small amount of money in the past (but not now), to help with supporting the centre's library.

Our other big competitive advantage is that we have the most experienced collection of senior academics (including seven professors) and former very senior military officers and defence officials (including a former chief of the defence force and three former deputy secretaries of defence) in Australia. This lends tremendous prestige to both our scholarly and policy-relevant research, and to our postgraduate and undergraduate teaching. This is an attainment of which Bob O'Neill should be justly proud, having brought the centre from childhood to maturity in his tenure from 1971 to 1982.

---

28 Dibb, Paul (2006) 'SDSC in the Nineties: A Difficult Transition', in Meredith Thatcher and Desmond Ball (eds), *A National Asset: Essays Commemorating the 40th Anniversary of the Strategic and Defence Studies Centre*, Canberra: The Australian National University, p. 96.

6

Robert O'Neill and the Australian Official War Histories: Policy and Diplomacy

Peter Edwards

Like the citizens of many nations around the world, Australians are marking the centenary of the Great War of 1914–1918. With rather less fanfare, Australians are also marking the centenary of the start of a tradition of official war histories, which have had a fundamental role in shaping the way that Australians have thought about the nation's involvement in war since 1914. Robert O'Neill's contribution to that tradition was a major turning point in the development of that tradition, in at least two important respects.

When war broke out in 1914, Australia was engaged in a general election, which brought the Australian Labor Party back to office. One of its first decisions was the appointment of an official war correspondent. The Labor Government referred this decision to the relevant union, the Australian Journalists' Association, who conducted a ballot. The outcome was a victory for the *Sydney Morning Herald* journalist Charles Bean over Keith Murdoch (the father of Rupert) of the Melbourne *Herald* and the Sydney *Sun*. When the Minister for Defence, Senator George F. Pearce, met Bean on 20 September 1914, Pearce told Bean that he should not only file newspaper reports but also, after the war, write a history of Australia's part, which would become 'a permanent record for libraries, schools, and the nation generally'.[1]

This was the origin of the 12-volume *Official History of Australia in the War of 1914–18*, of which Bean would be the general editor. He would also be the author of the six volumes that form the backbone of the series, dealing with the Australian Imperial Force on the Gallipoli peninsula and on the western front in France and Belgium. Those volumes were based on Bean's own notebooks, as well as the mountains of official records, such as the unit diaries. Bean was an extraordinarily dedicated and courageous reporter, who personally witnessed virtually every major battle in which the Australians were engaged, other than Fromelles.[2]

At this time, Australian history was practically unknown in Australian universities. For decades to come, it would be, at best, a small adjunct to British imperial history. Newspapers, by contrast, were thriving. Bean, born in Australia but educated at Clifton College and Oxford University, was an exemplar of an Anglo-Australian tradition of journalism that contributed serious commentary on national affairs. By 1914, Bean had published three books based on his own reporting.

The authors appointed to write the other volumes generally had similar backgrounds. As far as possible, Bean chose eyewitnesses rather than prominent participants, usually correspondents who had no interest in defending the reputations of senior officers but who knew at first hand what the men in the trenches (literally or metaphorically) had endured. Henry Gullett and F. M. Cutlack, who wrote the volumes on the Australian Imperial Force in Sinai, Palestine, and Syria, and

---

1   Connor, John (2011) *Anzac and Empire: George Foster Pearce and the Foundations of Australian Defence*, Melbourne: Cambridge University Press, p. 47.
2   Inglis, K. S. (1979) 'Bean, Charles Edwin (1879–1968)', *Australian Dictionary of Biography*, Vol. 7, Melbourne: Melbourne University Press. Available at: adb.anu.edu.au/biography/bean-charles-edwin-5166/text8677. See also Coulthart, Ross (2014) *Charles Bean*, Sydney: HarperCollins.

the Australian Flying Corps respectively, had similar backgrounds to Bean, as did Thomas Heney, who was appointed to write the volume on the home front but died before he could complete it.[3]

The central theme of the 1914–1918 history, especially of Bean's massively detailed volumes, was the character of the men he observed under the stress of war. In Bean's view, the Australians, especially those from the bush, had developed the qualities they had inherited from their British forebears: the character of the young nation had undergone its greatest test and had passed with flying colours. Despite the vast scope of the conflict, in which hundreds of thousands of Australians served and more than 60,000 were to lose their lives, Bean's approach depended on close attention to the individuals engaged in battle. The descriptions in the narrative and the accompanying sketches were supported by footnotes on the individuals named, showing that this great citizens' army comprised 'a fair cross-section of our people … [such that] the company commander was a young lawyer and his second in command and most trusted mate a young engine driver and so on'.[4]

It was not an approach that took much interest in, or had much room for, questions of strategy, or the involvement of Australians in high command, or civil–military relations. The author of the volume on the home front, Sir Ernest Scott, did include the exploits of Prime Minister W. M. Hughes in London and Paris, but more in the context of Australian domestic politics than of anything that might be called Australian strategic policy.[5]

---

[3] See their respective entries in the *Australian Dictionary of Biography*: Hill, A. J. (1983) 'Gullett, Sir Henry Somer (Harry) (1878–1940)', *Australian Dictionary of Biography*, Vol. 9, Melbourne: Melbourne University Press. Available at: adb.anu.edu.au/biography/gullett-sir-henry-somer-harry-448/text11157; Sweeting, A. J. (1981) 'Cutlack, Frederic Morley (1886–1967)', *Australian Dictionary of Biography*, Vol. 8, Melbourne: Melbourne University Press. Available at: adb.anu.edu.au/biography/cutlack-frederic-morley-5859/text9963; Stewart, Ken (1983) 'Heney, Thomas William (1862–1928)', *Australian Dictionary of Biography*, Vol. 9, Melbourne: Melbourne University Press. Available at: adb.anu.edu.au/biography/heney-thomas-william-6635/text11429.
[4] Quoted in Inglis, K. S. (1979) 'Bean, Charles Edwin (1879–1968)', *Australian Dictionary of Biography*, Vol. 7, Melbourne: Melbourne University Press. Available at: adb.anu.edu.au/biography/bean-charles-edwin-5166/text8677.
[5] Scott, Ernest (1936) *Australia during the War*, Sydney: Angus and Robertson

Bean's volumes, with their covers (as an early reviewer pointed out) the colour of dried blood, achieved substantial sales. To have them on one's bookshelves was an act of personal commemoration which complemented the nation's great commemorative institution, the Australian War Memorial, in the creation of which Bean was the moving force.

In what they omitted almost as much as in what they recorded, Bean's volumes had a major influence on how Australians thought of themselves and their young nation, especially its role in war. They helped to confirm the notion that Australia's primary role in conflict was to provide expeditionary forces who would fight alongside, and in close coordination with, those of Britain and the other Dominions.

By the time Bean finished the last of his six volumes, the world was again at war. It was a mark of the respect that he and his history had engendered that in 1943 the War Cabinet decided, on the recommendation of the Australian War Memorial (and almost certainly at the instigation of Bean himself) to appoint an official historian of this second global war. The man appointed, Gavin Long, had a similar background to Bean, that of a well regarded journalist and correspondent. Long was also an eyewitness to several campaigns, although it was not possible for one man to cover as many of the Australian battlefields as Bean had.

Many of those appointed to write other volumes in what eventually became a 23-volume series also had a background in journalism. The author of the home front volumes, Paul Hasluck, had experience of high-level diplomacy, rare for an Australian of his time, as well as the academic credentials of a professor of history or political science, but much of his reputation in the 1940s was based on his important role as a journalist at the *West Australian*.[6]

Although Hasluck would later became Australia's foreign minister, there was little on Australia's international relations in his two volumes on *The Government and the People*, which were focused on Australia's domestic politics. Australia's relations with Britain and the United States received relatively little attention, and were discreetly handled. Substantial — and sometimes controversial — books on the

---

6   Bolton, Geoffrey (2014) *Paul Hasluck: A Life*, Perth: UWA Publishing.

6. ROBERT O'NEILL AND THE AUSTRALIAN OFFICIAL WAR HISTORIES

high politics of war, including such matters as the relations of prime ministers Robert Menzies and John Curtin with Winston Churchill, or Curtin's relations with Douglas MacArthur, emerged much later, from a new generation of academic historians.[7] Gavin Long himself wrote a book on Douglas MacArthur, in which he expressed opinions widely held by Australian servicemen, but which were probably considered inappropriate for an official history.[8] It appears that, in the 1950s and 1960s, there was little appetite in official circles for a detailed account of the sometimes fraught relations between Australia and the countries that Menzies, in his peacetime term as prime minister from 1949 to 1966, liked to describe as Australia's 'great and powerful friends'.

It was perhaps symbolic that both Bean and Long died within months of each other in 1968. In the 1960s, Australian history, which had been steadily growing in Australian universities since the 1940s, was now flourishing and attracting popular attention outside the academy. The first volumes of Manning Clark's *A History of Australia*, published in 1962 and 1968, generated controversy, while Clark's teaching helped to inspire a new generation of Australian historians.[9] The late 1960s were years of rebellion and dissent, as the postwar generation of baby boomers came to adulthood, with many attending the burgeoning universities. Having known only peace and prosperity, they would probably have been restive in any case, but the Vietnam War crystallised their discontent and focused them on questions of war and peace. Amid an atmosphere of widespread dissent and anti-war demonstrations, the Strategic and Defence Studies Centre was established at The Australian National University in 1966, the nation's first major think tank on strategic policies.

Also in Canberra, the Australian War Memorial was recovering from its post-1945 doldrums and undergoing a major revival in its role as not only a museum but also a research centre in Australian military history. In his last years, Gavin Long encouraged the memorial's collaboration with the new public and academic interest in Australian military history. Long was involved in the award of the memorial's

---

7   See Horner, David (1992) *High Command: Australia's Struggle for an Independent War Strategy, 1939–45*, Melbourne: Allen & Unwin, and a number of later works by Horner, David Day, Anne Henderson, and others.
8   Gavin Long, *MacArthur as Military Commander*, Batsford, London, 1969.
9   McKenna, Mark (2011) *An Eye for Eternity: The Life of Manning Clark*, Melbourne: Miegunyah Press

first three research grants to 'a journalist, a soldier and schoolmaster turned academic, and a young scholar who would become a historian of distinction', an indication of the new breadth and diversity of background and interest in the field.[10]

This was the social, political and academic environment when Robert O'Neill was appointed in 1970 to write an official history of Australia's involvement in the Korean War. In the following year, he became head of the Strategic and Defence Studies Centre, the position he held until 1982. During those 12 years he would dedicate much of his research and writing time to the Korean War official history.

It is deceptively easy today to overlook the significance of O'Neill's appointment. For a start, it was by no means certain that the government of the day would undertake an official history of Australian involvement in the Korean War. By 1970, it was clear that Korea was the first of a series of post-1945 conflicts, which differed in many respects from the two world wars. Korea was certainly no minor affair, but it was on a markedly different scale from the two world wars. As in 1914–1918, the land war was much larger than those on the sea or in the air, but Australia's contribution was made not by a vast army of citizens who had been recruited 'for the duration', but by a relatively small, professional army, created only in 1948. Korea was the first of what historians would call Australia's 'wars of diplomacy',[11] in which the initial commitment and its subsequent higher direction would be interwoven with an increasingly assertive foreign policy, with alliance management and a sharp focus on the region to Australia's north the dominant elements.

To write the official history of Australia's involvement in this new type of war, the government chose a new type of historian. In his mid-30s when appointed, Robert O'Neill had not been there as a journalist or war correspondent: he was a schoolboy at the time of the Korean War. A graduate of the Royal Military College, Duntroon, who had served with distinction as a young officer in the Vietnam War,

---

10   Stanley, Peter (2003) 'Gavin Long and History at the Australian War Memorial', in Jeffrey Grey (ed.) *The Last Word?: Essays on Official History in the United States and the British Commonwealth*, Westport, Conn.: Praeger, pp. 113–14.
11   Grey, Jeffrey (2008) *A Military History of Australia*, third edition, Melbourne: Cambridge University Press, p. 220, uses this term to describe the conflicts in Malaya, Borneo, and Vietnam, but it is arguably no less applicable to Korea.

O'Neill had credibility with the services, but his principal qualification was something unknown to earlier generations of Australians — a doctorate in history, which had led to scholarly publications. His Oxford PhD thesis, subsequently published as a book, had been on the relationship between the German Army and the Nazi Party.[12] In short, he had outstanding credentials in the academic study of the high politics and civil–military relations that lay behind a military commitment. O'Neill knew the importance of recording and analysing not only the experience of those who served, but also the high-level decision-making that led to service personnel being placed in harm's way.

During the decade and more that O'Neill spent researching and writing, he discovered so much important and interesting material at this level that he realised that there should be, not just a chapter or two, but an entire volume on the strategic and diplomatic aspects of the commitment. The War Memorial Council agreed. The projected single volume was divided into two, one on strategy and diplomacy, and the other on combat operations.

Today it is easy to overlook the innovative character of a major scholarly volume of Australian diplomatic and strategic history. Diplomatic history was a tender, young shoot in Australian universities, where any scholarly interest in the history of Australia's foreign policy was more likely to be found in political science departments than in history departments. The gibe that Australia had no foreign policy other than slavish subservience to its powerful allies was commonly heard. Few works on Australia's diplomatic history, based on substantial archival research, had been published. The first volumes of *Documents on Australian Foreign Policy* began to appear in the mid-1970s, the fruit of a program initiated by Paul Hasluck as Minister for External Affairs (as Foreign Affairs was then known) from 1964 to 1969. Hasluck's long parliamentary career delayed the publication of the second volume of his contribution to the official history of Australia in the 1939–1945 war, and he subsequently wrote several important books of memoirs. Even when serving in high office, he remained essentially a historian who believed strongly in the importance of the written record.

---

12 O'Neill, Robert (1969) *The German Army and the Nazi Party, 1933–39*, London: Cassell.

Strategic history was even more neglected. The decade in which O'Neill was carrying out his research, the 1970s, was also a time of unprecedented scholarly discussion of Australian strategic and defence policy. In both academic and policy-making circles, a strong view was emerging that the era of forward defence was over, and Australia had to look to a new strategic concept, which would become known as 'the self-reliant defence of Australia'. This concept and its implications lay at the heart of the first White Paper on Defence to be brought down by an Australian government, in 1976. Vigorous debate followed on the ramifications and implications of this doctrinal shift and the associated reorganisation of Australia's defence organisation, implemented amid considerable controversy following a major review in 1974.[13]

The Strategic and Defence Studies Centre, with O'Neill at its head, was central to much of this discussion. In 1976, the centre held a major conference on 'The Defence of Australia: Fundamental New Aspects', resulting in a publication under that title, edited by O'Neill, the following year.[14] While the theme of this conference, as of so much discussion in the 1970s, was that Australian strategic and defence policies were moving into a new era, this environment clearly influenced O'Neill's research and analysis of the conflict of 1950–1953. If Australian strategic, defence, and foreign policies were about to move into a new era, it was essential that Australians should have a good understanding of the era that was passing. The forward defence era could be seen as ending with the fall of Saigon in 1975. Few events were more important in its initiation than the negotiation of the ANZUS Treaty and the commitment to the Korean War.

O'Neill's first volume of *Australia in the Korean War 1950–53* was therefore fundamental to a generation of scholarship on Australian strategic and diplomatic history.[15] It remains an indispensable account of the negotiation of the ANZUS Treaty, a fundamental element of Australian policies for decades to come, but its historiographical importance did not end there. O'Neill's detailed analysis of Australia's

---

13   Edwards, Peter (2006) *Arthur Tange: Last of the Mandarins*, Sydney: Allen & Unwin, chapters 10, 11, and 13.
14   O'Neill, R. J. (ed.) (1977) *The Defence of Australia: Fundamental New Aspects*, Canberra: Strategic and Defence Studies Centre, The Australian National University.
15   O'Neill, Robert (1981) *Australia in the Korean War 1950–53*, Vol. I: Strategy and Diplomacy, Canberra: The Australian War Memorial and the Australian Government Publishing Service.

diplomatic dealings, especially with London and Washington, showed that Canberra did not simply knee-jerk in response to directives from its allies. There were difficult choices to be made. Winston Churchill's peacetime government in London, for example, strongly opposed the idea that Australia (or New Zealand) should sign a security treaty with the United States to which Britain was not a party. The commitment to the Korean War was deliberately handled in a manner designed to show Washington that Canberra made its own decisions on such matters, independently of London. In subsequent years, Australia had to decide where it stood on matters where the United Kingdom and the United States were at odds, such as General MacArthur's threats of using atomic weapons and his 'push to the Yalu'.

By his detailed treatment of such matters, O'Neill demonstrated that war histories, like wars themselves, are what would now be called a whole of government exercise. The service, the sacrifice, the experience of those wearing uniform is, of course, central to a war history; but so too are the decisions that send those service personnel into combat. The roles of the politicians, the diplomats, the civilian officials, and the senior military officers are all important parts of the story. The careful study of what they did, or failed to do, is essential not only to understand what actually happened, but also as the foundation for the study of current and future policy. O'Neill's record of the work of P. C. (later Sir Percy) Spender as Minister for External Affairs and of young diplomats such as James (later Sir James) Plimsoll in Korea, for example, is a major contribution to Australia's diplomatic history.

The second volume of O'Neill's Korean War history, entitled simply *Combat Operations*, also shows the influence of a different style of authorship.[16] As in the two world wars, the land, sea, and air theatres are treated in three separate parts, as Australian units of the three services operated alongside the sister services of allied countries rather than as a joint force. But in each case O'Neill devotes considerable attention not only to the experiences of Australian units and individuals, but also to some of the wider military and diplomatic issues that affected the operational experience. The extent to which Australian servicemen were able to influence the allied coalition's tactical and operational

---

16 O'Neill, Robert (1985) *Australia in the Korean War 1950–53*, Vol. II: Combat Operations, Canberra: The Australian War Memorial and the Australian Government Publishing Service

approaches was an enduring theme of O'Neill's history, as it had been of his own experience as the intelligence officer of a battalion serving in Vietnam.

The impact of O'Neill's Korean War history on the Australian tradition of official war histories can be seen in the fourth series to be commissioned. Originally designated to cover the Malayan Emergency of 1948–1960 and the Vietnam War (to which Australian forces were committed between 1962 and 1972), it was later extended to include the Indonesian Confrontation of 1963–1966. It was then designated the *Official History of Australia's Involvement in Southeast Asian Conflicts 1948–75*. These conflicts, like others of the post-1945 era, have been referred to both as 'wars of diplomacy' and 'wars of decolonisation'.[17] The international context and Australia's management of both its major alliances and its relations with the new, post-colonial governments emerging in the region to Australia's immediate north were of obvious importance and interest.

O'Neill was a member of the selection panel which recommended the appointee for this history. In light of what has been recorded above, it is perhaps unsurprising that the selected historian, the present writer, had a background in diplomatic rather than operational history. I was the principal author of two volumes dealing with the political, strategic, and diplomatic aspects of the three conflicts, while other authors covered the operational and medical areas. The two strategic–diplomatic volumes, *Crises and Commitments*, and *A Nation at War*, were consciously written in the tradition of O'Neill's first Korean War volume.[18]

At the time of writing, a fifth series of Australian official war histories, *The Official History of Australian Peacekeeping, Humanitarian and Post-Cold War Operations*, is in the course of publication, with David Horner as the official historian and general editor. The government has also announced that a sixth series will be commissioned, to cover

---

17   See footnote 11 on wars of diplomacy in Anderson, Fay and Richard Trembath (2008) *Witnesses to War: The History of Australian Conflict Reporting*, Melbourne: Melbourne University Publishing.
18   Edwards, Peter with Gregory Pemberton (1992), *Crises and Commitments: The Politics and Diplomacy of Australia's Involvement in Southeast Asian Conflicts 1948–1965*, Sydney: Allen & Unwin in association with the Australian War Memorial; Edwards, Peter (1997) *A Nation at War: Australian Politics, Society and Diplomacy During the Vietnam War 1965–1975*, Sydney: Allen & Unwin in association with the Australian War Memorial.

the commitments to East Timor, Iraq, and Afghanistan. It can be anticipated that diplomatic and strategic considerations will be amply covered in these works, perhaps more prominently in the sixth series, although they are likely to be integrated into the volumes dealing with operations rather than as stand-alone volumes on the model of the Korean War and Southeast Asian Conflicts series. No official war historian today or in the foreseeable future is likely to omit the strategic, diplomatic, and civil–military dimensions of a conflict, as had been the practice of O'Neill's predecessors, Charles Bean and Gavin Long, and their respective colleagues.

The appointment of Robert O'Neill as the official historian of Australia's involvement in the Korean War, and the way in which he carried out that task, marked a major turning point, not only in the tradition of Australian official war histories, but also in Australian strategic and diplomatic historiography. He was the first of the Australian official war historians to have academic qualifications of a high order, whereas his predecessors had typically been distinguished journalists and war correspondents. Secondly, he pioneered the coverage in official histories of the strategic and diplomatic policy-making that led Australian forces to be involved in conflicts, with the same precision and authority as had always been given to the experience of those forces. From the vantage point of the second decade of the twenty-first century, it would be easy to overlook the full significance of O'Neill's contribution to an important element in Australians' understanding of their nation's place in the world.

7

The Evolution of Australian Official War Histories

David Horner

Robert O'Neill was the third of Australia's six official war historians, and directly or indirectly had a major influence on at least four of the official history series — his own and the three succeeding official histories. When O'Neill was appointed official historian for the Korean War in 1969, Australia had already had two official historians — Charles Bean and Gavin Long. O'Neill would need to draw on the experiences of his two successors, but also make his own decisions about what was needed for this new history. The two previous official histories provided much guidance.

The first official historian, Charles Bean, was general editor and principal author of the *Official History of Australia in the War of 1914–1918*, published between 1921 and 1942 in 15 volumes. This official history set the benchmark for later Australian official histories. Bean believed that his history had at least six objectives. First, it was largely a memorial to the men who had served and died. Second, he needed to record in detail what the Australians had done, in the belief that no other nation would do so. Third, the narrative needed to provide sufficient evidence to sustain the arguments presented in it. Fourth, as the war had been 'a plain trial of national character, it was necessary to show how the Australian citizen reacted to it'. This meant that Bean needed to bring to life the experiences of the men in the front line.

Fifth, Bean hoped that his history might 'furnish a fund of information from which military and other students, if they desired, could draw'. Finally, if possible, he wanted to tell the story from the Turkish and German sides as well as Australia's.[1]

By comparison with previous European official histories, Bean's history was unique in that it gave equal weight to the experiences of the soldiers and the decisions of commanders, and did not consciously try to draw lessons for future officers and commanders. The First World War series consisted of seven volumes on army operations, one each on the navy, the flying corps, the campaign in New Guinea, and the home front, as well as a photographic record. Bean wrote six of the army volumes. Only one, the home front volume, was written by a university-based historian. Three medical volumes were initiated some years later and were brought under Bean's general editorship. There was little coverage of higher strategic issues, partly because the Australian Government was only marginally involved in them.

Bean's history established an expectation that there would be a similar series for the Second World War, and he was instrumental in initiating it. On his recommendation, in March 1943 the government appointed Gavin Long as official historian for the Second World War. Following Bean's lead, Long travelled through the Southwest Pacific conducting interviews with officers and soldiers, and recording them in 134 diaries and notebooks. The Second World War official history, *Australia in the War of 1939–1945*, published between 1952 and 1977, consisted of 22 volumes, including seven on the army, two on the navy, four on the air force, two on the government and the people, two on the economy, and one on science and industry. Long wrote three of the army volumes, and 13 other authors wrote the remaining 19 volumes. Only the economic and science and industry volumes were written by university-based historians. As Bill Sweeting (one of Long's research assistants) wrote: 'It was the largest historical project ever undertaken in Australia.'[2]

---

1   Bean, C. E. W. (1961) *Anzac to Amiens*, Canberra: Australian War Memorial, p. viii.
2   Sweeting, A. J. (2000) 'Long, Gavin Merrick (1901–1968)', *Australian Dictionary of Biography*, Vol. 157, Melbourne: Melbourne University Press. Available at: adb.anu.edu.au/biography/long-gavin-merrick-10856/text19269.

While Bean continues to receive recognition for his achievement, with the publication of four biographies and discussion in numerous books and articles, Long has received less recognition. But his work was equally as impressive. His own accounts brought the experience of individuals alive in the same manner as Bean, and he raised contentious issues that set the agenda for further research, such as command problems and whether the final campaigns were necessary.[3]

The treatment of the home front was groundbreaking research. Australia's involvement in the Second World War was more complex than in the First World War. Australia's role as part of a larger allied coalition needed to be described, and the political story was fundamental to the history. To a greater extent than Bean, Long faced the problem of dealing with intelligence sources, but it is possible that he was never informed about the breaking of the German and Japanese codes, which only started to be revealed in the 1970s. Further, while the Secretary of the Department of Defence, Sir Frederick Shedden, who had been secretary of the War Cabinet, provided Long with whatever documents he requested, he did not offer Long documents that Long did not know existed. Although Long had originally planned a separate volume on general defence policy, this did not eventuate. No doubt Shedden hoped that his own history of Australian defence policy, written after he retired, would fill this gap, but it did not prove suitable for publication.[4]

Following the precedent of Bean's history, the government undertook to provide Long with 'reasonable access to official records', and decided that 'the exercise of censorship by the Government is to be limited to the preservation of disclosure of technical secrets of the three services which it is necessary to preserve in the post-war period'. Long acknowledged that while he and his colleagues had been given access to official papers, they were 'conscious of the special responsibilities which rest upon writers of a national history'.[5] These were to become the guiding principles for the later official histories.

---

3   See Long, Gavin (1963) *The Final Campaigns*, Canberra: Australian War Memorial.
4   Horner, David (2000) *Defence Supremo: Sir Frederick Shedden and the Making of Australian Defence Policy*, Sydney: Allen & Unwin, chapter 15.
5   Long, Gavin (1952) *To Benghazi*, Canberra: Australian War Memorial, pp. x, xi.

In the decades after the Second World War, the idea of writing official histories of Australia's involvement in the Korean War, the Malayan Emergency, Confrontation, and the Vietnam War languished. The First and Second World Wars had been great national endeavours involving hundreds of thousands of citizens. By contrast, the Korean War and the Malayan Emergency were fought by regular servicemen, and the nation at large was not closely involved. In the Vietnam War, the regulars were supplemented by national servicemen. The contentious nature of the war meant that there was no immediate call for an official history.

Robert O'Neill played a key role in reviving the idea of writing official histories of these more recent conflicts. As a teenager, he had become interested in the official histories of the two world wars. He graduated from the Royal Military College (RMC), Duntroon, in 1958 and from 1961, as a Rhodes Scholar, he was a graduate student at the University of Oxford. His supervisor, Norman Gibbs, the Chichele Professor of the History of War, was then working on a volume of the British official history of the Second World War. O'Neill met Michael Howard, who would also write a volume in the British official history. (Both Howard and O'Neill would later become Chichele Professor of the History of War.) O'Neill also met Brian Melland, of the Historical Section of the British Cabinet Office, and Noble Frankland, the author of a volume of the British official history and the Director of the Imperial War Museum. O'Neill had close contact with Sir Basil Liddell Hart, a professed critic of official histories, based on his own experience of the First World War, and the published volumes on that war.

O'Neill returned to Australia in 1966 and served with the 5th Battalion, Royal Australian Regiment (5RAR) in South Vietnam in 1966–1967. In 1966, his PhD thesis at Oxford was published as *The German Army and the Nazi Party, 1933–1939*,[6] and the success of this book encouraged him to write a book about his battalion's experiences in Vietnam. The result was *Vietnam Task*, published in 1968.[7]

---

6   O'Neill, Robert (1966) *The German Army and the Nazi Party, 1933–1939*, London: Cassell.
7   O'Neill, Robert J. (1968) *Vietnam Task: The 5th Battalion, Royal Australian Regiment, 1966–67*, Sydney: Cassell.

After Vietnam, O'Neill went to the RMC Duntroon as a lecturer, where the History Department of the Faculty of Military Studies was headed by Professor L. C. F. (Len) Turner, who had been joint author of three volumes of the South African official history of the Second World War. (As a cadet at Duntroon at this time, I was taught by Turner and O'Neill.) Turner and O'Neill agreed that work needed to start on official histories of Australia's more recent conflicts, and chronologically, the first one was the Korean War. In the meantime, the Army's Director of Infantry, Colonel David Thomson, had persuaded O'Neill to begin a history of the Royal Australian Regiment.

While in Britain in the early 1960s, O'Neill had met Air Vice-Marshal Geoff Hartnell, who was at Australia House and on the Board of Trustees of the Imperial War Museum. By 1969, Hartnell was a member of the Council of the Australian War Memorial and he took up the case for the official history of the Korean War. The Memorial Council and Director Bill Lancaster successfully sought funds for a Korean War history, and O'Neill and Turner were asked to accept the task. Turner withdrew, but O'Neill agreed to continue the task alone and was officially appointed in December 1969. He stopped work on the history of the Royal Australian Regiment. Eighteen years later, the then director of infantry asked me to write the history of the Royal Australian Regiment. I enlisted other authors to assist and the book, *Duty First,* was duly published in 1990.[8] Early parts of the book were based on an unpublished manuscript, 'History of the Royal Australian Regiment, 1945–1950', written by O'Neill in 1969.

O'Neill had already accepted an appointment in the Department of International Relations at The Australian National University. Once he arrived in early 1970, he found that Dr Tom Millar was stepping down as Head of the Strategic and Defence Studies Centre (SDSC) to become Director of the Australian Institute of International Affairs. The Head of International Relations, Professor Hedley Bull, asked O'Neill to take over as Head of SDSC. O'Neill then started work on two major tasks, headship of SDSC, and the official history of the Korean War.

---

8   Horner, David (ed.) (1990) *Duty First: the Royal Australian Regiment in War and Peace,* North Sydney: Allen & Unwin.

In anticipation of the appointment of an official historian for the Vietnam War, O'Neill also began to agitate for work to begin on collecting historical material. This yielded results, and Lieutenant Colonel Robin Morison was sent to Vietnam in charge of record making and gathering. O'Neill visited him there in 1971 to give a little guidance on what would be most valuable for a war historian. O'Neill advised the army to set up an oral history project, and over the next two years Morison interviewed more than a score of senior officers who had served in Vietnam. Morison was joined in this endeavour by Major Ian McNeill, who would later write one and part of another of the combat volumes of the Vietnam War official history.

Because the Korean War history was being undertaken on a shoestring budget, O'Neill had to proceed alone, although after a few years he was joined by a research officer, Darryl McIntyre. O'Neill worked on the official history at the Australian War Memorial or government offices (where he researched external affairs and defence files) during the morning and ran SDSC in the afternoon. Later, on study leave in Britain, he worked in the Imperial War Museum and the British Ministry of Defence, where he researched British documents, including the war diaries of British formations of which the Australian battalions were part (and which were not available in Australia).

Bean and Long had first-hand experience of many operations. O'Neill had not served in the Korean War, but had operational service in Vietnam. Unlike Bean and Long, however, O'Neill had a PhD in history and had written books on military history before he was appointed. Coming to the task some 20 years after the Korean War and having no personal experience of the war, O'Neill drew on his training as an academic historian. Clearly, he needed to research the files of the various Australian Government departments and also those of the United Kingdom, but to supplement the information in the files he sought to interview the participants. He was assisted by two former secretaries to the Department of External Affairs, Sir James Plimsoll and Sir Alan Watt, and especially by the former Minister for External Affairs, Sir Percy Spender, who played the key role in committing Australian troops to the Korean War and in bringing the ANZUS Treaty to fruition.

As he researched these files, O'Neill realised that the diplomatic and strategic aspects were the most important part of the story. He observed that 'there was very little interaction between Australian strategic policy and the combat operations of Australian forces in the Korean war', and hence any 'attempt to produce an integrated history, treating Australian policy development and Australian military operations as part of a continuous pattern of related activity, would have been highly artificial'.[9] As a consequence, the first volume of *Australia in the Korean War 1950–1953*, published in 1981, dealt with strategy and diplomacy, and the second volume, published in 1985, covered combat operations of the three services.

Volume II was divided into four parts — the land, air wars, sea wars, and a final part on prisoners, medical aspects, and post-armistice operations. It maintained the tradition of telling the story from the soldiers' perspective. As a former army officer who had seen active service of his own, O'Neill understood army operations, but he also needed to comprehend naval and air operations for those sections of his history. Bean had left the writing of the naval and flying corps volumes to other authors, just as Long had left the naval and air force volumes to those with specialist knowledge. While commanders' diaries and reports of proceedings were vital sources, O'Neill conducted interviews or sought advice from more than 70 participants.

The official history was an outstanding achievement, which not only upheld the very high standards of its predecessors, but set new standards. For example, the Korean War official history had a detailed bibliography and footnotes to documents, which had not generally been the case in the earlier official histories. It was important to put the experience of the servicemen on record, and in this respect the history has become the key source for information on the Australian operations — just as the Bean and Long histories have been the starting point for future research. But beyond this, the history was a major advance in the historiography of Australian diplomacy during a time when Australia was developing its own foreign policy. Volume I is still the most authoritative account of the establishment of the ANZUS alliance.

---

9   O'Neill, Robert (1981) *Australia in the Korean War 1950–1953*, Vol. I: Strategy and Diplomacy, Canberra: The Australian War Memorial and the Australian Government Publishing Service, p. xv.

Most importantly, the Korean War history revived the concept of official histories in a modern setting. It provided a bridge between the official histories of the world wars and those of Southeast Asian conflicts and beyond. Like the world wars, the Korean War history dealt with only one war. But, like subsequent series, the Korean War history showed that the political and diplomatic history was just as important as recounting what happened on the battlefield.

I received my first glimpse of the challenges of writing an official history when O'Neill supervised my master's thesis from 1974–1975, and my PhD thesis from 1978–1980 (the latter undertaken at ANU). After Duntroon, I had served as an infantry officer in Vietnam, and during those periods of postgraduate study I was still serving in the Australian Army. At that time, O'Neill was working on his official history. He discussed some of the challenges and at one stage asked me to read the army sections of Volume II. I am not sure that I had any useful comment to make at that point of my development as a historian. My interest in official histories was sparked, however, when I found that Gavin Long's plan to write a volume on strategic and defence policy had not been fulfilled, and that he had not been given full access to the papers of Sir Frederick Shedden. I determined that my PhD thesis on Australian strategic policy-making in the Second World War, for which I had access to the Shedden papers, would try to fill this gap in the Australian official history. It was published in 1982 as *High Command: Australia and Allied Strategy 1939–1945*.[10] My time working with O'Neill helped shape my approach when I later became an official historian.

In 1982, Dr Peter Edwards was appointed official historian for the Vietnam War, 10 years after the last combat troops withdrew. O'Neill was not directly involved in persuading the government to approve the history, but he was a member of the selection committee for the official historian and provided guidance. The *Official History of Australia's Involvement in Southeast Asia Conflicts 1948–1972,* marked a further step in the development of Australian official histories. Edwards, like O'Neill, was a Rhodes Scholar. He had a PhD in history and had written or edited books on Australian diplomatic history; but he had no military service and had not visited Vietnam during the Vietnam

---

10   Horner, David (1982) *High Command: Australia and Allied Strategy 1939–1945*, Canberra: Australian War Memorial.

War. This was not, however, an impediment to producing a thorough history, as he concentrated on strategy, diplomacy, and politics. Of his other six principal authors, only Ian McNeill had served in the Vietnam War, but all had university training as historians.

Edwards confirmed the model set by O'Neill in emphasising the importance of strategy and diplomacy. His history covered three conflicts — the Malayan Emergency (1948–1960), Confrontation (1963–1966), and the Vietnam War (1972–1975) — and his first volume on politics and diplomacy dealt with the background to the deployments in these conflicts. As with the earlier official histories, the Vietnam series dealt separately with the three services in Vietnam. The series ran to nine volumes, two on politics and diplomacy, one on the Emergency and Confrontation, three on land operations in Vietnam, one on air operations in Vietnam, one on naval operations in the Southeast Asia region, and one on medical aspects.

Both the O'Neill and Edwards histories suffered from the parsimony of governments. Edwards received no direct funding for several of his authors, so he persuaded two authors to write volumes as part of their university research projects, and the author of the RAAF volume was funded by the RAAF. The result was that although the first volume, *Crises and Commitments*, was published in 1992, 10 years after the beginning of the project, the last volume, *Fighting to the Finish*, did not appear until 2012, more than 40 years after the last combat troops withdrew from Vietnam. By this time, the youngest men who served in Vietnam were in their 60s. There was one advantage in this. The author, Ashley Ekins, was able to make use of recently available Viet Cong histories, deal with the arguments in other books, and tie up loose ends. But a long-delayed history should not be a model for the future. The series was deeply researched, measured in judgments, respectful of the achievement of the Australian service people, and superbly presented.

Successive official historians have sought to persuade governments to initiate new histories. Edwards tried to persuade the government to initiate an official history of Australian peacekeeping operations, but in 1992 the Minister for Veterans' Affairs declined to support a history while the Vietnam official history was uncompleted.[11]

As the Vietnam official histories started to appear, some historians questioned whether official histories had outlived their usefulness. For example, in 1994, the academic historian John Murphy argued that Edwards failed to provide a full portrait of Australian society and politics, and that his series consisted of books that were divided into specialist sub-disciplines of diplomatic and military history. Murphy concluded:

> Bean and Long were both journalists, writing for a wider audience; McNeill and Edwards are writing within more specialised discourses. In these senses the tradition of official history seems problematic and near to exhaustion. Where before it meant an attempt to explain the social experience of war, it has been diverted into the scholarly study of war as seen from the commanding heights of the cabinet, bureaucracy and armed forces.[12]

Glen St J. Barclay of the University of Queensland made a similar criticism. He acknowledged that the official historians of both world wars 'set a magnificent standard', but asserted that 'it could not be sustained'. It was possible, he said, 'to write exclusively and in vast detail about Australia's involvement in the two World Wars because Australians had played a significant part in their own right in many campaigns in both conflicts', but, he added, 'it would not be possible to write exclusively about Australian involvement in conflicts in which Australian units operated as marginal elements in a vast largely Allied operation' without producing an account for which the audience 'would certainly be prone to miss the point'. Thus, while O'Neill's

---

11   In 1991, the Senate Standing Committee on Foreign Affairs, Defence and Trade recommended that the Vietnam official historian be commissioned to write the history of Australian peacekeeping.
12   Murphy, John (1994) 'The New Official History', *Australian Historical Studies* 26(102), pp. 123–4.

volume *Strategy and Diplomacy* had been an 'unqualified success', his second volume, *Combat Operations,* although well done, was 'precisely a regimental history' which omitted the larger picture.[13]

The argument that Bean and Long were trying primarily to explain the social experience of war is hard to sustain, given their detailed treatment of operations. It seems that Murphy and Barclay were arguing that O'Neill and Edwards failed because they did not exactly follow, or more generally because it was no longer possible to follow, the model of previous histories. Did that mean that the concept of official histories had outlived their usefulness? Or could it be that there were new models with their own utility?

This was one of the questions I needed to deal with in 2002 when the Australian War Memorial engaged me to conduct a study into the feasibility of an official history of Australian peacekeeping. By that time I had retired from the Australian Army and was working in SDSC at ANU. As part of my feasibility study, I sought advice from both O'Neill and Edwards.

The arguments in favour of a new official history seemed persuasive. Despite the relatively few casualties — in all less than a dozen deaths — the operations were often extremely arduous and dangerous, and the absence of heavy casualties could be attributed about equally to excellent planning and training, and plain luck. Further, while Australia suffered few casualties, the conflicts involved very large numbers of deaths, including some of the great tragedies of the twentieth century. For example, hundreds of thousands were killed in Rwanda. The psychological impact on the Australians was considerable and many peacekeepers had been diagnosed with post-traumatic stress disorder.

The nature of Australian military operations had changed. We are unlikely to again see operations on a scale of the world wars. The operations in recent years, however, had played a large part in defining Australia's place in the world, and were similar to those that were likely to occur in the future. More broadly, Australia had shown that it was a good international citizen, and decisions had not been

---

13 Barclay, Glen St John (1995) 'Australian Historians and the Study of War, 1975–88', *Australian Journal of Politics and History* 41, pp. 240–53.

taken lightly. For example, there was probably more government consideration given to Australia's commitments to Somalia and Cambodia than was given to Australia entering the First World War. Many operations required complicated defence planning. An official history would need to discuss the reasons for the conflicts and the background to Australia's involvement. On a more personal level, the men and women of the Australian Defence Force (ADF) had become widely admired for their professionalism, reliability, and compassion. They had been truly representing Australia abroad. The history would therefore need to describe the activities of the Australians in the operations, even when relatively small numbers were deployed.

We now live in a society in which people demand more recognition than in the past. Service people expect medals and compensation for injuries. They feel that they too deserve to be treated as Anzacs. The feeling among veterans that service in peacekeeping operations was special and had not been recognised sufficiently was illustrated by the formation of the Australian Peacekeeping and Peacemakers Association in October 1997.

An official history of peacekeeping would face some intellectual challenges. By contrast with the first four series, the fifth series would need to deal with at least 50 missions in about 27 conflicts (as was the case when I did the feasibility study in 2002), many taking place at about the same time in a wide range of geographic areas. The fifth series would cover a period of more than 60 years — from 1947 to 2006 — and the authors would need to comprehend the domestic and international political environments across this entire period.

One obvious difference was that the first four series dealt with wars in which Australia was a participant. Within the bounds of proper scholarship, these could be partisan histories. To my knowledge, no-one suggested that Gavin Long and his authors should go easy on describing instances of Japanese barbarism because to do so might offend the Japanese. By contrast, the fifth series needed to deal, to a large extent, with missions in which the Australians were not protagonists in the conflict, but stood between the protagonists. Often Australia tried to maintain good relations with both sides of a conflict. How was the history to deal with situations in which Australian peacekeepers might have reported on the poor behaviour of one of the sides? In a similar vein, all the Australian deployments had been part of a multinational force, often composed of strange bed-fellows. Should we report on the unsatisfactory conduct of our allies?

One key question to be addressed was whether Australia's contributions actually made a difference. This question was never explicitly examined in the previous official histories, although they provide sufficient evidence for readers to draw their own conclusions. What difference did the Australians make by their presence in, say, the United Nations Truce Supervision Organisation in the Middle East? What was the value of Australia's contribution in Western Sahara, where the deadlock continues to the present day, even though the Australians withdrew more than two decades ago? And if the value of Australia's contribution was qualitative, rather than quantitative, who is able to make the judgement? Do we rely on the Australian troops' estimation of their own worth?

The first four official histories series described conflicts within particular paradigms for the use of force. These paradigms have undergone significant changes. The strategic environment since the end of the Cold War has seen the emergence of forms of warfare whose characteristics include ethnic conflict within countries; the influence of international media; the Revolution in Military Affairs and the development of network-centric warfare; the use of the precision strike; the use of special forces rather than large-scale deployments; the campaign against international terrorism; the increasing importance of operations other than war; the increasing importance of joint and coalition operations; the increasing role of non-government organisations (NGOs); and the deployment of women on operations. These characteristics were not present in the conflicts described in the earlier official histories.

In addition, there were special characteristics of peacekeeping that needed explanation, including the problems caused by restrictive rules of engagement, with soldiers being required to observe atrocities but not being permitted to intervene; the command and management problems of operating under United Nations rather than national control; the problem of 'mission creep' — for example, a humanitarian operation that might turn into a peace enforcement operation; the political sensitivity of many operations, with the government wishing to retain good relations with the protagonists; the problems of operating as part of a coalition that might include countries with entirely different political and military cultures; situations in which almost every action has political ramifications; and the involvement of many agencies, including other UN agencies and NGOs. These considerations meant that the old models of the official histories were no longer appropriate. A new and innovative approach would be needed for a modern official history.

The Australian War Memorial accepted my feasibility study, and in March 2004 I was appointed official historian. But government parsimony reached an all time high. No government money was specifically allocated for the project. The Director of the Australian War Memorial, Major General Steve Gower, and I cobbled together funds from various sources — the Australian War Memorial (from its operating budget), the Department of Defence, ANU, and the Australian Research Council — to allow the project to begin. I was able to engage authors and research assistants, but for only a limited period. As with the Vietnam history, all the authors had university training as historians. Dr Bob Breen had been a Regular Army officer and had spent considerable time visiting Australian forces on various operational deployments. Two other authors had Army Reserve service. The final *Official History of Australian Peacekeeping, Humanitarian and Post-Cold War Operations* consisted of:

- *Volume I: The Long Search for Peace: Observer Missions and Beyond: 1947–2006*
- *Volume II: Australia and the 'New World Order': From Peacekeeping to Peace Enforcement: 1988–1991*
- *Volume III: The Good International Citizen: Australian Peacekeeping in Asia, Africa and Europe, 1991–1993*
- *Volume IV: The Limits of Peacekeeping: Australian Missions in Africa and the Americas: 1992–2006*
- *Volume V: The Good Neighbour: Australian Peace Support Operations in the Pacific Islands, 1980–2006*
- *Volume VI: In Their Time of Need: Australia's Overseas Emergency Relief Operations, 1918–2006.*

7. THE EVOLUTION OF AUSTRALIAN OFFICIAL WAR HISTORIES

At the time of writing (December 2015), Volumes II and III had been published, Volume V was with the publisher, Volume VI was being cleared by government departments, and it was hoped that final drafts of Volumes I and IV would be completed by 31 March 2016.

This structure revealed substantial differences from earlier series. The government's policy considerations for each mission were included as part of the story of each mission, although each volume also had several chapters discussing the government's general approach to peacekeeping. There was no separate treatment of the different services. Some missions were conducted by mainly army or naval units, but in general the ADF now deployed in joint service task groups. There was no medical volume or section. Medical units deployed to northern Iraq and Rwanda, but they were covered in the same manner as other missions — i.e. as part of the general peacekeeping story. There were, however, appendices on post-traumatic stress disorder and Gulf War syndrome. It might be noted that the Australian operations in East Timor which began in 1999 were not included in this series, no doubt because of government sensitivities about offending Indonesia. I tried to have East Timor included in the series but was unsuccessful.

By the time I was appointed official historian in 2004, I had become convinced that work needed to begin on another official history, covering Australian military operations in Afghanistan and Iraq. Following the terrorist attacks in New York and Washington DC on 11 September 2001, the ADF sent troops into Afghanistan in October 2001. The troops departed in 2002, but returned to Afghanistan in 2005 and served there until 2014 when the commitment formally ended (although some troops remained). In 2003, Australia joined with the United States and the United Kingdom in taking part in the invasion of Iraq. Most of the Australian force withdrew soon after the initial campaign, but forces returned to Iraq in 2005 and remained there until 2009. Due to the political sensitivity of many of the operations, the Australian public, and indeed the troops themselves, had no idea what operations had actually been conducted, or why.

After agitating for many years, in 2011 I persuaded the Australian War Memorial to commission a feasibility study into an official history of Iraq and Afghanistan. I undertook the study in 2012 and concluded that an official history could be justified on three broad grounds. First, the experience of past official histories re-affirmed the requirement for detailed, authoritative accounts of Australia's military operations — a need strengthened by the increasing importance of policy issues and the requirement to provide authority for compensation and pension benefits. There was a public expectation that Australia's official history tradition would continue. Second, the operations in Iraq and Afghanistan, involving perhaps 30,000 Australians over 10 years, had clearly been of sufficient magnitude and complexity to warrant an official history. Third, because of restrictions on Australian journalists, the history of these activities had not been covered adequately in existing works.

There were compelling reasons why an official history should begin as soon as practicable. The operations had been running for more than a decade, casualties had been mounting and the Australian public had a right to know how and why the operations had been conducted. The ADF personnel who served there deserved to have their stories told. The operations were complex and long-running, and as each year passed it would become increasingly difficult to locate the information necessary to write an authoritative history. Most records in government departments are now held digitally, and there are particular problems in accessing highly classified records on digital systems.

Several reasons were advanced as to why such a history should not be written at that time. Some people argued that sufficient time needed to pass before past events could be seen in proper historical context. Yet previous governments had approved research for the official histories of the First and Second World Wars to begin during those wars. If an official history of Iraq and Afghanistan were to be authorised in 2013, the events of 2001–2002 would likely be covered in the first volume of the history. This volume would be published at the earliest in 2020 — some 18 years after the events concluded.

Certain officials argued that the events surrounding the operations in Iraq and Afghanistan were too sensitive, and might still be sensitive in 20 years' time. Australian operations were conducted as part of an allied coalition and it would be too difficult, perhaps impossible, to reveal the negotiations with Australia's coalition partners. More so than in the past, recent operations have been driven by intelligence; the sources and nature of this intelligence should remain secret. If an official history were to be approved there might be problems in clearing it for publication. Indeed, the experience of the peacekeeping official history showed that government departments were likely to try to censor the history, notwithstanding the cabinet minute stating that there was to be no censorship. Although we now live in an era of greater government transparency, governments have become even more determined to keep their decision-making considerations secret.

The Council of the Memorial agreed that a history was feasible and should begin as soon as possible, but attempts to obtain government approval were delayed by two changes of government during 2013 — Prime Minister Julia Gillard was replaced by Kevin Rudd in mid-2013 and in turn he was defeated in a general election by the Coalition, led by Tony Abbott. In April 2015 the Abbott Government approved and agreed to fund the official history of Iraq and Afghanistan, and added funding for a volume on East Timor. At the time of writing, the government had not announced the new official historian. The new official history will be a major undertaking — one which will bring about a further evolution in the nature of Australian official histories.

Robert O'Neill had no direct influence over the official history of Iraq and Afghanistan. But there was considerable indirect influence. His agitation in 1969 had led to the Australian War Memorial Council taking the key role in presenting the case to the government, and that approach from the council has persisted through to the present time, leading to the Vietnam, peacekeeping and Iraq/Afghanistan official history series. As O'Neill's student, I was strongly influenced by his approach to official histories and historical scholarship in general. I was able to use that knowledge and experience not only as official historian of peacekeeping, but also in setting the ground work for the Iraq/Afghanistan series. Robert O'Neill has made an outstanding contribution to scholarship and public debate in the field of strategic studies (as discussed in other chapters). His major contribution in keeping Australian official histories alive, contributing to their evolution, and in fostering them should not be overlooked.

8

The Postwar Evolution of the Field of Strategic Studies: Robert O'Neill in Context

Catherine McArdle Kelleher

Introduction

This chapter views the postwar evolution of strategic studies as an academic field to illuminate the intellectual and organisational context of Bob O'Neill's scholarly achievements and organising adventures. Bob has been deeply involved in this evolution for over five decades, and has enjoyed a truly global view. Quite apart from his own research, he has been a significant animateur of research and teaching, with an amazing record of attracting and supporting students and colleagues, women as well as men, in Australia, the United Kingdom, the United States, and throughout Asia. Bob is also renowned as the builder and organiser of multiple collaborative efforts and numerous institutions across disciplines and across continents. It has been a remarkable career, but all the more remarkable for the far reaching lessons he has drawn, the wise counsel he has given, and the sense of integrity that Bob has made the standard for judgment and analysis.

I — and a number of others in this volume — have had the distinct pleasure of being along on the journey at different times and in different places. The context in which he has operated has too often been forgotten; he has led or fought many of the critical battles in postwar strategic studies, always with the same calm and vision. Presenting the evolutionary timeline of the field will time his career, detailed in other essays in appropriate measure.

I apologise that what I present here is far too much of an American view to do Bob's career justice. It is also a personal view based on experiences that sometimes, but not always, have paralleled his. I hope thereby to challenge him to present his version and to write about the rest of the story as he sees it. It has not always been a smooth or a supportive context, especially given his advocacy for a more open and inclusive field, and his embracement of diversity, with emphasis on a more than a 'Europe first' or 'great powers' approach to strategy, and arguing for a greater transparency where possible. But for him, it has always been a journey of seizing and creating new opportunities, with enthusiastic appreciation of the farthest shore ahead. I suspect, too, that it has never been dull.

The Focus of Strategic Studies in the Postwar Period

Writings in the last decades have usually portrayed strategic studies as a child of the 1950s, driven by the almost unimaginable consequences of the nuclear revolution, and glowing most brightly in the risks and successes of the Cold War. In reality, the neat symmetric package of history and ideals is only part of a much longer history.[1] Beginning in the 1920s and 1930s, the building of strategic studies parallels the harnessing of technology, and the recruitment of the best and the brightest in the natural sciences to the preservation of the state and its interests. It was supported by many of the dominant American foundations and Anglo-Saxon scientific societies, those who had earlier transformed science and its advancement into a public good and a public goal. It was thus largely developed in an Anglo-Saxon

---

1   The classic postwar analysis through early Vietnam is Hedley Bull's masterly (1968) 'Strategic Studies and its Critics', *World Politics* 20(4), pp. 593–605, extended by Betts, Richard (1997) 'Should Strategic Studies Survive?', *World Politics* 50(1), pp. 7–33, and from a different perspective Buzan, Barry and Lene Hansen (2009) *The Evolution of International Security Studies*, New York: Cambridge University Press.

context, with legacy contributions from Britain, the United States, and the Commonwealth countries, all pursuing particular variants reflective of their own new or re-drawn roles in the Cold War and after.

Community members themselves differ on the significance of the contributions made and the range of the policy successes scored. Is it just nuclear policy or a wider domain on the use of any kind of force — the state's natural monopoly — to preserve the state? Is there more than a practical limit to how close to government policy one needs to be or should be? What are legitimate cost–benefit comparisons for social scientists and historians? The long shadow of Vietnam and its ideological battles alone highlights the critical and recurring divides and debates that have occurred and re-occurred.[2]

Most scholars agree on a core of tasks and principles, basically a set of democratic convictions and optimism about the role of social scientific contributions to policy, that has set them apart from continental or Asian practices and aspirations.[3] The key tenets presented here are in their most abstract form:

1. Security writ large is not just the province of the professional military but of informed, engaged citizens. It is not just for a Cincinnatus who comes to the rescue and then returns to his field. In democratic states in particular, it is the responsibility of every citizen, and for those who can, it is a right and honourable profession. Required is the citizen soldier, the public service official, the committed educator, and the impartial policy scientist who must take on the task of advisor and critic.

2. Knowledge that is gained or created in the social and behavioural sciences (the policy sciences) is to be applied in a constant campaign against external threat, experienced at home or abroad. That comes in part through government, but it can and in some ways must come from the outside through daily operations — the research and findings of universities, think tanks, private study groups and foundations, and the leadership of informed individuals.

---

2   The shadows of the 'wars of choice' of the twenty-first century are now almost as long, given the use of social science expertise in interrogation techniques that crossed into torture, and in sanctioning ethnic tensions to extremes.

3   See here the threads running through Freedman, Lawrence (2013) *Strategy*, New York: Oxford University Press, and those undergirding Nye, Joseph (1989) 'The Contribution of Strategic Studies: Future Challenges', Adelphi Paper 29(235), pp. 20–34.

3. The goal is to develop critical thinking and focus attention on the important, not just the urgent. Ideally, neither individuals nor organisations should surrender the right to speak truth to power. Nor should they be tied directly to, or subservient to, present government policy, but rather be able to continually stretch toward future goals, and to adopt best practices wherever they come from.
4. In the end, policy represents the result of a broad lens and informed choice, perhaps involving necessary compromise given time and circumstance, but aiming for an optimised solution to the degree possible. It almost inevitably has a political frame, and costs and consequences to be regularly attributed. Uncertainty is to be confronted and narrowed; risk is to be assessed and weighed systematically against other options.

At least for those over 40, most of these principles, while impossibly abstract, have a familiar ring. In the United States and a somewhat more cynical Britain, this corresponds to the aspirations of the civic virtue movement of the late nineteenth century and the 1920s and 1930s. Education and transparency, and sometimes the distance from politicians and political games, it was argued, would yield the best result for a wise decision-maker. One example may suffice: Robert Brooking's conviction, as a merchant magnate in the Midwest, of the need to establish a single institution at the seat of government in Washington DC, to offer the best information and advice to government, and simultaneously to train successor generations of analysts to do the transparent, consistent, scientific analysis needed to identify new problems and unanticipated threats.[4]

Less ethereal perhaps is the tie to the all-out mobilisation against the threat to the state posed by the twin demons of communism and fascism in the 1930s and the Second World War, and the recruitment of many to the cause who had previously seen policy problems as someone else's problem.[5] There had always been such a tie, expressed often in personal relationships in Britain, but it was now greatly expanded and magnified as the war continued. The United States, in

---

[4] The Brookings Institution was at one period actually a degree-granting university, first as a wing of Washington University in St Louis, and then after the institution was founded in 1927 on its own.

[5] See David Ekbladh's analysis of foundations and individuals in the pre-Second World War American stirrings in (2011–2012) 'Present at the Creation', *International Security* 36(3), pp. 107–41.

its first golden age, represented a more dramatic shift. A handful of the best universities and centres — Harvard, Yale, Stanford, Columbia, University of Chicago, MIT, the Hoover Institution, the Princeton Institute for Advanced Study and its predecessor — provided eager players who were anxious to step nearer to government and to serve. Government, but also major philanthropic groups — in the US, Carnegie and Rockefeller, joined later by Ford — provided the needed funds. University and foundation heads alike acted as talent scouts and persuasive disseminators.[6] There was analysis and intelligence work, but also broader outreach programs of lectures and public policy education, integration of refugees with the most parochial of Americans in political life, and continuing watch over popular moods and tolerance of suffering.[7]

Evolution of the Field: Students, Subjects, and Support

By the time Bob (and I) entered strategic studies as a full-time graduate student player in the 1960s, the field and the supporting infrastructure had attracted significant stature, as well as infrastructure and funding. Some have argued the 1960s and 1970s represented the second golden age of strategic analysis. University centres of excellence existed in growing numbers on both sides of the Atlantic and throughout the Commonwealth. The task was to develop strategic studies as a crucial (and most interesting) sector of a broadened discipline of global international relations. The Third World, the non-aligned movement, nationalism, and terrorism were as valid as issues for study as the old standbys of international law, international organisations, and the diplomacy of the great powers of Europe. There were new curricula, deliberately violating the narrow professionalism of the

---

6 Ibid. Ekbladh details the pre-war contributions of, among others, Edward Mead Earle, Bernard Brodie, Harold Lasswell, Nicholas Spykman, and William T. R. Fox.

7 At one point, one of the pre-eminent researchers on public opinion, Hadley Cantril of Princeton, was actually brought with his team into the White House to provide daily measures of popular support.

more traditional war colleges,[8] focused on the military, political, and economic challenges to the security of the state, and the options available to protect and defend its interests. In the United States, the student base was expanded quite decisively with the extensive funding available under several national laws, particularly under the *National Defense Education Act*, a piece of legislation designed as a response to Sputnik and loss of space superiority in 1958.

Funding was plentiful. Government agencies, especially those related to defence and intelligence, saw education as a recruitment tool for later employment or mobilisation, and project support as providing wider options for decision-makers. Carnegie, Rockefeller, and a host of other foundations, with some government prompting, offered funds to support study and study-related field work overseas. Ford pursued both these goals at a new extensive program of centres to ensure area studies of the highest quality — literature, culture, and personalities as well as military traditions and strategic arsenals. There were also government funds for publishing houses and magazines,[9] and regular free distribution of relevant analysis for both the governmental sector and the informed audiences strategic studies was so anxious to attract.

One new feature was the development of international specialised centres for research and policy debate, funded by governments and foundations, especially the International Institute of Strategic Studies (IISS), which Bob O'Neill led with such skill and grace in the 1980s. Founded by Alastair Buchan in 1958, it was originally focused largely on Britain, with selected American visitors. But it quickly went global, attracting more Americans, those from the dominions, co-optees from the Third World, and eventually, the communist sphere.

IISS was not the usual foreign affairs and diplomacy centre, such as the Council on Foreign Relations or Chatham House, which had its roots in the genteel debates of the 1920s and the somewhat rowdier

---

8   The service war colleges were themselves ultimately transformed in the 1970s and the 1980s to teach to a broader strategic studies vision, one emphasising history, economics, and political science, as well as doctrine and operations management. The 'Turner revolution' at the Naval War College in Newport, Rhode Island, in the early 1970s is perhaps the best known in detail. See Hattendorf, John B. et al. (1984) *Sailors and Scholars: The Centennial History of the U.S. Naval War College*, Newport: Naval War College Press.

9   Perhaps the most dramatic revelation was the discovery in the late 1960s of CIA's Cold War financial support for the arts, especially magazines (*Encounter* and *Der Monat*, for example), that until then had been viewed as bastions of intellectual commentary and liberal criticism.

discussion in the 1930s. It was rather a membership organisation with an expert staff, designed to mobilise, educate, inform, and influence in strategic studies. The target audience, convened annually, was originally the elite who needed to be educated on the external threats to the NATO alliance and individual countries. It later expanded to working officials, promising students, and young policy hopefuls. Most were civilians and men, initially with only the rarest female stars, with Coral Bell of Australia, Margaret Gowing of Oxford, and Flora Lewis of the *New York Times* in the regular ranks. There were a range of specialist publications, which eventually included *Survival*, a magazine that ranked with *Foreign Affairs*, and the Adelphi Papers on emerging topics or crises, commissioned globally. There were also items for the analyst's right hand: annual tomes of information that established ground truth, thus creating a common global data base, through *Strategic Survey* and *The Military Balance*.

RAND in Santa Monica, California, was and remained something quite different, close to government but often standing on its own well into the 1980s. There were other specialised shops close to particular services — Center for Naval Analyses to the Chief of Naval Operations, and Institute for Defense Analyses to the Chairman of the Joint Chiefs — but RAND, even in its earliest incarnations, had a commitment to broaden the dialogue and improve analysis. It used its openness to draw the best and near-best practitioners, and the most innovative applications from economics, game theory, mathematics, operations research, and psychology. At a distance well removed from Washington DC, its ability was set to range more freely than inside-the-DC-beltway analysis, and its overall enthusiasm for experimentation, gaming, good writing, and effective presentation attracted intellectual fans in and outside of the United States. Early on, it was the envy and the model for close-to-government think tanks in France, Germany, and Japan. Many RAND publications were unclassified and broadly circulated.[10] Further, the RAND staff was diverse, with notable women analysts, such as Roberta Wohlstetter and later Lynn Davis.

RAND also represented a new civil–military model of analytic engagement. Led and populated originally by veterans of war-time policy analysis and retired military personnel, it drew almost all its

---

10   RAND itself became a graduate studies program, gaining accreditation in 1975.

funding from Project Air Force or other government monies. In some divisions there was a marked military presence, although seemingly never at the expense of direct analysis. Lunchtime debate at RAND was unique, with civilians totally in charge, no uniforms required, and no set work hours or effort to coordinate vacation time.

Divisions were generated by the war in Vietnam and the lingering questions it raised. The challenges came from those who vigorously opposed the war, reformers within the strategic studies community, and protestors within universities generally.[11] The charge was what they deemed the perversion of strategic studies independence, its analytic processes, and the subsequent suppression of dissent and challenge.[12]

The rifts and splits within and across disciplines over these issues went deep. The reformers saw what they defined as the insidious militarisation of American intellectual life and the sins of loyalty to government dogma and objectives, not the use of science and knowledge to the limits of independent inquiry in the service of ethical goals. The traditionalists and the operators responded with challenges to the loyalty of those who questioned legitimate government goals that had been and were still supported by popular majorities. They rejected those who set their own ethical preferences and refused to acknowledge the critical risks to state interests at stake.

By the mid-1970s, at RAND and elsewhere, it had become too often a dialogue of the deaf. The choice of which path to follow, at least in the United States, was stark. In public, distinctive subcultures emerged, with universities now rejecting centres or projects with government funding or the assignment of students to Reserve Officers' Training Corps units, and research centres were too superficially divided into good non-profits or presumably less good for profits. For the reformers, the ironic twist was that much of the government-specific funding and

---

11 Daniel Ellsberg had been a contributor at OSD and had initially worked for Nixon in 1969. Ellsberg tried — at first unsuccessfully, then, in 1971, successfully through the *New York Times* — to leak the study, against massive opposition from administration. The break-in of Ellsberg's psychiatrist's office, conducted to gather evidence against Ellsberg, constituted only one of Nixon's efforts to discredit Ellsberg and his colleague, Leslie Gelb.
12 See the analysis of these charges in the critiques published by two younger American historians: Rohde, Joy (2013) *Armed with Expertise: The Militarization of American Social Research during the Cold War*, Ithaca: Cornell University Press; Bessner, Daniel (forthcoming) *Democracy in Exile: Hans Speier and the Rise of the Defense Intellectual,* Ithaca: Cornell University Press.

projects critical for strategic studies disappeared from public view, into classified realms of compliant contractors, essentially withheld from debate, question, or democratic oversight. Traditionalist analysts, on the other hand, far too often found themselves held back by those now in an instinctive defensive crouch against any change or the new, and with a preference for safe subjects or consensual judgements. Some of the splits and fights continue in muted tones into the present, as is most recently evident in the argument in anthropology and sociology over the orientation and uses of the Human Terrain Research projects during the war in Afghanistan.

University centres themselves were developing ranges of specialties and areas of analytic specialisation. Bob experienced this first in Canberra and later when leading his own Oxford program. Student interest and recruitment was high, especially transatlantic student interest, at both the undergraduate and graduate levels. Cambridge, Massachusetts, long an IISS rampart, often claimed first place. In the 1950s and 1960s, the Harvard complex (Law School, Graduate Faculty, and in the 1970s, the JFK School) and the MIT Center for International Studies allowed cross registration; the faculties represented a major node of arms control study and discussion outside of Washington, which was almost unfailingly influential through its alumnae, increasingly not all male, in Washington. The relevant officials had often been their classmates or their students. A parallel development to the Cambridge clusters came with the increasing interest in strategic studies at the Center for International Security and Arms Control at Stanford, partnering with the growing centres at the University of California campuses at Berkeley and San Diego, and within the somewhat more conservative view of the Hoover Institution.

The analytic networks spread globally and grew at a steady pace in the 1970s, and less so in the early 1980s. *International Security*, born in Cambridge, joined *Survival*, a journal more academic in focus, and a number of smaller journals emerged and flourished. Bob was among the creators of a wide-reaching informal Asian group, made up of influential players, students, and former students (many who had come to Australia for training) that stretched across disciplines and borders. It was often a path for influence, or at least for an intellectual fellowship that opened doors to collaboration and cooperation.

It sometimes even stimulated negotiated outcomes, although without the multilateral exchanges and tendencies that NATO and especially Bob's IISS had informally fostered from the early 1960s onward.

In the Reagan era of the 1980s, Washington hosted not just partisan or contractor job shops (American Enterprise Institute, Heritage Foundation, Cato Institute) or the non-partisan greats (Brookings, Carnegie Endowment for International Peace), but for the first time, also several university centres. Georgetown and its Center for Strategic and International Studies (soon to become independent and more engaged in the daily political fray) were at the more conservative pole. At the other end, the emerging Center of International and Security Studies at Maryland worked closely with the National Academies of Sciences in the Soviet Union and in Washington on technical weapons and scientific expert exchanges, as well as broader programs within the framework of cooperative security.

As the 1980s drew to a close, the strategic studies field began to change again. Most programs essentially moved closer to the subfields of traditional international relations: arms control and disarmament, non-proliferation, or detailed studies of civil unrest and political change. Something close to Bob's first graduate research interests engaged us both with increasing significance: the awakening detente relations with Gorbachev and the Soviet Union, and the new frictions between politicians and military leaders. In critical London meetings, Bob highlighted the number of new control agreements in nuclear and conventional areas that increased the chance for future change, and downplayed the now traditional European security scenarios and even the traditional defence budgets. These issues were not new to those of us who had been patiently observing and working to deepen slow changes over the last two decades. But the big questions had to do with new frameworks and new methods of verification, of further limits on tests and technologies, and conflicts outside of Europe. Would or could Russia enter the European 'home'? And what was to be Eastern Europe's future?

One driver of change in this was the substantial new funding available through the MacArthur Foundation's Peace and Security Program. Under Ruth Adams, MacArthur funded 12 new or renewed university programs globally, established an international fellowship competition that would eventually award over 140 graduate fellowships over

10 years through the Social Science Research Council, and provided generous funding for international collaborative research for the next 20 years. The Carnegie Corporation, under David Hamburg, and Ford, under McGeorge Bundy and Enid Schoettle, became co-conspirators, highlighting security partnerships and the new security cooperative options for Russia and the United States. Bob, first at IISS and then Oxford, was a stakeholder and an advisor in these foundation efforts. Often in tandem with Lawrence Freedman, he regularly testified to intellectual need and to scholarly value, devised new curricula, and argued for the analytic standards that should be required. MacArthur's goal was to broaden the basis of security studies to include new external global threats: the environmental crisis, resource crises, civil security and unrest, and the new chemical and biological risks overshadowed for so long by the nuclear threat.

New divisions occurred within strategic studies in response. Some found this shift in overall focus to be a turning away from the primary threat of avoiding nuclear conflicts and risks. An underground controversy in the United States and Europe bubbled for several years over whether the true essence of strategic studies was analysis only on the use of force and its conditions, or requirements for military structures and future planning.[13] But the reach of the field clearly broadened and the fellowship tracks definitely strengthened the efforts at diversity.

One of the many MacArthur initiatives in which Bob and I had a major hand, with Ernest May and Uwe Nerlich, was the multi-year Nuclear History Program. It joined scholars and some retired military officials from the US, France, Britain, and Germany in the attempt to make clear each country's nuclear past and set about training and supporting a new generation of scholars in writing original monographs. Bob's students produced three or four of the best theses. Perhaps 15 top flight monographs were produced across the four countries, and research continues today based on the materials that were declassified or found. Energising other foundations to action, MacArthur underwrote the DC National Security Archive, a trove of recently declassified documents from all four countries, and encouraged younger scholars to write theses or books on a range of nuclear topics, some 25 works in all.

---

13   A notable scholar and commentator said to me at the time: 'MacArthur will have us all doing embroidery.'

The Washington effort was gradually reflected in the other capitals as well. This was a major shift toward openness, when almost everything had been previously closed or hidden behind the 30-year rule.[14] It constituted a true transformation from earlier scattered efforts and years-long frustrating attempts to get the declassifications. Bob clearly also pursued these lessons in the work he later did with the Imperial War Museum in London and on other official historical boards.

From the end of the Cold War until almost the present, strategic studies has been in a relatively muted phase, not unusual in times when threat of direct conflict is low and defence forces and monies are in relative decline. Bob himself remained active in research and outreach, from Canberra as founding Chairman of the Australian Strategic Policy Institute, and from Sydney as a Director of the Lowy Institute, as well as his role in the prestigious commissions on the future role of nuclear weapons (Canberra Commission) and the strategic challenges inherent in a multipolar world, especially in Asia. But what conflicts there were — the wars of Yugoslav succession in the 1990s, and the 'wars of choice' in Afghanistan and Iraq under George W. Bush in the first decade of the twenty-first century — were, for much of the strategic studies community, throwbacks to the expeditionary wars of the past, or not worthy of extended analysis. University studies remained static or fell away; the career paths into government or independent analytic futures were markedly narrower. Funding for anything but non-proliferation and arms control was limited. Europe was at the 'end of history' and the only great strategic questions concerned the adjustment of a shrunken Russia to its new global status and the rapid rise of China, along with the other emergent economic powers.

What has brought renewed interest and growing university enrolments in the last several years is the growth of international crises and transformative political change, beginning perhaps with the seismic shifts of the Arab Spring. Strategic studies has been particularly focused on the steady strategic growth of China — always close to Bob's agenda — and the actions of a red-toothed Vladimir Putin in Crimea, Ukraine, and Syria in challenging or negating the framework of cooperative security in Europe. Strategic studies itself

---

14   Throughout the George W. Bush Administration, there was, however, a successful effort, often led by those close to Vice President Cheney and Secretary of Defense Rumsfeld, to reverse historical declassification and to reclassify critical documents and files.

has lost some venues — with the exception of newcomers Stanton, Robertson, and long-time stalwart Carnegie, foundations are on the whole less interested in funding fellowships or supporting continuing surveys and core-building studies. University faculties are generally satisfied when there are one or two 'strategic' experts on their rolls. Yet there are new or renewed institutions — a nuclear boot camp or two, new publications and commentaries on the Web and social media networks, and a growth in practitioners and students interested in re-examining traditional wisdom on the workings of deterrence, the impact of new technologies, the possibility of limited nuclear war, or the future of formal arms control and disarmament. There seems to be deep, continuing interest in strategic studies, and more than enough work to be done to understand the challenges of new forms of warfare, from cyber to hybrid, and of the new risks but also new responses to proliferation through monitoring and formal and informal control. And then there are the tasks of re-inventing, for new generations of politicians and younger voters, many of the original precepts of strategic studies that they have largely forgotten or have never known.

The New Agenda

What is the shape of the new agenda that strategic studies confronts? What are the prospects for even partial solutions or resolutions over the next decade and beyond? Seven critical areas come easily to mind which we can identify here only in telegraphic form. Only one or two are areas in which Bob has not already done significant thinking and work, or challenged his students and colleagues. Briefly tagged are:

1. Strategic analysis in a multipolar framework: two-sided games are no longer enough.
2. Understanding a more complex past — sufficient history?
3. The creation and breaking of taboos, blurring the nuclear/conventional divide, defining the new nuclear era of congruent safety and security.
4. The inclusion paradox — how to ensure and exploit diversity in thinkers and operators and the new divisions in civil/military roles?
5. Who will fight the next war — the man/machine mix?

6. Escalation theory and distributed lethality models — will it be better or worse in 2025?
7. The rediscovered but un-integrated threat — economic weapons, sanctions, and market denial.

To take up only several of these themes sketched in the briefest detail:

Almost from the outset, strategic studies has persisted with models for analysis and education that are at their core most appropriate for two-sided conflict and cooperation. Very little attention has been devoted to incorporating insights from multi-layered, multi-player games in which there are complex and interactive payoffs for both cooperation and competition. These are very hard problems, and not a declared arena for solutions by consensus.

But it is hard to see how in the strategic framework of the present we can avoid trying to unpack these problems in a more rigorous and systematic way. The rise of a maturing ambitious China and the effects of a deliberately disruptive Russia pose choices not faced by the United States since the early 1970s and the Nixon/Kissinger balancing acts. The George W. Bush/Dick Cheney dream of technological dominance as the answer seems less relevant in the era of hybrid or cyber warfare or the creation of new strategic islands.

In the past two decades there have been valiant efforts to develop resources for historical understanding about the use of force in concrete situations, particularly in the assessment of risk. But there are fewer than there must be in order to systematise and codify lessons about nuclear decision-making and its risks. We have also concentrated largely on a diagnostic approach — what went wrong, and what must be avoided. Little research or teaching has emphasised what must go right, the minimum that allows us to create scenarios for the realistic avoidance of bad choices or practices. Here we are stuck in Cold War protocols and the wisdom of dead strategists, or worse, the results of single-outcome gaming, and dogmas from the age of nuclear plenty in a bipolar world.

Moreover, historic analyses need time and space, and careful focus on interrelationships. Few institutions now exist that can and do follow the path of systematic estimate and experimentation — that is, assessing the interrelationships between the use of force and outcomes — except if led by a resolute leader (for example, the Turner revolution in naval education at Newport) or team (for example, the related efforts in diplomatic history of Gaddis and Kennedy at Yale). Major themes require continuity and repeated intellectual attacks. To cite only a few: In the wake of the still-untested Iran deal, will the tenets of the nuclear revolution still hold? Will deterrence change at lower numbers or a slowing pace of proliferation? What are the parallels to the tri-polar competition among the major powers in the Pacific?

What are the critical technologies for the future — and how will we not only control their application but also recognise them?

What efforts can we make now to adjust and adapt, and to understand the process for doing so with the framework of strategic studies? The age of mass mobilisation is well behind us, but what of mass education and even training on these crucial issues and the choices that will have to be made? We test weapons, but not intellectual or organisational processes for making choices; we train for consistency, but not innovation or confrontation with uncertainty, and we leave more than necessary room for muddling through at the point of decision.

Concluding Words

The longer context narrative here should highlight why we must now take the time and the best talent to consciously assess the patterns and lessons of the past and to define the analytic tasks for the future. Change, while it appears to be rapid, occurs rather more slowly than we believe. Its assessment requires the best applications of the knowledge gained in intellectual research and observation (as well as operational practice) wielded by civilian and military analysts. New options and new choices may exist; inevitability exists only in literature and partisan history. Bob's career path, and the achievements of the cadre of students and colleagues he has brought along with him, assure us that there are always informed choices to be made, and options to be assessed toward better outcomes, if we have but the wit to find them.

9

Strategic Studies in Britain and the Cold War's Last Decade[1]

Lawrence Freedman

For decades, from 1982, Bob O'Neill played a central role in the British strategic studies community, first as Director of the International Institute for Strategic Studies (IISS) and then as Chichele Professor of the History of War at Oxford. He also served, usually as chair, on the boards of numerous other organisations, including IISS, the Imperial War Museum, and the Centre for Defence Studies at King's College. I have described elsewhere the remarkable qualities Bob brought to any organisation in which he had a part to play, and his unique talent for leadership:

> Bob was always in control and always polite, though occasional signs of irritation were allowed to intrude in the face of specious arguments or when time was being wasted with mini-speeches. Potential objections were anticipated and parochial concerns deflected. He was particularly effective at making an organisation feel good about itself and its staff pleased with a job well done. At the same time, while sustaining morale and boosting the public profile, he would never allow an organisation to go into denial and put off addressing its problems. About these problems, whether to do with personnel or finance, he would stay well informed. Part of Bob's success was his

---

1 Thanks to Jeff Michaels for his comments.

ability to develop rounded assessments of the people he was working with, even to junior levels, aware of their strengths as well as their weaknesses and the links between the two.[2]

This leadership was of particular importance at a time when the established framework for thinking about security was undermined, and then set aside. This period started with the Cold War, edging towards a new and dangerous peak. Then not only did the sense of danger start to subside, but the Cold War itself came to an abrupt, although fortunately rather graceful, conclusion. This was followed by a whole series of new issues bursting on to the agenda, courtesy of Saddam Hussein, Slobodan Milosevic, and then Osama bin Laden. Leadership in these circumstances required steadiness, so that people did not get giddy with the pace of change, yet crucially it also depended on appreciating the possibilities and the challenges in the new situation.

My aim in this chapter is to convey the state of the strategic studies community in Britain as Bob O'Neill arrived to take up his role as Director of IISS, with some observations about how it changed over the subsequent decade. This community was, and still is, made up of the defence specialists and students of international relations in universities and think tanks. Bob's arrival at IISS was coincident with my own at King's College London as Professor of War Studies, and for much of this period I was on the Council of IISS. This chapter therefore inevitably reflects my perspective as both an observer and a participant.

I

At the start of the 1980s, many of the most influential figures in the defence debate were retired military officers with distinguished war records. Field Marshal Lord Carver, a former Chief of Defence Staff, was regularly cited as a critic of nuclear policy.[3] General Sir John Hackett's fictional account of *The Third World War* (which NATO just won) was a bestselling vehicle for making the case for higher defence

---

2   Freedman, Lawrence (2006) 'Bob O'Neill and the Art of Academic Leadership', *Australian Journal of International Affairs* 60(1), pp. 13–17.
3   Carver, Michael (1982) *A Policy for Peace*, London: Faber.

spending.[4] Meanwhile, the number of academic specialists in defence and strategy was small. The overseas priorities of universities had been shaped by the demands of empire more than the threat of war. They provided for those with the administrative competence and language skills to run the colonies. In many university departments there were scholars who had spent time in Africa and Asia and had picked up on their languages and cultures. By contrast, chairs — never mind whole departments — dedicated to war were rare. Standing out was the Chichele Chair of the History of War at Oxford, occupied by Sir Michael Howard in 1980. His appointment as Regius Professor of History left the post unfilled until it was taken up by Bob O'Neill in 1987. Howard had also established the other chair with war in its title while at King's College London. Aware of the college's unsatisfactory foray into military studies during the interwar years, he created the War Studies Department during the 1950s and became its first chair in 1965. Shortly after, it was Howard who after persuaded Defence Secretary Denis Healey to get the Ministry of Defence to sponsor a number of academic posts in this field. This program continued through the 1980s, effectively coming to an end with the seed funding for the Centre for Defence Studies at King's College (in collaboration with the London School of Economics and Political Science (LSE)) in 1990.[5]

By the early 1980s, there were centres of excellence around the country in particular areas, including defence economics at Aberdeen, arms control at Lancaster, and Soviet studies at Birmingham. At Edinburgh, John Erickson had established himself as a leading interpreter of Soviet military history and thought.[6] Looking back, it is striking how little academic work was under way on the conduct, as opposed to the politics, of the conflict which had taken British lives and consumed much governmental energy — 'the Troubles' (a typical British euphemism) in Northern Ireland. The field of terrorism studies, now a more crowded field, was dominated by Paul Wilkinson, then at Aberdeen before he later set up a centre at St Andrews.[7]

---

4   *The Third World War*, London: Sidgwick & Jackson, was first published in 1978 and then in an updated version in 1982.
5   On the background, see Howard, Michael (2006) *Captain Professor: The Memoirs of Sir Michael Howard*, London: Continuum International Publishing Group, p. 195.
6   *The Guardian* (2002) 'Humanities: John Erickson'. Available at: www.theguardian.com/news/2002/feb/12/guardianobituaries.humanities.
7   Wilkinson, Paul (1977) *Terrorism and the Liberal State*, London: John Wiley.

The Department of War Studies at King's was then still small, with Barrie Paskins, a defence lecturer on the ethics of war, with three other colleagues.[8] When Howard had become the first defence lecturer at All Souls in Oxford in 1968, the Chair of War Studies he had created was filled by Laurence Martin. It became vacant when Martin left to become Vice Chancellor of Newcastle University in 1978. It was revived in 1982 as the personal project of Air Marshal Sir Neil Cameron when he became principal of the college. That is how I came to move from the Royal Institute of International Affairs, better known as Chatham House, to King's.

King's also had a link with the Royal Naval College Greenwich, the only staff college to have a dedicated academic department. The Department of History and International Affairs had been led by Brian Ranft, who had a part-time position at King's when I arrived. He was followed in this position by Peter Nailor. One of Nailor's colleagues, Geoff Till, a former King's student, took up the part-time position when Ranft retired to ensure that maritime studies were on the curriculum (a role later taken up by Andrew Lambert). Till succeeded Nailor at Greenwich in 1989 and then became one of the main architects of the academic support function at the new Joint Services Command and Staff College, which merged all three staff colleges in the late 1990s. With King's now responsible for this function, Till became a full Professor at King's, and the first Dean of Defence Studies. Up to this point, there was little internal academic support at the other staff colleges. Brian Holden Reid was seconded from King's to the Army Staff College at Camberley, where he was resident historian from 1987 to 1997. The army did have substantial departments at the Royal Military College at Sandhurst, teaching cadets. Its staff included the leading military historian John Keegan, until he left to join the *Daily Telegraph* in 1986. Another member of the Sandhurst staff, Chris Donnelly, was the leading expert on the Soviet military system.[9] The naval equivalent at Dartmouth also had a strong teaching staff, including the naval historian Eric Grove. Meanwhile, the RAF relied

---

8   Michael Dockrill, Brian Bond, and Wolf Mendl.
9   Donnelly's influence was considerable. In 1979, he became head of the Soviet Studies Research Centre, also based at Sandhurst, and in 1989 became an adviser to the NATO Secretary-General, helping to manage the aftermath of the end of the Cold War.

on a series of impressive officers, starting with Tony Mason in 1976 and later including Andrew Vallance and Tim Garden, who developed links with the universities.

While the specialist defence community was small, the wider international relations community was growing and starting to organise itself as a discipline. The first conference of the British International Studies Association was held in 1975 at Lincoln College Oxford under the Chairmanship of Alastair Buchan, then at Oxford but also the founding director of IISS. The very first Department of International Relations had been created at Aberystwyth after the First World War. The Montague Burton Chairs at Oxford and the LSE, established in the 1930s, were accepted as the leading chairs in the profession. The Australian Hedley Bull took over the Oxford chair from Buchan after the latter's untimely death in 1978, only to himself die distressingly young from cancer in 1985.[10] At LSE, Philip Windsor, another IISS alumnus, led on security studies, while the Montague Burton Professor, Susan Strange, was creating a new field of internal political economy, moving the subject away from its preoccupation with states and security. Elsewhere, Joseph Frankel had built up a formidable department at Southampton, from which a remarkable number of later stars emerged, including Steve Smith.

Outside of academia, the think tank world was small but high powered. Chatham House was another product of the aftermath of the First World War. It had been set up to help avoid another major war. Under the economist Andrew Shonfield, it had broken its focus. Ian Smart, a former Foreign and Commonwealth Office (FCO) official who had been at IISS before becoming Shonfield's deputy, was one of the most original and articulate commentators on security issues during the 1970s. He set up a project on the future of British foreign policy, for which I was recruited, and then wrote the project's most important paper, a study of the options for Polaris replacement.[11] He could have become director, but instead became a consultant on nuclear energy matters, and dropped away from the defence world. Instead, journalist David Watt, who was well connected and a brilliant writer, but did not claim any specialist expertise, became the new director.

---

10 Ayson, Robert (2012) *Hedley Bull and the Accommodation of Power*, London: Palgrave.
11 Smart, Ian (1997) *The Future of the British Nuclear Deterrent: Technical, Economic, and Strategic Issues*, London: Royal Institute of International Affairs.

IISS had been established in the first place as a result of concern in the 1950s that defence policy in the nuclear age required a degree of specialist knowledge that was beyond existing institutions. Its international reputation was based on published output, notably the *Military Balance* and the Adelphi Papers, while its annual conference was the most important gathering of its kind, including senior figures from many governments and international organisations, as well as academics and think tank members. The directing staff comprised of a non-British director (Christoph Bertram of Germany, and then Bob) and a British deputy with an army background (Brigadier Kenneth Hunt, followed by Colonel Jonathan Alford), supplemented by a series of up and coming young Americans (in the first years of the 1980s this was Bob Nurick) and an international group of largely young research associates. It was an incubator for new faces in the transatlantic strategic studies community. In the early 1980s, it moved from its spartan accommodation in John Adam Street to smart new premises in Tavistock Street, close to both LSE and King's. It was also, once an endowment from the Ford Foundation was agreed, on a more secure financial footing than Chatham House, which, unlike its European interlocutors, did not get a large government subsidy.[12]

The other member of the London think tank triumvirate was the Royal United Services Institute (RUSI). It also lived on a tight budget, in this case with life support from the Ministry of Defence. In principle, it was the main outlet for military voices. In the 1970s, these had often been quite right-wing, especially under the strident leadership of Air Marshal Stuart 'Paddy' Menaul, who remained an active commentator on defence matters.[13] By 1982, the institute had returned to the more measured tones of the establishment, and was directed by another airman, Group Captain David Bolton. Other London think tanks, such as the Institute for the Study of Conflict,

---

12 From 1978 to 1982, I ran a small policy studies unit that did get a modest grant from the FCO.

13 Towards the end of his reign at the RUSI it was perceived that a less individualistic and a more collegiate approach was appropriate, and in 1976 he left to continue his work as publicist and defence commentator. Air Vice-Marshal SWB Menaul CB CBE DFC AFC (1987) 'RUSI Director-General 1968–1976: An Appreciation', *The RUSI Journal* 132(3), pp. 25–6.

provided a focus for strong anti-communist views,[14] but these were quite small and considered more as a source of strong opinions than independent analysis.

How influential were the think tanks? At the time I was not sure, as I suggested in a seminar on the role of the outsiders in policy-making at RUSI at the end of 1981.[15] My experience working at Chatham House during the late 1970s was that government was resistant to outside influences. This included parliament as well as academics and think tank members. On the nuclear issue, for example, there had been minimal parliamentary activity since 1965. Civil servants were prohibited from participating in the Chatham House study group that led to the production of Ian Smart's paper on the Polaris replacement. Even in small private gatherings put together under the aegis of one of the institutes, and despite the latitude made possible by invoking the Chatham House Rule,[16] the burden of official secrecy and political caution weighed heavily.

Having done my doctoral research on the United States, I was always struck by the ease with which I could get hold of information in Washington that would get the highest classification in the UK, as well as the ease of movement between the government and think tank worlds. In Washington, individuals with real expertise had a reasonable expectation of getting a spell in government and returning to the think tank world, at which point they could enrich public debate with their knowledge of the workings of government. Other than temporary appointments to the FCO's Planning Staff or Arms Control Unit, this was rare in the UK. Beyond that, the resources available to institutions such as RAND, to take the most famous American example, dwarfed those available to the British think tanks. They could not even aspire to undertake the sustained number-crunching that made them an adjunct to policy-making, or grow large on the basis of government

---

14 Michaels, Jeff (2014) 'Britain's Cold War Think Tank: Brian Crozier and the Institute for the Study of Conflict', in Luc van Dongen, Stéphanie Roulin and Giles Scott-Smith (eds), *Transnational Anti-Communism and the Cold War: Agents, Activities, and Networks*, London: Palgrave Macmillan.
15 Report of the Tripartite Seminar held at RUSI on 'Outsiders' Influence on Defence Policy: Part I', 11 November 1981; (1982) *RUSI Journal* 127(1).
16 'When a meeting, or part thereof, is held under the Chatham House Rule, participants are free to use the information received, but neither the identity nor the affiliation of the speaker(s), nor that of any other participant, may be revealed.' Chatham House, 'Chatham House Rule'. Available at: www.chathamhouse.org/about/chatham-house-rule#sthash.nzqXyGcB.0TSMHZAl.dpuf.

contracts. I recall being told by a Conservative MP when I was trying to arrange a briefing on the Polaris report that our efforts were paltry and pointless. We could never compete with RAND.

It is also important to keep in mind that all three institutes were membership organisations, who had to spend a lot of time providing a steady diet of speakers and seminars, as well as high-quality publications. IISS's *Military Balance*, for example, provided authoritative information on the state of the world's armed forces. Chatham House had also played a long role in recording developments in foreign policy as much as seeking to influence its conduct. In both Chatham House and IISS, the libraries were of immense importance, especially when it came to press cuttings. In the pre-Google age, these were the first port of call for anyone trying to study contemporary affairs. Researchers could not simply sit in their offices and find whatever information they wanted online, but had to go out and look for what they needed, armed with a note pad and, with luck, access to a decent photocopier.

In addition to their value as a safe arena for some interaction between independent researchers and policy-makers, the think tanks also offered international networks. IISS and Chatham House were linked not only to the main American centres, such as RAND and Brookings, but also the European institutes, such as the German Council on Foreign Relations, the German Institute for International and Security Affairs, and the French Institute for International Relations. The regular visits to London by individuals such as Karl Kaiser and Uwe Nehrlich from Germany, Thierry de Montbrial and Pierre Hassner from France, and Johann Jørgen Holst from Norway (later to become Norwegian Foreign Minister) brought a wider European perspective to UK debates on security. As I will discuss presently, there were also reasonably regular links with the foreign policy institutes in the Soviet Union and the Warsaw Pact.

II

By the early 1980s, the academic and policy debate was contained within the Cold War framework, which in itself carried the legacy of the terrible history of the twentieth century. It was a field of study originally animated by the problem of war. That meant exploring how relations between states went wrong. The academic study of international relations tended towards a commentary on the great powers that was both historically informed and sensitive to recent developments. The practitioners might express strong views, but their backgrounds were not dissimilar to other members of the establishment, and the tradition was donnish. While few academics entered government, there was movement in the other direction — for example, Peter Nailor had moved from the Ministry of Defence to take up a chair at Lancaster. The vocation was to pass on learning to the next generation while writing about topics of interest when in the mood to do so. Journalism was largely frowned upon as being somehow demeaning, although book reviewing was considered a high art. Although money was tight, university life was far less pressured. This was before the start of the successive research assessment exercises.

A shared feature of the senior figures in government and academia was the impact of their wartime experiences and the early stages of the Cold War on their world views. This was a generation that was, by the early 1980s, weary. They had lived through the country's heroic stand against Hitler and a time when British's international standing had not been in question. Many were still dogged by Dean Acheson's 1962 jibe about Britain having lost an empire and failed to find a role.[17] Dependence on the United States for security and influence was understood but resented, often manifesting itself in a distrust of the latest American intellectual fashion. Above all, there was a dismayed sense that the relative decline that the country had known since 1945, which had seen former enemies overtake Britain in prosperity, was bound to continue.

If there was a dominant disciplinary influence, it was history, with the more ambitious using familiar concepts to explore the different ways of thinking about the developing international system.[18] The so-called English school, which was only given its name in 1981,[19] was initially associated with Martin Wight, who had died in 1972.

---

17 Speech at West Point, 5 December 1962, in *Vital Speeches*, 1 January 1963, p. 163. On the consequences, see Hill, Christopher (1979) 'Britain's Elusive Role in World Politics', *British Journal of International Studies* 5(3), pp. 248–59.
18 For example, Frankel, Joseph (1970) *National Interest*, London: Macmillan.
19 By Roy Jones in (1981) 'The English School of International Relations: A Case for Closure', *The Review of International Studies* 7(1), pp. 1–13.

It reflected the idea that the international system could be viewed as a society with its own norms and conventions, and not just as a collection of autonomous states.[20] In some ways, it was less a school of thought than an intellectual temper, offering a somewhat pragmatic middle way between more dogmatic realists and idealists. It was not offering a radical new way of looking at international affairs.

The durability of the established frameworks was evident when it came to the analytical support for the critics of mainstream views. The idealist strand in British thinking about international affairs was sustained largely by two academic outfits, initially with a Quaker inspiration. The Richardson Institute for Peace Research, named after Lewis Fry Richardson, was established in 1959. It first found a home at Lancaster University and eventually went to Kent, where it became part of the Conflict Research Centre. Until 1982, its director was Michael Nicholson, who very much followed Richardson in his belief that quantitative analysis could be used to put the study of war and peace on a more scientific basis. In many ways, Nicholson, who had a background in economics, was a rare and early representative in Britain of the scientific approach that was gradually gaining traction in the United States.[21] The other component to what became the Conflict Research Centre was the more idiosyncratic work of John Burton, first at University College London from 1963 and then at Kent. Burton, who had been a senior member of the Australian Foreign Office, believed that a more holistic view of the world, and a sustained focus on basic human needs, could be the basis for new techniques of conflict resolution.[22]

---

20 The classic text is normally now seen to be Butterfield, Herbert and Martin Wight (eds) (1966) *Diplomatic Investigations: Essays in the Theory of International Politics*, London: Allen & Unwin. See Dunne, Tim (1998) *Inventing International Society: A History of the English School*, Basingstoke: Macmillan; Linklater, Andrew and Hidemi Suganami (2006) *The English School of International Relations: A Contemporary Reassessment*, Cambridge: Cambridge University Press.
21 Nicholson, Michael (1989) *Formal Theories in International Relations*, Cambridge: Cambridge University Press; *The Guardian* (2001) 'Social Sciences: Michael Nicholson'. Available at: www.theguardian.com/news/2001/oct/20/guardianobituaries.socialsciences.
22 Burton, John (1979) *Deviance, Terrorism and War*, London: Macmillan; *The Guardian* (2010) 'John Burton Obituary'. Available at: www.theguardian.com/world/2010/aug/22/john-burton-obituary.

The main centre of peace research was the Department of Peace Studies at Bradford University, founded by Quakers in 1973, with Adam Curle as the first chair. It barely survived its first few years. It was caught between its original Quaker inspiration and radicals who believed that there could be no peace without justice, and that justice could require armed struggle, and also between those who believed that the cause of peace could best be advanced through scholarship, and those who believed that their scholarship was secondary to activism.[23] The problem was aggravated by Curle's relaxed approach to the demands of academic life. In 1978, Curle retired and was replaced by a tough-minded former missionary, James O'Connell, who restored discipline and stressed the importance of scholarship. Without O'Connell, it is likely that the department would have survived, either because of its internal tensions or because of the hostility of the Thatcher Government, which took the view that this was not so much peace as appeasement studies. The government demanded that the University Grants Commission investigate Bradford to assess whether this could possibly be a serious academic department — it was.[24] From Bradford, Paul Rogers was to the fore with the most sustained critique of British and NATO nuclear policy.

The King's Department of War Studies and Bradford's Department of Peace Studies were often set against each other, as if they were polar opposites. The Department of War Studies was not activist, and contained a range of views. Wolf Mendl, the head of department up to my arrival, was a Quaker who shared O'Connell's combination of strong values and deep commitment to rigorous scholarship. Moreover, to the extent that nuclear deterrence was at issue, there were a number of common reference points. Supporters of deterrence were not arguing in favour of nuclear war. The issue was how best to prevent one. Nor were the critics opposed to the measures of arms control that helped stabilise rather than eliminate the nuclear relationship.

Indeed, arms control was the focal point for younger scholars with an interest in what might now be called 'hard power'. The British International Studies Association arms control group was led (with some help from me) by John Simpson at Southampton, already

---

23 Young, Nigel (1981) 'Educating the Peace Educators', *Security Dialogue* 12(2), pp. 123–35.
24 *The Guardian* (2013) 'James O'Connell Obituary'. Available at: www.theguardian.com/education/2013/sep/19/james-oconnell-academic-dies-87.

a leading expert in the non-proliferation field. The focus was telling. The intellectual challenge was to be found in managing the arms race and east–west relations. This was not a group that entered the arena to talk about war, but more to consider how it might best be prevented. The vital knowledge was of the properties of nuclear weapons and the doctrines of strategic stability, the coherence of alliances and the conventions of crisis management. There was little reason to talk of the conduct of war itself, because if the one for which we were most prepared came about, this would constitute a monumental failure of policy and a catastrophe from which there might be no recovery.

III

The sense of decline was reflected in the wider public debates on foreign and defence policy. These were still influenced as much by the logic of decolonisation as by the ebb and flow of the Cold War. In the late 1960s, the contraction of the empire led the Labour Government to conclude that it was pointless to sustain military garrisons in the Middle East and the Far East. It appeared that the country no longer had vital interests beyond Europe worth defending by force of arms. The sovereign base area in Akrotiri and Dhekelia would have been handed over to the government in Cyprus were it not for the awkward situation arising out of the 1974 Turkish invasion of Cyprus and the island's partition. The relentlessly narrow focus on the NATO area was confirmed in 1981 by the defence review undertaken by Sir John Nott, much to the chagrin of the Royal Navy. This also removed the last attempt at a maritime presence in the South Atlantic, *HMS Endurance*.

The review reflected a prominent theme of the defence debates of the 1970s, in which Professor David Greenwood at the University of Aberdeen had taken such a prominent role. Looking at the persistent pressure on the defence budget, struggling to stay close to the NATO norm of 3 per cent of GDP (and with a struggling GDP), he had pointed to the need to make hard choices on defence priorities, which were reflected in what seemed to be the core missions for the individual services — a long-range strike role for the RAF, sustaining the British Army of the Rhine, or the Royal Navy's surface fleet. The 1981 review came down against an expansive maritime presence, although this was, to a degree, to make way for a role on which the Royal Navy was less keen — responsibility for the national nuclear force.[25] In 1980, the government decided to replace the ageing SSBN force with Polaris missiles, with one carrying new US Trident missiles.[26]

This decision became bound up with the question of whether Britain had really come to terms with its reduced role in world affairs, as if Trident was a last defiant gesture in the long retreat from the glories of empire. It was also caught up with the revival of an anti-nuclear movement in the United Kingdom. At issue here was not only the national nuclear force but also the decision taken by the alliance to locate US ground-launched cruise missiles at Greenham Common and Molesworth bases in the UK, along with other European countries.[27] With President Ronald Reagan's hawkish administration and the Soviet invasion of Afghanistan raising international tensions, the nuclear issue soon dominated public debate. It had an immediate impact on the Labour Party in opposition, with Michael Foot, a long-time supporter of the Campaign for Nuclear Disarmament, now leader. This, along with the party's general antipathy towards NATO and the EU, was one reason for a number of key figures leaving Labour and starting the new Social Democrat Party.[28]

Although Margaret Thatcher's Conservative Government is credited with turning around Britain's economic position and international standing during the 1980s, neither would have been predicted at the start of the decade, when the economic policies pursued by her government appeared to have worsened the position. 1982 was a transitional year. By March the economy had begun to recover and with it the Conservative Party's position in the opinion polls. Then in April came the Falklands War. This came out of the blue, with a British task force sent to defend a territory few could locate on a map

---

25   For his study of the Nott Review, see Greenwood, David (1981) *Reshaping Britain's Defences*, Aberdeen Studies in Defence Economics, no. 19.
26   For a flavour of the debates on nuclear weapons leading to this decision, see Freedman, Lawrence (1980) *Britain and Nuclear Weapons*, London: Macmillan.
27   The key text for the movement was Thompson, Edward and Dan Smith (1980) *Protest and Survive*, London: Penguin. Thompson was a radical historian. Dan Smith had worked for the Campaign for Nuclear Disarmament and then at the Richardson Institute. The title was a play on the government's civil defence pamphlet, *Protect and Survive*, published in May 1980.
28   Some of the ideas that influenced Social Democrat Party defence policy are found in Segal, Gerald et al. (1983) *Nuclear War and Nuclear Peace*, London: Macmillan.

or knew was still owned by Britain. As surprising as the outbreak of war was, the task force was able to set sail quickly and was able to defeat Argentine forces decisively.

The Falklands raised issues about the conduct and utility of war well below the nuclear threshold, but neither the academic/think tank community nor the political class was geared to these issues.[29] Although important debates about conventional strategy were underway in the United States at the time, and despite Field Marshal Sir Nigel Bagnall's long campaign to introduce new operational concepts into the British army,[30] this was an area that civilian academics were largely content to leave to military practitioners. In practice, it was the nuclear debate, much more than the Falklands, that stirred up the British strategic studies community. Up to this point, the British line was to accept the idea that the nuclear age had turned out to be more stable than many had dared to hope. If there was a challenge it came from the 'neo-cons', a term already in use to describe the hard-line Democrats in the US who were dismayed at their party's soft line on the Soviet Union. Now the challenge came from the anti-nuclear movement. Their critique was not just of the policies of government, but of the craven intellectuals (such as me) who had turned into cheerleaders for deterrence.[31] Yet this was still largely a new twist to an established debate. It did not really push out the boundaries.

IV

Ten years later, the strategic studies community in Britain looked very different. It was much larger and more varied in its interests and concerns. Most of this can be put down to the end of the Cold War and the emergence of new — or re-emergence of old — types of conflicts,

---

29 The media commentators during the campaign were invariably retired officers. See Adams, Valerie (1986) *The Media and the Falklands Campaign*, London: Macmillan.
30 See Shamir, Eitan (2011) *Transforming Command: The Pursuit of Mission Command in the U.S., British and Israeli Armies*, Stanford: Stanford University Press, chapter 5. Those working closely with the military, such as Brian Holden Reid and Christopher Donnelly (who illuminated Soviet doctrine), were among the exceptions. Among specialists, Richard Simpkins, a retired army officer, was influential. See his (1985) *Race to the Swift: Thoughts on Twenty-First Century Warfare*, London: Brassey's Defence Publishers.
31 I noted my alarm that 'however liberal I might be when compared with American Hawks, I was quite reactionary when compared with European doves', in the introduction to Freedman, Lawrence (1986) *The Price of Peace: Living with the Nuclear Dilemma*, New York: Henry Holt, p. 13.

especially in the Balkans. Before addressing this major transformation in the international system, it is worth noting three other factors that influenced the community during the course of the 1980s.

The first was a more sceptical and searching approach in the media and in parliament. On the nuclear side, this was also helped by the readiness of the Conservative Government to defend their views on nuclear deterrence. Thus the Trident decision was accompanied in 1980 by an 'Open Government' document which laid out the rationale, and the program itself was subjected to an annual report by the Select Committee on Defence.[32] The confidence with which the case was made reflected the role of Michael Quinlan, the key figure in the Ministry of Defence, who had also been one of the prime movers behind the NATO decisions on cruise missiles.[33] There was also support for more analytical approaches to these and other policy issues in the flagship current affairs program *Weekend World*, hosted by Brian Walden, which drew on academic support as talking heads.[34]

The second factor was the growth of international relations as a popular discipline in its own right. At the start of the 1980s, higher education was squeezed hard by the government, and funding remained tight until late in the decade when Kenneth Baker, as Secretary of State for Education, called for an expansion of student numbers. This led to a rapid surge in student places over the next few years, as well as a number of former polytechnics acquiring university status. Strategic studies and international relations were beneficiaries of this surge. To take the example of King's, it was able to move from a niche master's degree to offer undergraduate courses in war studies, which in turn allowed it to expand the range of master's degrees.[35]

Third, the anti-nuclear movement pushed figures such as Mary Kaldor to the fore, and encouraged others to study defence policy with a critical stance. One idea, for example, was to take advantage of new

---

32 Defence Open Government Document 80/23 of July 1980.
33 On retirement, Quinlan set out his ideas in Quinlan, Michael (2009) *Thinking About Nuclear Weapons: Principles, Problems, Prospects*, London: Oxford University Press. See also Freedman, Lawrence (2011) 'The Intellectual Legacy of Michael Quinlan', in Bruno Tetrais, *Thinking About Strategy: A Tribute to Sir Michael Quinlan*, Paris: l'Harmattan.
34 The production team was remarkable for its talent, including Peter Mandelson and David Aaronovitch.
35 Oddly, one of the motivations for a move into undergraduate teaching was a concern that interest in the MA might drop off with the end of the Cold War.

technologies to avoid any appearance of having an offensive capability, while making it extremely hard for a would-be attacker to invade — so called 'non-offensive defence'.[36] In addition, a very different sort of critical security studies began to develop, in some ways akin to the one that had developed in the 1960s around the Vietnam War, as those opposed to the war questioned how society had become so warlike and whose interests were served by the constant resort to military means. This turned into a more general critique of the Western political order. The difference now was the stress on issues of gender and race as factors which shaped power structures.[37]

One example of this shift was Ken Booth, who had become an increasingly critical voice within the mainstream, but then began to take an increasingly radical stance.[38] Booth was at Aberystwyth, which became the centre of critical security studies in the UK.[39] Whereas a previous Head of Department, John Garnett, had praised the virtues of common sense and warned against the subject becoming too complex and esoteric,[40] now postmodernism was used to question Western habits of thought, stressing the emancipatory potential of international relations in contrast to supporting the status quo.[41] One of the challenges for this way of thinking was that it was removed from the main political parties in its language and concepts. In its most Foucault-driven manifestations, it was not always expressed in

---

36   See Barnaby, Frank and Egbert Bouker (1982) *Defence Without Offence: Non-nuclear Defence for Europe*, Peace Studies Paper No. 8, Bradford University; The Alternative Defence Commission (1983) *Defence without the Bomb: The Report of the Alternative Defence Commission*, London: Taylor and Francis.
37   On the changing character of security studies, see Buzan, Barry and Lene Hansen (2009), *The Evolution Of International Security Studies*, Cambridge: Cambridge University Press. Buzan has been an innovative figure in international relations who also contributed to strategic studies. See Buzan, Barry (1987) *An Introduction To Strategic Studies: Military Technology And International Relations*, London: Macmillan.
38   Booth, Ken (1991) 'Security in Anarchy: Utopian Realism in Theory and Practice', *International Affairs* 67(3), pp. 527–45.
39   For a while, a Welsh School was identified as distinct from an English School, until Booth decided there was nothing particularly Welsh about it.
40   Garnett, John (1984) *Commonsense and the Theory of International Relations*, London: Macmillan.
41   Richard Wyn Jones became a leading exponent of the Welsh School. See Jones, Richard Wyn (1999) *Security, Strategy and Critical Theory*, Colorado: Lynne Rienner.

a form that was intelligible to a lay audience.[42] With the growth of the universities came new forms of funding, and publications became a key indicator of value, whether or not they were actually read. If anything, the study of international relations became progressively detached from its practice.

The most important shift was in the nature of international relations. After the alarm that accompanied what Fred Halliday called the Second Cold War in the early 1980s[43] came the second shock of the complete end of the Cold War. Whatever may be said about the prescience of Western scholars in anticipating this development, there is an important story in the role of British academics in helping it along. As already noted, one role played by Chatham House and other think tanks was in keeping open some sort of dialogue with the Soviet bloc.[44] This was done through the regular round tables organised by Chatham House (the first of which had met in 1975), or the form of informal diplomacy practiced by John Erickson, who arranged meetings with Soviet figures in Edinburgh.[45] Some of this was done in response to what was seen as an overly hawkish attitude taken by Prime Minister Margaret Thatcher. Yet Thatcher held a number of day-long seminars with academics at Chequers on security issues and took note of what they said. It was at one of these seminars that Archie Brown of Oxford University expressed the view that change was coming in the Soviet Union, and that Britain should seek to cultivate the next generation. As a result of this, Mikhail Gorbachev was invited to London even before he had taken power in Moscow. At an extraordinary small meeting with specialists in the Soviet economy and arms control, Thatcher was fully briefed on the challenges that Gorbachev would

---

42 For a critique of this trend, see Wallace, William (1996) 'Review: Truth and Power, Monks and Technocrats: Theory and Practice in International Relations', *Review of International Studies* 22(3), pp. 301–21. Wallace warned against self-indulgence, detachment from political life, and refuge in abstractions, theories, and meta-theories. This prompted a lively debate, with key figures from Aberystwyth, such as Ken Booth and Steve Smith, arguing for a wider view of politics, focused more on civil society.
43 Halliday, Fred (1983) *The Making of the Second Cold War*, London: Verso.
44 See Pravda, Alex and Peter Duncan (1970) *Soviet-British Relations since the 1970s*, Cambridge: Cambridge University Press.
45 *The Guardian* (2002) 'Humanities: John Erickson'. Available at: www.theguardian.com/news/2002/feb/12/guardianobituaries.humanities.

face and the value of establishing a constructive relationship with him. The meeting with Gorbachev ended with Thatcher's famous proclamation that here was a man with whom she could do business.[46]

While it was hard to complain about the end of the Cold War, as the world suddenly seemed a safer place, there was an abrupt obsolescence of expertise. Hard-earned knowledge on verification and arms control, first strikes, and NATO doctrine appeared irrelevant. Then suddenly new types of expertise were required as Saddam Hussein invaded Kuwait, followed by its liberation by an American-led coalition, and then the Soviet Union and Yugoslavia fell apart. In addition to a grasp of actual military operations, rather than hypothetical nuclear exchanges, it was now necessary to have an understanding of regional conflicts, or how weak states could fall apart under pressure. The new issues involved questions of intervention in internal conflicts and then, later, the challenges of terrorism.

In some ways, the universities found it easier to respond to these challenges than the think tanks. This was partly because they were growing as the Cold War came to an end, but also because new disciplines — such as sociology and anthropology — were now needed to deal with the new types of conflict in which ethnicity seemed to play a prominent role, and knowledge of areas such as the Middle East and the Balkans was required. Although the think tanks soon caught up, and were able to use their international networks to develop the necessary links with post-communist Europe, at first the necessary expertise tended to be more at hand in the universities, where there was also a supply of research students and post-doctorates who began to take on the weight of hard research. In addition, university-based academics, including Bob O'Neill, once at Oxford, engaged directly with a new generation of curious students, including young officers at the staff colleges.

---

46   See Brown, Archie (2008) 'The Change to Engagement in Britain's Cold War Policy: The Origins of the Thatcher–Gorbachev Relationship', *Journal of Cold War Studies* 10(3). The episode is described also in Moore, Charles (2015) *Margaret Thatcher: The Authorized Biography*, Vol. II: Everything She Wants, London: Allen Lane, pp. 231–2. I was there, but played a minor role. My main recollection was that, at the end of the meeting, after formidable briefings by Brown, Alec Nove, and Michael Kaser on the travails of the Soviet Union, to which she listened intently, Thatcher asked if they still believed in 'world domination'.

V

This was a time of uncertainty and possibilities. My recollection, especially after 1985, is of a continuing conversation, conducted in the universities and think tanks, together with policy-makers and the media, about a world that was straining to escape from the constraints of the Cold War. The normal charge made against the strategic studies community of this period was that it failed to anticipate the collapse of the Soviet Union. Looking back, I am unconvinced of this. The first half of the 1980s was tough, with an ailing Soviet leadership stubbornly clinging to the old ways, and a hawkish American President who seemed less interested in a comfortable détente than victory in the Cold War. By the second half of the decade, it was evident that something was up, and, as we have seen, the astute Soviet-watchers of the period knew that the current system was untenable and would change when a new leadership took over. How it would change could not be known. It depended on decisions to be made, not least in the Kremlin. By the last years of the 1980s, few doubted that important changes were underway, and much time was spent speculating on how far Gorbachev would dare go in reforming the system.

In addition, security issues in a variety of regions were becoming detached from the East–West confrontation. This had become clear in the Middle East, where Iran and Iraq were at war for most of the decade. A glance at the Adelphi Papers of the 1980s illustrates the shift. In these pre-blogging years, there was a lag from commissioning to publication, which explains the number of papers on ballistic missile defence that came out a few years after Reagan's 'star wars' speech of March 1983. But there were also regular papers on regional changes, from East Asia to the Mediterranean, and two papers on the Iran–Iraq war. The 1988 IISS conference was on changes in the strategic landscape, published as Adelphi Papers the next year.

In practice, by the time the Cold War ended, it was less important for the management of the generality of international problems than it had been when it began. This meant that while the sudden surge of warmth between Moscow and Washington, and London, encouraged talk of a new era of peace, there were many international conflicts that had their own dynamic, independent of the wishes and interests of the great powers. Even in Europe, ideas that the collapse of communism could somehow be managed as a sort of controlled explosion, without too much disruption, turned out to be too optimistic. Having lost a form of international order that appeared stable because of the balance of terror, there was a search to describe a new world order that was as stable but based on something more positive than a mutual fear of nuclear war. The search is still on.

Figure 1: Robert O'Neill receiving a prize from the Governor General, Field Marshal Sir William Slim, Scotch College Melbourne Speech Day, December 1954.

Figure 2: Captain Robert O'Neill briefing 5 RAR company commanders before an operation, Nui Dat, Vietnam, 1966.

Figure 3: Lieut-General Hermann Flörke with Sally, Robert and daughter Jenny on a walk near Giessen, Germany, 1 July 1973.

Figure 4: Robert O'Neill with US Secretary of State George P. Shultz, Washington DC, 1983.

Figure 5: Robert O'Neill with President Chun Doo Hwan, Seoul, Korea, 1984.

Figure 6: IISS/ACA 'New Faces' Conference, Bellagio, Italy, July 1984.

Front row, from left to right: Co-organiser William Kincade, Guest Practitioner (Lord) Denis Healey, Co-organiser Robert O'Neill, future US Secretary of State Condoleeza Rice, future French Minister for Social Affairs and Health Marisol Touraine. In the back row, behind Denis Healey, is John Chipman, future Director General of the IISS.

Figure 7: Robert O'Neill with Prime Minister Yasuhiro Nakasone, Tokyo, 1986.

Left to right: Mr Masataka Kosaka of the Foreign Ministry; Professor Masashi Nishihara; Robert O'Neill; Sir Michael Palliser, IISS Council Chairman; Mr Kiichi Saeki, Council Member.

Figure 8: Robert O'Neill with former US President Jimmy Carter, Emory University, Atlanta GA, 1985.

Figure 9: Robert O'Neill with Deputy Premier Li Peng, Beijing, September 1986.

Figure 10: Robert O'Neill with former US Secretary of State Henry Kissinger, Tokyo, 1986.

Figure 11: Sir Michael Howard responding at a dinner to mark his 70th birthday, All Souls College, Oxford, December 1992.

At left is (Sir) Lawrence Freedman. At right is Robert O'Neill.

Figure 12: Robert O'Neill at opening of new offices for the International Peace Academy, New York, 1992.

At left is (Dr) Kate O'Neill. At right is Ambassador Olara Otunnu, President of the IPA.

Figure 13: Robert O'Neill, Honorary Colonel, The 5th Royal Green Jackets, Oxford, 1993–1999.

Figure 14: Robert O'Neill speaking at the Salzburg Seminar, 1994.

Figure 15: Robert O'Neill with Prime Minister Paul Keating, Sydney, before the first meeting of the Canberra Commission on the Elimination of Nuclear Weapons, 1995.

Foreign Minister Gareth Evans at right of second row, former US Defense Secretary Robert McNamara at right of third row.

Figure 16: Robert O'Neill greeted by Prime Minister John Howard after the final meeting of the Canberra Commission, Sydney, 1996.

Ambassadors Rolf Ekeus and Qian Jiadong are in centre.

10

The Uncomfortable Wars of the 1990s

John Nagl and Octavian Manea

The Spirit of the 1990s

After the shock and awe of Operation Desert Storm, in which one of us participated directly, the remainder of the 1990s confronted the West with a series of instabilities of a different nature. The post-Cold War security environment reflected less the typical challenges generated by strong powers that, for centuries, were at the core of the main international rivalries, and more a world of challenges produced by weak and failed states. Where the problems of the short twentieth century (1914–1991) were caused by states that were too strong and wanted to expand their borders, the problems of the decades that followed would be caused by states that were too weak to govern within their own borders. It was a world shaped not by the classical balance of power, as in the past, but increasingly by a balance of weakness. The new reality produced two immediate consequences. On one side, there was a shifting away from the paradigm of symmetric state-to-state conflict toward intrastate wars, where religious and ethnic identities, as well as communities and groups, were the key variables shaping the violence cycles.¹ Sectarian and ethnic security dilemmas, well orchestrated by interested elites, swamped the public space by amplifying group fears. It was the moment of cold-blooded opportunists such as Slobodan Milosevic, Ratko Mladic, and Mohamed Farah Aideed, who understood human nature and knew that the instinct of resorting to violence 'has been deeply seated in our stock for hundreds of thousands of years'.²

They just needed to nurture the right conditions and mobilise those fears against the right target for their own benefit. As Robert O'Neill put it:

> The leaders of religious, ethnic and immigrant communities, and of political parties or factions thereof, will continue to draw on this source of influence and exploit it both for indirect leverage in bargaining and for direct effect in conflict when all else seems likely to fail. Thus it is more at this level than that of nations that we must aim our policies in post-Cold War Europe.³

On the other side, the societal dimension of modern warfare took primacy of place. To win back its legitimacy, 'the government must address contentious, long ignored, but popular issues tied to key facets of national life (socio-political, economic, educational, juridical)'.⁴ In fact, it was this societal dimension that endangered Europe the most, particularly the

> avalanche of chaos falling on the West from the Centre, East and South ... The causes of such dangers lie primarily in the weak, defective political structures of most of the states on Europe's southern and eastern flank ... In many of them corruption and maladministration are rife. Several are disintegrating.⁵

---

1   Snyder, Jack (2007) 'International Sources of Interstate and Intrastate War', in Chester A. Crocker, Fen Osler Hampson and Pamela Aall (eds) *Leashing the Dogs of War: Conflict Management in a Divided World*, Washington: United States Institute of Peace Press, p. 19.
2   O'Neill, Robert (1998) 'Europe and the Wider World: The Security Challenge', in Ken Booth (ed.) *Statecraft And Security. The Cold War and Beyond*, New York: Cambridge University Press, p. 198.
3   Ibid.
4   Galvin, John R. (1986) 'Uncomfortable Wars: Toward a New Paradigm', *Parameters* 26(4), p. 6.
5   O'Neill, Robert (1998) 'Europe and the Wider World: The Security Challenge', in Ken Booth (ed.) *Statecraft And Security. The Cold War and Beyond*, New York: Cambridge University Press, pp. 198–9.

This structural reality would ultimately trigger the Western interventionism in former Yugoslavia, in Bosnia (1995) and Kosovo (1999), but it was also instrumental in laying the ground for successive NATO and EU enlargements to the east.

Unfortunately, Western military establishments were deeply entrenched in the interstate paradigm and resistant to move beyond their organisational culture.[6] But the new societal dimensions of warfare — requiring roles as diverse as peacekeeping, providing humanitarian assistance, disaster relief, post-conflict reconstruction, and counterinsurgency — were not amendable to solution by what General Anthony Zinni called 'a Cold-War era military machine'.[7] As Robert O'Neill put it:

> Gone are the days when NATO armies could plan around a single mission … [T]hey still have to be able to fight, of course, but they have to be able to do many other things as well, from re-building shattered cities to supervising elections … [T]heir inherited Cold War skills, structures and approaches can sometimes be irrelevant or even counterproductive. Future development has to address responsibilities that will be much more intrinsically political in nature, such as the promotion of democratisation, support for human rights, policing of international law and the apprehension of war criminals.[8]

The struggle between entrenched organisational culture and new strategic requirements became the hallmark of the civil–military gap that defined the debates inside the Clinton Administration during the 1990s, and marked the first generation of the next century.

---

6   Priest, Dana (2004) *The Mission: Waging War and Keeping Peace with America's Military*, New York: W.W. Norton & Company, p. 26.
7   Zinni, Anthony C. (2001) 'A Military for the Twenty-First Century: Lessons from the Recent Past', *Strategic Forum* 181. Available at: www.au.af.mil/au/awc/awcgate/ndu/sf181.htm.
8   O'Neill, Robert (1997) 'The Remaking of Modern Armies Post Cold War', in Peter Dennis and Grey Jeffrey (eds) *The Second Fifty Years: The Australian Army 1947–1997*, Canberra: Australian Defence Force Academy, pp. 3–4.

Black Hawk Down Meets Assertive Multilateralism

Bill Clinton did not run for the Presidency on his foreign policy credentials; to the contrary, 'it's the economy, stupid' was the focus of his campaign. The theme resonated with the American public, who were reluctant to support a muscular role on the global stage after victory in the Cold War. Richard Holbrooke, one of the core members of the Clinton team, captured well the public mood:

> In the decade before 9/11, Americans had turned away from the outside world after 60 years of continuous and expensive international involvement, from Pearl Harbor to the disintegration of the Soviet Union at the end of 1991. Americans were proud, of course, that their sacrifices had succeeded in defeating both fascism and communism during that long period, but they were exhausted and ready to turn inward.[9]

It was the end of history, the time of peace dividends, not of overseas interventions in non-strategic internal conflicts.[10] The only nation building to be done was here at home;[11] 'In the glow of having won the cold war, Americans felt that they could rest on the assurance of the security its superpower status provided.'[12]

The US mission in Somalia evolved from a purely humanitarian one to fighting local militias and hunting rogue leaders almost without Washington noticing the change.[13] The end result was the 'Black Hawk Down' moment on 3 October 1993, when 18 Americans were killed on the streets of Mogadishu while the image of angry mobs celebrating shocked America and the world. The net effect was an increased reluctance in congress to engage internationally, and public opinion decided to stay away from foreign entanglements. For President

---

9   Chollet, Derek and Samantha Powers (eds) (2011) *The Unquiet American: Richard Holbrooke in the World*, Philadelphia: Public Affairs, p. 227.
10   Soderberg, Nancy (2005) *The Superpower Myth: The Use And Misuse of American Might*, New Jersey: John Wiley & Sons, p. 18.
11   Chollet, Derek and James Goldgeier (2008) *America Between the Wars: From 11/9 to 9/11*, New York: Public Affairs, p. 57.
12   Soderberg, Nancy (2005) *The Superpower Myth: The Use And Misuse of American Might*, New Jersey: John Wiley & Sons, p. 20.
13   Chollet, Derek and James Goldgeier (2008) *America Between the Wars: From 11/9 to 9/11*, New York: Public Affairs, p. 93.

Clinton, this was an essential learning moment: 'I know we can intervene in these little countries with great ease and the first seventy-two hours go really well. But I am concerned what happens after that. I don't want to do Haiti unless I'm confident there's a plan for the day after.'[14] As Robert O'Neill would emphasise:

> There has always been a high correlation between success in war and ability to achieve a clean termination — although this has not been recognised widely until recently. We now acknowledge the importance of the exit strategy. Ideas on what makes a successful conclusion and how to disengage after achieving it need to be thought through before beginning a war or intervention, and not after it has begun to go awry.[15]

The direct outcome of this heightened sensitivity toward an exit strategy was Presidential Decision Directive 25. Adopted in May 1994, it focused on clarifying the criteria for US participation in multilateral peace operations. The document emphasised the need for clearly defined objectives, sufficient forces, and realistic criteria for ending American participation in overseas adventures. It was very much a product of its times, with Somalia and Vietnam traumas and the Powell Doctrine being the main drivers.[16] In fact, the combined legacies of the two perceived quagmires would greatly impact the American use of force in the 1990s, with 'memories of Mogadishu which hung over our deliberations like a dark cloud; and Vietnam, which lay further back, in the inner recesses of our minds', as Richard Holbrooke would later say about Dayton.[17]

There were two broad camps that shaped the debate inside the White House, related to the question of how to use unipolar power to respond to the challenges of the new security environment. On one side there was a generation shaped by a certain reading of the Vietnam quagmire. Against this formative experience, an entire generation of

---

14 Daalder, Ivo H. and I. M. Destler (2009) *In the Shadow of the Oval Office: Profiles of the National Security Advisers and the Presidents they Served: From JFK to George W. Bush*, New York: Simon & Schuster, p. 232.
15 O'Neill, Robert (1999) 'Success and Failure in War in the Twentieth Century', paper at the Second Symposium of War and Peace in the Twenty-First Century: Reflections upon the Century of War, Tokyo, October 7–8, 1999, p. 117. Available at: www.nids.go.jp/english/event/symposium/pdf/1999/sympo_e1999_3.pdf.
16 Davidson, Janine (2010) *Lifting the Fog of Peace: How Americans Learned to Fight Modern War*, Ann Arbor: University of Michigan Press, p. 84.
17 Ibid., p. 92.

officers became the guardians (to use the term of the historian Brian McAllister Linn) of a proper use of force, of a betrayed way of war that should not have been distracted by nation-building. For them, 'Vietnam provided a collective identity'[18] symbolising the essence of all wrongs and of how not to fight a war. For General Colin Powell, it reflected a 'belief in using all the force necessary to achieve the kind of decisive and successful result that we had achieved in the invasion of Panama and in Operation Desert Storm'.[19] It also expressed a promise: 'Many of my generation, the career captains, majors, and lieutenant colonels seasoned in that war, vowed that when our turn came to call the shots, we would not quietly acquiesce in halfhearted warfare for half-baked reasons that the American people could not understand or support', as Powell would write in his memoirs.[20] In this interpretation, incrementalism, the use of force in small progressive doses, was a recipe for disaster. It was the equivalent of 'not being allowed to fight to win'.[21] Instead, they favoured an overwhelming force paradigm, or 'the bully's way of going to war',[22] but only in circumstances that displayed realistic achievable political outcomes, clear exit strategies, and in the service of direct US vital national interests. The Weinberger-Powell doctrine reflected 'a utilitarian realistic yardstick',[23] an 'intervention test',[24] a set of guidelines that should be applied any time America would go to war. There were many inside the Clinton administration for whom the Powell Doctrine was raising questions — 'the kind of which we should have asked in Vietnam' as Tony Lake, Clinton's first national security advisor,

---

18   Linn, Brian McAllister (2009) *The Echo of Battle: The Army's Way of War*, Cambridge: Harvard University Press, p. 195.
19   Powell, Colin with Tony Koltz (2012) *It Worked For Me: In Life and Leadership*, ebook edition, New York: HarperCollins, loc. 2634.
20   Chollet, Derek and Samantha Powers (eds) (2011) *The Unquiet American: Richard Holbrooke in the World*, Philadelphia: Public Affairs, p. 214.
21   Davidson, Janine (2004), 'Giving Peace a Chance: The Modern Military's Struggle Over Peace Operations', *Small Wars and Insurgencies* 15(2), p. 176.
22   Buley, Benjamin (2008) *The New American Way of War: Military Culture and the Political Utility of Force*, New York: Routledge, p. 67.
23   Handel, Michael I. (2001) *Masters of War: Classical Strategic Thought*, London: Frank Cass, p. 246.
24   Smith, Rupert (2006) *The Utility of Force: The Art of War in the Modern World*, London: Penguin Books, p. 309.

put it.[25] From this perspective, the Bosnia and Somalia entanglements were simply a déjà vu of those specific political and military errors, a replay of the Vietnam War:

> [W]henever the military had a clear set of objectives ... as in Panama, the Philippine coup, and Desert Storm, the result has been a success. When the nation's policy was murky or nonexistent — the Bay of Pigs, Vietnam, creating a Marine presence in Lebanon — the result has been a disaster. In Bosnia, we were dealing with an ethnic tangle with roots reaching back a thousand years.[26]

In the 1990s, this reluctance to use force in outlier cases — especially in areas considered outside US vital interests — that didn't fit the very strict criteria developed by the Powell doctrine came to be described as Vietmalia syndrome.[27] In practice, this described 'the collective aversion to both nation building and casualties'.[28] At a deeper level, it reflected a profound reluctance on behalf of the US military to deal with the societal dimension of warfare — the underlying domestic political roots of the new wars — that the trends and realities pushed towards it at the forefront of the post-Cold War world. In short, it was a policy meant to ensure that the military would only fight the comfortable, speedy wars that they wanted to fight, on their terms: 'win decisively, and come home swiftly with few casualties and to great public approval.'[29] It was also the embodiment of a specific organisational culture, one suited for the political imperatives of the industrial war paradigm — for Desert Storm-like operations, but not for wars amongst the people 'where the object is the will of the people, where the enemy is operating as guerillas, or where conditions of acceptable governance are to be created and maintained'.[30]

---

25 Interview with Anthony Lake (2002) Miller Center, University of Virginia. Available at: millercenter.org/oralhistory/interview/anthony-lake-2002.
26 Soderberg, Nancy (2005) *The Superpower Myth: The Use And Misuse of American Might*, New Jersey: John Wiley & Sons, p. 23.
27 Chollet, Derek and Samantha Powers (eds) (2011) *The Unquiet American: Richard Holbrooke In The World*, Philadelphia: Public Affairs, p. 215.
28 Davidson, Janine (2010) *Lifting the Fog of Peace: How Americans Learned to Fight Modern War*, Ann Arbor: University of Michigan Press, p. 90.
29 Davidson, Janine (2013) 'Civil–Military Friction and Presidential Decision Making: Explaining the Broken Dialogue', *Presidential Studies Quarterly* 43(1), p. 143.
30 Smith, Rupert (2006) *The Utility of Force: The Art of War in the Modern World*, London: Penguin Books, p. 310.

On the other side of the Clinton Administration, there was a group with a different mindset that had a much more nuanced interpretation of what the American role in the post-Cold War world should be. They believed in affirming US leadership and power, including through the limited use of America's military power, in the service of 'assertive multilateralism'.[31] Their lessons were not Vietnam related, but reflected the legacies of Munich and the Holocaust as 'the benchmark horrors'[32] of a previous interwar period that was shaped by the absence of America from the world stage. It was a generation of policy-makers with Wilsonian tones, for whom human rights, democracy, and liberal values should be at the core of US foreign policy.[33] Its informal leader was Madeleine Albright, a refugee from Czechoslovakia and 'the hawk of the administration that was always pressing for stronger US action against repression, especially in Europe'.[34] What mattered most for them were the failures of past collective security organisations to act when international peace and security was threatened. From this perspective, the collapse of former Yugoslavia and its ripple effects (between 1991 and 1995 the death toll was close to a staggering 300,000) provided a textbook case: it was 'the greatest collective security failure of the West [in Europe] since the 1930s',[35] and many in the Clinton Administration were determined not to let happen again. This resonated deeply with the personal experiences of both Albright and Holbrooke, for whom the past European tragedies of communism and Nazism were deeply ingrained in the background of their families. In Holbrooke's case, the sense of European history was even more amplified — both of his parents were refugees from Nazism, and his wife, Kati Marton, was a Jewish refugee from Hungary, a country left within the Iron Curtain's deadly embrace.[36] At the same time, they were part of a generation that believed that past European tragedies

---

31 Chollet, Derek and James Goldgeier (2008) *America Between the Wars: From 11/9 to 9/11*, New York: Public Affairs, p. 69.
32 Ibid.
33 Ibid., p. 82.
34 Soderberg, Nancy (2005) *The Superpower Myth: The Use And Misuse of American Might*, New Jersey: John Wiley & Sons, p. 15.
35 Chollet, Derek and James Goldgeier (2008) *America Between the Wars: From 11/9 to 9/11*, New York: Public Affairs, p. 269.
36 Chollet, Derek and Samantha Powers (eds) (2011) *The Unquiet American: Richard Holbrooke in the World*, Philadelphia: Public Affairs, p. 165.

demonstrated that the maintenance of stability in Europe is a multilateral problem. There is no invisible hand to keep its nations from colliding with each other. If all interpretation of state behaviour is done on a unilateral basis by other states, suspicions and mistrust will accumulate.[37]

At the time, the philosophical gap between the two schools of thought came to be symbolised by the historical exchange between the risk-averse mindset of General Colin Powell (the Chairman of the Joint Chiefs of Staff), and Madeleine Albright (the US Ambassador at the UN) who famously asked: 'What's the point of having this superb military that you're always talking about if we can't use it?'[38]

A compromise was ultimately mediated, preparing the ground for the coercive diplomacy campaigns in Bosnia and Kosovo, the hallmarks of a new post-Cold War interventionism. It was a prudent embracing of those who advocated a humanitarian intervention doctrine, a combination between

> those who bring a heartfelt passion to the issues but then an essential skepticism and moderation as they apply their minds to the issues. Because when you move from ideals to ideology you get in trouble. That was certainly the great lesson of Vietnam.[39]

Nobody will better sum up this compromise that captured the logic of the Clinton wars, than General Wesley Clark: 'if you line up international law, good diplomacy, and modern military power, you can achieve strategically decisive results without decisive force.'[40]

Over time, the interpretation of threats that the instabilities in the Balkans posed to NATO and to US interests gradually changed. The new consensus reflected the conviction that, left unchecked, the spilling over effects could challenge regional stability in Europe: 'mindful of the fact that seen decades earlier, violence in the region had triggered a world war, Clinton recognised that Milosevic's

---

37 O'Neill, Robert (1998) 'Europe and the Wider World: The Security Challenge', in Ken Booth (ed.) *Statecraft And Security. The Cold War and Beyond*, New York: Cambridge University Press, p. 196.
38 Buley, Benjamin (2008) *The New American Way of War: Military Culture and the Political Utility of Force*, New York: Routledge, p. 80.
39 Interview with Anthony Lake (2002) Miller Center, University of Virginia. Available at: millercenter.org/oralhistory/interview/anthony-lake-2002.
40 Priest, Dana (2004) *The Mission: Waging War and Keeping Peace with America's Military*, New York: W.W. Norton & Company, p. 258.

dream of Greater Serbia and his campaign of ethnic cleansing could have grave consequences for the rest of Europe'.[41] For Tony Lake, the National Security Advisor in the first Clinton Administration, the danger was clear: 'the war in Bosnia could have sparked a wider conflagration in Europe, affecting some of America's NATO allies and many of the continent's new democracies.'[42] Imagining the result if the international community had not intervened:

> [T]he Serbs would have continued their offensive; more than a million and a half Kosovars would today be sitting in camps or starving in the hills with no hope of return; Milosevic would be strengthened; and in a region with many unresolved ethnic tensions, potential dictators would have learned the lesson that massive violence will draw no response from the international community.[43]

A Syria *avant la lettre* at NATO's doorstep.

In Bosnia and Kosovo, the core signature of the American way of war during the 1990s was the use of airpower and precision guided munitions (PGMs) to coerce and compel an adversary. In part, the choice was rooted in the risk-adverse mindset, or the body bags syndrome, displayed by the US military in campaigns that essentially were wars of choice that did not reflect American vital national interests (such as Lebanon or Somalia). On the other hand, there was a belief that in the post-Desert Storm age of PGMs, airpower could make a huge difference by providing a clean, surgical strike capability to be used in limited coercive diplomacy campaigns designed to compel the other side to change behaviour or negotiate. It captured the mindset of the senior civilian officials in the Clinton Administration — the so-called Surgical Strike School — who assumed a high degree of precision in the application of limited force, but also an ability to 'achieve limited political objectives' without escalating the effort.[44] The major flaw of this approach was that it fundamentally ignored the human domain, those societal forces that make people tick and move communities

---

41 Soderberg, Nancy (2005) *The Superpower Myth: The Use And Misuse of American Might*, New Jersey: John Wiley & Sons, p. 77.
42 Lake, Anthony (2000) *Six Nightmares*, New York: Hachette Book Group, p. 114.
43 Steinberg, James (1999) 'A Perfect Polemic: Blind to Reality on Kosovo', *Foreign Affairs* 78(6), pp. 128–33. Available at: www.foreignaffairs.com/articles/kosovo/1999-11-01/perfect-polemic-blind-reality-kosovo.
44 Zenko, Micah (2010) *Between Threats and War: U.S. Discrete Military Operations in the Post-Cold War World*, Stanford: Stanford University Press, p. 24.

at the grass-root level ('ethnic divisions, traditional relationships, ideology, religion, attitudes, nationalism, beliefs, family structure, customs, culture') while the core focus of the US military remained on 'machines, organization, equipment, maximizing firepower, reducing casualties, accurate employment of weapons on target'.[45] The combined outcome of the Powell-Weinberger Doctrine and the Surgical Strike School was an army unprepared for campaigns 'more politically complicated than Desert Storm ... Although the military knew how to win battles, it had no sense of how to use American power to achieve political objectives — to win wars.'[46]

Arguably one of the most influential thinkers at the time was John Warden, an air force fighter pilot whose ideas about the use of airpower were instrumental in developing the Desert Storm's air campaign. He understood the enemy as a system, as a collection of multiple centres of gravity, of points 'where the enemy is most vulnerable and where an attack will have the best chance of being decisive'.[47] The five rings[48] that Warden listed — leadership, key industrial production, infrastructure, population, and fielded forces — would be at the forefront of the coercive acupuncture campaigns of the 1990s. For example, during Operation Deliberate Force in Bosnia (September 1995), NATO disrupted the ability of the Bosnian Serbs to move their forces around the battlefield by effectively destroying their communications network.[49] The emphasis was on cutting the communication between 'the brain' and 'the muscles' — as Adrian R. Lewis later put it, 'the objective of operations was to destroy the system of nerves that transmitted orders from the brain to the muscles, severing the links between the decision makers and the fighting forces'.[50] But what added to the coercive leverage of NATO was the synergy effect achieved in conjunction with the ground offensives of the Muslim and Croat forces that threatened the balance of power on

---

45 Lewis, Adrian R. (2007) *The American Culture of War: The History of U.S. Military Force from World War II to Operation Iraqi Freedom*, New York: Routledge, p. 391.
46 Nagl, John (2014) *Knife Fights: A Memoir of Modern War in Theory and Practice*, New York: Penguin Books, p. 46.
47 Quoted in Kagan, Frederick W. (2006) *Finding the Target: The Transformation of American Military Policy*, New York: Encounter Books, p. 114.
48 Ibid., p. 121.
49 Ibid., p. 187.
50 Lewis, Adrian R. (2007) *The American Culture of War: The History of U.S. Military Force from World War II to Operation Iraqi Freedom*, New York: Routledge, p. 389.

the battlefield.⁵¹ The altered context played directly into the Bosnian Serbs' fears of being dominated by competitive ethnicities, so rather than completely losing their defensive capacity, they decided to bargain and negotiate.⁵² For some in the Clinton Administration, the lesson was about the power of technology to compel an adversary to alter his behaviour:

> Imagine you were a Bosnian Serb in the 1995, as US troops used electronic warfare to find and cripple your radar and anti-aircraft missiles, and then hit you with accurate long-range strikes against which you had no effective response. No wonder you'd have concluded you stood a better chance of survival at the negotiating table than on the battlefield.⁵³

The Kosovo campaign was a much more complicated story. For Slobodan Milosevic and NATO, the symbolic stakes were much higher. Kosovo was the historical birthplace for the Serbian nation. NATO, an alliance in its 50s that year, couldn't let the bloodshed and the ethnic cleansing orchestrated by Milosevic to continue without impunity. Its entire relevance in the post-Cold War world as a collective security organisation would have been otherwise questioned. The use of airpower was again considered as the ideal tool for changing Milosevic's calculus. A Western ground component was excluded from the start because of the major political cleavages that might have caused the consensus in the Alliance to collapse.⁵⁴

There is another reason for which Washington was not fond of the idea of a ground option:

> [F]rom the air we had a thousand to one advantage on Milosevic. Once we got into those mountains of Yugoslavia where the Germans had been savaged — we were on the ground — our advantage was no longer a thousand to one. Maybe it was two to one. It would have been a daunting prospect to go over the Albanian Alps and send a land force into Belgrade ... Once the Serbs got us on the ground, the possibility

---

51   Byman, Daniel L. and Matthew C. Waxman (2008) 'Kosovo and the Great Air Power Debate', in Thomas G. Mahnken and Joseph A. Maiolo (eds) *Strategic Studies: A Reader*, London: Routledge, pp. 169–70.
52   Kagan, Frederick W. (2006) *Finding the Target: The Transformation of American Military Policy*, New York: Encounter Books, p. 187.
53   Lake, Anthony (2000) *Six Nightmares*, New York: Hachette Book Group, p. 81.
54   Daalder, Ivo H. (1999), 'U.S. Diplomacy before the Kosovo War', *Brookings Institution*, 28 September. Available at: www.brookings.edu/research/testimony/1999/09/28balkans-daalder.

for guerrilla attacks, insurgency, there were all these tunnels that had been dug in World War II to protect against invasion. It would have been a bloody mess.[55]

But this gave Milosevic a certain window of opportunity to try to divide the Alliance and force the West to accept a different reality on the ground — a new ethnic balance. It followed a highly incremental, low-intensity, politically micro-managed military campaign, 'one that began small, the antithesis of Colin Powell's insistence on overwhelming force'.[56] The focus was very much on the centres of gravity highlighted by John Warden, but in reverse priority, starting with 'the outermost ring and gradually worked into the inner rings — critical infrastructure, command and control nodes, and finally, just at the end of the campaign, the leadership itself'.[57] A fierce debate started between General Wesley Clark (at the time NATO's Supreme Allied Commander Europe) and Lt. Gen. Michael Short (at the time in charge of directing the air operations against Serbia). Clark wanted the airpower to be used primarily against the Serbian forces (tanks and irregular light units) operating in Kosovo against the Albanian local population, while for Short 'the jewel in the crown' was represented by the high-impact, but politically sensitive targets in downtown Belgrade.[58] Gradually the campaign evolved closer to hitting the regime as the factories of Milosevic's cronies.[59] It was not until Milosevic understood, however, that NATO had the political resolve to wage a ground campaign that he finally capitulated.[60] Blair and Clinton were publicly talking about all options being on the table. There was a larger, highly visible, choreographic effort designed to persuade Milosevic that the Alliance was dead serious: elements of the 82nd Airborne Division were deployed in the region while 25,000

---

55 Interview with Samuel R. Berger (2005) Miller Center, University of Virginia. Available at: millercenter.org/oralhistory/interview/samuel-r-berger.
56 Priest, Dana (2004) *The Mission: Waging War and Keeping Peace with America's Military*, New York: W.W. Norton & Company, p. 258.
57 Kagan, Frederick W. (2006) *Finding the Target: The Transformation of American Military Policy*, New York: Encounter Books, p. 191.
58 Priest, Dana (2004) *The Mission: Waging War and Keeping Peace with America's Military*, New York: W.W. Norton & Company, pp. 264–5.
59 Interview with Samuel R. Berger (2005) Miller Center, University of Virginia. Available at: millercenter.org/oralhistory/interview/samuel-r-berger.
60 Daalder, Ivo H. and I. M. Destler (2009) *In the Shadow of the Oval Office: Profiles of the National Security Advisers and the Presidents they Served: From JFK to George W. Bush*, New York: Simon & Schuster, p. 243.

NATO troops were dispatched in Albania and Macedonia.[61] Still, the Kosovo air campaign was an ugly victory (as Ivo Daalder and Michael O'Hanlon would say at the time): 78 days of targeting; 26,600 bombs and missiles; 10,000 Kosovar Albanians killed; and more than 863,000 civilians leaving Kosovo during the campaign.[62] The larger lesson to be taken at a time when Washington seemed to be again seduced by its promises might be that airpower should always be used in synergy with other instruments of power, because in Kosovo 'the air campaign by itself had not achieved the desired political and military ends, and that the determination to fight an air-only campaign rendered air power itself significantly less effective'.[63]

In retrospect, the legacy of the Clinton interventionism — Haiti, Bosnia, Iraq, Kosovo — was about establishing a new playbook, re-writing the old rules of the road, and pushing for redefining the rights and obligations of state sovereignty — the building block of the international order. 'Nobody gave us a book when we came in. The old way clearly wasn't working. The world had fundamentally changed. The way you do business has to change, but how you do it took a while', reflected Nancy Soderberg, Deputy Assistant to the President for National Security Affairs.[64] It was an imperative for a world where the main threats to international peace and security were generated from within states, by governments that were knocking out their own people. Figuring out and implementing the new rules was a messy process, but ultimately 'he brilliantly moved the United States from the Cold War into the post-Cold War, or 21st-century era'.[65] By 1999, the nature of conversation was fundamentally changed. There was an increasing emphasis on a doctrine of international community. British Prime Minister Tony Blair captured the new zeitgeist:

---

61 Byman, Daniel L., and Matthew C. Waxman (2008) 'Kosovo and the Great Air Power Debate', in Thomas G. Mahnken and Joseph A. Maiolo (eds) *Strategic Studies: A Reader*, London: Routledge, p. 167.
62 Priest, Dana (2004) *The Mission: Waging War and Keeping Peace with America's Military*, New York: W.W. Norton & Company, p. 266.
63 Kagan, Frederick W. (2006) *Finding the Target: The Transformation of American Military Policy*, New York: Encounter Books, p. 194.
64 Interview with Nancy Soderberg (2007) Miller Center, University of Virginia. Available at: millercenter.org/oralhistory/interview/nancy-soderberg.
65 Ibid.

> The most pressing foreign policy problem we face is to identify the circumstances in which we should get actively involved in other people's conflicts. Non-interference has long been considered an important principle of international order ... But the principle of non-interference must be qualified in important respects. Acts of genocide can never be a purely internal matter.[66]

This is the spirit that harnessed what was later codified as the Responsibility to Protect (R2P) norm — when national governments fail in their fundamental duty to protect their own citizens or are the perpetrators of large scale killing against them, it is the right of international community to intervene in order to substitute this responsibility[67] — which, years later, was instrumental in preparing the ground for the NATO intervention in Libya in 2011.

The campaigns against Iraq during the 1990s can also be understood through the framework of R2P. Saddam Hussein never stopped being a focus for the Clinton Administration, but was mainly perceived as a containable threat to its own citizens in the south (the Shia population) and in the north (the Kurds). It is in this context that 'the Clinton administration contemplated military action against him only to uphold the no-fly zones and to contain his ambition to build weapons of mass destruction'.[68] The No Fly Zones (NFZs) were a reflection of the belief that sovereignty didn't provide local leaders a blank check to use force against their own people. Overall, the NFZs established in Iraq were highly successful in keeping Iraqi airpower outside the northern and southern parts of the country, but were much less successful in deterring ground troops from attacking the Shia and Kurd populations.[69]

During the 1990s, global terrorism was on the rise. The plot to destroy the World Trade Center (February 1993) and the attacks against US embassies in Kenya and Tanzania (August 1998) reflected the new trend. Bin Laden himself became a target for the US Government,

---

66 PBS Newshour (1999) 'The Blair Doctrine', 22 April. Available at: www.pbs.org/newshour/bb/international-jan-june99-blair_doctrine4-23/.
67 Rice, Susan E. and Andrew J. Loomis (2007) 'The Evolution of Humanitarian Intervention and the Responsibility to Protect', in Ivo Daalder (ed.) *Beyond Preemption: Force and Legitimacy in a Changing World*, Washington DC: Brookings Institution Press, p. 83.
68 Chollet, Derek and James Goldgeier (2008) *America Between the Wars: From 11/9 to 9/11*, New York: Public Affairs, p. 206.
69 Zenko, Micah (2010) *Between Threats and War: U.S. Discrete Military Operations in the Post-Cold War World*, Stanford: Stanford University Press, p. 29.

but, absent a 9/11 provocation, nobody was willing to use force on an extensive scale against Afghanistan as the state that presumably hosted him. Even the offshore strikes against the terrorist training camps were criticised on the Hill. However, at the end of Clinton Administration, Sandy Berger warned Rice: 'You're going to spend more time during your four years on terrorism generally and al-Qaeda specifically than any other issue.'[70]

The interventions in Bosnia, Haiti, Somalia, Iraq, and Kosovo were also instrumental in clarifying 'a new understanding of America's place in the world'.[71] For Albright and Holbrooke, the crises of the post-Cold War world showed the need for decisive US leadership, and prepared the ground for affirming America as an indispensable power in managing the most pressing threats to international peace and security:

> The world's richest nation, one that presumes to great moral authority, cannot simply make worthy appeals to conscience and call on others to carry the burden. The world will look to Washington for more than rhetoric the next time we face a challenge to peace.[72]

From Containment to Enlargement

None of the military interventions launched by the Clinton Administration during the 1990s has any meaning outside of the enlargement framework that, in the end, captures the essence of his terms. In a way, this can be seen as a larger effort of the first truly post-Cold War presidency to shape the new era and articulate a coherent vision of the role of America in a new world.[73] From its early days, the Clinton Administration made a constant, conscious search for developing a substitute to the containment doctrine that provided a clear-cut strategic rationale for the Cold War. The White House

---

70   Daalder, Ivo H. and I. M. Destler (2009) *In the Shadow of the Oval Office: Profiles of the National Security Advisers and the Presidents they Served: From JFK to George W. Bush*, New York: Simon & Schuster, p. 248.
71   Chollet, Derek and James Goldgeier (2008) *America Between the Wars: From 11/9 to 9/11*, New York: Public Affairs, p. 206.
72   Zenko, Micah (2010) *Between Threats and War: U.S. Discrete Military Operations in the Post-Cold War World*, Stanford: Stanford University Press, p. 29.
73   Chollet, Derek and James Goldgeier (2008) *America Between the Wars: From 11/9 to 9/11*, New York: Public Affairs, p. 65–6.

needed to come up with a new grand strategy construct, as well as a core organising principle, able to set the direction for the US post-Cold War foreign policy. It is in this context that, in September 1993, Anthony Lake, the Assistant to the President for National Security Affairs, proposed a new guiding principle:

> Throughout the Cold War, we contained a global threat to market democracies; now we should seek to enlarge their reach, particularly in places of special significance to us. The successor to a doctrine of containment must be a strategy of enlargement — enlargement of the world's free community of market democracies.[74]

An important emphasis here was on providing the institutional regional framework that was able to stabilise, encourage, and consolidate new democracies in key regions. In part, this is the role that NATO played in Central and Eastern Europe (CEE) over the last 20 years. In this interpretation, NATO is much more than a traditional political and military alliance or standard collective defence organisation. That is certainly at its core, but deeply embedded in its historical DNA is a transformative power: 'Even as NATO held the line against the Soviet Army, it drew France and Germany together. It helped integrate Italy and, eventually Spain, into the community of democracies. It gave shattered economies the confidence to recover.'[75] Specifically, in the former Warsaw Pact countries, by incentivising the reforming of military establishments, the restructuring of civil–military relations and playing the role of 'a magnet to build their democracies, settle their border disputes and deal with their minorities issues in an appropriate way',[76] NATO would secure the domestic transitions[77] under way in a highly sensitive region. The CEE countries were disposed in the near proximity of the Balkans, which at the time were massively ravaged by ethnic wars. The danger of spilling over was very real, especially in countries such as Romania and Hungary, where nationalistic impulses and zero-sum optics flooded the public space. It was in this sense that

---

74 Remarks of Anthony Lake, Assistant to the President for National Security Affairs, 'From Containment to Enlargement', Johns Hopkins University, School of Advanced International Studies, Washington DC, 21 September 1993.
75 Remarks of James B. Steinberg, Director, Policy Planning Staff, US Department of State, 'Advancing NATO's Adaptation', Atlantic Council of the United States, 13 June l996.
76 Interview with Samuel R. Berger (2005) Miller Center, University of Virginia. Available at: millercenter.org/oralhistory/interview/samuel-r-berger.
77 Ikenberry, G. John (2001) *After Victory: Institutions, Strategic Restraint and the Rebuilding of Order After Major Wars*, Princeton: Princeton University Press, pp. 236–7.

NATO enlargement acted as an engine for change by transforming societal impulses and empowering the reformist forces. Ultimately, the NATO expansion secured those countries and incentivised them to fix some of those structural weaknesses that plagued the former communist countries and were instrumental in the collapse of former Yugoslavia. Over time, the success of NATO enlargement prepared the ground for the EU expansion. In the end, the Clintonian enlargement framework reflected the spirit of the order — building projects designed to stabilise post-1945 international relations.[78] It was a way to tame the ghosts of the past, the legacies of 'unresolved and often conflicting historical resentments, ambitions, and, most dangerous, territorial and ethnic disputes', but at the same time spread the seeds of transformative forces, without which 'these lands remain vulnerable to the same problems, often exacerbated by an obsession with righting historical wrongs, real or mythical'.[79]

It was debates over the Balkan wars that marked John Nagl's return to Oxford to study again under Professor O'Neill in 1995. Having served in a cavalry squadron that led the eventual American intervention, Nagl was keenly aware of the debates enumerated here, and cognisant of the lessons O'Neill taught from his own experience as a young army officer in Vietnam. It was the combination of O'Neill's combat experience in that war and Nagl's own in Operation Desert Storm that convinced Nagl, with O'Neill's support and advice, that counterinsurgency would soon return to the forefront of strategic thought. That led to the writing of a doctoral dissertation that would eventually be published as *Learning to Eat Soup with a Knife: Counterinsurgency Lessons from Malaya and Vietnam.*[80]

Redefining the role of NATO for a post-Cold War world has a second dimension that was very much at the core of the debates inside the Clinton Administration. From its early days, NATO was the main instrument designed to contain and deter Soviet power in Europe.[81] But in a world defined less by traditional aggression and more by the

---

78   Ikenberry, G. John (2001) 'What would a New Transatlantic Bargain Look Like?', in Mark D. Ducasse (ed.) *The Transatlantic Bargain*, Rome: NATO Defense College, p. 83.
79   Chollet, Derek and Samantha Powers (eds) (2011) *The Unquiet American: Richard Holbrooke in the World*, Philadelphia: Public Affairs, p. 179.
80   Nagl, John (2005) *Learning to Eat Soup with a Knife: Counterinsurgency Lessons from Malaya and Vietnam*, Chicago: Chicago University Press.
81   Ibid.

'adverse consequences of instabilities that may arise from the serious economic, social and political difficulties, including ethnic rivalries and territorial disputes',[82] NATO had to respond to new market niches, to the out of area instabilities that threatened European security. It was in this context that 'the purpose of NATO was being defined in Bosnia and in Kosovo'.[83] It was no longer about containing Russian power, but about crisis management in an unstable neighbourhood. In a way, NATO was still in the business of containment, but the enemy was not related to states that were too strong, but the chaos generated by states that were too weak.[84] In short NATO had to adapt to an environment where 'local conflicts, internal political and economic instability, and the return of historical grievances have now replaced Soviet expansionism as the greatest threat to peace in Europe'.[85] The new profile that NATO adopted in the 1990s is very close to what Professor Robert O'Neill was proposing at the time, an Alliance for Development[86] able to respond and remedy to the entrenched maladministration and pervasive weakness of the states in the land between Western Europe and Russia. He understood immediately the need to go beyond the core traditional military competencies that were part of the NATO traditional brand. Ultimately, the whole NATO adaptation reflected the spirit of the Alliance for Development because the entire process 'aimed at the long-term building of secure, prosperous states which ultimately can either take their place as members of the EU, or enter into long, close and peaceful association with it'.[87]

But the post-Cold War NATO transformation was not without controversy. George Kennan was one of the most visceral critics of that decision. He considered the NATO enlargement as 'the most fateful

---

82   NATO (1991) 'The Alliance's New Strategic Concept'. Available at: www.nato.int/cps/en/natolive/official_texts_23847.htm.
83   Interview with Samuel R. Berger (2005) Miller Center, University of Virginia. Available at: millercenter.org/oralhistory/interview/samuel-r-berger.
84   Nagl, John (2014) *Knife Fights: A Memoir of Modern War in Theory and Practice*, New York: Penguin Books, pp. 237–8.
85   Chollet, Derek and Samantha Powers (eds) (2011) *The Unquiet American: Richard Holbrooke in the World*, Philadelphia: Public Affairs, p. 176.
86   O'Neill, Robert (1998) 'Europe and the Wider World: The Security Challenge', in Ken Booth (ed.) *Statecraft And Security. The Cold War and Beyond*, New York: Cambridge University Press, p. 207.
87   Ibid., p. 206.

error of American policy in the entire post-cold-war era',[88] a tragic mistake that would humiliate and alienate Russia and empower the anti-reformist nationalist elites. After the Crimea annexation, that entire revisionist school was resurrected. They vindicate Kennan's insight considering NATO expansion as 'a bad idea with predictable bad results',[89] a punitive peace that exploited Russian disarray and one that Moscow had little choice but to swallow. But imagine how the CEE region would have looked in the absence of a NATO enlargement to the east. It would have been a gigantic Ukraine-like grey zone, a ring of hollow states with very weak, corrupted structures ripe for insidious subversion and intimidation in the proximity of the Russian Empire. In short, it would have provided the perfect target, the ideal playground for hybrid warfare. As Robert Kaplan pointed out recently, 'what the Putin regime likes the most is weak democracies'.[90] These provide the right societal foundation for orchestrating all kinds of intelligence operations, for subversion, for corruption, for buying off politicians and influence. Seen in retrospect, NATO was responsible for clearing and holding the former Warsaw Pact countries by keeping them outside of the Russian influence, while in the successive stages, the EU was responsible for building European modernised countries.

Lessons in Post-Cold War Interventionism: The 1990s as a Preview of the Post-9/11 COIN Era

Nobody described better the relevance of the 1990s for the type of campaigns that shaped the post-9/11 security environment than US Secretary of Defense Robert Gates. In a 2007 speech, he emphasised that, after Vietnam,

> the Army relegated unconventional war to the margins of training, doctrine, and budget priorities ... This approach may have seemed validated by ultimate victory in the Cold War and the triumph of Desert Storm. But it left the service unprepared to deal with the

---

88 Kennan, George F. (1997) 'A Fateful Error', *The New York Times*, 5 February.
89 Bremmer, Ian (2015) *Superpower: Three Choices for America's Role in the World*, Great Britain: Portfolio Penguin, p. 14.
90 Kaplan, Robert D. (2015) 'The Future of Geopolitics in the Lands Between Baltic and Black Seas', keynote speech presented to CEPA Forum, Washington DC, 2 October.

operations that followed: Somalia, Haiti, the Balkans, and more recently Afghanistan and Iraq — the consequences and costs of which we are still struggling with today.[91]

The last decade of the twentieth century reflects a perpetual clash between the guardians of the traditional American way of war as the antithesis of Vietnam (one focused on 'a strategy of annihilation' and obsessed by 'how to secure victory in its desired fullness'[92]) and a different generation who understood that Desert Storm was not the return of the old days, of 'good, clean soldiering' in the spirit of the Second World War, but an aberration and 'the final salute of the Cold War military'.[93] It was just a preview of a new age, where campaigning was messy and slow, like eating soup with a knife, and where the core mission was less about destroying armies and more about helping to rebuild nations and societies.

Most of the 1990s interventions (Somalia in particular, but including Haiti, Bosnia and Kosovo) should have forced America to rethink the definition of what success means in the context of the post-Cold War battlefields. Winning in the so-called MOOTWs (Military Operations Other Than War) was no longer about military success in itself, but about the ability to focus on the societal dimensions of warfare, local dynamics, and political vacuums. General Rupert Smith, a veteran of the Balkans, emphasised that the hallmark of the post-Cold War interventionism was about establishing 'a condition in which the political objective can be achieved by other means and in other ways'.[94] Over time, everything came to depend 'on progress on local parties' political steps, not on a superpower's military prowess'.[95] By themselves, military means were hardly enough. They could secure the environment and provide a 'breathing space', but

---

91 Small Wars Journal Editors (2007) 'SECDEF Robert Gates, 10 Oct 07 AUSA Speech', *Small Wars Journal*. Available at: smallwarsjournal.com/blog/secdef-robert-gates-10-oct-07-ausa-speech.
92 Weigley, Russell F. (1973) *The American Way of War: A History of United States Military Strategy and Policy*, New York: Macmillan, p. 22.
93 Clancy, Tom with General Tony Zinni (Ret.) and Tony Koltz, *Battle Ready*, New York: Berkley Books, p. 488.
94 Smith, Rupert (2006) *The Utility of Force: The Art of War in the Modern World*, London: Penguin Books, p. 270.
95 Soderberg, Nancy (2005) *The Superpower Myth: The Use And Misuse of American Might*, New Jersey: John Wiley & Sons, p. 36.

> the military mission on its own, will not achieve a strategic objective ... The goal should be broader: the future of society itself. In a strategic sense, a peacekeeping operation is more about political progress and economic programs than it is about troops in blue berets.[96]

As a consequence, the expectations for fast exit strategies should have been changed as the 1990s interventionism revealed 'the international forces must remain in place, not only until military tasks are completed but also until the indigenous political will and structures exist to support a stable government and a local security force to keep the peace'.[97]

Haiti perfectly illustrates this point. The Clinton Administration 'prematurely declared that our mission had been accomplished'.[98] For the White House, the return of Jean Bertrand Arstide, the legitimate elected leader, was considered the end of the process, when in fact it should have been another intermediate step towards building 'a normal country, capable of fending for itself and governing itself decently'.[99] But without a significant US presence on the ground for the long haul, to shape the environment, incentivise and pressure the necessary reforms, the country 'slipped back into civil unrest and corrupt, incompetent, often violent politics'.[100] For some of the decision-makers at the time, the lesson was clear: 'The Clinton Administration should not have left Haiti to its own devices and its deeply flawed leadership, thereby allowing an initial success to turn into failure.'[101] This would become a familiar snapshot for the counterinsurgents of the post-9/11 era. Stability operations are not just about building strong host nation institutional capacities, but also legitimacy and good governance. Time and time again, whether in Kosovo, Afghanistan, or the post-surge Iraq, the host nation leadership will choose to behave as a predatory government, operating 'as a collection of patronage networks that systematically extract resources from the population for the benefit of those networks and the power brokers who run them'.[102] Tony Lake

---

96 Lake, Anthony (2000) *Six Nightmares*, New York: Hachette Book Group, p. 193.
97 Ibid., p. 94.
98 Talbott, Strobe (2008) *The Great Experiment: The Story of Ancient Empires, Modern States, and the Quest for a Global Nation*, New York: Simon & Schuster, p. 302.
99 Ibid., p. 303.
100 Ibid.
101 Ibid.
102 Biddle, Stephen (2014) 'Afghanistan's Legacy: Emerging Lessons of an Ongoing War', *The Washington Quarterly* 37(2), p. 80.

10. THE UNCOMFORTABLE WARS OF THE 1990S

summarised his take away from Haiti as: 'we were to see how much easier it is to help a nation build the structures of democracy than it is to change a political culture.'[103]

The 1990s operations also reflected the need to change the roles and missions the militaries were expected to perform. At their core, they remained fighting machines along the lines of the traditional American way of war, but in addition there was an entire new spectrum of responsibilities, most of them 'much more intrinsically political in nature'.[104] As one of the officers formed during post-Cold War operations, Tony Zinni discovered that on the MOOTW battlefields of the 1990s, he had to deal with 'political problems, with humanitarian problems, with economic reconstruction, with social problems'.[105] In Somalia, he served on 'the political, security, judicial and police committees ... met with women's groups, schoolteachers' and other professional groups, to hear complaints and get cooperation for projects',[106] and he coordinated extensive psyops, civic action, and rebuilding projects. And all these from an officer that came from a military that regarded the Second World War as 'the last Good War — the last with moral clarity, an easily identified and demonized enemy, unprecedented national unity ... World War Two was the way you fight a war.'[107] It was his generation's legacy, a tradition he was taught that must be preserved. It was also the kind of 'clear-war fighting mission' that the military was comfortable with and constantly searching for. Nothing prepared him for the ubiquitous rebuilding and reconstruction tasks in a world where peacekeeping, peace enforcement and 'vague, confusing military actions heavily overlaid with political, humanitarian and economic considerations' defined the new normal.[108]

---

103 Lake, Anthony (2000) *Six Nightmares*, New York: Hachette Book Group, p. 140.
104 O'Neill, Robert (1997) 'The Remaking of Modern Armies Post Cold War', in Peter Dennis and Grey Jeffrey (eds) *The Second Fifty Years: The Australian Army 1947–1997*, Canberra: ADFA, p. 4.
105 Remarks by General Anthony C. Zinni (2004) 'From the Battlefield to the Negotiating Table: Preventing Deadly Conflict', Joan B. Kroc Distinguished Lecture Series, University of San Diego, 15 April.
106 Clancy, Tom with General Tony Zinni (Ret.) and Tony Koltz, *Battle Ready*, New York: Berkley Books, p. 299.
107 Ibid., p. 483.
108 Ibid., p. 498.

There is another key component emphasised by the MOOTW battlefields that will become a common denominator in every post-9/11 stability operation — the imperative to devise a comprehensive approach that will blend and synchronise civil and military efforts in recognition of the fact that the military tools are barely enough. Analysing the 1990s, Professor Robert O'Neill clearly understood that the new security environment called for comprehensive skills 'on a wide series of fronts, civil and military',[109] bringing together specific expertise in democratic practice, law, local government, public health, communal relations, religious affairs, urban development, economics and business development, policing and military affairs.[110] At the same time, stabilising a country required strategic patience for the long haul, being able to plan, correlate sequences and manage broadly 'on several time scales — the long term for economic and social development, the mid term for military force development and political reforms, and the short term for peacekeeping, conflict resolution or peace enforcement'.[111] For a counterinsurgent of the 1960s, 1970s, or from the post-9/11 era, this would be simply déjà vu. He would have understood instantly the primacy of political and administrative aspects, but also the need for an integrated civil–military framework that ties together the different lines of operations 'diplomacy, information operations, intelligence, financial and military — to achieve predominantly political objectives'.[112] The problem is that, in reality, that degree of cohesiveness between very different civilian and military cultures is very hard to develop in theatre. In Bosnia, for example, there was never a coordinating whole of government machinery 'that brought the civilian, nongovernmental and military resources of the United States and Europe together' to force change.[113]

---

109 O'Neill, Robert (1998) 'Europe and the Wider World: The Security Challenge', in Ken Booth (ed.) *Statecraft And Security. The Cold War and Beyond*, New York: Cambridge University Press, p. 200.
110 Ibid., p. 201.
111 Ibid., p. 207.
112 Nagl, John (2005) *Learning to Eat Soup with a Knife: Counterinsurgency Lessons from Malaya and Vietnam*, Chicago: Chicago University Press, p. 16.
113 Priest, Dana (2004) *The Mission: Waging War and Keeping Peace with America's Military*, New York: W.W. Norton & Company, p. 256.

Nonetheless, most of the MOOTWs of the 1990s provided formative experiences for an entire generation of officers, immersing them in new operational challenges beyond the type to which they were accustomed. These challenges proved to be the ultimate harbingers of things to come at a highly different intensity, complexity, and scale after 9/11. In fact, the generation that would later serve in Afghanistan and Iraq 'cut their teeth on a decade of other than war missions'.[114] For Lieutenant Colonel David Petraeus, the Operations Chief for the UN force in Haiti, it was an opportunity to learn

> what nation building is all about: nation building was very prominent there, and here is where I got my first experience, actually truly conducting a complete comprehensive civil-military campaign: train their police units, reform the penitentiary system which was a disaster at the time, rebuild rule of law, re-establish basic services (electricity, food, shelter, water) in a country that was at the basic level of public services imaginable.[115]

The American troops dispatched in Kosovo as peacekeepers under the NATO umbrella soon discovered the contours of what Dana Priest described as an enduring invisible battlefield, an underground world of parallel structures and shadowy governance networks — like the Ministry of Public Order — controlled by former Kosovo Liberation Army (KLA) separatists and their Mafia-like organisations[116] that 'intimidated, threatened, assaulted and sometimes allegedly killed anyone who questioned their rule'.[117] It is here in the microcosm of Kosovo that the American troops were exposed to the need to protect the local communities and population. In the mixed town of Vitina, 'they escorted every day Serb children to school, and every week they took families to Serbia proper or Macedonia to shop or visit relatives'.[118] It is in the Balkans that American troops had to build relations amongst the people, with the local church and shopkeepers, understand the puzzle of local grievances, loyalties, and family

---

114 Davidson, Janine (2010) *Lifting the Fog of Peace: How Americans Learned to Fight Modern War*, Ann Arbor: University of Michigan Press, p. 95.
115 Manea, Octavian (2013) 'Reflections on the 'Counterinsurgency Decade': Small Wars Journal Interview with General David H. Petraeus', Small Worlds Journal. Available at: smallwarsjournal.com/jrnl/art/reflections-on-the-counterinsurgency-decade-small-wars-journal-interview-with-general-david.
116 Priest, Dana (2004) *The Mission: Waging War and Keeping Peace with America's Military*, New York: W.W. Norton & Company, p. 271.
117 Ibid., p. 309.
118 Ibid., p. 317.

connections, while mediating and managing deep communal tensions between angry ethnic communities in town hall meetings.[119] As the post-9/11 veterans would soon discover:

> You win these kinds of wars by drinking tea, lots of tea. Ultimately, to earn the support of the population, you have to gain their trust and the way you gain their trust is by developing personal relationships. You must be more than a uniform and it is important for the leaders to take their helmets off, take their protective glasses off, body armor off and demonstrate that they trust people whose support they are trying to earn.[120]

Often the top US officer in charge of Vitina had to be 'mayor, police chief, judge and jury'.[121] Kosovo was where the American troops had to understand and navigate very detailed, grass-root, connect-the-dots linkages across the human terrain, especially the underground administrative hierarchy, in order to dismantle the real spoilers of local peace and stability. But this required a different set of skills that were closer to 'old fashioned detective work'.[122] Most of these snapshots will be familiar to any veteran of the post-9/11 stability operations or to any student of counter-insurgency. For example, fighting in Khalidiyah, a town lost in the Sunni triangle, was more 'akin to breaking up a Mafia crime ring than dismantling a conventional enemy battalion or brigade'.[123] Be it Talibans, Al-Qaeda in Iraq, Vietcong, or the subversive underground networks of former KLA fighters, they all understood that first and foremost they are in a competition for governance, and what they had to do was to establish 'a competitive system of control over population'. In the end 'when a country is being subverted it is not being outfought; it is being out-administered'.[124]

---

119 Ibid., p. 315.
120 Manea, Octavian (2010) 'Interview with Dr. John Nagl', *Small Wars Journal*. Available at: smallwarsjournal.com/jrnl/art/interview-with-dr-john-nagl.
121 Priest, Dana (2004) *The Mission: Waging War and Keeping Peace with America's Military*, New York: W.W. Norton & Company, p. 315.
122 Ibid., p. 309.
123 Nagl, John (2005) *Learning to Eat Soup with a Knife: Counterinsurgency Lessons from Malaya and Vietnam*, Chicago: Chicago University Press, p. 13.
124 Fall, Bernard B. (1998) 'The Theory and Practice of Insurgency and Counterinsurgency', *Naval War College Review*, Winter. Available at: www.au.af.mil/au/awc/awcgate/navy/art5-w98.htm#rettop.

10. THE UNCOMFORTABLE WARS OF THE 1990S

Overall, the lessons of the last decade of the twentieth century suggest, as Robert O'Neill anticipated, that the imperative — in public policy circles, armed services, think tank community, and media — was to develop 'a new science of security which fits the new era, in much the same way that military strategy of the pre-nuclear era had to adapt to the Cold War'.[125]

---

125 O'Neill, Robert (1998) 'Europe and the Wider World: The Security Challenge', in Ken Booth (ed.) *Statecraft And Security. The Cold War and Beyond*, New York: Cambridge University Press, p. 207.

11

A Mission Too Far? NATO and Afghanistan, 2001–2014

Mats Berdal

Introduction

The history and politics of the Western Alliance in the early years of the Cold War provided the backdrop to some of the more specific questions that, under the gentle, inspiring, and highly efficient supervision of Bob O'Neill, informed my doctoral project at Oxford. Benefiting from the release of newly declassified material, I was able to concentrate on the day-to-day politics, dynamics, and actual workings of the Alliance in greater detail than had previously been possible. Bob's training and experience as an historian proved immensely valuable to my efforts.

At some stage in the course of my work, in between time spent in various American and European archives, we decided that I ought perhaps to consult a body of literature subsumed under the rather grand heading of 'alliance theory'. My thesis, after all, was to be submitted in international relations, and some useful propositions and hypotheses might be gleaned from the literature. Much of this literature reflected and was inspired by the aspiration — still very much prevalent in sections of the American political science community — to lend scientific rigour to the study of international relations, eschewing what Hedley Bull had famously defined as the 'classical approach' to the subject.[1]

When it came to the *viva voce*, one of the examiners asked, in probing and typically perceptive fashion, whether the theoretical writings on alliances that I had consulted had really added much to my thesis, let alone to an understanding of the workings of NATO? The implication of the question suggested he thought they had not, and, of course, he was right. I was relieved rather than frustrated. My sense at the time was that Bob, though a historian by training, was always instinctively more comfortable with the classical approach. This approach emphasised the critical importance of a historical perspective in the study of international politics but, in Bull's words, was distinguished by the 'explicit reliance upon the exercise of judgement and by the assumptions that if we confine ourselves to strict standards of verification and proof there is little of significance that can be said about international relations, [and] that general propositions about the subject must therefore derive from a scientifically imperfect process of perception and intuition'.[2]

The approach seemed to me to capture the intellectual temper that infused Bob's reflections on strategy and international politics, as is evident from his writings and contributions to the many debates on the challenges facing the Western Alliance at the time when he was serving as Director of the International Institute for Strategic Studies (IISS) in the 1980s. It is an approach that remains, especially in its emphasis on the importance of historical context and perspective, relevant to an understanding of NATO's post-Cold War history, including the record of its difficult, costly, and drawn out involvement in Afghanistan.

---

[1]   Bull, Hedley (1966) 'International Theory: The Case for the Classical Approach', *World Politics* 18(3).
[2]   Ibid., p. 361.

NATO and Afghanistan: Context, Focus, and Argument in Brief

Created following the International Conference on Afghanistan — held in Bonn — and commanded by NATO since August 2003, the International Security Assistance Force (ISAF) formally completed its mission at the end of 2014. Marking the occasion at a meeting of the North Atlantic Council on 17 December 2014, Jens Stoltenberg, NATO's newly appointed Secretary-General, insisted that Afghanistan was now 'more stable and prosperous than ever'.[3] In his annual report, issued a few weeks later, the Secretary-General again noted how the Alliance had successfully achieved what it had set out to do in Afghanistan.[4] Given the scale, cost, and longevity of NATO's deployment, an upbeat end of mission report from the chief executive was, perhaps, only to be expected. Even as ISAF was preparing to lower the flag in Kabul, however, the claim that stability (whatever that might mean) had been brought to Afghanistan looked distinctly unconvincing. Since then, developments have only reinforced the fear — widespread among long-standing observers of Afghan history, politics, and society — that few of NATO's achievements, limited as they are, will prove sustainable in the medium to long term. Indeed, one year on from ISAF's withdrawal, there has been a sharp decline in the security situation throughout the country. A faltering, aid-dependent economy wrestling with record levels of unemployment and corruption, a steep increase in the number of people seeking to leave the country, political instability at the centre, and no substantive progress in peace and reconciliation talks with the Taliban, were all combining to ensure that state collapse remained a very real possibility.[5] Responding to the deteriorating situation, the Obama Administration decided to delay the withdrawal of US forces from the country in October 2015.

---

3   NATO (2014) 'Opening Remarks by NATO Secretary General Jens Stoltenberg at the Meeting of the North Atlantic Council with Past and Current Non-NATO ISAF Contributing Nations', 17 December. Available at: www.nato.int/cps/en/natohq/opinions_116104.htm?selectedLocale=en.
4   NATO (2015) 'The Secretary General's Annual Report 2014', 30 January. Available at: www.nato.int/cps/en/natohq/opinions_116854.htm.
5   Chatham House (2015) 'Developments in and Prospects for Afghanistan', Asia Programme Meeting Summary, 10 November. See also SIGAR (2015) 'Report of the Special Inspector General for Afghanistan Reconstruction (SIGAR)', 30 July, pp. 93–5. Available at: www.sigar.mil/pdf/quarterlyreports/2015-07-30qr.pdf.

A full and exhaustive discussion of the reasons behind this bleak picture is beyond the scope the present chapter, whose focus is confined to NATO's mission, activities, and record. The chapter is concerned, in particular, with two issues raised by the history of the Alliance's involvement and the decidedly mixed legacy it leaves behind. While these are closely, indeed inextricably linked, they merit separate treatment for the purposes of analysis.

The first of these concerns the sources of the failure to meet the objective of bringing peace and stability to the country. These are necessarily varied and complex, and the trajectory of developments in Afghanistan over the past decade and a half plainly cannot be ascribed to NATO actions or inactions alone. Chief among NATO's failures — and of special interest here — has been a fundamental inability to recognise and engage with the drivers and dynamics of conflict and violence within the country, including the ways in which NATO contributed to mounting insecurity through its actions and those of its member states.

The second issue concerns the politics and functioning of the Alliance. While NATO's long-established planning mechanisms, force generation, and staff procedures 'worked',[6] and while combat experience was gained and inter-operability improved, the Alliance's overall effort was deeply fragmented. This was a reflection of underlying and never properly reconciled divisions over objectives among allies. Put differently, NATO never functioned as an effective coalition of allies bound together by a common strategic vision and clarity of objectives in Afghanistan; it always remained less than the sum of its parts. At one level, this reality reflected differing views about the appropriate level of ambition for NATO in Afghanistan, with the US consistently sceptical of what was dismissively termed (and not just by the Bush Administration) the nation-building ambitions of many European allies. Many of those allies, in turn, deplored the dominant and overriding influence in US decision-making of a much more narrow counter-terrorism perspective, especially within the Pentagon, CIA, and the US military. Equally important in terms of explaining

---

6   For a perceptive and illuminating discussion of how 'the system worked', looking at the escalation of international involvement after 2001, and drawing upon Leslie Gelb's famous 1971 article tracing America's deepening involvement in Vietnam, see Suhrke, Astri (2011) *When More is Less: The International Project in Afghanistan*, London: Hurst & Co., pp. 4–5. For Gelb's original article, see Gelb, Leslie H. (1971) 'Vietnam: The System Worked', *Foreign Policy* 3.

NATO's fragmented approach, however, were the domestic political pressures and considerations, often extraneous to Afghanistan itself and developments there, which shaped the commitments of individual allies to NATO's mission.

The Evolution of NATO's Afghanistan Mission

In order to explore these issues more fully, it is necessary to start by tracing the evolution of NATO's mission to Afghanistan. This is a history of initial engagement, escalating involvement and rapid withdrawal, which can usefully be divided into three periods.

2001–2003: Engaging Allies in 'appropriately flexible ways'

NATO only assumed responsibility for ISAF in Kabul in 2003, and did not complete the gradual expansion of its mission to cover the whole of Afghanistan until October 2006. However, any attempt to understand the history of the Afghanistan mission must start with the strategic decisions that were taken, and those that were not, by the US in response to the terrorist attacks of 11 September 2001.

The shock, scale, and horror of those attacks led to a near universal outpouring of sympathy and support for the US. This was exemplified by the Security Council's prompt condemnation of the attacks as 'threats to international peace and security' and its reaffirmation of the US's right of individual and collective self-defence.[7] On the very same day that the Security Council passed its resolution, the North Atlantic Council invoked Article V of the Washington Treaty for the first time in its history. The so-called 'collective defence provision' stipulated that an 'an armed attack against one or more of them in Europe or North America shall be considered an attack against them all'.[8] Much was made at the time, and since, about this unprecedented move on the part of the Alliance. As a demonstration of support and solidarity with the US, the symbolism could not have been greater. And yet, the military and operational significance of the Article V

---

7   UN Security Council Resolution 1368, 12 September 2001.
8   The North Atlantic Treaty, 4 April 1949, Article V.

invocation soon proved negligible. As preparations for military and covert actions in Afghanistan got under way in the weeks following the 9/11 attacks, the Bush Administration had no desire to involve NATO directly in operations through its collective assets, or command and planning structures. Paul Wolfowitz, Deputy Defence Secretary at the time, summed up the administration's view of NATO and its role on the eve of the attack on Afghanistan:

> We think we had a collective affirmation of support with what they said with Article Five, and if we need collective action we'll ask for it. We don't anticipate that at the moment ... We need cooperation from many countries but we need to take it in appropriately flexible ways.[9]

Wolfowitz's comments and the subsequent unfolding of the campaign in 2001 point to two aspects of US policy that help explain the dynamics of Alliance relations for the entire period of NATO's involvement.

First, in taking the 'battle to the terrorists, to their networks and to those states and organizations that harbor and assist terrorist networks',[10] the US did not wish to be constrained. The Authorization for Use of Military Force (AUMF), passed by congress on 14 September 2001, was open-ended, both in terms of time and geographical scope.[11] Operation Enduring Freedom (OEF), formally launched with the attack on Afghanistan on 7 October 2001, was a counter-terrorism mission broadly conceived. Indeed, to US decision-makers it was 'the opening salvo in a global war on terror'.[12] Following the toppling of the Taliban regime and the inauguration of an interim Afghan Government in late December 2001, thought gradually turned to how stability might be extended throughout the country. Even so, OEF's central focus on 'disrupting, dismantling and defeating Al-Qaeda and Taliban' — fuelled by the desire for retribution and revenge, especially in the early days — remained a dominant strategic priority throughout

---

9   Paul Wolfowitz, Press Conference, NATO HQ, 26 September 2001, quoted in Kreps, Sarah E. (2011) *Coalitions of Convenience: United States Military Interventions after the Cold War*, Oxford: Oxford University Press, pp. 95–6.
10   Washington Post (2001) 'Text: Rumsfeld's Pentagon News Conference', 18 October. Available at: www.washingtonpost.com/wp-srv/nation/specials/attacked/transcripts/rumsfeld_text101801.html.
11   The AUMF remains in force.
12   Stapleton, Barbara J. and Michael Keating (2015) *Military and Civilian Assistance to Afghanistan 2001–14: An Incoherent Approach*, London: Chatham House, p. 2. Available at: www.chathamhouse.org/sites/files/chathamhouse/field/field_document/20150722MilitaryCivilianAssistanceAfghanistanStapletonKeating.pdf.

11. A MISSION TOO FAR? NATO AND AFGHANISTAN, 2001–2014

the period of NATO's engagement. The Bush Administration's aversion to nation-building was well known before 9/11, and explains why it successfully resisted calls for ISAF to be expanded outside Kabul before 2003. Scepticism about ambitious postwar objectives was also widely shared, notably by Robert Gates who, upon taking office as Secretary of Defence in 2006, was quick to conclude that 'our efforts [in Afghanistan] were being significantly hampered by muddled and over-ambitious objectives'.[13] Defining the strategic objectives for Afghanistan set the US apart from many European NATO allies. Gates himself, looking back, felt the divergence of views between European approaches 'that looked a lot like nation-building' and much narrower US objectives remained 'an important and underlying source of friction and frustration' within NATO.[14]

Second, Wolfowitz' remarks made it clear that while the US welcomed the support of individual allies in its global and open-ended war on terror, NATO as an alliance — with its limited collective assets, well-established planning procedures, and consultative mechanisms — was more likely to complicate, even restrict, US freedom to respond as it saw fit. The prevailing view held by American officials of NATO's Kosovo operation in 1999, especially in the Pentagon and within the military, reinforced this sentiment. Now, in the post-9/11 world, the mission would always 'determine the coalition', as Rumsfeld made clear from the outset.[15]

Over time, as security deteriorated and challenges mounted in Afghanistan and Iraq, following its invasion by the US and the UK in 2003, the importance and uses of allies became more apparent: they could help legitimise the need for continuing involvement internally to congress (which controlled the purse strings) and to an increasingly war-weary public; they could assume the burden of nation-building tasks; and some allies might even provide useful assets (for example, contributing intelligence and special operations forces). At the end of the day, however, NATO *per se* was of limited use and interest, a sense

---

13   Gates, Robert (2014) *Duty*, London: W. H. Allen, p. 203.
14   Ibid.
15   Washington Post (2001) 'Text: Rumsfeld's Pentagon News Conference', 18 October. Available at: www.washingtonpost.com/wp-srv/nation/specials/attacked/transcripts/rumsfeld_text101801.html.

captured by Gates' admission that he struggled to stay awake during NATO meetings, finding them 'excruciatingly boring', as 28 countries rattled through their pre-prepared scripts.[16]

There is a final aspect to the early phase of operations in Afghanistan and the strategic choices then made by the US, which crucially shaped the context of NATO's expanding involvement from 2003 onwards. What was soon dubbed the 'Afghan Model'[17] of operations — a very light conventional footprint, relying instead on special operations forces, precision weapons, and local allies, in the form of the Northern Alliance, to overthrow the Taliban regime — combined with a rejection of nation-building and an unwillingness to invest in the search for a broader, more inclusive political settlement following the collapse of the Taliban in 2001 had very important long-term consequences. The Bush Administration's postwar plan, as one perceptive study would later put it, 'seems to have been to pass control of the country as quickly as possible to local proxies who had assisted international forces and thereafter to retain a residual counter-terrorism mission'.[18] In the process of doing so, US forces entered into alliances with local and regional strongmen and warlords, men such as Ismail Kahn and Gul Aga Shirzai, many of whom had risen to prominence during the horrific civil war that had engulfed the country after 1992.[19] This development and the dynamic set in motion by cultivating relations with venal, predatory, and violent warlords set the stage for renewed conflict. As Alex Strick van Linschoten and Felix Kuehn concluded when examining developments after the fall of the Taliban regime, the 'strategic mistake of handing over the government to former strongmen and warlords ... aided the Taliban's return'.[20] Crucially, bringing warlords and their tribally based

---

16   Gates, Robert (2014) *Duty*, London: W. H. Allen, p. 194.
17   Biddle, Stephen (2003) 'Afghanistan and the Future of Warfare', *Foreign Affairs* 82(2), pp. 31–45. Available at: www.foreignaffairs.com/articles/afghanistan/2003-03-01/afghanistan-and-future-warfare.
18   Wilton Park (2015) 'Capturing the Lessons from the Helmand Provincial Reconstruction Team (PRT)', Wilton Park Report WPR1322, p. 11.
19   On Gul Agha Sherzai and the local impact of his alliance with US forces in their war on terror, see Gopal, Anand (2014) *No Good Men Among the Living: America, the Taliban and the War through Afghan Eyes*, New York: Metropolitan Books, pp. 107–10.
20   van Linschoten, Alex Strick and Felix Kuehn (2012) *An Enemy We Created: The Myth of the Taliban/Al Qaeda Merger in Afghanistan, 1970–2011*, London: Hurts & Co., p. 254. See also van Bijlert, Martine (2009) 'Unruly Commanders and Violent Power Struggles: Taliban Networks in Uruzgan', in Antonio Giustozzi (ed.), *Decoding the New Taliban*, London: Hurst & Co., pp. 158–60.

patronage networks into positions of power at the local and district level gave rise to a distinctive political economy of conflict that would continue to confound NATO's attempts, starting in 2003, to stabilise the country through aid, reconstruction, and development assistance (as discussed more fully below).

2003–2009: Expanding Mission, Growing Insurgency

NATO assumed command of ISAF in August 2003. Soon thereafter it was authorised by the UN Security Council under Chapter VII to expand ISAF's presence outside 'Kabul and its environs' with the aim of establishing security and extending the writ of the government to 'all parts of Afghanistan'.[21] By October 2006, following a phased anticlockwise expansion — starting in the north in 2004 and ending with a surge in the south and east in 2006 — ISAF's area of responsibility covered the whole of the country. Accompanying the process was the creation of a complex and top-heavy structure of regional command headquarters, contributing to making NATO forces, in the words of one senior official, 'high on tail, low on teeth'.[22] Formally under ISAF's command by late 2006 were also some 25 Provincial Reconstruction Teams (PRTs) operating from local bases. These were multinational teams, combining civilian and military elements, led by individual nations, whose role was to 'deliver a "stabilisation effect"' by facilitating 'reconstruction, security, governance, aid and development'.[23] As such, the PRTs were critical to NATO's stated ambition of 'extending the influence of the central government'.[24]

The expansion of NATO's role after 2003 requires explanation.[25] After all — and it is an argument that has often been made since — the Taliban had been toppled, its foot soldiers had scattered and al-Qaeda was, if not defeated, weakened and without a safe haven in the country.

---

21 UNSC 1510, 13 October 2003.
22 Interview with NATO Official, June 2015.
23 Wilton Park (2015) 'Capturing the lessons from the Helmand Provincial Reconstruction Team (PRT)', Wilton Park Report WPR1322, p. 5.
24 Speech at IISS by NATO Secretary General, Jaap de Hoop Scheffer, 12 February 2004.
25 Numbering some 5,000 and confined to Kabul in September 2003, NATO ISAF troop levels grew to 33,000 in 2006, and would eventually peak — following the 2009–11 surge — at more than 130,000 in July 2011.

A combination of three factors drove NATO's growing involvement. The first was a strong, if confused and strategically inchoate, sense among allies that the Alliance needed to carve out a more clearly defined role for itself in the post-9/11 security landscape. To this end, the Prague meeting of NATO Heads of State and Government, held in November 2002 and dubbed the 'transformation summit', famously signalled NATO's readiness to go out-of-area in order to take on new and global challenges.

The second factor was related. With US attention and resources increasingly focused on Iraq and, soon after its invasion in 2003, fully absorbed by the catastrophic consequences of state collapse in that country, pressure mounted for NATO allies to pick up the burden in Afghanistan. The readiness to do so was aided by the deep divisions that existed over US actions in Iraq (in contrast to the emerging narrative of 'a good war' in Afghanistan), but also the growing realisation among European allies that Afghanistan was not 'mission accomplished' in late 2001. This was the third factor that drove NATO's deepening involvement: a sense among European allies, that, above all, 'the interveners now had an obligation to deliver more than a government of warlords'.[26] To meet that obligation, NATO developed and regularly updated its Comprehensive Strategic Political Military Plan for Afghanistan once it had assumed command of ISAF. Its vision and underlying idea, as summarised by Keating and Stapleton, remained basically unchanged:

> [O]n the basis of reconstruction and development, the Afghan government would extend its legitimacy and authority countrywide, thereby enabling its international partners to help build a sustainable stability that would foster economic development. This 'end state' would allow a military exit with continued foreign assistance typical of other post-conflict fragile states.[27]

---

26 Wilton Park (2015) 'Capturing the lessons from the Helmand Provincial Reconstruction Team (PRT)', Wilton Park Report WPR1322, p. 11.
27 Stapleton, Barbara J. and Michael Keating (2015) *Military and Civilian Assistance to Afghanistan 2001–14: An Incoherent Approach*, London: Chatham House, p. 4.

The script did not pan out as envisaged. Instead, the period between 2006 and 2009 saw NATO confronted with a 'growing and resilient insurgency'.[28] Even as troop and aid levels rose, and a comprehensive approach that emphasised integrated working between the military and civilian arms of NATO's effort was formally adopted, the much vaunted stability effect proved ever more elusive. As combat operations intensified, especially in the south of the country, security continued to deteriorate. Indeed, it is a striking fact, as Graeme Smith observed, and which ought to have given pause for thought, that 'every increase in troop numbers in southern Afghanistan brought a corresponding increase in violence'.[29]

2009–2014: COIN and Transition to 'Afghan lead for security'

By early 2009, with a new administration in power in Washington, an increasingly war-weary public, and a president intellectually and emotionally committed to bringing America's 9/11 wars to an end, the situation in Afghanistan was deemed to 'demand urgent attention and swift action'.[30] An immediate increase in US troop numbers (of some 17,000) was ordered in March 2009, along with a reaffirmation of the central aim of US policy: 'to disrupt, dismantle and defeat al Qaeda in Pakistan and Afghanistan, and to prevent their return to either country in the future.'[31] To this end, the counter-terrorism operations emphasising kill and capture were also intensified, as the skills and methods developed in Iraq were transferred to Afghanistan. In July 2009, Stanley McChrystal, shortly after assuming command of NATO ISAF, was asked to conduct a multidisciplinary assessment of the

---

28   McChrystal, Stanley (2009) 'Commander's Initial Assessment', Commander NATO ISAF, Afghanistan/US Forces, 30 August. Available at www.washingtonpost.com/wp-dyn/content/article/2009/09/21/AR2009092100110.html.
29   Smith, Graeme (2013) *The Dogs are Eating them Now: Our War in Afghanistan*, Berkeley: Counterpoint, p. 169. Remarkably, even the intensive 'kill-and-capture' campaign of 2010–11, which saw thousands of night raids and operations aimed at breaking the back of the insurgency, did not lead to 'a significant downturn in violence or insurgent attacks'. van Linschoten, Alex Strick and Felix Kuehn (2012) *An Enemy We Created: The Myth of the Taliban/Al Qaeda Merger in Afghanistan, 1970–2011*, London: Hurts & Co., p. 315.
30   'Statement by the President on Afghanistan', 17 February 2009, White House Press Release.
31   'Remarks by the President on a New Strategy for Afghanistan and Pakistan', 27 March 2009, White House Press Release.

situation in Afghanistan and present military options.[32] Faced with the prospect of 'strategic defeat', McChrystal concluded that a 'significant change to our strategy and the way we think and operate' was needed.[33] He called for a 'comprehensive counter-insurgency (COIN) campaign' focused on protecting the population, strengthening the Afghan National Security Forces (ANSF) and 'improving governance at all levels'.[34] Following a protracted and deeply divisive internal debate about the way forward, Obama endorsed the new approach. Reflecting his long-term desire to end US combat commitments, and conscious of growing war-weariness among the public, he opted for a more limited troop surge of 30,000. At the same time, he made it clear that the drawdown of US troops and transfer of responsibility for security to ANSF would start no later than July 2011.

Where the US led, NATO allies followed. In support of Obama's surge, NATO ministers pledged to deploy another 7,000 troops.[35] The shift in focus towards transition and eventual withdrawal was formally endorsed by NATO members at the Lisbon Summit in November 2010. It was agreed that Afghan forces would assume 'full responsibility for security across the whole of Afghanistan' by the end of 2014.[36] At the time, NATO ministers insisted that the pace of transfer of responsibility to Afghan security forces would be 'conditions-based, not calendar-driven', and that transition would not simply 'equate to withdrawal of ISAF-troops'.[37] Domestic political pressures and war weariness in NATO countries, however, ensured that the transitional process never stood much chance of being truly conditions-based.[38]

---

32 McChrystal, Stanley (2009) 'Commander's Initial Assessment', Commander NATO ISAF, Afghanistan/US Forces, 30 August. Available at www.washingtonpost.com/wp-dyn/content/article/2009/09/21/AR2009092100110.html.
33 Ibid.
34 Ibid.
35 In 2009, the NATO Training-Mission Afghanistan also activated. It was set up to train and help professionalise Afghan security forces in preparation for the transfer of responsibility for security.
36 NATO (2010) 'Lisbon Summit Declaration', 20 November. Available at: www.nato.int/cps/en/natolive/official_texts_68828.htm.
37 Ibid.
38 For the condition of the Afghan army one year on from ISAF's departure, see Amiri, Sharif (2016) 'NATO Report Slams Afghan Army as Mission Incapable', *Tolo News*, 10 January. Available at: www.tolonews.com/en/afghanistan/23228-nato-report-slams-afghan-army-as-mission-incapable.

Indeed, the quip that President Obama's strategy for the Afghan endgame was best summed up by 'surge, bribe and run'[39] proved uncomfortably close to the mark.

Explaining NATO's Record in Afghanistan: The Sources of Failure

How do we explain the failure on the part of NATO and its partner nations to bring stability to Afghanistan between 2001 and 2014? While a full and detailed answer to this question is beyond the scope of the present chapter, the history and pattern of involvement sketched above point to three sets of issues which, though closely related, merit separate attention:

- the debilitating impact of conflicting and competing objectives on Alliance cohesion and unity of purpose, notably between the US and its European allies;
- the inability of individual allies operating within their geographic areas of responsibility, and of NATO as a whole, to appreciate and grapple with underlying sources of violence and conflict in Afghanistan; and
- the inherent difficulties of applying NATO's approach to stabilisation and COIN in the case of Afghanistan.

Conflicting and Competing Objectives

The central fault-line, in terms of the overall political objective for the campaign, remained the tension between the US focus on counter-terrorism, broadly defined, and a more ambitious set of state- and peace-building objectives held by coalition partners. This gave rise to conflicting priorities on the ground and a fragmentation of effort from the outset. The tension was not always easily gleaned from upbeat and soothing NATO communiqués that emphasised the Alliance's 'comprehensive approach to crisis management' and its delivery

---

39 Brahma Chellaney quoted in Thakur, Ramesh (2015) 'With the Benefit of Hindsight: Chronicling Afghanistan Errors', in Jack Cunningham and W. Maley (eds), *Australia and Canada in Afghanistan: Perspectives on a Mission*, Toronto: Dundrun Press, p. 220.

of 'stabilisation and reconstruction effects'.⁴⁰ But it was always there. Given the dominant influence of the US in terms of decision-making power and resources (especially following the surge in 2009–2010),⁴¹ the counter-terrorism perspective would always trump other considerations, within the Alliance as well as within internal administration debates on Afghan policy. The counter-terrorism perspective remained premised on a broad and permissive definition of terrorists and insurgents — one that never seriously questioned 'the supposedly unbreakable link between the Taliban and al-Qaeda'.⁴² As a result, the scope for exploring a wider political settlement to end the war, as called for by Richard Holbrooke in the face of internal opposition in 2010, and strongly favoured by European allies, was always limited and never won through at critical moments.

In terms of operations and activities, the tension between strategic priorities gave rise to, and were reflected in, a complicated and dysfunctional set of command and control arrangements that included multiple and separate chains of command, both within theatre and between capitals and theatre. Most obvious in this respect was the separation of OEF from NATO's ISAF mission, though it was evident at other levels too, notably in the deployment and activities of US Special Operations Forces (elements of which reported directly to Tampa, Florida) and, significantly, in workings of the nationally led PRTs.⁴³ The variety of models and approaches adopted by different PRTs were, to a degree, a function of location, resources, and national styles. As a result, they operated with a high degree of autonomy and only loose direction from ISAF regional headquarters. Adaptation to circumstances is to be valued in many contexts but, as Jackson and Gordon perceptively noted in 2007, for NATO states to extoll virtues of

---

40   NATO (2010) 'Lisbon Summit Declaration', 20 November. Available at: www.nato.int/cps/en/natolive/official_texts_68828.htm.
41   In the words of one of NATO's Senior Civilian Representatives (SCR), as US military and civilian assistance efforts increasingly came to dwarf that of others, allies and coalition partners were left 'outside the magic circle comprised of the US ambassador and the US military commander in Kabul where the actual decision-making took place'. NATO SCR quoted in Stapleton, Barbara J. and Michael Keating (2015) *Military and Civilian Assistance to Afghanistan 2001–14: An Incoherent Approach*, London: Chatham House, p. 5.
42   van Linschoten, Alex Strick and Felix Kuehn (2012) *An Enemy We Created: The Myth of the Taliban/Al Qaeda Merger in Afghanistan, 1970–2011*, London: Hurts & Co., p. 326.
43   On the subject of command and control, drawing attention also to the striking lack of unity *within* US forces in Afghanistan, see Cowper-Coles, Sherard (2011) *Cables from Kabul: The Inside Story of the West's Afghanistan Campaign*, London: Harper Press, pp. 163–5.

diversity was also 'a ruse for justifying both national agendas and the absence of an effective strategic framework in which the PRTs could operate'.[44] The bilateral provision of aid, reconstruction, and security assistance by PRTs within their respective areas of responsibility created national bubbles, further undermining attempts at achieving strategic coherence overall.

Ed Butler, who led the British Task Force that deployed to the south in 2005 and 2006, would later reflect on the overall consequences:

> [T]he main challenge to the creation of a coherent political–military strategy was the existence of multiple missions set by all the different stakeholders and nations, all with their own definitions of success and failure. In other words, there was a 'split planning effort' from the start. At the operational level, we used the term 'duality of mission' to describe this tension: NATO's objective of nation-building and reconstruction *vis-à-vis* the US objective of counter-terrorism. The ends, ways and means of the two missions were diametrically opposed.[45]

Drivers of Violence and Insecurity: Local Context, Political Economy, and Nationalism

The contribution of NATO and partner nations to security and stabilisation efforts in Afghanistan — collectively and individually within their respective sectors of operations — was critically undermined from the outset of ISAF's expansion outside Kabul by a persistent failure to properly grasp some key, underlying drivers of conflict. This was even more notably so from 2006, when combat operations intensified. Two aspects of this deserve special attention.

The first was the way in which local context and the distinctive political economies of conflict within Afghanistan drove violence and insecurity throughout the provinces. The latter was shaped by complex ethno-tribal grievances, local politics, and power struggles, often with deep historical roots, and all set within the patronage-based and nepotistic post-Taliban political order that emerged in 2001 and 2002. This reality contrasted sharply with the dominant narrative

---

44 Jackson, Matthew and Stuart Gordon (2007) 'Rewiring Interventions?: UK Provincial Reconstruction Teams and "Stabilization"', *International Peacekeeping* 14(5), p. 649.
45 Butler, Ed (2015) 'Setting Ourselves up for a Fall in Afghanistan', *RUSI Journal* 160(1), p. 49.

through which NATO, led by the US (and within the US, led by the Pentagon and the military), understood and approached the Afghan conflict. Aptly termed the 'insurgency narrative'[46] by Mike Martin, this effectively reduced the struggle in Afghanistan to, on the one hand, a legitimate government seeking to build the foundations of a modern, democratic, and liberal-looking state, supported in that endeavour by the West, and, on the other, a retrograde, ideologically-driven Taliban insurgency, benefiting from sanctuaries in and support from Pakistan. While this view was not without some foundation in fact, it profoundly and fatally simplified what was actually driving dynamics in places where NATO operated. As one study of the British experience between 2006 and 2014 in Helmand — though of much wider relevance to an understanding of NATO's overall campaign — perceptively emphasised:

> The localised nature of the insurgency and the local grievances and rivalries that shaped how different local actors aligned and realigned themselves in relation to the 'government' and 'Taliban' figures frequently had far less to do with the macro-dynamics of insurgency and counter-insurgency than they did with complex local political dynamics including the narco-economy and power relations between rival social groups.[47]

This failure to understand the interaction of the conflict's micro-dynamics with patronage politics and struggles over power and resources at the centre, meant that the actions of NATO allies often played into and contributed to the entrenchment of violent and exploitative political economies in perverse and unintended ways. The most striking, and now well documented, examples of this are effects of UK-led counter-narcotics policies. The initial attempts at eradication, pursued in Helmand where opium production and the narcotics industry was the main source of livelihood to thousands of farmers, and of power and profits to officials and strongmen inside

---

46   Martin, Mike (2014) *An Intimate War: An Oral History of the Helmand Conflict*, London: Hurst & Co, p. 195.
47   Wilton Park (2015) 'Capturing the lessons from the Helmand Provincial Reconstruction Team (PRT)', Wilton Park Report WPR1322, p. 4. In fact, as the study concluded, 'the "Taliban" fought for a variety of reasons and while there were certainly "ideological" fighters in Helmand who were committed to the Quetta Shura, the majority of insurgents may have fought less out of commitment to the Taliban ideology than (as they saw it) on the basis of local issues, including a desire to protect their crops or localised grievances relating to access to land and water or more provincial level horizontal inequalities'. Ibid., p. 21.

and outside the province, provide a pertinent example. As discussed more fully below, this much more complex picture of the sources and dynamics of insecurity fundamentally challenged the premises on which NATO's stabilisation, as well as NATO and American COIN efforts, were predicated.

The second aspect, more difficult to pin down and measure, but no less important, was the role played by NATO and the Western-led intervention generally in stimulating Afghan nationalism and anti-foreign sentiment, especially in the Pashtun belt in the south.[48] Familiarity with Afghan history should, but never seems to have, alerted outsiders to the likely importance of the innate resistance to foreign intrusion and control in the country. It was perhaps a failure linked, as Anatol Lieven has suggested, to the tendency to treat Afghanistan as a 'landscape of the mind, onto which Westerners could project a variety of agendas and fantasies'.[49] This said, suspicion and resentment towards the international coalition, and certainly the intensity it acquired over time, were not given. Taliban's removal in 2001 was generally welcomed, and hope appears to have been widespread that an extended period of civil war would finally come to an end and a more just political dispensation emerge. Several factors soon served to undermine that hope.

One of these was the return to power and influence of the warlords and strongmen that had been so prominent during the deeply destructive civil war of 1992–1996. The basic attitude taken towards these warlords and strongmen by the US was pithily summed up by Ahmed Rashid: 'a cheap and beneficial way to retain US allies in the field who might even provide information about al Qaeda.'[50] By 2004, their abusive, predatory, and corrupt behaviour was fuelling the Taliban revival, and feeding into suspicion and conspiracy theories about the real motives of NATO's presence.

---

48 On this, see findings of Graeme Smith's so-called 'Taliban survey' based on interviews conducted with Taliban fighters in 2007 and 2008 and discussed in Smith, Graeme (2013) *The Dogs are Eating them Now: Our War in Afghanistan*, Berkeley: Counterpoint, chapter 8.
49 Lieven, Anatol (2010) 'Insights from the Afghan Field', *OpenDemocracy*. Available at: www.opendemocracy.net/anatol-lieven/insights-from-afghan-field.
50 Rashid, Ahmed (2008) *Descent into Chaos*, London: Allan Lane, p. 129. See also Gopal, Anand (2010) 'Flash to the Past: Missed Opportunities for Reconciliation', *Afghanistan Analysts Network*. Available at: www.afghanistan-analysts.org/flash-to-the-past-missed-opportunities-for-reconciliation/.

Local nationalisms and anti-foreign resistance were also powerfully stimulated by the conduct and fall-out of military operations, especially from 2006, when the number of civilian casualties from NATO operations began to rise steeply. An authoritative study drawing upon surveys in five of Afghanistan's provinces (Helmand, Paktia, Uruzgan, Balkh, and Faryab) conducted between 2008 and 2010, found that the behaviour of troops, especially in areas where levels of insecurity were high, was widely viewed as disrespectful of 'Afghan culture, religion, and traditions', and became an significant 'driver of insecurity'.[51] As an inevitable result, trust in NATO-ISAF declined. In the words of one former provincial governor, interviewed in January 2009: 'people are slowly but surely coming to the conclusion that they are an occupied country. As a result of the bombings, house searches, being bitten by dogs, people are thinking that the US is worse than the Soviets.'[52] While the problem was recognised by many, attempts to address it remained half-hearted, and the conduct of operations continued to cause resentment and 'push people to join the insurgency'.[53] Recognising the counterproductive effects of air strikes and night raids on efforts to win hearts and minds, General McChrystal temporarily tightened restrictions on the use of force by US troops soon after assuming command of ISAF. These, however, were soon lifted again by General Petraeus who, upon replacing McChrystal in mid-2010, ordered a sharp increase in number of night raids by special operations forces in an attempt to decapitate the insurgent leadership before the drawdown of troops began in earnest.

It is worth adding here that whatever the diversity of views within the Alliance about mission objectives, and whatever degree of experimentation took place in individual PRTs, most Afghans, key regional actors (and, indeed, much of the wider international community) never distinguished clearly between NATO, and the US and its broad counter-terrorism focus. This perception was plainly not

---

51   Fishstein, Paul and Andrew Wilder (2012) *Winning Hearts and Minds?: Examining the Relationship between Aid and Security in Afghanistan*, Medford: Feinstein International Centre, Tufts University, p. 35. Available at: fic.tufts.edu/assets/WinningHearts-Final.pdf.
52   Quoted in ibid.
53   This was among the more notable findings of Graeme Smith's aforementioned 'Taliban survey', see Smith, Graeme (2013) *The Dogs are Eating them Now: Our War in Afghanistan*, Berkeley: Counterpoint, p. 205. See also Lieven, Anatol (2010) 'Insights from the Afghan Field', *OpenDemocracy*. Available at: www.opendemocracy.net /anatol-lieven/insights-from-afghan-field.

without basis in fact, however much it also concealed a more complex picture — there were, for example, differences in behaviour among contingents, with some notably more aggressive than others.[54]

The Assumptions of Stabilisation and COIN

The fundamental, though on closer inspection far from unproblematic, assumption that governed NATO's mission in Afghanistan was that aid, development, and reconstruction would progressively help stabilise insecure areas. Doing so, like a virtuous cycle, would simultaneously serve to strengthen the legitimacy and authority of central government.[55] The PRTs, focusing resources on development projects that would produce quick wins — roads, hospitals, wells, and local infrastructure projects of different kinds — were the instruments through which the stabilisation effect would be delivered. The belief that aid and Quick Impact Projects (QIPs) could help win hearts and minds also underpinned the COIN strategy explicitly adopted in 2009, and saw astonishing amounts of money injected into local economies in support of reconstruction projects (in the US case through the so-called Commanders Emergency Response Program).

The assumption was problematic for at least two closely connected reasons. In the first instance, it rested on (or seemed to take for granted) the view that the government of Hamid Karzai enjoyed political legitimacy. In fact, the Karzai Government was widely and increasingly seen by many as weak, corrupt, and abusive. Following the toppling of the Taliban in 2001, Northern Alliance commanders quickly set about consolidating local power bases, using tribal networks, and access to central government to seize the state apparatus in local districts and provinces. This in turn enabled them to capture and influence the distribution of aid and development funding. The upshot was to alienate those outside the patronage networks of corrupt and violent strongmen, and to further weaken the legitimacy of an already weak central government. This helps explain why the aforementioned

---

54   On aggressive behaviour of troops, see Smith, Graeme (2013) *The Dogs are Eating them Now: Our War in Afghanistan*, Berkeley: Counterpoint, p. 162, and see Chandrasekaran, Rajiv (2012) *Little America: The War Within the War for Afghanistan*, London: Bloomsbury, p. 277.
55   Indeed, this assumption is central to 'clear–hold–build', which in 2009 was NATO's 'preferred operational approach' to counter-insurgency. See Ucko, David H. (2013) 'Beyond Clear–Hold–Build: Rethinking Counterinsurgency at the Local Level', *Contemporary Security Policy* 34(3), p. 526.

study of aid and reconstruction in five of Afghanistan's provinces found so 'little concrete evidence … that aid projects were having more strategic level stabilisation or security benefits such as winning populations away from insurgents, legitimising the government, or reducing levels of violent conflict'.[56] Quite the opposite was the case, with 'more evidence of the destabilizing rather than the stabilizing effects of aid, especially in insecure areas where the pressures to spend large amounts of money quickly were greatest'.[57]

The second factor flowed directly from this. NATO proceeded in Afghanistan on the assumption that insecurity and sources of instability emanated from a resurgent Taliban, rather than a much more complex and multilayered set of sources. Such sources included rapacious government officials, and long-standing ethnic, tribal, and local grievances, fuelled by an exploitative political economy. This reality doomed a population-centred counterinsurgency campaign aimed at drawing the population away from insurgents and towards the government. As Karl Eikenberry, American Ambassador to Kabul from 2009 and 2011, and with two tours of military duty to Afghanistan before that, noted:

> 'Protect the population' makes for a good bumper sticker, but it raises the question: Protect it from whom and against what? It certainly meant protecting the Afghan people from marauding Taliban insurgents. But what about criminal narco-traffickers, venal local police chiefs, or predatory government officials?[58]

Not surprisingly, expressing such views earned him few friends at the Pentagon and among senior officers committed to COIN during the internal strategy debates. He had nonetheless honed in on a critical problem underlying the COIN philosophy as applied to Afghanistan.

Underlying all of this, and much of the discussion above, was the deeper failure to appreciate the political nature and drivers of conflict, that is, the extent to which violence was driving the competition over power

---

56 Fishstein, Paul and Andrew Wilder (2012) *Winning Hearts and Minds?: Examining the Relationship between Aid and Security in Afghanistan*, Medford: Feinstein International Centre, Tufts University, p. 3.
57 Ibid.
58 Eikenberry, Karl W. (2013) 'The Limits of Counterinsurgency Doctrine in Afghanistan', *Foreign Affairs* 92(5). Available at: www.foreignaffairs.com/articles/afghanistan/2013-08-12/limits-counterinsurgency-doctrine-afghanistan.

and resources among elites.⁵⁹ Recognition of this dynamic should have encouraged the pursuit, with the same fervour and aggression as the military campaign, of a political strategy aimed at reconciliation and a more inclusive political settlement.

The Politics and Functioning of the Alliance

The discussion above has focused on why an unprecedented amount of resources and effort on the part of NATO and partner countries, invested at great human cost over a period of 13 years, produced results so much at variance with the declared objectives of bringing lasting peace and stability to Afghanistan.⁶⁰ Addressing that question is obviously of the highest priority. The question is not, however, precisely the same as asking how NATO functioned as an alliance and why the mission unfolded in the way it did. To answer that question, two additional drivers of institutional response need to be factored into the analysis.

In the first instance, and as noted earlier, NATO's growing involvement in Afghanistan from 2003 was linked to the widespread post-9/11 perception, shared by NATO capitals, that the Western Alliance needed to demonstrate its continuing relevance in the face of new and global challenges in the interests of institutional survival, 'in particular, those posed by terrorism and the proliferation of weapons of mass destruction'.⁶¹ No longer held together by the unifying perception of a common Cold War threat, and with a more recent patchy record of operations in the Balkans to show for its efforts, NATO needed to prove its credibility. Assuming a greater role in Afghanistan came to be seen as the test of NATO's transformation in the face of changing security threats and risks that transcended the Euro-Atlantic area. High-flown summit declarations notwithstanding, deep differences

---

59   A point also strongly emphasised in Fishstein, Paul and Andrew Wilder (2012) *Winning Hearts and Minds?: Examining the Relationship between Aid and Security in Afghanistan*, Medford: Feinstein International Centre, Tufts University, pp. 57–9.
60   As an illustration of the sums involved, by mid-2015 the cumulative appropriations for US 'relief and reconstruction' alone had reached some $110 billion. SIGAR (2015) 'Report of the Special Inspector General for Afghanistan Reconstruction (SIGAR)', 30 July, p. 78. Available at: www.sigar.mil/pdf/quarterlyreports/2015-07-30qr.pdf.
61   'The Prague Summit and NATO's Transformation — A Readers Guide', NATO, 2003, p. 26.

between the US and European allies about how best to 'manage global security and risk' were difficult to conceal, even as NATO decided to operate 'out-of-area'.

Speaking at the IISS annual conference in September 2007, Jaap de Hoop Scheffer, the NATO Secretary-General, suggested that consensus was in fact emerging within the Alliance about its future direction:

> Old terms, such as 'in-' and 'out-of area' no longer apply. All allies acknowledge that, in a globalized world, such definitions have become artificial. They all agree that NATO must be prepared to address security challenges at their source, whenever and wherever they arise.[62]

It was a heroic effort, even if one allows for the platitudinous style demanded by the setting and the occasion. It was not, however, a terribly convincing claim, neither at the time nor when the full force of NATO's fragmented approach and decidedly mixed record in Afghanistan exposed the shallowness of the consensus on NATO's global role. The Prague summit itself had been held against the backdrop of deep rifts among allies about US plans for Iraq. Reaching agreement on a strategic vision did not become any easier in the years that followed. The manifest difficulties of meeting objectives in Afghanistan, with allies increasingly drawn into a full-blown insurgency after 2006, over time added to the sense of that NATO might not, after all, be politically suited and structurally equipped to take on 'security challenges at their source, whenever and wherever they arise'.[63]

This realisation also helps to explain the curious mixture of relief and apprehension, but also rediscovered sense of purpose, permeating NATO's Brussels headquarters by the time the ISAF mission was drawing to a close. Sentiments widely, if not explicitly, articulated in NATO capitals included relief at having disengaged from a costly, divisive, and failing mission in Afghanistan. This was balanced by apprehension and a renewed sense of purpose presented by Russia's forceful assertion of its 'great power' credentials, exemplified by its transparently illegal annexation of Crimea in March 2014 and

---

62 NATO (2007) 'Managing Global Security and Risk', speech by NATO Secretary General, Jaap de Hoop Scheffer, at IISS Global Strategic Review, 7–9 September.
63 This is discussed more fully in Berdal, Mats and David Ucko (2009) 'NATO at 60', *Survival* 51(2).

continuing support for pro-Russian separatist forces in eastern Ukraine. In terms of Alliance cohesion and dynamics, the Russian challenge, while deeply troubling, was also more familiar. Crucially, it engages more directly and unequivocally with what are viewed as the core national interests of the Alliance's members, especially in Eastern Europe.

The second internal driver of institutional response alluded to above was more critical to NATOs actual performance in Afghanistan. This was the range of domestic political pressures and interests held by Alliance members, which framed their contributions to operations in Afghanistan. Unsurprisingly, national interests and perspectives on the mission were not merely — in many cases not even primarily — driven by developments and realities in Afghanistan itself. For European allies, even though they might not share US campaign priorities, supporting US efforts and being seen to do so was always an important consideration in decision-making regarding Afghanistan. This was partly as an act of solidarity but it was also, quite obviously, seen as a matter of profound political interest. According to Sherard Cowper-Coles, who served as UK Ambassador to Kabul and as Special Representative for Afghanistan and Pakistan between 2007 and 2010, 'eagerness to please the Americans' was one of two 'institutional factors' that help explain UK policy towards Afghanistan.[64] This kind of consideration was not unique to the UK, though each individual ally had to balance it against a different set of domestic priorities and pressures, from electoral cycles and coalition politics, to growing war weariness and financial constraints. The choices made by NATO countries regarding their deployments to Afghanistan — where to deploy, with what resources, and under what caveats — thus reflected a complex mix of domestic political considerations and constraints.[65] This in turn contributed to the fragmented nature of mission. Those countries deploying to the south in 2006, for example, where fighting

---

64 Cowper-Coles, Sherard (2015) 'Reflections from Afghanistan', in *Rethinking State Fragility*, London: The British Academy, p. 22. Available at: www.britac.ac.uk/intl/rethinking-state-fragility.cfm.
65 The other institutional factor singled out by Cowper-Coles was the British military, in particular the British Army, which, on the basis of the principle of 'use them or lose them', saw Afghanistan as 'a chance not just to engage the Taliban, but also to engage the Treasury, the Royal Navy, and the Royal Air Force'. Ibid., p. 23.

was most intense — Denmark, Canada, the Netherlands, UK, and the US — soon formed an inner core of allies, which met separately and from whose decisions other allies were, and felt, excluded.

Concluding Thoughts

Bob left the IISS for the dreaming spires of Oxford in 1987. Supported and encouraged by him, I travelled the other way in 1992, leaving Oxford and my pre-occupation with NATO and the Cold War of the 1950s for a fellowship at the IISS, where I turned to the United Nations and the disorder of the post-Cold War era.

One consequence of the UN's inability to meet the high expectations of the organisation in the immediate aftermath of the Cold War, was to encourage analysts and governments to call for more effective multilateral mechanisms and institutions to meet new post-Cold war challenges. The search intensified notably following the peacekeeping disasters in Somalia, Rwanda, and former Yugoslavia between 1992 and 1995. Given its capabilities, planning, and tested decision-making structures, NATO, which had already lent its capabilities to the UN in the Balkans, was seen by many as a natural candidate to take on 'crisis management and peacekeeping' tasks. The view that NATO could step in where the cumbersome, ineffective, and under-resourced UN had failed, however, tended to ignore two characteristics common to both organisations, and which crucially continue to influence their functioning. Although profoundly different in many outwardly respects, they are both inter-governmental and deeply political institutions. As such, the range of interests held by their member states — reflecting different historical perspectives, values, and understandings of threats and challenges to international peace and security — will always complicate the search for coherence and unity of effort. The history of NATO's mission in Afghanistan has shown that in this respect, at least, there are parallels to draw between otherwise markedly different organisations.

12
Theory and Practice, Art and Science in Warfare: An Etymological Note

Beatrice Heuser

La théorie est le pied droit et l'expérience le pied gauche,
il faut avoir les deux pieds pour marcher
(Georg Friedrich von Tempelhof)[1]

Strategic thinking, or 'theory' if one prefers,
is nothing if not pragmatic.
(Bernard Brodie)[2]

In this Festschrift for Robert O'Neill, my post-doctoral adviser and patron during the years when I had to spread my wings and leave the safe nest of studenthood, my contribution concerns a subject that we have discussed many times as he guided me on my first lectures in the area of strategic studies. Both of us had been doctoral students of Michael Howard, and both of us read German, so we could discuss Clausewitz and his contribution to the field — which one must concede is outstanding, however critical one might be of parts of Clausewitz's writing. When I asked him for advice on my earliest teaching in strategic studies, Bob once encouraged me to look at definitions of strategy, in theory and

---

1   von Tempelhof, Georg Friedrich (1997 [1783]) *Geschichte des Sieben-jährigen Krieges,* Vol. I, Osnabrück: Biblio, p. 203.
2   Brodie, Bernard (1974) *War and Politics,* London: Cassell, p. 452f.

practice, art, and science. Here is the 'homework' which, a quarter of a century on, I would like to present to him, with all my thanks and appreciation for the wonderful guidance he has given me over the years.

Etymology

In writings on war, we find the claim made that war is an art. Other authors stress the need for a science of war. This article explores these claims and the reasoning behind them. It will sketch how these terms were used in relation to the terms 'strategy' and 'tactics'.

The difference between theoretical reflection and practical application of the results of the reflection is traditionally conveyed by the terms 'science' and 'art'. A brief reminder of the etymology of both terms is useful here, as the current usage of both terms in English is the exact opposite of its original use. The French and English word 'art' hails from the Latin *ars*, the most important meaning of which, for our purposes, is skill, practical ability to do something, a meaning reflected in the French and English word 'artisan' or skilled craftsman. Originally, the 'Arts' subjects were thus ones that implied practical skills, like the ability to speak a language, or to paint a picture ('fine art'). The equivalent German word, *Kunst*, was related to *Können*, the ability to do something.

The French and English word 'science', by contrast, originally implied abstract knowledge and reflection upon a subject, the *theory* (as opposed to the *practice* of art). It is derived from the Latin *scientia*, knowledge or wisdom, and has its equivalent in the German *Wissenschaft*. Abstract logic, mathematics, theoretical reflections upon the laws of nature (i.e. physics — still called 'natural philosophy' at some Scottish universities) were all sciences, and stood in clear contrast to applied subjects (i.e. arts) such as engineering, founding cannon, building fortifications, or indeed, organising for and waging war, the skills expected from a general.

This does not mean, however, that everybody used these terms consistently. A conflation or confusion of the terms can be trace back to the late Middle Ages. Dodging the choice between art and science, Jean de Bueil in his *Jouvencel* of 1466 told his readers that 'the conduct of war [should be] artful and subtle, which is why it is

12. THEORY AND PRACTICE, ART AND SCIENCE IN WARFARE

appropriate to conduct it by *art and science* [my emphasis]'.[3] A century later, the Englishman John Smythe similarly stated the need for arts and sciences of war, without explaining what he meant by either.[4] In 1616, Colonel Johann Jacobi von Wallhaussen noted, tautologically: 'The art of war is an art or science about how to wage war.'[5] The French marshal Feuquières' works, written before 1711, were described by his posthumous publishers as dealing with 'l'Art militaire', while Feuquières himself claimed to be dealing with 'la science de la guerre', which he subdivided into theory and practice.[6] In the early eighteenth century, Maurice of Saxony, Marshall of France, used both terms — his 'dreams' had the *art* of war as their subject — but then noted that '[a]ll *sciences* have principles and rules; war alone has none'.[7]

We find a similar muddle of terms in the *Reflections on the Art of War*, originally of 1797, by Georg Heinrich von Berenhorst (1733–1814) from Anhalt-Dessau who pursued his very successful military career in Prussia. Berenhorst only used the expression 'tactics' (and not 'strategy', the utility of which had apparently not yet dawned on him), which he defined as including the choice of weapons,

> the way of combining them; any rule, instructions and exercises for the soldier ... with regard to the use of his arms, in his posture and the movement of his body ... I should like to call this elementary tactics. Tactics further means: the principles according to which a century, a cohort, a company or a battalion breaks up, moves, reconfigures ... according to which one deploys cohorts, battalions in the order of battle and lets them advance towards the enemy who is within a shot's or a throw's reach, or lets them retreat: all that pertains to the actual fight, all that will decide on a particular day, at a particular hour, that which the *higher sciences of war* and *skills of army leadership* aim for — higher in the sense that they are based on tactics. These *higher sciences* to me are the *art* of marching with the entire army or substantial parts thereof, to advance, to retreat ... of establishing ... strongholds; of choosing campsites; of using the surface of the earth

---

3   de Bueil, Jean (1887 [1493]) *Le Jouvencel par Jean de Bueil*, Paris: Renouard, p. 15.
4   Smythe, Sir John (1964 [1590]) *Certain Discourses Military*, Ithaca, NY: Cornell University Press, pp. 3–5.
5   von Wallhaussen, Johann Jacobi (1616) *Das heutige Kriegswesen in einer Perfecten und absoluten Idea begriffen und vorgestelt*, Hanau: Selbstverlag, p. 1.
6   de Pas, Antoine, Marquis de Feuquières (1731) *Mémoires sur la Guerre où l'on a rassemblé les Maximes les plus nécessaires dans les operations de l'Art Militaire*, Amsterdam, Fracois Changuion, title page and p. 2.
7   de Saxe, Maurice (1756) *Rêveries sur l'Art de la Guerre*, The Hague.

according to its features; of passing streams and rivers: finally, the great *art* of making apposite, reliable plans and to ... adapt them cleverly to new developments, or to abandon them and to replace them by others [my emphasis].[8]

To add to the terminological confusion, authors writing in Germanic languages contributed a further term: *Kriegskunde,* knowledge of war (with the word 'Kunde' used much in the sense as the Greek *logía*).[9] We find in Brussels, to this day, a street called rue de la Stratégie in French, and *Krijgskundestraat* — street of the knowledge of war — in Flemish. The US Joint Chiefs of Staff in their *Dictionary of the U.S. Military Terms for Joint Usage* of 1964 defined 'strategy' as both 'art and science', in peace and war, in the pursuit of political aims.[10] Napoleon himself had little interest in philosophical clarity. He confusingly stated that '[s]trategy is an art', while noting a few lines further on that the great generals of the past had turned 'warfare into a true science'.[11] US Joint Chiefs of Staff were thus in good company when in 1964 they issued the following claim in a doctrine manual:

> Strategy is the *art and science* of developing and using political, economic, psychological, and military forces as necessary during peace and war, to afford the maximum support to policies, in order to increase the probabilities and favourable consequences of victory and lessen the chances of defeat [my emphasis].[12]

The Prussian officer and military author August Rühle von Lilienstern (1790–1847) remarked on this terminological confusion in much writing on the subject. At the time when Rühle was writing, people began to contrast a workman's skills in performing the same tasks over and over, and the creation of something unique with flair, intuition,

---

8   von Berenhorst, Georg Heinrich (1978 [1827]) *Betrachtungen über die Kriegskunst, über ihre Fortschritte, ihre Widersprüche und ihre Zuverlässigkeit,* Osnabrück, Biblio Verlag, p. 7f.
9   Cancrin, Georg Ludwig Graf (1818) 'Allgemeine Uebersicht der Kriegskunde zu Lande', in Rühle von Lilienstern, *Aufsätze über Gegenstände und Ereignisse aus dem Gebiete des Kriegswesens,* Berlin: Ernst Siegfried Mittler, pp. 95–101.
10 Luttwak, Edward (2001) *Strategy: The Logic of War and Peace,* Cambridge: Harvard University Press, pp. 239–41.
11 Foch, Ferdinand (1909) *De la Conduite de la Guerre: La manœuvre pour la Bataille,* Paris: Berger-Levrault, p. 3.
12 Quoted in Handel, Michael (1996) *Masters of War: Classical Strategic Thought,* second edition, London: Frank Cass, p. 36.

and genius; the use of word *Kunst* was already moving towards the latter sense, while it was still seen, at the same time, as the opposite of *Wissenschaft* or science.[13]

Nevertheless, what all these writers were in search of were principles and rules governing warfare that could be taught and passed on to subsequent generations. As we have already noted, two schools can be distinguished, those who defined warfare as an art, and those who emphasised the reflexive, theoretical (scientific) skills needed to underpin the practice of warfare.

Science in Warfare

The quest for a science of war can be traced back to antiquity. The first century AD Roman author Frontinus, who wrote in Latin but used the odd Greek word (such as 'strategy') when no Latin word existed, wrote about the science of war — *rei militaris scientia*.[14]

In the Middle Ages, the author(s) of the *Book of the Order of Chivalry*, which may have originated in the Spanish-speaking world of the thirteenth century, saw 'the order of knyghthode' as a 'scyence' that deserved to be 'wreton and redde in scoles lyke as the other scyences'.[15] Subsequently, the introduction of fire power, especially hand-held arquebuses and muskets, made drilling soldiers very important: only thus could the relatively rapid firing of these still very unwieldy personal arms be ensured. The resulting movements of lines of soldiers, with the man in the front firing and those behind him reloading and keeping out of the firing line while successively moving forward to take his place, constituted geometrical patterns, the filigree of the battlefield, as the French called it. Other features of Baroque warfare also invoked geometry: the calculation of firing distances and the targeting of cannon, in turn important for the angles of the wide and flat fortifications of Vauban and his contemporaries;

---

13 von Lilienstern, Rühle (1818) 'Ueber Theorie und Praxis, über den Unterschied zwischen Wissenschaft und Kunst', in *Idem: Aufsätze über Gegenstände und Ereignisse aus dem Gebiete des Kriegswesens*, Vol. 1, Berlin: Mittler, vol. 1, pp. 41f., 45, 71–4.
14 Frontinus, Sextus Iulius (1925 [ca. A.D. 84–96]) 'Stratagematon' in Charles E. Bennett (trans. and ed.) *Frontinus: The Stratagems and the Aqueducts of Rome*, London: William Heinemann, p. 2f.
15 Anon (c. 1483) *Book of the Order of Chivalry*, p. 23.

the zig-zagging trenches constructed for sieges to approach the adversary's ramparts without making oneself vulnerable to his defensive fire; the movement of troops and their concentration in the area of the potential battlefield; and the supply lines and distances of depots to the battlefield, all these involved geometric calculations. Henry Duke of Rohan thus spoke about the '*science* of the general', which consisted of the understanding and ability to apply such aspects of warfare.[16]

In the age of Newton, Euler, and Boyle, military writers sought increasingly to find scientific axioms applicable to warfare, just as the former had discovered hard and fast rules governing mathematics, inanimate nature in general, or gasses in particular. Warfare was thus increasingly seen as a subject of academic study and mathematical training, and military academies opened their doors. In 1740, Bardet de Villeneuve published his 12 volumes on *Military Science*, in which he drew extensively on the works of the Spanish officer and diplomat Santa Cruz de Marcenado.[17] Twenty years later, Paul Gédéon Joly de Maizeroy, the translator of Emperor Leo VI's *Taktika*, to whom we owe the introduction of the term 'stratégie' to French and thus into the Western vernacular languages, used the term 'military science' in his *Essais militaires*.[18] And after the Napoleonic Wars, an anonymous author, writing in Vienna, explained that 'strategy is the science of war', and it was this subject to which he devoted his three-volume study of past wars.[19]

Despite heavy competition from those who insisted that warfare was only an art, not a science, the science school battled on. The Italian naval historian and Dominican priest, Alberto Guglielmotti, writing between 1856 and 1889, defined strategy as

> The supreme military *science* which invents the way of guiding the forces on the battlefield to victory. [Strategy] is similar to dynamics which ... studies the laws of movement, space, time in an abstract way,

---

16   de Rohan, Henri Duc (1972 [1636]) *Le Parfaict Capitaine,* Osnabrück, Biblio Verlag, p. 262.
17   de Villeneuve, Bardet (1740) *La Science militaire*, Vol. 1 : Cours de la science militaire, The Hague: Jean van Duren. For a biography and excerpts of Santa Cruz de Marcenado in English translation, see Heuser, Beatrice (2010) *The Strategy Makers*, Santa Monica: ABC-Clio, pp. 124–46.
18   de Maizeroy, Paul Gédéon Joly (1762) *Essais militaires, ou l'on traite des armes défensives,* Amsterdam: Gosses.
19   Anon. (1814) *Grundsätze der Strategie erläutert durch die Darstellung des Feldzugs von 1796 in Deutschland*, Vol. 1, Wien: Anton Strauss, pp. vii, 3.

and then moves to mass, speed, impact, resistance, friction. Strategy calculates the axes and dispositions of attack from the basis to the objective; it controls the lines of communication and the withdrawal routes; it compares, in a solution given to a strategic problem, the advantages and disadvantages and resolves in concrete terms, on the terrain, the fundamental problem of the movement of forces over faster routes, in the shortest time, in order and in a timely manner to win. This applies as much to [war on] the land as at sea [my emphasis].[20]

Similar ideas can be found among his French contemporaries, such as General Lewal.[21]

The late nineteenth century, with its exponential growth in the number and spread of new technological inventions, if anything made the scientific even more popular. In the early twentieth century, German and British authors wrote about *Strategical Sciences* and the *Science of War*.[22] Marxism-Leninism and the individuals, movements, and states inspired by it even claimed that history was a science, and consequently also saw military science as essential underpinnings of warfare. In German parlance to this day, science encompasses both 'natural sciences' and 'the sciences of the spirit', what in Britain would be called the arts and humanities. The claim that warfare has to be studied 'scientifically' thus seems to be the oldest, as well as the more modern approach.

Warfare as an Art

Yet the emphasis on the practical side of war studies also has a distinguished pedigree that came to the fore especially during the Renaissance, and is still going strong. In the early 1400s, the first modern strategist, Christine de Pizan, wrote about the 'art of war',

---

20 Ferrante, Enzio (1993) 'La pensée navale italienne: II. De Lissa à la Grande Guerre', in Hervé Coutau-Bégarie, *L'Evolution de la Pensée navale*, Band III, Paris: Economica, p. 106f.
21 Lewal, Général J. L. (1892) *Introduction à la Partie positive de la Stratégie*, Paris: Librairie militaire L. Baudoin, p. 61f.
22 von Caemmerer, Rudolf (1904) *Die Entwicklung der Strategischen Wissenschaft im 19. Jahrhundert*, trans. Karl von Donat, Berlin: Baensch; von Caemmerer, Rudolf (1905) *The Development of Strategical Science*, London: Hugh Rees; Henderson, G. F. R. (1905) *The Science of War: A Collection of Essays and Lectures, 1892–1903*, London: Longmans, Green; Fuller, J. F. C. (1925) *The Foundations of the Science of War*, London: Hutchinson.

'military art', and the 'art of chivalry'.[23] A century later, Berault Stuart, one of the captains employed by the King of France, and Niccolò Machiavelli in Florence would follow this usage with their respective books on the *Art of War*.[24] By the seventeenth century, it was normal to be referring to the art of war, not only in Italian but also in French, English, and German.[25]

What they all had in common was the quest for transmittable rules and principles which could help future practitioners of warfare. Yet Jacques François de Chastenet de Puysegur, Marshal of France, who between 1693 and 1743 wrote principles and rules on the art of war, claimed that he had previously not come across any such principles in any areas of the art of war, except in the sub-area of siegecraft.[26] At the time of the French Revolution, Georg Heinrich von Berenhorst, in trying to establish a set of rules and principles governing warfare, followed the precedent of Machiavelli and Puysegur in referring to *Kriegskunst*, the art of war, and for a long time this term would dominate writing in German on the subject. Behrenhorst was mainly concerned with arguing that there was a body of knowledge and insights that can be passed on to younger generations. He noted that hitherto, most cultures had mainly passed on lessons learnt empirically from experiences of previous wars and battles, rather than trying to rise above such empiricism and attempting to approach warfare from the perspective of theoretical approaches, such as those of geometry or geography.[27]

---

23   de Pizan, Christine (1997 [1404]) *Le Livre des Faits et Bonnes Mœurs du roi Charles V le Sage*, Eric Hicks & Thérèse Moreau (trans. and ed.), Paris: Stock, p. 158ff; de Pisan, Christine, *L'Art de la Chevalerie selon Végèce* (1488 [1410]), Paris: Antoine Verard.
24   Stuart, Berault, Seigneur d'Aubigny (1976 [1508]) *Traité sur l'Art de la Guerre*, Elie de Comminges (ed.), Den Haag : Martinus Nijnhoff; Machiavelli, Niccolò (1521) *Libro della Arte della Guerra*, Florence: li Heredi di Philippo di Giunta.
25   Hexham, Henry (1642) *The Principles of the Art Militarie, Practised in the Warres of the Vnited Netherlands*, Part 1, second edition, Delft; Part 2 (1642) Delft: Antony of Heusden; à Troupitzen, Laurentius (1638) *Kriegs Kunst, Nach Königlich Schwedischer Manier...*, Franckfurt: Mattheo Merian; de Billon, Jean (1613) *Les Principes de l'Art militaire*, Lyon: Berthelin; Mallet, Allain Manesson (1684) *Les travaux de Mars, ou l'art de la guerre*, Paris: Denys Thierry.
26   de Chastenet, Jacques François, Marquis de Puységur or Puysegur (1748) *Art de la Guerre, par principes et par règles*, Paris: Charles-Antoine Jombert, p. 3.
27   von Berenhorst, Georg Heinrich (1789) *Betrachtungen über die Kriegskunst über ihre Fortschritte, ihre Widersprüche und Zuverlässigkeit*, Vol. 1, second edition, Leipzig: G. Fleischer the Younger.

12. THEORY AND PRACTICE, ART AND SCIENCE IN WARFARE

Henri Baron de Jomini, the foremost and first great analyst of Napoleonic warfare, first published his definitions on the subject in 1805 and defined strategy as

> the art of making war upon the map, and comprehends the whole theater of operations. Grand Tactics is the art of posting troops upon the battlefield according to the accidents of the ground, or bringing them into action, and the art of fighting upon the ground in contradistinction to planning upon a map.[28]

Elsewhere, Jomini wrote: 'Strategy ... is the *art* of bringing the greatest part of the forces of an army upon the important point of the theater of war or the zone of operations [my emphasis].'[29] Jomini thus came down on the side of those who regarded strategy — and waging war — as an art, not a science. Jomini's definitions would dominate the nineteenth century.

The American naval strategist Alfred Thayer Mahan (1840–1914), writing at the end of the nineteenth century, provided perhaps the most elaborate defence of the concept that warfare should be seen as an art. He followed Jomini in many respects, and picked up in particular on the Jominian argument about strategy as an art, not a science:

> *Science* is sure of nothing until it is proved ... it aims at absolute certainties, — dogmas, — towards which, through numerous experiments, it keeps moving. Its truths, once established, are fixed, rigid, unbending, and the relation between cause and effect are rather laws than principles; hard lines incapable of change, rather than living seeds. *Science* discovers and teaches truths which it has no power to change; *Art*, out of materials which it finds about it, creates new forms in endless variety. It is not bound down to a mechanical reproduction of similar effects, as is inanimate nature, but partakes of the freedom of the human mind in which it has its root. Art acknowledges principles and even rules; but these are not so much fetters, or bars, which compel its movements aright, as guides which warn when it is going wrong. In this living sense, *the conduct of war is an art*, having its spring in the mind of man, dealing with very various circumstances, admitting certain principles; but, beyond that, manifold in its manifestations, according to the genius of the artist and the temper of the materials with which he is dealing. To such an effort dogmatic prescription is

---

28   Henri, Antoine, Baron de Jomini (1868 [1837]) *The Art of War*, Capt. G. H. Mendell and Capt. W. P. Craighill (trans.), Philadelphia: J. B. Lippincott, pp. 69–71.
29   Ibid., p. 322.

unsuited; the best of rules, when applied to it, cannot be rigid, but must have that free play which distinguishes a principle from a mere rule [my emphasis].[30]

Here we see the inversion of the meaning of the two terms that was creeping into the English language: increasingly, 'art' came to mean something done with instinct, intuition and talent (even genius), not by rote, reflection, or reasoning.

Other very technical definitions abounded in the later nineteenth and early twentieth centuries, such as that of the Britons Sir Edward Hamley, General J. F. Maurice,[31] his namesake General Frederick Barton Maurice,[32] and G. F. R. Henderson, who by 'strategy' understood 'the *art* of rightly directing the masses of troops towards the objects of the campaign'.[33] At the outset of the twentieth century, Lt. Col. Walter James wrote:

> The *art of war* is usually divided into two parts — strategy and tactics. Strategy deals with the military considerations which determine the choice of the offensive or defensive, the selection of the country in which to fight, the objects against which the armies should be directed, and embraces the Plan of Campaign or General Idea which dominates the conduct of the operations. Broadly speaking, therefore, strategy is concerned with the movement of troops before they come into actual collision, while tactics deals with the leading of troops in battle, or when battle is imminent [my emphasis].[34]

Equally, Captain (later Sir) Basil Henry Liddell Hart, whose most important works stem from the 1920s, 1930s, and 1940s, defined strategy as '[t]he *art* of distributing and applying military means to fulfil the ends of policy [my emphasis]'.[35] Liddell Hart was pessimistic about the existence of a science of war, not because he did not ardently

---

30 Mahan, Alfred Thayer (1918) *Naval Strategy Compared and Contrasted with the Principles and Practice of Military Operations on Land*, Boston: Little, Brown and Co., p. 299f.
31 Maurice, J. F. (1891) *War*, London: Macmillan, p. 7.
32 Maurice, F. B. (1929) *British Strategy*, London: Constable & Co., p. 3.
33 Henderson, G. F. R. (1905) *The Science of War: A Collection of Essays and Lectures, 1892–1903*, London: Longmans, Green, p. 39.
34 James, W. H. (1904) *Modern Strategy*, second edition, Edinburgh: William Blackwood and Sons, p. 17f.
35 Hart, Basil Liddell (n.d. [1944]) *Thoughts on War*, London: Faber and Faber, p. 229.

12. THEORY AND PRACTICE, ART AND SCIENCE IN WARFARE

wish to promote it, but because he did not feel that humanity had made much leeway with it. Four years before the outbreak of the Second World War, he wrote:

> A study of military history brings ample confirmation of Rebecca West's *[bon] mot*: 'Before a war military science seems a real science, like astronomy, but after a war it seems more like astrology' … There is, doubtless, a science of war; but we are a long way from discovering it. Apart from the mere technique of utilizing weapons, what passes for 'military science' is hardly more than the interpretation of conventions nurtured by tradition and warped by sentiment, patriotic and professional.[36]

Liddell Hart's contemporary, the French admiral and Clausewitz-disciple, Raoul Castex (1878–1968) came down firmly on the 'art' side of the 'art-or-science' debate, with strategy as the 'art of the general', an art that had its own theory, however, which facilitated its learning in the absence of copious personal experiences.[37]

A Cold War example of the arts–science debate comes from Belgium, where the analyst of strategy, Henri Bernard, emphasised that war and conflicts are not physical experiments which can be repeated step by step and in all physical conditions — if that were the case, one could speak about a science in the modern sense of empirically based on repeatable experiments. But the conduct of war pairs material, physical forces (which are quantifiable) with moral forces, it is a 'struggle of wills', and thus has unquantifiable dimensions.[38]

At the end of the Cold War, the British political scientist Robert Neild used a wider definition still: 'Strategy is the *art* of pursuing political aims by the use or possession of military means [my emphasis].'[39] The broadest use of the terms 'strategy' and 'art' were made by the British strategist Lawrence Freedman: 'strategy is the *art* of creating

---

36   Ibid., p. 45.
37   Castex, Raoul (1937 [1929]) *Théories stratégiques*, Vol. 1, second edition, Paris: SEGMC, p. 20f.
38   Bernard, Henri (1965) *Guerre Totale et Guerre Révolutionnaire*, Brussels and Paris: Brepols, p. 5.
39   Neild, Robert (1990) *An Essay on Strategy as it Affects the Achievement of Peace in a Nuclear Setting*, Basingstoke: Macmillan, p. 1.

power' [my emphasis].[40] In the Anglophone countries, the notion that strategy is an art still prevails over its Marxist-Leninist designation as a science.

A Science and an Art, or Strategy as one and Tactics as the Other?

Authors other than the muddle-headed, such as Jacobi von Wallhausen and Berenhorst, saw both science and art as necessary in warfare. Some tied them in with the distinction between strategy and tactics.

Those writing in German began to use the terms 'strategy' and 'tactics' much in the way of Emperor Leo VI, from about the time his work was translated into German in five volumes in 1777–1781. We thus find 'strategy' and 'tactics' used by the Prussian mathematician Heinrich von Bülow (1752–1807), who sought to bring calculable order, logic, and clarity to the art (or practice) of war. Around 1800, he wrote:

> The *science* of military movements of two armies at war outside our range of view, or, if you prefer, out of the range of the shot of the big guns etc. is strategy. The *science* of the military movement in the presence of the enemy, in his full view, or, if you prefer, within the firing range of his big guns, is tactics [my emphasis].

From this he derived the not very profound rule of thumb that strategy could be divided into 'two main parts: the march and the camp'.[41] Later he used a second definition, equating *'science* of war' with *'theory'*, and *'art* of war' with its *'application'*.[42]

Their contemporary, Archduke Charles (1771–1847), a veteran of the Napoleonic Wars, in 1806 defined 'strategy' as 'the *science* of war: it designs the plan, circumscribes and determines the development of military operations; it is the particular science of the supreme commander [my emphasis]'. 'Tactics', by contrast, he defined as 'the *art* of war. It teaches the way in which strategic designs are to be executed;

---

40 Freedman, Lawrence (2004) *Deterrence*, Cambridge: Polity Press; Freedman, Lawrence (2013) *Strategy: A History*, Oxford: Oxford University Press.
41 von Bülow, Dietrich Heinrich Frhr (1799) *Geist des neuern Kriegssystems hergeleitet aus dem Grundsatze einer Basis der Operationen*, Hamburg: Benjamin Gottlieb Hoffmann, pp. 83f., 89.
42 Ibid., p. xiv.

it is the necessary skill of each leader of troops [my emphasis].'[43] We thus find a correlation between 'strategy' and 'science', and 'tactics' and 'art'. Similarly, writing in 1809, August Wagner divided warfare into an enduring component — pertaining especially to its purpose — which he saw as the subject of the 'science of war'; and a component constantly changing with 'the shape of weapons and encounters', which he saw as the domain of the 'art of war'.[44]

To clarify matters, Rühle von Lilienstern devoted a lecture to the question of the difference between art and science, in the context of a lecture series on war that he published in 1818.[45] Honing in on the officer's need for science/reflection and understanding of the issues at hand on the one hand, and his need for the capacity for applying this through art/action/its practice, Rühle argued that neither was enough on its own, and both only made sense if they had each other: 'Any practice without theory lacks rules and is vague [unsicher], its success lies in the hands of fortune; any theory without a possible and without an intended practice remains empty, sterile, pointless speculation.' He introduced a helpful simile: without theory/science and reflection, the practitioner would be confronted with the skill sets he was taught like an artisan with a large tool kit which was thrown at his feet in complete disarray. Only by putting it in order and by reflecting systematically and scientifically on the problem at hand would he be able to identify the tools that would be needed for the operation he planned. Rühle further argued that a survey of the history of warfare could lead to two different products: one, a narrative or description (historiography), another, a reflection on a higher level, addressing the questions whether laws had been at work, and why and for what purpose things had been done (what today one might expect to find in the social sciences).[46]

---

43 Archduke Charles (1882 [1838]) 'Das Kriegswesen in Folge der französischen Revolutionskriege', in Freiherr von Waldtstätten (ed.), *Erzherzog Karl: Ausgewählte militärische Schriften*, Berlin: Richard Wilhelmi, p. 57; Archduke Charles (1882) *Ausgewählte militärische Schriften*, Berlin: R. Wilhelmi, pp. vii, 3.
44 Wagner, August (1809) *Grundzüge der reinen Strategie*, Amsterdam: Kunst- und Industrie-Comptoir, pp. vii ff.; see also Anon. (1814) *Grundsätze der Strategie erläutert durch die Darstellung des Feldzugs von 1796 in Deutschland*, Vol. 1, Wien: Anton Strauss, p. vii.
45 von Lilienstern, Rühle (1818) 'Ueber Theorie und Praxis, über den Unterschied zwischen Wissenschaft und Kunst', in *Idem: Aufsätze über Gegenstände und Ereignisse aus dem Gebiete des Kriegswesens*, Vol. 1, Berlin: Mittler, vol. 1, pp. 56, 37–75.
46 Ibid., pp. 46–8.

At the same time, Rühle was convinced that practice nourished reflection, and that reflection would inspire action, so that to be fruitful, both would ideally have to interact; but, crucially, one could complement one's practical experience and theoretical reflection with that of others through the medium of lecture and literature. Theory was thus, for him, a distillation from experience — the essence of experience. (Rühle's metaphor evokes the process whereby a salt is distilled from its liquid solution.) This essence, this elixir, would be so strong that no lesser mind would be able to digest it, and for that reason some might reject theory as they simply could not get their heads around it. On the one hand, any theory that was not rooted in experience (i.e. in empirical knowledge), which was the mere figment of the imagination of an armchair strategist (*Stubengelehrter*), would easily shatter when it clashed with hard facts. It would be useless as a directive for action. On the other hand, one's understanding of one's own experience could not fail to be enriched by good theory, and would allow analysis on a higher level, and at once more insightfully. Rühle's advice was thus to approach both theory and supposed lessons drawn from one's own experiences critically, and to check theory against reality. He advised his readers to compare one's own limited experiences with those of others (and with examples recorded in literature), as exceptions exist for all rules, and chance deviations from the norm will occur, and no one person can amass sufficiently large experience to come to (what we would now call statistically relevant, large-n) conclusions. Moreover, even if 99 experiences confirm one rule, in war there is no certainty that the hundredth case will would be dominated by another. Bottom line, Rühle argued, nothing would replace the individual office's analytical skills, his good critical judgment, informed by both practical experience and by theory.[47]

Another logically coherent attempt to define the roles of science and art in warfare can be found a century later, when French General Jean Colin tackled the subject in his *Transformations of War* of 1911. To him, war was the object both of a science and an art. Science, he wrote, 'seeks laws, identifies and classifies facts; art chooses, combines and produces'.

---

47   Ibid., pp. 53–7, 62f.

12. THEORY AND PRACTICE, ART AND SCIENCE IN WARFARE

> There is a *science* of war which studies the means of action and the elements of war, analyses the events of past wars, compares them, and draws conclusions about the relations of cause and effect, sometimes succeeding in establishing general laws. *Art*, more or less using the results produced by science, at the moment of action chooses the procedures that seem suitable to diverse particular cases. [*Art*] is the application to action of the actor's natural gifts and of assimilated knowledge. Depending on each individual instance, the latter will play a more or less important role. *Science* finds in *art* a more or less direct application … sometimes *art* can do without *science*, sometimes it is reduced to the [pure] application of scientific findings [my emphasis].[48]

Interestingly, we also find the inversion of this relationship in French literature. General Bonnal, lecturing at the Paris Ecole de Guerre in 1892–1893, told his students that '[s]trategy is the *art* of conceiving; tactics the *science* of execution [my emphasis]'.[49] Creating further terminological confusion, in the late Russian Empire, General Mikhail Ivanovich Dragomirov dismissed the concept of a 'science' of war out of hand, instead endorsing the concept of a 'theory of war'.[50]

But the debate was by no means settled. Sir Julian Corbett (1854–1922) commented on the art–science debate:

> [T]he classical strategists insist again and again on the danger of seeking from [their so-called science] what it cannot give. They even repudiate the very name of 'Science'. They prefer the older term 'Art'. They will permit no laws or rules. Such laws, they say, can only mislead in practice, for the friction to which they are subject from the incalculable human factors alone is such that the friction is stronger than the law.[51]

Corbett wrote that 'the mistrust of theory' that is so characteristic of the British,

> arises from a misconception of what it is that theory claims to do. It does not pretend to give the power of conduct in the field; it claims no more than to increase the effective power of conduct. Its main

---

48   Colin, Jean (1989 [1911]) *Les transformations de la guerre*, Paris: Economica, p. 4.
49   Castex, Raoul (1937 [1929]) *Théories stratégiques,* Vol. 1, second edition, Paris: SEGMC, p. 6.
50   Quoted in Foch, Ferdinand (1918 [1900]) *Principes de la Guerre: Conférences faites en 1900 à l'École supérieure de Guerre,* fifth edition, Paris: Berger-Levrault, p. 8.
51   Corbett, Sir Julian S. (1988 [1911]) *Some Principles of Maritime Strategy.* Annapolis, MD: US Naval Institute Press, p. 8.

practical value is that it can assist a capable man to acquire a broad outlook whereby he may be the surer his plan shall cover all the ground, and whereby he may with greater rapidity and certainty seize all the factors of a sudden situation.[52]

It was impossible, however, to ignore the debate. Corbett for one, like Mahan before him, emphasised the need for a common vocabulary to discuss war plans, and this needed to be produced through 'theoretical study'.[53]

In Russia's communist era, Marxist-Leninist definitions continued to follow narrow definitions of strategy and tactics, adding the intermediary level of operation. They described strategy as the preparation and conduct of war in general, operations the conduct of war on a theatre level, while tactics was the organisation and conduct of battle in detail. The essence of both was the same: armed conflict. In parallel, they used the terms 'military art' referring to 'the theory and practice of preparing and conducting military operations', and 'military science' referring to 'the system of knowledge about the character and laws of war'. Strategic, operational and tactical level warfare were all part of military art, taught through military doctrine, subject to the rules identified (objectively) by military science.[54] The Chief of the Soviet General Staff Marshal Nikolaj Orgakov (1917–1994) wrote as late as in 1979: 'War strategy' (*voyennaya strategiya*) is 'that part of military *art* which determines the principles of the preparation [of war] and the conduct of war and the campaign in its entirety [my emphasis]'. Echoing Clausewitz, he continued: 'Strategic military actions are the fundamental means for the achievement of the purposes of the war.'[55]

Other reflections on the importance of theory and its relation to practice could be found in the West. The American Clausewitz-scholar Bernard Brodie wrote at the end of the Vietnam War:

---

52 Ibid., p. 3f.
53 Ibid., pp. 6–8.
54 Quoted in Leebaert, Derek (ed.) (1981) *Soviet Military Thinking*, London: George Allen and Unwin, p. 14f.
55 Quoted in Backerra, Manfred (1983) 'Zur sowjetischen Militärdoktrin seit 1945', *Beiträge zur Konfliktforschung* 1, p. 48. This definition is still very close to that supplied by Clausewitz. In book two of *On War*, he defined 'strategy' merely as 'the use of engagements for the object of the war' — a very technical approach. See von Clausewitz, Carl (1976 [1832]) *On War*, Michael Howard and Peter Paret (trans. and ed.), Princeton University Press, pp. 128, 177.

Strategic thinking, or 'theory' if one prefers, is nothing if not pragmatic. Strategy is a 'how to do it' study, a guide to accomplishing something and doing it efficiently. As in many other branches of politics, the question that matters in strategy is: Will the idea work? More important, will it be likely to work under the special circumstances under which it will next be tested? These circumstances are not likely to be known or knowable much in advance of the moment of testing, though the uncertainty is itself a factor to be reckoned with in one's strategic doctrine. Above all, strategic theory is a theory for action.[56]

From this, the Anglo-American strategist Colin S. Gray developed his term 'strategic theory' in a didactic context, defined as follows: 'Strategic theory helps educate the strategist so that he can conceive of, plan, and execute strategy by his command performance.'[57]

The Invention of the Social Sciences

It is a testimony to the genius of the Prussian philosopher-general Carl von Clausewitz (1780–1831) that he overcame this confusion of terminology and these semantic quarrels by cutting the Gordian knot. In his great *On War,* Clausewitz simply concluded that neither term was satisfactory, speaking out against this separation between arts and sciences: 'No matter how obvious and palpable the difference between knowledge [science] and ability [art] may be ... it is still extremely difficult to separate them entirely in the individual ... [I]f it is impossible to imagine a human being capable of perception but not of judgment or vice versa, it is likewise impossible to separate art and knowledge altogether.' He conceded,

> creation and production lie in the realm of art; science will dominate where the object is inquiry and knowledge. It follows that the term *'art* of war' is more suitable than *'science* of war' ... But we must go on to say that strictly speaking war is *neither an art nor a science* ... [W]ar ... is part of man's social existence. War is a clash between major interests, which is resolved by bloodshed — that is the only way in which it differs from other conflicts. Rather than comparing it to art we could more accurately compare it to commerce, which is also a conflict of human interests and activities, and it is *still* closer to

---

56 Brodie, Bernard (1973) *War and Politics*, London: Cassell, p. 452f.
57 Gray, Colin S. (2010) *The Strategy Bridge: Theory for Practice*, Oxford: Oxford University Press.

politics, which in turn may be considered as a kind of commerce on a larger scale. Politics, moreover, is the womb in which war develops ... [my emphasis].

This is where we encounter the idea about the relationship between politics and war for which Clausewitz is most famous.[58]

One might thus argue that Clausewitz was one of the fathers of the social sciences, which sought to come out of the impasse of seeing human endeavours as either something to be studied scientifically, or as something for which only the quest for practical prescriptions made sense. In a different way, Clausewitz thus brought Rühle's dialectic between empirical knowledge and theory-based analysis to a new synthesis, thereby laying great parts of the foundations of strategic studies as we have come to know them.

---

58 Clausewitz, Carl (1976 [1832]) *On War*, Michael Howard and Peter Paret (trans. and ed.), Princeton University Press, p. 128. For a draft version of this passage, see Hahlweg, Werner (ed.) (1990) *Carl von Clausewitz: Schriften, Aufsätze, Studien, Briefe,* Vol. 2, Part 2, Göttingen: Vandenhoek & Rupprecht, pp. 668–70.

13

A Pivotal Moment for Global Nuclear Arms Control and Disarmament Policies: The Contribution of Robert O'Neill

Marianne Hanson

Introduction

As a strategist and leading academic in the field of security studies, Robert O'Neill was at the forefront of the re-imagining of the role of nuclear weapons, a re-imagining which has gathered strength since the 1990s, and which has shaped the current aspirations (if not yet the full practice) of leaders of the nuclear weapon states. Robert O'Neill's standing in the international strategic studies community and his willingness to reconsider prevailing assumptions about the utility of nuclear weapons have been instrumental in urging the nuclear weapons debate away a focus on Cold War deterrence thinking, and towards envisaging a nuclear weapon free world. Through his membership of the 1995–1996 Canberra Commission on the Elimination of Nuclear Weapons and the 1998 Tokyo Forum for Facing Nuclear Dangers, and his position on the Advisory Board of the 2008–2010 joint Australia–Japan International Commission on Nuclear Non-proliferation and

Disarmament, Robert O'Neill has played a key role in articulating how the changing nature of international security urgently requires us to re-think the role of nuclear weapons.

It is not an exaggeration to say that his scholarly research and commission activities have been highly influential in creating the climate where today, the leaders in almost every state have firmly declared their intention to seek a world without nuclear weapons. This aspiration is no longer something that is seen as naïve, radical, or strategically unwise (although there certainly are some die-hards who do retain a faith in nuclear weapons, and there is a long way to go before we reach a nuclear free world). The need to eliminate all nuclear weapons is a policy now firmly pursued even by hawks such as Henry Kissinger,[1] numerous military leaders,[2] various serving and former US national security advisers, secretaries of state and defense, and prominent world figures.[3] It was a position made most evident by President Obama's clear call, in Prague in 2009, for a world without nuclear weapons,[4] a most extraordinary statement made possible by the preceding years of debate and study on the role of nuclear weapons conducted by Robert O'Neill and others like him.

Nuclear Weapons During the Cold War

Like most strategists in the Cold War era concerned with the tension between the US and USSR and their allies, and the accompanying reliance on nuclear deterrence, Robert O'Neill's work focused very much on elements of arms control and nuclear postures. This is not to say, of course, that such strategists who saw value in nuclear deterrence were entirely happy about its logic or its potential dangers. Nuclear deterrence was never an entirely uncontroversial issue. But in a time of vertical proliferation of nuclear weapons — where at its height

---

1   Shultz, George P., William J. Perry, Henry A. Kissinger and Sam Nunn (2007) 'A World Free of Nuclear Weapons', *Wall Street Journal*, 2 January. Available at: www.wsj.com/articles/SB116787515251566636.
2   Canadian Coalition for Nuclear Responsibility (1996) 'Statement by Generals and Admirals of the World Against Nuclear Weapons', 5 December. Available at: www.ccnr.org/generals.html.
3   As evidenced by the membership of Global Zero: www.globalzero.org/.
4   Obama, Barack (2009) 'Remarks by President Barack Obama in Prague', Whitehouse Press Release, April 5. Available at: www.whitehouse.gov/the-press-office/remarks-president-barack-obama-prague-delivered.

in the mid-1980s, the number of such weapons on the planet grew to around 70,000, with the vast majority of them being held by the US and the USSR[5] — it was imperative to understand the dynamics of nuclear acquisition, deployment, and postures practised by those states which possessed nuclear weapons. These tens of thousands of weapons had a destructive power hundreds of times greater than the bombs used against Japan in 1945. And although the chief tension was that between the two superpowers, the addition of Britain (1952), France (1960) and China (1964) into the nuclear club during the Cold War added to the complexity of strategic thinking and calculation. In effect, one could not be a scholar of international security during the Cold War without considering the key role that nuclear weapons, or at least the threat of using nuclear weapons, played in that conflict.

These weapons were central to the security policies of the nuclear weapon states, which came to dominate strategic thinking and international affairs in a way that no other weapon has done. The Cold War became synonymous with the ever-present threat of catastrophic nuclear war, and planning to prevent it (and sometimes even to wage it — with nuclear war-fighting strategies, limited nuclear war, and even the idea of a winnable nuclear war all deliberated) occupied the minds of military thinkers and practitioners for decades. Their analyses and calculations ranged over notions such as deterrence, extended deterrence, flexible response, massive retaliation, counter-force and counter-value strategies, second-strike capabilities, and other elements that came with the onset of the atomic age, against a backdrop of the massive upward spiral in the numbers of nuclear weapons.

The core element was, of course, the idea of nuclear deterrence, the threat to use nuclear weapons against an adversary to dissuade that adversary from taking any undesired action, and especially to deter it from attacking one's own state or allies.[6] Deterrence rested on a delicate psychological balance and, if it failed, would bring unparalleled disaster not only to the states concerned, but also to the wider world. As recognised by fellow Australian, Hedley Bull,

---

5   Bulletin of the Atomic Scientists (2015) *Nuclear Notebooks: Nuclear Arsenals of the World*. Available at: thebulletin.org/nuclear-notebook-multimedia.
6   Classic works on nuclear deterrence include Schelling, Thomas (1966) *Arms and Influence*, New Haven: Yale University Press; Schelling, Thomas and Morton Halperin (1961) *Strategy and Arms Control*, New York: The Twentieth Century Fund; and Freedman, Lawrence (2004) *Deterrence*, New York: Polity Press.

with whom Robert O'Neill was to work at the International Institute for Strategic Studies in London and The Australian National University, and whose insightful work on arms control Robert O'Neill would masterfully survey and re-present in 1986,[7] the 'most important immediate goal of arms control' was to 'stabilise the relationship of mutual deterrence between the superpowers'.[8] Preventing nuclear war was the overwhelming objective, even if this meant exploring how to convince one's opponent that nuclear attack would be unleashed if one was duly provoked.

At its core, nuclear deterrence and its accompanying strategies relied on the promise of mutually assured destruction, or what came to be known as the MAD doctrine. Deterrence required, if it was going to be effective, clear communication between adversaries, a capacity to inflict the damage promised — that is, the actual nuclear weapon capability — and the credibility that such punishment would indeed be undertaken. The price to be paid for relying on deterrence was a robust stockpile, one which could withstand, if necessary, a first strike from one's adversary, and still be able to deliver a second strike in retaliation. This threat to use nuclear weapons (even in response to a nuclear attack) was always contentious, but for Bull, as O'Neill notes,[9] there was 'clearly a distinction between nuclear weapons intended for deterrence and nuclear weapons for use in combat'. The first category, Bull believed, had merit as an essential component of stability between the superpowers; in the absence of a durable peace between the US and the USSR, the pursuit of nuclear arsenals was a rational, if precarious, strategy. Deterrence also required that each state was to remain vulnerable to attack from the other if strategic stability was to be maintained; in this sense, and as Bull had noted, anti-missile defences were 'subversive of the real purpose of nuclear weapons', that purpose being to provide stable deterrence.[10]

---

7   O'Neill, Robert (ed.) (1986) *Power and Policy: Doctrine, the Alliance, and Arms Control*, London: Macmillan.
8   Bull, Hedley (1961) *The Control of the Arms Race: Disarmament and Arms Control in the Missile Age*, London: Weidenfeld & Nicolson, p. 8.
9   O'Neill, Robert (ed.) (1986) *Power and Policy: Doctrine, the Alliance, and Arms Control*, London: Macmillan, p. 5.
10 Ibid.

There remains no consensus among practitioners or scholars about the usefulness, workability, or moral standing of the policy of nuclear deterrence. Whether it was the determining factor that prevented war between the great powers, or whether it was ever truly reliable as a strategy, remain contentious questions.[11] Nevertheless, any serious engagement with international relations during the Cold War could not avoid a focus on the complex and high-stakes issue of nuclear deterrence. As one of the most prominent and respected figures in strategic studies, Robert O'Neill's notable contributions at the time to these questions included *The Strategic Nuclear Balance: An Australian Perspective*,[12] the first comprehensive examination conducted in Australia of American, Soviet, and Chinese nuclear capabilities and policies, and their impact on nuclear arms control and non-proliferation; *New Directions in Strategic Thinking*;[13] *The Conduct of East–West Relations in the 1980s*;[14] *Power and Policy: Doctrine, the Alliance and Arms Control*;[15] the aforementioned work, *Hedley Bull on Arms Control*;[16] and numerous chapters and special lectures.

The 1970s and 1980s also saw the emergence of formal attempts to reduce the likelihood of nuclear war between the nuclear powers, and to prevent nuclear proliferation. The bilateral Strategic Arms Limitation Talks had resulted in the SALT Treaties of 1972 and 1979, both aimed at regulating the nuclear arms race between the US and the Soviet Union. For its part, the nuclear Non-Proliferation Treaty

---

11 Useful critiques of the role of nuclear weapons in the Cold War include those made by McGwire, Michael (1985) 'Deterrence: The Problem — Not the Solution', *International Affairs* 62(1), pp. 55–70; Lebow, Richard Ned and Janice Gross Stein (1995) 'Deterrence and the Cold War', *Political Science Quarterly* 110(2), pp. 157–81; and Price, Richard and Nina Tannenwald (1996) 'Norms and Deterrence: The Nuclear and Chemical Weapons Taboos', in Peter J. Katzenstein (ed.), *The Culture of National Security: Norms and Identity in World Politics*, New York: Columbia University Press. Some have even pointed to what has been called the essential 'irrelevance' of nuclear weapons as a determining factor in whether or not the superpowers went to war with each other. Mueller, John (1988) 'The Essential Irrelevance of Nuclear Weapons: Stability in the Postwar World', *International Security* 13(2), pp. 55–79.
12 O'Neill, Robert (ed.) (1975) *The Strategic Nuclear Balance: An Australian Perspective*, Canberra: Strategic and Defence Studies Centre, The Australian National University.
13 O'Neill, Robert and D. M. Horner (eds) (1981) *New Directions in Strategic Thinking*, London: Allen & Unwin.
14 O'Neill, Robert (1985) *The Conduct of East–West Relations in the 1980s*, Hamden, Connecticut: Shoestring Press.
15 O'Neill, Robert (ed.) (1986) *Power and Policy: Doctrine, the Alliance, and Arms Control*, London: Macmillan.
16 O'Neill, Robert and David Schwartz (eds) (1987) *Hedley Bull on Arms Control*, London: Palgrave Macmillan.

(NPT) of 1970 committed member states — other than the existing five nuclear powers, often referred to as the P5 because these are the same states which enjoy the right of permanent membership and veto power in the UN Security Council — to refrain from pursuing nuclear weapons. The Stockholm Conference in 1986 on Confidence and Security Building Measures, conducted by the OSCE (Organization for Security and Co-operation in Europe) was instrumental in forging processes of trust and verification between the Western and Eastern blocs, and led to the very important 1989 Conventional Forces in Europe (CFE) Treaty, bringing a long-overdue focus on the need to address conventional weapons and forces held by the opposing blocs. Between the Stockholm and CFE Treaties was the very important 1987 Intermediate-Range Nuclear Forces (INF) Treaty which agreed to eliminate completely the intermediate-range nuclear missiles held by the US and USSR.

While the CFE Treaty was clearly important as part of Gorbachev's focus on ending the Cold War, and the INF Treaty was a landmark agreement,[17] the other treaties, at least in some ways, seemed to fall short of expectations. The SALT treaties did not bring about real reductions in the nuclear arsenals of the superpowers (although the successor Strategic Arms Reduction Talks (START) treaties which commenced in 1991 have done so). While it is true that the NPT has successfully limited the number of nuclear weapon states in the world (only four states — Israel, India, Pakistan and North Korea — have joined the nuclear ranks) it did nothing to curb the vertical proliferation of nuclear weapons, which reached a staggering peak of around 70,000 some 15 years *after* the NPT had been agreed. Nor has the NPT been able to bring the P5 nuclear weapon states to eliminate all of their weapons, something which they are obliged to do under Article VI of that treaty and by other legal decisions. It is this particular failure — the nuclear weapon states, despite their numerous pledges, are clearly not moving to zero (even though their

---

17   Unfortunately, even the successes of the CFE and the INF Treaties have stalled recently, as tensions between the US and Russia rise. These developments cannot be examined here, but useful summaries are provided by Collina, Tom Z. (2012) *The Conventional Forces in Europe (CFE) Treaty and the Adapted CFE Treaty at a Glance*, Arms Control Association Fact Sheet. Available at legacy.armscontrol.org/factsheet/cfe; Collina, Tom Z. (2014) 'Russia Breaches INF Treaty, US Says', *Arms Control Today*, September. Available at: legacy.armscontrol.org/act/2014_09/News/Russia-Breaches-INF-Treaty-US-Says.

arsenals have shrunk considerably), and there are thousands of nuclear weapons, even 25 years after the end of the Cold War — which has produced a renewed focus on nuclear weapons for Robert O'Neill.

Rethinking the Role of Nuclear Weapons

When the Cold War ended — unexpectedly, almost abruptly, but with much celebration — there arose the opportunity to take stock of the position in which the world now found itself, and to reconsider those assumptions and policies that had prevailed in international relations for the previous 40-odd years. This profound change in the structure of world politics allowed us the opportunity to reflect seriously on what kind of a world we now wished to live in, and what steps would be necessary to sustain and increase the peace brought by the ending of the superpower confrontation. In reality, however, this did not happen — at least not in any systematic or meaningful way. Many of the troubled issues that existed during the Cold War — such as the Israeli–Palestinian conflict, the simmering resentment against Western, and especially US, policies and presence in the Middle East more broadly, the grave inequalities between states and people of the world where extreme poverty and vulnerability existed for many and immense wealth and political influence prevailed for some — did not receive the attention they deserved, now that the threat of global annihilation seemed to have passed. This was especially true in two key and interrelated areas: Russia was more or less isolated after the Cold War, as NATO and the EU expanded eastwards at an unwise pace, and nuclear weapons continued to remain the central component of security policy for the nuclear weapon states, even though the very *raison d'etre* for these arsenals was now a thing of the past.

We had seen, however, the glimmer of an alternative nuclear future during the negotiations for the INF Treaty between Ronald Reagan and Mikhail Gorbachev in Reykjavik in 1986. There, both leaders had advanced the idea that it was not only possible, but indeed feasible and desirable, to seek full nuclear disarmament. Disagreements over various issues, especially Reagan's plans for missile defence, resulted in a more modest achievement — the elimination of intermediate range forces — but, as Nikolai Sokov notes, the meeting at Reykjavik had 'become a symbol of sorts — an example that nuclear disarmament is within reach as long as political leaders have courage to make such a decision and break through bureaucratic politics and the maze of arcane nuclear balance theories'.[18] Reykjavik came to represent a tantalising opening for the complete elimination of nuclear weapons, led by the two superpowers,[19] but it was an opening that was not taken seriously or pursued at the time; nor was it revived by the nuclear weapon states, even when the Berlin Wall fell and the East–West confrontation came to an end a few years later.

Nevertheless, the idea was kept alive by some: the Pugwash Conferences on Science and World Affairs produced a seminal work examining the desirability and feasibility of a nuclear free world,[20] while the Henry L. Stimson Center, established in Washington DC in 1989, launched a substantial project on this same idea. The centre, as its website states, is geared toward 'providing policy alternatives, solving problems, and overcoming obstacles to a more peaceful and secure world'. In 1994, it began to examine the conditions under which the world might move toward the balanced and progressive elimination of nuclear weapons. Its Steering Committee brought out three reports.[21] Among those on this Steering Committee were Robert McNamara, US Secretary of Defense from 1961–1968, and General Andrew Goodpaster, Supreme Allied Commander, Europe (SACEUR), from 1969–1974. The presence of such individuals from the policy and military fields was an important element in this new process.

---

18 Sokov, Nikolai (2007) 'Reykjavik Summit: The Legacy and a Lesson for the Future', *Nuclear Threat Initiative*. Available at: www.nti.org/analysis/articles/reykjavik-summit-legacy/.
19 For useful accounts of these negotiations, see Bunn, George and John B. Rhinelander (2007) *Reykjavik Revisited: Toward a World Free of Nuclear Weapons*, World Security Institute and Lawyers Alliance for World Security. Available at: cisac.fsi.stanford.edu/sites/default/files/Bunn-Rhinelander-Reykjavik_Sept07.pdf; Goodby, James E. (2007) 'Looking Back: The 1986 Reykjavik Summit', *Arms Control Today*, September. Available at: legacy.armscontrol.org/act/2006_09/Lookingback.
20 Rotblat, Joseph et al. (1993) *A Nuclear Weapon Free World: Desirable? Feasible?* Oxford, Westview Press.
21 Stimson Center (1995) *Beyond the Nuclear Peril: The Year in Review and the Years Ahead*, Stimson Report 15, Steering Committee of the Project on Eliminating Weapons of Mass Destruction. Available at: www.stimson.org/images/uploads/research-pdfs/Report15.pdf; Stimson Center (1995) *An Evolving US Nuclear Posture*, Stimson Report 19, Steering Committee of the Project on Eliminating Weapons of Mass Destruction. Available at: www.stimson.org/images/uploads/research-pdfs/Report19.pdf; Stimson Center (1997) *An American Legacy: Building a Nuclear Weapon Free World*. Available at www.isn.ethz.ch/Digital-Library/Publications/Detail/?ots591=0c54e3b3-1e9c-be1e-2c24-a6a8c7060233&lng=en&id=93672.

The Canberra Commission Report

In turn, it appears that these studies came to influence the thinking of Australian Prime Minister Paul Keating and his Minister of Foreign Affairs, Gareth Evans. Their creation of the Canberra Commission reflected a sense of optimism that nuclear elimination was possible. The NPT had been extended indefinitely in 1995, and Australia had helped to bring about a treaty to eliminate another kind of weapon of mass destruction, the Chemical Weapons Convention, in 1993. The Labor Government saw Australia as an activist middle-power, a 'good international citizen'. But the event that most led to the creation of the Canberra Commission was the resumption of French nuclear testing in the South Pacific. Keating noted:

> No image in the twentieth century has seared our collective consciousness like that of the mushroom cloud. And in our minds that image of the bomb defined the Cold War ... We assumed that because the Cold War was over, the weapons that defined it had miraculously disappeared as well ... the realisation that this was not so came with the announcement by President Chirac, on 13 June 1995, that France would conduct a series of eight underground nuclear tests at Muroroa atoll in French Polynesia.[22]

Keating gathered a group of prominent, informed thinkers and practitioners into an independent commission and tasked them with assessing the options for a nuclear free world. He conceded that over the years, various anti-nuclear groups had campaigned for this, and had prepared many reports on nuclear dangers (and, indeed, civil society groups continue to be highly active in this field), but importantly, up until that time, no *government* had ever put its name to a report backing elimination. He stated:

> I wanted to put the authority of a sovereign government behind the push to rid the world of nuclear weapons ... I thought we had an unprecedented and possible unrepeatable opportunity to begin to move to a new strategic environment which offered not just a reduction in the number of nuclear weapons, but their elimination.[23]

---

22 Keating, Paul (1998) 'Eliminating Nuclear Weapons: A Survival Guide for the Twenty-First Century', Public Lecture, University of New South Wales, 25 November. Available at: www.keating.org.au/shop/item/eliminating-nuclear-weapons---25-november-1998.
23 Ibid.

Robert O'Neill, then Chichele Professor of the History of War at All Souls College, Oxford, was an obvious choice for membership of the Canberra Commission. Not only was he a gifted Australian scholar in international relations, holding prestigious positions at Oxford, the International Institute for Strategic Studies, and The Australian National University, but he was also an experienced soldier and strategist. He had first-hand knowledge of arms control, nuclear non-proliferation, nuclear strategy, and nuclear policy. In 2007, looking back on the Canberra Commission initiative, Robert O'Neill was to state: 'it was clear to me that the role of nuclear weapons had changed since the end of the Cold War and it was high time to re-examine their utility. Proliferation had become a greater danger and the possibility of nuclear weapons falling into the hands of terrorists was another new factor to be addressed.'[24]

Others among the 17 commissioners were former prime ministers, ambassadors, eminent scientists, and civilian and military leaders. Two of the commissioners had been part of the US military establishment: Robert McNamara, and General Lee Butler, former Commander in Chief of the US Strategic Air Command. Former Chief of the Defence Staff and head of British Armed Forces, Field Marshal Lord Carver, was an additional military voice. Their appointment was deliberate. The Keating Government recognised that the report would need to demonstrate its credibility to the security and defence policy communities if it was to be taken seriously.

Over the course of several months, the commissioners met to consider ways to reduce the dangers posed by the ongoing retention of nuclear weapons. It should be noted that at the outset, there was no clear consensus among the commissioners about the nature or extent of the problem, or about the steps which should be taken. But after several meetings, intense deliberation, and review of the technical and political issues canvassed by an extensive range of background papers, the commissioners' unanimous view presented in their report was that a balanced, phased, and verified elimination process was clearly necessary.

---

24 O'Neill, Robert (2007) 'World Order Under Stress: Issues and Initiatives for the Twenty-First Century', Cunningham Lecture, The Academy of the Social Sciences in Australia.

The *report*'s essential message was as follows: as long as any one state has nuclear weapons, other states will want them also; as long as nuclear weapons exist, there is a chance that they will be used, either deliberately or by accident; and, that any use of nuclear weapons would be catastrophic.[25] The report examined the strategic, technological, and political arguments usually put forward in support of retaining nuclear weapons, and made a comprehensive and persuasive case against them. It argued that without elimination, the world faced increased threats of proliferation, nuclear terrorism, and nuclear use.

As part of the growing debate on the issue of elimination, the report consolidated and extended the view that the utility of nuclear weapons — an issue that was never wholly or logically resolved, even during the Cold War — was even less convincing today.[26] After all, despite their possession of vast nuclear arsenals, states have accepted stalemate or even defeat (the US in Vietnam, Soviet Union in Afghanistan, and France in Indo-China, when strategic and moral calculations ruled out any use of nuclear weapons in these conflicts) and have suffered calamitous assaults upon their territory (for instance, in September 2001 in the US, when the presence of a vast nuclear arsenal did nothing to deter terrorism and was utterly unhelpful in responding to it). Moreover, the new kinds of security threat faced by the world meant that nuclear weapons and nuclear deterrence were at best redundant, and at worst, obstacles to international security.[27] The only utility accorded to nuclear weapons was that they possibly deterred against a nuclear attack by another nuclear state. But even in this case, the elimination of these weapons would be a positive gain. If nuclear weapons served no useful purpose, then retaining them would be costly, would invite further proliferation, and would sooner or later result in them being used.

---

25   Department of Foreign Affairs and Trade (1996) *Report of the Canberra Commission on the Elimination of Nuclear Weapons*, Canberra.
26   For detailed examinations of the commission's origin, arguments, and impact, see Hanson, Marianne and Carl J. Ungerer (1998) 'Promoting an Agenda for Nuclear Weapons Elimination: The Canberra Commission and Dilemmas of Disarmament', *Australian Journal of Politics and History* 44(4), pp. 533–51; Hanson, Marianne and Carl J. Ungerer (1999) 'The Canberra Commission: Paths Followed, Paths Ahead', *Australian Journal of International Affairs* 53(1), pp. 5–17.
27   Hanson, Marianne (2002) 'Nuclear Weapons as Obstacles to Security', *International Relations* 16(3), pp. 361–79.

While urging that as strategic circumstances change, so too must strategic thinking, the Canberra Commission report laid out a series of practical immediate, reinforcing, and final steps which could be taken to move towards a nuclear weapon free world. Immediate steps — such as devaluing the role of nuclear weapons in security policies, taking nuclear forces off alert, removing warheads from delivery vehicles, hastening reductions between the US and Russia, negotiating a Comprehensive Test Ban Treaty and a Fissile Material Cut-Off Treaty, and providing mutual no-first-use pledges, were all things that the nuclear weapon states could do without damaging their security prospects.[28]

The commissioners agreed that while nuclear weapons could not be dis-invented, we could certainly devalue, phase-out, eliminate, and outlaw their possession and use. In the same way that prohibition regimes have been put in place for other weapons of mass destruction — chemical and biological weapons — prohibitions adhered to even by the most powerful states in the international system, so too could nuclear weapons be stigmatised and relegated to the annals of history. The fundamental thinking behind this concept, which has carried through to the present day, was that humans have the power to determine their future and to seek a world in which security can be achieved without recourse to inhumane weapons, which in any case are bound to have disastrous global impacts if they are ever used. We cannot dis-invent chemical or biological weapons, nor indeed the gas ovens used by the Nazis, but human sensibility and condemnation can produce legal constraints against what are increasingly seen to be inhumane, abhorrent, and unacceptable practices. Indeed it is this key idea which has led to the Humanitarian Initiative against nuclear weapons (discussed below). And in any case, as the commissioners pointed out, the sophisticated level of modern conventional weaponry is more than adequate to make it the first choice for military action: deterrence can be achieved with conventional weapons, as can any response to aggression and/or any instance of a state which seeks to develop nuclear weapons after a nuclear free world has been achieved.[29]

---

28 Department of Foreign Affairs and Trade (1996) *Report of the Canberra Commission on the Elimination of Nuclear Weapons*, Canberra.
29 For more detailed analysis of the utility of nuclear weapons and how this in turn shaped the commissioners' findings, see Hanson, Marianne (2002) 'Nuclear Weapons as Obstacles to Security', *International Relations* 16(3); Hanson, Marianne (2005) 'Regulating the Possession and Use of Nuclear Weapons: Ideas, Commissions, and Agency in International Security Politics: The Case of the Canberra Commission', in Ramesh Thakur, Andrew F. Cooper and John English (eds), *International Commissions and the Power of Ideas*, Tokyo: Nations University Press.

The Australian Government had changed during the course of the Canberra Commission's deliberations, and Keating and Evans were no longer in power. The new conservative Liberal Government, which had sought to distance itself from its Labor predecessor, was lukewarm in its promotion of the report. Notwithstanding this, analysts from around the world recognised the value of the report as an independent analysis of the nuclear issue by distinguished and hard-headed experts.[30]

The Tokyo Forum on Facing Nuclear Dangers

The Canberra Commission had made the point that a world that was divided into states that had nuclear weapons and those that did not was unsustainable. In other words, while we had been successful in limiting the number of states that possessed nuclear weapons, we should not assume that this could be contained indefinitely. The five acknowledged nuclear weapon states under the NPT could not reserve to themselves the unique security benefits that nuclear weapons allegedly brought, while at the same time denying these same benefits to other states. The bargain of the NPT had been that non-nuclear states would promise never to acquire nuclear weapons, in exchange for the nuclear weapon states giving up their nuclear arsenals (albeit at some unnamed point). The nuclear states were to move to nuclear disarmament, and also assist non-nuclear weapon states wanting to utilise nuclear energy for peaceful purposes. The extension of the NPT in 1995 had been a reassertion of this bargain. Although some states were reluctant to extend the regime indefinitely — because extension clearly favoured the nuclear weapon states — they ultimately agreed to the extension, *inter alia,* on the basis that the nuclear armed states would fulfil their promise to disarm.

Yet this promise remains unfulfilled, even 25 years after the Cold War ended. Certainly the nuclear states have reduced their stockpiles considerably during this time — we now have 'only' around 16,000

---

30   Indicative was the assessment in the *Bulletin of the Atomic Sciences* which labelled the report as a 'no-nonsense road map'. Moore, Mike (1996) 'A Boost for Abolition', *Bulletin of the Atomic Sciences* 52(6).

nuclear weapons in existence[31] — but the pace of reductions has been slow. Moreover, most of the practical steps (suggested by the Canberra Commission and subsequent reports) have not been taken by the nuclear weapon states. Nuclear forces remain on high alert; all these states continue to modernise their nuclear arsenals, still touting the alleged benefits of their nuclear weapons in their security policies; the Comprehensive Nuclear-Test-Ban Treaty has not entered into force; and we have no Fissile Material Cut-off Treaty. The disillusion felt by many non-nuclear states has been palpable, and the vast majority of these have now given up hope that disarmament can be reached via the promises of the NPT.

India had long denounced the unequal nature of the NPT and a system that allowed the P5 to retain their arsenals while denying nuclear weapons to any other states. This sense of injustice, together with the rise to power of the hard-line Bharatiya Janata Party, led to India conducting nuclear tests in mid-May 1998, an event which propelled Pakistan to follow suit later that month. The proliferation of nuclear weapons to the South Asian continent (Israel had also developed a nuclear weapons capability, but refused to confirm or deny this) raised concerns throughout the world. It was denounced by most states, including by the nuclear weapon states, and prompted the then Prime Minister of Japan, Ryutaro Hashimoto, to establish a new commission, the Tokyo Forum for Nuclear Non-Proliferation and Disarmament, in August 1998. The forum met four times and produced its report in July 1999, *Reducing Nuclear Dangers: An Action Plan for the Twenty-First Century*.[32]

Once again, Robert O'Neill was asked to contribute his experience and advice, although most members of the Tokyo Forum were newcomers to this kind of disarmament diplomacy and had not participated in the Canberra Commission. There were disagreements between some of the forum's members, but all subscribed to the general thrust of the report, namely, that the proliferation recently seen in South Asia was a harbinger of future dangers and that renewed attention had to be given to the issue of nuclear weapons. The forum differed from the

---

31 Arms Control Association (2015) *Nuclear Weapons: Who has What at a Glance*. Available at: www.armscontrol.org/factsheets/Nuclearweaponswhohaswhat.
32 Ministry of Foreign Affairs of Japan (1999) *Facing Nuclear Dangers: An Action Plan for the Twenty-First Century: The Report of the Tokyo Forum for Nuclear Non-Proliferation and Disarmament*. Available at: www.mofa.go.jp/policy/un/disarmament/forum/tokyo9907/.

Canberra Commission in that it was a direct response to proliferation, and focused more on the dangers of proliferation, but essentially it reiterated what the Canberra Commission had painstakingly pointed out less than three years earlier. If the Canberra Commission appeared at a time of substantial optimism in world politics, the forum was a response to a deteriorated security landscape. The forum noted that 'much has changed since the Canberra Commission issued its important report in 1996', and that 'troubling signs are now evident on many fronts'.[33]

Its first key recommendation was that the world must '[s]top and reverse the unravelling of the Nuclear Non-Proliferation Treaty regime by reaffirming the treaty's central bargain'. To do this, the nuclear weapon states were urged to demonstrate 'tangible progress in nuclear disarmament', and non-nuclear states pressed to work actively to discourage any further nuclear proliferation. The practical steps outlined in the Canberra Commission report were again urged, but there was an additional focus on stopping and reversing the proliferation in South Asia (Recommendation 11) and specific attention was paid to the dangers of missile proliferation and missile defence. In sum, this forum essentially amplified the Canberra Commission's message further; it too drew positive acclaim from various organisations and analysts.

Ultimately, however, and despite the best efforts of Canberra Commissioners and Tokyo Forum members, the nuclear weapon states paid little heed to their recommendations. Security conditions worsened in subsequent years, with the rise of jihadi-driven terrorism against the West and accompanying turmoil within the Middle East, the decision taken by North Korea in 2006 to join the ranks of the nuclear weapon states (and its four sets of nuclear tests, the most recent conducted on 6 January 2016), and an ongoing deterioration in US–Russian relations. Unfortunately, none of these developments help to persuade the leaders of the nuclear weapon states to take seriously the need for nuclear elimination, even though none of them could be addressed effectively by the use of nuclear weapons. The possession of an all-purpose nuclear security blanket — no matter how unsuitable such weapons are for preventing or responding to crises — continued to dictate the policies of these states.

---

33 Ibid.

While modest reductions continued by the US and Russia (especially via the New START Treaty), none of the relatively cost-free practical steps have been taken, much to the dismay of most of the world's states. A number of other studies reiterated the points first made prominent by the Canberra Commission,[34] and the important arguments in favour of elimination first made in 2007 by the highly authoritative American figures, George Shultz, William Perry, Henry Kissinger, and Sam Nunn, drew considerably on the groundbreaking work which O'Neill and others had done earlier.

A Renewed Emphasis on the Elimination of Nuclear Weapons: The Joint Australia–Japan International Commission on Nuclear Non-proliferation and Disarmament

The election of a new Labor Government in Australia in 2007 saw a further attempt to address these issues. Former Foreign Minister Gareth Evans (who had overseen the Canberra Commission and served on the Blix Commission) was supported by new Prime Minister Kevin Rudd in reasserting Australian leadership in nuclear elimination by establishing the Joint Australia–Japan International Commission on Nuclear Non-proliferation and Disarmament (ICNND). Eminent individuals invited to the Commission's Advisory Board included Henry Kissinger, Sam Nunn, and George Shultz, as well as George Robertson (former British Secretary of Defence and Secretary-General of NATO). Again, Robert O'Neill was enlisted to join this group, bringing with him his long years of scholarship in the field, and his positions on the Canberra Commission and Tokyo Forum. It is testament to O'Neill's esteemed standing that he has played such an important role right from the beginning of these endeavours, via the Canberra Commission, through to the most recent and extremely comprehensive

---

34   These included the Canadian Parliamentary Report, *Canada and the Nuclear Challenge: Reducing the Political Value of Nuclear Weapons for the Twenty-First Century*, which had appeared in December 1998, and the *Weapons of Mass Destruction Commission Report: Weapons of Terror: Freeing the World of Nuclear, Biological and Chemical Arms* (commonly known as the Blix Report) of July 2006.

approach taken by the ICNND. Its report[35] bears the hallmarks of the careful consideration given to these matters by Robert O'Neill, and his contributions constitute a very important thread linking these works from 1995 through to the 2010 report, and beyond. His published work in this field after the Cold War, especially *Alternative Nuclear Futures*[36] and *World Order Under Stress*,[37] add to his authoritative contributions to these crucial questions.

Clearly, these various reports have been instrumental in bringing about a re-thinking of the role of nuclear weapons in the post-Cold War era, and have resulted in the affirmation of the goal of a nuclear weapon free world by state leaders, military personnel, and notable others, including some unlikely sources. What we continue to see, however, is that even as the idea of zero nuclear weapons is becoming normalised, as leaders pledge their willingness to disarm, we are still a long way from the realisation of a nuclear free world. As a result, the 2015 Review Conference of the nuclear NPT saw a record number of states and organisations express their dismay and disappointment with the nuclear weapon states. O'Neill had pointed out in his Cunningham Lecture that 'the double standard built into the NPT is likely to prove fatal to the current regime'.[38] And so it appears to be the case. Many states have now lost hope that the NPT can bring about disarmament, as the P5 states seem unwilling even to adopt the practical steps long urged upon them. In response, 121 states have now signed the international pledge to ban nuclear weapons, an initiative that arose as the result of three important conferences held to examine the humanitarian consequences of nuclear weapons. This Humanitarian Initiative is likely to result in a nuclear weapon ban-treaty within a few years.

The nuclear weapon states will not support such a move. But this is an important development. While the nuclear states will not sign such a treaty, they are likely to be increasingly constrained by

---

35 International Commission on Nuclear Non-proliferation and Disarmament (2010) *Eliminating Nuclear Threats: A Practical Agenda for Global Policymakers*. Available at: icnnd.org/Pages/default.aspx.
36 Baylis, John and Robert O'Neill (eds) (2000) *Alternative Nuclear Futures: The Role of Nuclear Weapons in the Post-Cold War World*, Oxford: Oxford University Press.
37 O'Neill, Robert (2007) 'World Order Under Stress: Issues and Initiatives for the Twenty-First Century', Cunningham Lecture, The Academy of the Social Sciences in Australia.
38 O'Neill, Robert (2007) 'World Order Under Stress: Issues and Initiatives for the Twenty-First Century', Cunningham Lecture, The Academy of the Social Sciences in Australia.

a legal provision formally outlawing nuclear weapons. And while a ban-treaty will not, of course, lead automatically or immediately to elimination, it will assist in the process of further stigmatising and eventually outlawing the possession and use of nuclear weapons. In the past, the establishment of a legal prohibition has preceded the eventual elimination of a particular weapon (this has been the case with landmines, cluster munitions, biological and chemical weapons) and this is also likely to be a watershed development in the moves towards a nuclear free world.

Ultimately, of course, it is only the leaders of the nuclear weapon states who can take these steps, and commissioners and scholars can do no more than advocate for what they see as the most prudent course of action. But this does not mean that we should disregard the effects of these activities. They have been vital in raising public consciousness and keeping this issue alive, and in providing clear and achievable goals for the steady phasing-out of all nuclear arsenals. The activities of Robert O'Neill and others like him, and the works they have produced, remain an important body of knowledge which continues to inform current debates and decisions taken by advocacy groups, individuals and, increasingly, by states who are keen to see advances in disarmament.

Conclusion

One of the problems that has become evident over the years is that governments appear not to take seriously what expert security specialists have to say, even though these experts have decades of experience behind them, can point to the lessons of history, and are often able to take a detached and dispassionate view of issues. This was observed by Robert O'Neill with reference to the invasion of Iraq in 2003.[39] He noted that there was widespread opposition to the Iraq War, and that he and the majority of his colleagues opposed that action on a number of grounds. Unfortunately, '[t]he US and allied governments simply put their fingers into their ears and took no notice of what experts had to say, while their soldiers and others … have borne the fearful cost of this disregard'. He argues that there has

---

39   O'Neill, Robert (2007) 'World Order Under Stress: Issues and Initiatives for the Twenty-First Century', Cunningham Lecture, The Academy of the Social Sciences in Australia.

13. A PIVOTAL MOMENT FOR GLOBAL NUCLEAR ARMS CONTROL

been, 'a propensity of the leading Western governments participating, including our own [Australian Government] to ignore sound advice at the outset and then, when in trouble, to pretend that everything is going much better than it is'.

The same can be said of the nuclear elimination issue: nuclear states appear to believe that the nuclear status quo can be maintained indefinitely, and that the risks are low. In this sense, those who continue to rely on nuclear weapons to keep the peace, and who appear not to be worried by the prospect of accidental or terrorist use, are surely not realists, but might be better described as idealists. Such idealism is misplaced; we have been immensely fortunate that nuclear weapons have not been used since 1945. Hedley Bull made the point as early as 1961 that 'the danger of nuclear war by accident is more serious than that of deliberate and premeditated attack'.[40] This thought has also clearly influenced Robert O'Neill. Numerous close calls have occurred,[41] and it beggars belief to suggest that continuing with sanguine policies will save us from disaster. Robert Oppenheimer noted in 1946: 'It would seem to me visionary in the extreme, and not practical, to hope that methods which have so sadly failed in the past to avert war will succeed in the face of this far greater [nuclear] peril.' It is vital, as a fellow Canberra Commissioner, Richard Butler noted, to 'reverse history's greatest accident' by outlawing and eliminating nuclear weapons.[42]

But the reluctance to take the advice of experts who have closely studied these issues continues. Even the repeated calls for elimination made by Kissinger and his colleagues appear to have fallen on deaf ears. If these weapons — which might or might not have played a role in stabilising relations during the Cold War — are of little or no use today, and if their retention will lead to further proliferation, possible terrorist acquisition, and mistaken or deliberate use, and if today's security concerns require and can be met by a robust conventional capability — which

---

40 Bull, Hedley (1961) *The Control of the Arms Race: Disarmament and Arms Control in the Missile Age*, London: Weidenfeld & Nicolson, p. 207.
41 Highly recommended are Schlosser, Eric (2013) *Command and Control: Nuclear Weapons, the Damascus Accident, and the Illusion of Safety*, New York: Penguin; and Lewis, Patricia et al. (2014) *Too Close for Comfort: Cases of Near Nuclear Use and Options for Policy*, London: Chatham House. Available at: www.chathamhouse.org/publications/papers/view/199200.
42 Butler, Richard (1996) *The Elimination Of Nuclear Weapons: Reversing History's Greatest Accident*, The Sir Robert Madgwick Lecture, delivered at the University of New England, Armidale, 1 May.

it is abundantly clear the great powers do possess — then there is no strategic need to maintain costly, imprecise, clumsy (in terms of military utility), dangerous and manifestly inhumane nuclear weapons.

Robert O'Neill and David Schwarz reminded us that Hedley Bull's contribution to the debate on arms control 'was based on a deep scepticism not only about those who urged rearmament, but also about those who advocated arms control and disarmament measures'.[43] It is quite clear that this approach has also informed Robert O'Neill's own work. For him, it has not been enough simply to accept prevailing practices, or to acquiesce to any fashion of the times and leave unexamined those things which deserve to be re-examined. By being willing to reconsider the role of nuclear weapons in a changed strategic landscape, he has given us a prudent assessment and a clear course to follow. He noted that Bull 'emphasized the need to re-examine the analytic assumptions underlying' various theories and practices, and it is clear that he has done the same thing when he reappraised the role of nuclear weapons. Reversing his previous thinking on the utility of these weapons required some courage, and a willingness to risk the ire of peers who continued to hold fast to the old doctrines.

There were many who were fortunate to study under the guidance of Robert O'Neill over the years, and who benefitted greatly from his intellectual energy and critical abilities. And we can continue to draw inspiration and strength from his post-academic activities. In 1981 he wrote that 'all who are professionally concerned with strategic thinking, particularly those who work in universities and the media' are obliged to 'make a major effort to stimulate wider discussion' of the security problems that beset the world.[44] Robert O'Neill has done this most admirably in alerting the world to the nuclear dangers which continue to exist long after the Cold War has ended, and his efforts have paved the way for the acceptance, at least at a declaratory level, of the idea of eliminating nuclear weapons. We can seek to follow his example and hope that one day, his and our prescriptions for a safer world might be heeded.

---

43   O'Neill, Robert and David Schwartz (eds) (1987) *Hedley Bull on Arms Control*, London: Palgrave Macmillan.
44   O'Neill, Robert and D. M. Horner (eds) (1981) *New Directions in Strategic Thinking*, London: Allen & Unwin.

14

Robert O'Neill's Institutional Leadership: The End of the Cold War and the Re-emergence of a Global World Order

John Hillen

International affairs are influenced by many factors, not the least of them Harold McMillan's warning, 'events, dear boy, events'. Statesmen, political leaders, military commanders, theorists, and influential writers on the topic play their role in the unfolding shape of the international arena. So too institutions — empires, states, militaries, government ministries, universities at times, international organisations, sub-state organisations, religious groups, and other popular movements — might all wield a geopolitical agenda and purpose that forms and sculpts history. But the role of the private institution — the so-called think tank — is a relatively new phenomenon, perhaps some 60–70 years old

The role of the private research institution in helping shape international affairs, rather than simply analysing their passing after the facts, is less well known. However, when one turns to look at the career of Robert (Bob) O'Neill AO, and considers his decade at the helm, as Director and then Chairman of the International Institute for Strategic Studies (IISS), one can see how a think tank — and its leader — can play a very outsized role in actually determining global affairs; or, at the very least, laying the intellectual and policy groundwork for tremendous shifts in geopolitics, and by doing so, helping these shifts come about.

During the time that Bob O'Neill was Director of IISS (1982–1987) he uniquely positioned the institute to accommodate a reasoned but passionate set of debates and deliberations about a very different grand strategy pursued by President Ronald Reagan and the United States — strategic questions that were at the time driving the European members of the Atlantic Alliance and some in the US further and further apart. O'Neill did not let the institute become fractured by this challenge, but rather led IISS to make intellectual space for fairly examining the new elements of Reagan's strategy and US actions, even while subjecting them to rigorous strategic analysis. His leadership paid dividends, keeping IISS not only relevant but, indeed, still central to questions of superpower rivalry and potential nuclear conflict; the Reagan grand strategy was able to unfold to good effect — pushed, questioned, and shaped by the work of IISS.

At almost the same time, recognising the likely erosion of the criticality of the institute's founding *raison d'etre* (managing the nuclear balance between rival superpowers), O'Neill also positioned IISS for influence and access elsewhere in the strategic world — displaying the foresight to anticipate a more multipolar world in the near future. He expanded and built the institute's finances, research agenda, membership base, and governance structure to make the narrowly focused Atlantic Alliance think tank become the most influential and truly global public policy research institute in international affairs. Any one of these feats would have been notable, but to do both in tandem sets the bar for visionary institutional leadership and influence.

By the end of his tenure as director, the IISS research agenda, conference schedules, complexion of IISS membership, and governance were all changing to encompass much of the strategic world that did *not* represent only the competition between US and Soviet blocs of influence. In his term as Chairman of the IISS Council (1996–2001), O'Neill expanded on this diversification of IISS's traditional NATO-based and nuclear issues-oriented membership, research expertise, and convening authority. Working with the director at the time, O'Neill helped create the para-diplomatic regional dialogues in Asia and the Middle East for which IISS is so well known today, and made the institute the preeminent global strategic research institutes of its time.

However, in 1982, when Bob O'Neill arrived to take over IISS, none of that was assured, let alone in the cards. It would be a formidable leadership challenge just to keep the institute from being riven by the strategic upheavals of that time.

IISS and the Advent of the Reagan Doctrine

Sir Michael Howard, one of IISS's founders, has described the purpose of the institute at its inception and the events that led to its founding.[1] IISS would study the military problems and strategies of the world — especially those the nuclear age, exclusively a European issue at the time of IISS's founding in 1958. The institute's quarterly journal was tellingly named *Survival*, and its premier research publication, *The Military Balance*, was the indispensable public accounting of the world's military forces. The philosophical heritage of the institution was hard-headed and realistic (they knew disarmament was impractical), but the research agenda was ultimately interested in *avoiding* war — especially nuclear war. For the 24 years between IISS's founding and the arrival of Australian infantry veteran Bob O'Neill as its director, it was one of the world's preeminent research institutions that had global membership, but a Western European outlook on issues of the nuclear arms race, strategies of deterrence, and superpower rivalry.

The rise to power of President Ronald Reagan in 1980–1981 posed a challenge to the intelligent, hotly debated, but likely near-consensus among IISS members in 1980 about the suitability of the various permutations of détente tried by all American administrations since Eisenhower. President Reagan promised the end of détente and a strategy of confrontation. His predecessor, Jimmy Carter, had offered a softer version of détente than his predecessors, saying in 1977 that the US should be 'free of that inordinate fear of communism'.[2]

---

1   Howard, Michael (2006) *Captain Professor: A Life in War and Peace*, London: Continuum, pp. 153–65.
2   Carter, Jimmy (1977) Speech at Notre Dame University, University of South California Santa-Barbara American Presidency project records, 21 May.

Reagan accused Carter of accommodating the Soviet Union's worst behaviours and resisting the connection between Marxist and communist movements around the world and the USSR. Mainstream Republicans did not escape Reagan's criticisms. His conservative allies, a political insurgency of sorts within the Republican Party, made much of President Ford declaring in a debate with Carter that Eastern Europe was not under Soviet domination and insisting in the follow up that Poland, Romania, and Yugoslavia were free from Soviet interference.

The impression of weakness inherent in Carter's version of détente, exacerbated by the Soviet invasion of Afghanistan and the taking of American hostages in Iran in 1979, doomed Carter's re-election chances in the opinion of many historians. In 1980, Ronald Reagan stormed to a huge victory over President Carter, promising to return America to strength and greatness again — in large part by vigorously resisting the USSR, Soviet-inspired movements, and supporting anti-communist movements the world over. Reagan noted:

> As the foundation of my foreign policy, I decided we had to send as powerful a message as we could to the Russians that we weren't going to stand by anymore while they armed and financed terrorists and subverted democratic governments. Our policy was to be one based on strength and realism. I wanted peace through strength, not peace through a piece of paper.[3]

To an institution such as IISS, enjoying a highly intelligent and now somewhat rehearsed existence as a centre of strategic thinking about arms control, the nuclear balance, and theories of deterrence, this aggressive rhetoric and the implicit Reagan policy of confrontation was a challenge to absorb. As IISS veteran Sir Lawrence Freedman has written:

> The status of the Institute depended on its ability to pay attention to its core business, which had always been focused on transatlantic relations and the conduct of the Cold War. The context was a sharp discontinuity in American policy. During the 1970s the Institute had worked naturally within the mainstream transatlantic consensus, which was focused on the appropriate mix of détente and defence, which led to a concentration on the conduct of arms control.

---

3   Reagan, Ronald (1990) *An American Life: The Autobiography*, Kindle edition, New York: Simon & Schuster, loc. 3778–80.

Yet during the Jimmy Carter years (in which many IISS alumni served) this consensus began to be challenged. Key figures in the membership were taking an increasingly sceptical view of both Soviet intentions and in consequence the role of arms control and the durability of deterrence (notably Albert Wohlstetter among the senior figures and Colin Gray, who was briefly on the staff, among the Young Turks). The debate became increasingly polarised, and by the early 1980s this polarisation had spread to transatlantic relations. In Ronald Reagan's Washington the new mainstream view was to doubt Soviet motives, question the value of arms control and prepare for a period of intensive arms racing. Only Margaret Thatcher's government showed any sympathy, yet even in Britain the official line remained pro-détente and pro-deterrence.

This created real political difficulties for IISS. It needed to work with the US government, which was wary of consorting with organisations which were perceived to be promoting erroneous visions, and the major charitable foundations, which were often more attached to the policies of the 1970s and who saw their role as being to challenge and rein in the provocations of the Reaganauts. On the streets there was an increasingly vocal movement protesting against nuclear weapons and claiming that official policies were propelling the world to disaster. There were many pitfalls in this situation for an international institute, which had to be sensitive to the political and intellectual currents in a range of countries if it was to satisfy an increasingly diverse membership, without losing its way and purpose.[4]

The first few years of the Reagan Administration did not do much to settle nerves or smooth over varying opinion, and a National Intelligence Council report of the time acknowledged, with understatement, substantial 'differences between the United States and our West European allies'.[5] By 1982, as O'Neill was being recruited to be IISS's first non-European Director of the IISS, Cold War tensions were at their height as the American administration drove hard to reverse what it saw as Soviet ascendency and American decline. Reagan's new Secretary of State George Schultz described the attitude of the administration and conflict with Europe thusly:

---

4   Freedman, Lawrence (2006) 'Bob O'Neill and The Art of Academic Leadership', *Australian Journal of International Affairs* 60(1), pp. 13–17.
5   Brands, Hal (2014) *What Good Is Grand Strategy?: Power and Purpose in American Statecraft from Harry S. Truman to George W. Bush*, Ithaca: Cornell University Press, p. 115.

Throughout the cold war era, America's responsibilities as a superpower had been fulfilled with impressive success. But fear of flagging will or failure had become pervasive. The American presidency had become a story of successive agonies: the assassination of John F. Kennedy; the anguished departure of Lyndon Johnson at the nadir of the Vietnam War; Richard Nixon's de facto impeachment; Gerald Ford's healing but brief stewardship; and Jimmy Carter's miseries, which, with a weak smile, he spread across the American and international scene. In June 1980, I had said in a speech to the Business Roundtable, 'All around us, and plain for all the world to see, is confusion about our aims, deterioration in our world position, and deep concern, perhaps fear, that we are no longer able to establish a tough-minded sense of direction and stick to it.' Now, in mid-1982, we were still besieged by problems and buffeted by events. Ronald Reagan's program, off to a strong start at home, was struggling abroad. President Reagan had set out to restore America's strength, optimism, and 'can do' spirit. He was strengthening our defence capabilities, invigorating the morale of our men and women in uniform, and carrying the message of political and economic freedom around the world. But the president's foreign policy refused to lift off and soar. I felt the United States held the winning hand, but it was proving a difficult hand to play. Bitterness marked the discord between the United States and our European allies over the proposed construction of a gigantic 3,500-mile pipeline running from Siberia through rugged terrain to carry gas, Soviet gas, into Europe. The American and European economies were in a recession, and the pipeline contract meant good jobs during a time when they were hard to get.[6]

Yet the upcoming year, 1983, would be critical for nuclear arms negotiations: close U.S.–European coordination would be essential. New Soviet missiles, SS-20s, had been deployed and, since the 1970s, explicitly and directly targeted on Europe. These intermediate-range missiles could not reach the United States. Their purpose was to intimidate West Europeans as part of an ongoing Soviet effort to drive a wedge between the United States and our NATO allies. U.S. missiles, as agreed by all NATO members, were scheduled to be deployed beginning in late 1983 on European soil as a counter to these Soviet deployments. Crucial negotiations would determine whether the arms race would be speeded up or scaled back. The pressing need for coherence and unity in the alliance would be practically impossible to manage, I knew, unless we could dissipate the acrimonious atmosphere

---

6   Shultz, George P. (2010) *Turmoil and Triumph: My Years as Secretary of State*, Kindle edition, New York: Scribner, loc. 128–35.

with the Europeans created by the pipeline dispute. U.S.–Soviet relations had gone into the deep freeze when the Soviets invaded Afghanistan just after Christmas of 1979. Now the Soviet-backed crackdown in Poland further deepened the cold. Relations between the two superpowers were not simply bad; they were virtually non-existent. West German Chancellor Helmut Schmidt said to me in May 1982, 'The superpowers are not in touch with each other's reality. The Soviets can't read you. More human contact is needed.' 'The Soviet system is incompetent and cannot survive,' I had said in a speech at Stanford in 1979. 'In the struggle with communism freedom is the ideological victor in the world.' Now, three years later, in 1982, I had not changed my mind. The Soviets had to be made to realise that they could not succeed with aggression, nor could they win an arms race. But we did not want to spark conflict through fear or miss opportunities to resolve outstanding problems. President Reagan recognised the Soviet Union for what it was: aggressive, repressive, and economically bankrupt, but militarily powerful, with an arsenal of strategic nuclear weapons able to devastate us in thirty minutes. We must recognise that reality, I knew, but we should also be ready to deal with the Soviets more constructively if the opportunity arose. We had to gather support for this approach: from Congress, the press, and the public. Global stability depended on how we dealt with the Soviets.[7]

It was into this cauldron that Bob O'Neill was thrown in 1982 — plucked out of the antipodes and moved to the centre of the Cold War as director of the preeminent European think tank, studying its nuclear and military ramifications. His appointment was not unanimously supported, some perhaps thinking that if the aggressiveness of the Reagan doctrine threatened to riven the European-based membership, then it would take an insider to prevent such an outcome. But, O'Neill had notable bonafides as a Cold War scholar and strategist,[8] and he would need those to cement his position as a determined director, even while preparing to change and expand the focus of the institute to other military and strategic matters.

---

7   Ibid., loc. 148–54.
8   Bob was the editor or co-editor of a number of books on nuclear arms and Cold War strategy issues, including O'Neill (ed.) (1974) *The Strategic Nuclear Balance: An Australian Perspective*, Canberra: Strategic and Defence Studies Centre, The Australian National University; and O'Neill, Robert and David Schwartz (eds) (1987) *Hedley Bull on Arms Control*, London: Palgrave Macmillan.

O'Neill inherited an IISS membership that was largely resistant to the Reagan administration approach, which contrasted sharply to the carefully created strategic, military, and technical framework of détente that IISS had been a key player in constructing over the past decades. Even so, in the institute's research agenda and conference presentations, O'Neill made space for a rigorous and serious discussion of the new and highly controversial American strategy that was two years underway when he took charge. Too smart a leader to ever show anything but an even hand (to this day, I don't know how Bob really felt about it in his strategic heart at the time), he prepared the way for discussions that were scrupulously fair, and by doing so, the institute was able to show more openness to the new American strategy than others did at the time.[9]

It cannot be stressed how different the Reagan approach was to the consensus of the time. Reagan described his thinking in his autobiography. It was not considered a sophisticated view — especially by foreign policy sophisticates.

> The Soviet Union we faced during my first winter in office was guided by a policy of immoral and unbridled expansionism. During that first year, we embarked on a broad program of military renewal to upgrade our land, sea, and air forces and adopted a foreign policy aimed at making it clear to the Soviets that we now viewed them through a prism of reality: We knew what they were up to, we were not going to accept subversion of democratic governments, and we would never accept second place in the arms race. At the same time, recognising the futility of the arms race and the hair-trigger risk of annihilation it posed to the world, I tried to send signals to Moscow indicating we were prepared to negotiate a winding down of the arms race if the Soviets were also sincere about it — and proved it with deeds. These policies were linked: Because we now viewed the Soviets through the prism of reality, we knew we would never get anywhere with them

---

9   Bob later became a forceful and leading voice for the abolition of nuclear weapons on the Canberra Commission of 2006, so I don't think he'll ever be accused of being overly sympathetic to the hard line of Reagan's policies. But he was scrupulously fair. Ironically, Reagan made much of his own nuclear weapon abolitionist ambitions, including to Gorbachev during their first meetings. See Lettow, Paul (2006) *Ronald Reagan and His Quest to Abolish Nuclear Weapons*, New York: Random House.

at the arms control table if we went there in a position of military inferiority; if we were going to get them to sue for peace, we had to do it from a position of strength.[10]

The European-led near-consensus reflected in most IISS work at the time[11] maintained that the American position was strong enough — and improving it military or technologically would only upset the balance of power that the institute had so carefully analysed. O'Neill noted in his 1984 conference summary that IISS member Albert Carnesale 'summed up the European argument thus: "Western Europe objects to any change in a security system that seems to be working well enough as it is, therefore the burden of proof is on those who propose change."'[12]

However, fundamental to accepting the legitimacy of Reagan strategy and providing the beginnings of such 'a burden of proof' was that one had to accept that the Soviet Union had been measurably in the military ascendancy during the 1970's. As Hal Brands has written:

> Reagan was prepared to enter into arms-control negotiations on these and other weapons, but in the meantime he deemed it imperative to restore the leverage that came with military power. 'A sound East-West military balance is absolutely essential,' he stated; strength was the indispensable precondition to everything Reagan hoped to do.[13]

IISS, of course, was the premier independent measuring stick of the balance of military power. With the deployment of Soviet SS-20 missiles in Europe in the early 1980s, and the USSR's involvement in conflicts from Central America through to Afghanistan, that might not be so hard to prove in theory — but the Reagan response to it still powerfully challenged the mainstream consensus. For the most part, IISS members could live with the current balance of power as being balance. O'Neill, in guiding the work, research agenda, membership

---

10 Reagan, Ronald (1990) *An American Life: The Autobiography*, Kindle edition, New York: Simon & Schuster, loc. 7998–8006.
11 There has never been a true consensus on any issue in IISS — made up as it is of individual staff researchers and thousands of members. But on the nuclear balance question, détente, and deterrence, there was — as Lawrence Freedman referred to — as close to near-consensus as IISS members could get when compared with the Reagan approach.
12 O'Neill, Robert (1985) 'Conference Report', in *New Technology and Western Security Policy*, Part III: Papers from the IISS 26th Annual Conference in 1984, Adelphi Paper 189, London: IISS.
13 Brands, Hal (2014) *What Good Is Grand Strategy?: Power and Purpose in American Statecraft from Harry S. Truman to George W. Bush*, Ithaca: Cornell University Press, p. 111.

contributions, and conferences of the institute that would address the Reagan strategy, did not give voice to the idea that Reagan and Shultz were crying wolf or over-inflating Soviet ascendancy for political purposes (although many in Europe thought exactly that). As O'Neill noted at the 1983 annual conference in his report: 'Whatever their political significance, Soviet advances are real and, from an American perspective, the "balance" had altered unfavourably. Should the United States aim at superiority and not merely maintenance of parity remains the most important, albeit unresolved question.'[14]

Overall, and perhaps due to his strategic upbringing on the other side of the world, O'Neill exhibited more scholarly detachment from the transatlantic consensus and therefore ended up, in retrospect, appearing to enjoy more foresight or open-mindedness than most IISS experts or conferees in these mid-1980s gatherings. Summing up the attitude of annual conferees in 1983, O'Neill wrote: 'Little optimism was felt in the committee for the possibility of inducing change in Eastern Europe. At best the fruits for such Western policies (i.e. Reagan pressure) would be marginal although, of course, over a long time, the margins would accumulate.' Still, O'Neill opened the door to the Reagan line and its proponents, noting in the same proceedings:

> Yet the future may hold revolutionary changes in and for Eastern Europe rather than evolutionary ones. The Soviet Union's likely response to such changes is essentially unpredictable. She might simply muddle through or down, sensing inevitable decline in her empire she might consider alternatives.[15]

Although the IISS debates were heated at the time, and definitely unsettled well into the late 1980s, O'Neill's even-handed approach made space for the Reagan strategy to be examined seriously, and for IISS to be used as a critical sounding board. I see no evidence that the majority of the members, especially those European members who came of age forging the transatlantic mainstream consensus that Reagan so powerfully challenged, were ever convinced that the Reagan approach would be anything but disruptive to a well-thought out strategic near-consensus about how to resist Soviet aggression

---

14 O'Neill, Robert (1984) 'Conference Report', in *The Conduct of East–West Relations in the 1980s*, Part III: Papers from the IISS 25th Annual Conference in 1983, Adelphi Paper 189, London: International Institute for Strategic Studies.
15 Ibid.

without the confrontation Reagan appeared to promise. But, in the end, O'Neill's approach allowed for the institute's analysis and work to be part of what was indeed a coherent, if controversial, grand strategy from the administration — and one that ultimately was successful. As Hal Brand's recent archival examination of the administration has shown:

> These sources (NSC documents from the early 1980s) illustrate that there was a Reagan grand strategy — a comprehensive, long-term vision for U.S. policy toward Moscow. This strategy drew heavily on Reagan's own ideas and involvement, and utilized all elements of national power. It was premised on the idea that the Soviet Union was far weaker than it had looked in the late 1970s, and that the United States could take advantage of that weakness by exerting pressure in the military, economic, political, and ideological realms. This was the unifying rationale behind the major elements of Reagan's statecraft, from his enormous military buildup, to his eponymous doctrine of supporting anti-Soviet insurgents in the Third World, to his strident rhetorical condemnations of Moscow and other measures. The primary goal of these initiatives was not to force the collapse of the Soviet Union (as some hard-liners advocated), but to provide diplomatic leverage that could be used to moderate Soviet behavior and reduce Cold War tensions on terms favorable to the United States. In essence, Reagan's grand strategy — spelled out in presidential decision directives issued in 1982 and 1983 — was meant to capitalize on America's competitive advantages vis-à-vis Moscow, to reverse the tide of the Cold War, and then to begin the process of forging a more stable superpower relationship.[16]

SDI and IISS

The Reagan military build up, especially the deployment of Pershing intermediate range nuclear missiles in Western Europe, was controversial in IISS and the world over, but the administration's Strategic Defense Initiative (SDI) elicited even more emotion and aggravation among those who thought the nuclear balance was carefully and responsibly

---

16 See Brands, Hal (2014) *What Good Is Grand Strategy?: Power and Purpose in American Statecraft from Harry S. Truman to George W. Bush*, Ithaca: Cornell University Press, p. 103. I view this work as one of the few neutral treatments of Reagan's strategy and the end of the Cold War, positioned as it is between the hagiographies by Reagan's allies and the still spiteful analysis of his critics, who cannot bring themselves to acknowledge even a slight contribution of his strategy to the peaceful end of the Cold War.

understood by both super powers. SDI was as important to Reagan's strategy as it was disruptive to the nuclear balance consensus. Reagan later wrote: 'some people may take a different view, but if I had to choose the single most important reason, on the United States' side, for the historic breakthroughs that were to occur during the next five years in the quest for peace and a better relationship with the Soviet Union, I would say it was the Strategic Defense Initiative, along with the overall modernisation of our military forces'.[17]

However, in 1983–1984, even the perception of a technological advantage on one side of the Cold War, which could upend several decades of game theory and nuclear strategy, was an overwhelmingly unwelcome development for those who had built the existing transatlantic nuclear consensus. Many, including much of the IISS membership, channelled their disapproval into scepticism about the technological potential itself. Bob O'Neill took the issue head on — neither promoting the technology or the strategic changes it might portend, but also not resisting a mature discussion of its potentiality. It was no mean feat to walk this political tightrope. As Lawrence Freedman recalled:

> To some extent coming from Australia helped Bob establish his authority as Director of IISS. This nationality carried paid-up membership of the Western alliance but a degree of distance from the immediate transatlantic rows. Yet his effectiveness went beyond nationality, or even his natural diplomatic skills, to an understanding of the role of the Institute as a forum for debate and research. This was different to the stance taken during the IISS's pioneering years of the 1960s when it failed to address in its publications the most divisive issue of the time, the continuing war in Vietnam. A good example of Bob's approach, with which I happened to get involved, was the response to President Reagan's strategic defense initiative (SDI), better known as 'star wars', which as widely seen to be both foolhardy and provocative. Rather than refuse to take the issue seriously, which was for a time the inclination of European governments, Bob raised the money for an extensive, almost smothering program, of analysis, which eventually came to be published in a series of Adelphi Papers. Some of these contributed to moving the debate along, addressing the technical questions of missile defences as well as the more overtly

---

17 Reagan, Ronald (1990) *An American Life: The Autobiography*, Kindle edition, New York: Simon & Schuster, loc. 7994–7.

political and doctrinal. By the time this program was complete (which was never the case with the SDI itself) the world had moved on and East/West relations were moving into a more constructive phase. The key point was that nobody felt excluded, the important issues had been ventilated and the credibility of the Institute as a forum where these matters were addressed was enhanced. At the 1984 annual conference, for example, American policy-makers first began to engage with the anxieties of their allies over the implications of this particular policy.[18]

Bob O'Neill's willingness to take on SDI instead of deriding it technologically and strategically, or dismissing it as fantasy unworthy of strategic consideration, as many institutes of the time did, is a good example of his subtle but strong institutional leadership. He did not take sides, but rather gave numerous perspectives their day in the sun — and subjected each to analysis and critique. In the end, this approach not only helped IISS successfully navigate the challenge to it from the Reagan doctrine and the heightened Cold War tensions when Bob became director, but kept the institute coherent enough for Bob to implement his second great example of international strategic leadership during his time as IISS Director and later Chairman.

Preparing IISS for the Re-emergence of a Global World Order

Bob O'Neill's second major institutional move was to revitalise and build the infrastructure of the institute — financial resources, information technology, research staff, publications, and membership — by expanding and revitalising the core purpose and expertise of IISS. Starting as he did in the mid-1980s, and gaining momentum as Reagan and Gorbachev began to thaw the superpower tensions of the early 1980s, Bob repositioned the institute as a truly global body — in research expertise and membership — while still focusing on military issues and problems of strategy.

---

18   Freedman, Lawrence (2006) 'Bob O'Neill and The Art of Academic Leadership', *Australian Journal of International Affairs* 60(1), pp. 13–17.

Financially, the institute had not lived exactly hand to mouth in its first 25 years before O'Neill became director, but was close to it at times. And what resources it did enjoy — research grants, publications income, and membership fees — were related to the institute's core expertise in European security, the Atlantic Alliance, the nuclear balance of power, and the superpower rivalry.

O'Neill set about trying to draw in money to match a large challenge grant from the Ford Foundation that would give IISS its first true capital fund, and thereby control over the direction of its research agenda and the possibility of expanding the expertise of the institute beyond its core area. O'Neill succeeded in raising the funds, and hired a research staff to reinforce the expanded agenda of the institute, and build up competencies in other areas of strategy and military affairs. In particular, he raised funds from the Rockefeller Foundation for a regional security program, including an assistant director for regional security. He set about expanding the annual conference agenda, which had a long lead time (see below), but in the meantime he commissioned Adelphi Papers on Security in East Asia, the two Koreas, South African and other African security issues, and the Middle East — among other non-nuclear balance of power in Europe topics.

O'Neill also set out to improve other elements of the infrastructure at IISS beyond its financial base. When he arrived at IISS there were no computers, and so information technology as an important component of public policy research was introduced by O'Neill. He also took steps to widen the appeal and distribution of research and publications — many of which had been styled in the 1960s and were not part of an updated sales and distribution network.

Knowing that ultimately he was leading a membership based organisation, O'Neill launched a drive to add more IISS members from East Asia and the Middle East. Over some objections, he pushed for Chinese members and contributions, starting in the mid-1980s. He also worked to diversify the IISS Council, which along with the Trustees of IISS was the body of foreign policy notables who acted as the governing and advisory body for the institute. Council members were added from Asia and the Arab countries of the Middle East.

One of the most telling and profound expressions of IISS focus and activity — of its leadership, research staff, and membership interests — was the annual conference. Habitually held in Europe and almost always focused on some aspect of the nuclear arms race or super-power rivalry, the annual conference appropriately captured the intellectual energy of IISS and its members.

Bob inherited this Euro-nuclear-superpower focus. Prior to his arrival, as part of the usual pattern, in 1978, the topic of the conference was 'Prospects of Soviet Power in the 1980s'. In 1979, the institute met in Switzerland to discuss 'The Future of Strategic Deterrence'. The 1980 annual conference in Italy marked a bit of a departure from the usual nuclear balance issues, looking at conflict in the Third World, but through the lens of super power rivalry. A 1981 conference in the US explored America's security. The 1982 conference in The Hague looked at 'Defense and Consensus: The Domestic Aspects of Western Security'. The 1983 annual conference, Bob's first as director, was held in Ottawa and focused on 'The Conduct of East–West Relations in the 1980s'. With annual conferences some three years in the making and planning, at this time Bob started plans to re-orient the annual conference and the institute in general. 1984 saw the institute meet in Avignon to consider 'New Technology and Western Security Policy',[19] and 1985 saw the last of the classic cold war nuclear-balance IISS European conferences in Berlin, with a focus on 'Power and Policy: Doctrine, the Alliance, and Arms Control'.

In 1986, the O'Neill agenda for expanding and revitalising IISS's institutional reach and infrastructure came visibly onto the scene with the annual conference held in Kyoto, Japan, and featured many new (non-European) faces. 'East Asia, the West, and International Security' featured Henry Kissinger and speakers from Japan, China, Australia, and elsewhere. In O'Neill's summing up of that landmark conference, he departed from the standard nuclear balance language of IISS over the previous 28 years and referred to different strategic shaping factors, such as 'economic and social factors' that would 'dramatically' affect the relative standing of states and their security in Asia. He had a nuanced look at alliance structures, technology, economics, reform, 'the market revolution in China', and development

---

19 Read 'East–West' here in IISS patois of the time as 'Soviet Bloc–Western Bloc'. A few years later, Bob would be at pains in his 1986 conference write up to redefine 'East' for the institute as what was classically known as the Far East/Asia.

in the region. His approach foreshadowed a more subtle geopolitical and grand strategic approach to analysis than the more scientific nuclear throw-weight formulas of the European balance of power.[20]

The following year IISS was back in Europe with a conference in Barcelona — but one that strategically looked south, not east across central Europe. The focus of that 1987 conference (Bob's last as director) was security in the Mediterranean and the Middle East, and featured Israeli and Arab speakers, among others. O'Neill still allowed for some committee examination of Soviet–US–Europe Cold War issues, as they were still central to global security during this time of new IISS expansion. But O'Neill's push to have IISS expand its scope of research, its intellectual aperture, and its membership perspective paid dividends, even in its historically core area of expertise. The new global perspective pushed by O'Neill ironically allowed the institute to perhaps to lift its focus from the nuclear balance ledger book if you will, and see more broadly the whole of the strategic enterprise and the global arena. The work on the military dimensions of the super power rivalry presented at the southern-focused Mediterranean conference proved to be prescient — or at least Bob O'Neill was able to present it that way in the proceedings. Although an unexpectedly quick and dramatic beginning-of-the-end to the Cold War was still two years away, O'Neill remarked in his conference summing up that in reference to the US–Soviet conflict, 'we may well be at one of history's hinge points'.[21]

As the Cold War ended, a few subsequent IISS conferences sensibly returned to focus on the end of the superpower rivalry, but Bob had set the stage — a world stage — for IISS, and there would be no looking back. The funding of this expansion and revitalisation, the research staffing and scholarship that bolstered it, the new scope of the membership and governance that he had put into place made it a truly global think tank, just at the time the end of the Cold War brought about a diffusion of power and strategic challenge in the world. In the mid to late 1980s not everyone could see this, and many thought IISS need not change its research and membership focus. Critics of Bob's moves claimed that IISS was not the UN, and should not expand its focus.

---

20 See O'Neill, Robert (1987) 'Concluding Remarks', in *East Asia, The West, and International Security*, Adelphi Paper 212, London: IISS.
21 O'Neill, Robert (1998) 'Conclusion' in *Prospects for Security in The Mediterranean*, Adelphi Paper 231, London: IISS.

Bob's foresight was rewarded, of course, with the end of the Cold War and the rise of multiple centres of power and strategic challenge in the world. During his time as Chairman of the Council (1996–2001), many intelligent voices were doubting the relevance of military-centred research institutes due to the sheer unlikelihood of major power conflict.[22] O'Neill, together with energetic new Director John Chipman, conceived the idea for using the IISS's global convening power he had built as director a decade prior, in order to sponsor ministerial-level regional security conferences — starting in Asia. The marquee events on the international security calendar and of the institute are now those conferences — the Shangri-La Dialogue for Asian/Pacific security issues and the Manama Dialogue for Persian Gulf and Middle East security issues.

Institutional leadership is difficult. Especially of membership based institutes that largely operate by committee and a type of informal near-consensus. Any scholar can forcefully express an opinion in a book, a journal article, or a conference paper — coherence lends itself to individual efforts. But to lead multifaceted and complex institutions composed of thousands of opinionated members and donors in a coherent direction, all the while building and broadening the institution's infrastructure, appeal, membership, and influence, is a real feat.

For Bob O'Neill to have kept IISS as intact as he did during the challenge to the transatlantic consensus presented by the early Reagan years is something that should be recognised and saluted. It was difficult, and yet he did it elegantly. For him to not only keep the institute whole but to also accommodate a fair and rigorous treatment of the heretical strategies of the Reagan doctrine such that they could actually be improved by the analysis and debate of IISS is a marvel of leadership — both strong and subtle. And, finally, for him to simultaneously expand the institute's reach and appeal in such a way that it was ideally prepared for the multipolar world that was to emerge soon after his directorship ended was a final transcendent act of intuitional leadership at its finest.

---

22 See, for example, Friedman, Thomas (2005) *The World is Flat*, New York: Farrar, Straus and Giroux; and Fukuyama, Francis (1992) *The End of History and the Last Man*, New York: Free Press. A better guide to the fleeting nature of the peace dividend phenomenon is Howard, Michael (1978) *War and The Liberal Conscience*, New York: Columbia University Press.

15
Lessons for Iraq and Afghanistan

Carter Malkasian and Daniel Marston

Robert O'Neill did not take part in the Iraq or Afghan wars. Yet he has had an abiding influence over how the United States and the West have approached the past 15 years of war. His experiences, books (*Vietnam Task* and *General Giap*), and most importantly, his teaching guided a cadre of scholar-practitioners involved in the Iraq and Afghan wars. His teachings lay at the root of many of the reforms that took place. Without him, the United States and the West would have been far less able to meet the challenges of the recent wars. Through six decades, O'Neill has been a father of strategic thinking on insurgency, carefully teaching and guiding from behind.

We met Professor O'Neill in the late 1990s as young graduate students coming to Oxford to work under his supervision. We were two of his last students. By that time, he had served in Vietnam, taught at The Australian National University, run the International Institute for Strategic Studies (IISS), and taken the Chair of the Chichele Professor of War at Oxford. As Americans, we had been exposed to Vietnam in our earlier studies, but our first true instruction in insurgency and counter-insurgency came from Professor O'Neill. With that in mind, this chapter will trace the development of his thinking and chart his influence on strategy in Iraq and Afghanistan.

Vietnam

O'Neill's deployment to Vietnam as an infantry officer from 1966 to 1967 forms the starting point of his thinking on insurgency. He was there for a year with the 5th Battalion, Royal Australian Regiment (5RAR). O'Neill chronicled the deployment in *Vietnam Task*, published shortly after the battalion returned to Australia. As noted in Tony White's chapter, O'Neill wrote most of the book while on active duty in Vietnam; his account documents his attempt to steer an objective path through a campaign in which he was deeply involved. *Vietnam Task* was never intended to be definitive. O'Neill wrote it intending that it would serve as a record of a moment in the war, in one part of the campaign and in one unit's experience of which he was part.

Vietnam Task has had a significant impact on our thinking and research, during work on our degrees and beyond.[1] In the late 1990s, the Vietnam War was still a divisive topic for many in the United States. Having grown up in the shadow of the war, we had heard the often contentious discussions taking place in families and neighbourhoods, as well as in academe. We have read and re-read *Vietnam Task* and learned different things from it each time, as the context of our own experiences working in Iraq and Afghanistan have developed, as well as when we have carried out our own research into the Vietnam War.

Vietnam Task is an important addition to the larger body of work on Vietnam and has stood the test of time, not only as a personal memoir, but as a study of insurgency, counter-insurgency, and adaptation. O'Neill laid out several key concepts in *Vietnam Task,* especially regarding analysis and the need for constant learning and adaptation in the midst of war.[2] There is one particular chapter that we consider timeless, Chapter 13 'A re-evaluation of strategy', which has helped shape our thinking on numerous issues over the past two decades.

Context

A key theme of Chapter 13 is the need to understand context. In his discussion of the main effort of a campaign, O'Neill stressed that:

---

1 O'Neill, Robert J. (1968) *Vietnam Task*, Melbourne: Cassell.
2 Ibid.

15. LESSONS FOR IRAQ AND AFGHANISTAN

the most fundamental question seemed to be the determination of our aim. Was it to kill Viet Cong [VC], to bring the main force to battle, to isolate the main force from the people, to assist in civil reconstruction, to restore Government control to villages or to cut VC supply lines? As strategy can be most effectively applied only with knowledge of the opponent's aim, it was important to consider exactly what the VC were attempting to do in order to achieve a victory.[3]

He then described how, in Vietnam, the allied coalition had to contend with an enemy that could field guerrilla forces as well as main forces, and how '[VC] main force regiments … [w]ere not to win the support of the people, but to throw back the forces of the Government and by a process of continued expansion and amalgamation to inflict final crushing defeat on the Government Army'.[4]

In making these points, O'Neill articulates the complexity of the war in Vietnam and the need for a multilayered approach to the campaign: 'the most direct means of winning the war lies in eliminating the Viet Cong cadres from the villages, positive Government action to administer the population cannot be put into effect until the main force Viet Cong regiments in a particular locality have been neutralised and are kept from interfering with the restoration of Government control.'[5] (We will come back to this last important point.) This could be construed to align with the mantra repeated for much of the Iraq and Afghanistan campaigns: 'clear, hold, build'. We would agree, but only to a point; O'Neill is always clear that issues in Vietnam are specific to that time, place, and campaign, and care is necessary in applying lessons from one campaign to another.

Adaptation

Adaptation and creative thinking is another major theme of Chapter 13 in *Vietnam Task*. In presenting this theme, O'Neill placed it within the context of his battalion's culture of debate, declaring that '[Lt Colonel John Warr, commanding officer] had been stimulating discussion of our methods ever since the battalion had been raised and scarcely a week passed in which he did not ask me what our aim

---

3 Ibid., p. 182.
4 Ibid., p. 183.
5 Ibid., p. 184.

in Phuoc Tuy was and then debate the matter'.⁶ Halfway through the tour, Lt Colonel Warr asked O'Neill to write a paper outlining the aims of the campaign, then used it to frame a debate among all the platoon and company commanders in the battalion.

That paper also served as a framework for how the battalion could succeed. In his 2006 address to the IISS, O'Neill recounted how he crafted five points to guide the strategy of his battalion over the second half of their deployment:

1. Our principal challenge was not the Viet Cong main force and the North Vietnamese Army but the political cadres which the Viet Cong had inserted into towns and villages.
2. Our prime task had to be the removal of enemy political cadres from the towns and villages.
3. Our second priority was to help with reconstruction and development so that the local people's needs would be met effectively and they might come to feel that a non-communist government would give them a better chance of a good life than a communist one.
4. Major offensive operations in or near populated areas were highly counter-productive in terms of winning popular support.
5. Other kinds of operations, especially those aimed at eliminating Viet Cong cadres and winning popular support, were much less costly to ourselves in casualties and therefore much more sustainable politically by our own and allied governments.

Within these five points lie concerns about overly conventional operations, unpopular governments, and avoiding harm to civilians that we would both later hear in O'Neill's lectures at Oxford.

In later years, O'Neill argued that the American public stopped supporting the war in Vietnam from 1968 onward because too little had been achieved at too great a cost. In his view, the five points above offered ways to conduct operations and achieve successes at a reasonable cost.⁷ In sum, O'Neill left Vietnam with a strong

---

6   Ibid., p. 182.
7   O'Neill, Robert (2006) 'World Order and the War on Terror: Prospects and Perspectives', lecture at International Institute for Strategic Studies, 29 November.

appreciation for context (especially its political and social aspects), adaptation, and a set of five operational guidelines that might have helped get to a happier outcome.

After Vietnam and the publication of *Vietnam Task*, O'Neill wrote a book on the North Vietnamese military leader, Vo Nguyen Giap, and won a teaching position at The Australian National University.[8] He next turned his focus to the Korean War, but he continued to refine his thinking on Vietnam and insurgency.

Oxford

In 1987, O'Neill became the Chichele Professor of War at All Souls College, Oxford University. A major theme in his lectures and seminars was the difficulty of handling insurgencies and their prominence in modern warfare. What cannot be overstated is that in the 1990s O'Neill was one of the few professors in history, political science, or strategic studies teaching about insurgency. Indeed, before September 2001, it was not uncommon to hear top scholars dismiss the idea that the United States would ever face an insurgency again. This was the era of the revolution in military affairs and 'shock and awe'. Too many generals, policy-makers, and scholars lived in the afterglow of the impressive US success in the 1991 Gulf War. In contrast, O'Neill believed that, because great powers find it too expensive and counterproductive to fight each other, insurgency and terrorism had become the dominant form of warfare. With foresight, he argued that insurgency and terrorism were at the cutting edge of international politics and would not go away for decades. Therefore, students needed to understand insurgency and be thoroughly familiar with the most important recent historical examples.

Wary of generalisation, O'Neill used historical cases to ground his thoughts. In his class on the history of modern war, Malaya and Vietnam were the subject of multiple lectures. For the Americans studying under O'Neill, Malaya was a largely unknown conflict. Vietnam, of course, was not. O'Neill was always clear that issues in Vietnam are specific to their time and place, and that care is necessary in applying lessons from one campaign to another. Context is everything: war is

---

8   O'Neill, Robert J. (1969) *General Giap: Politician and Strategist*, Melbourne: Cassell.

ever-changing and the experiences of the various forces would change based upon which province and which year they served in Vietnam. War is grey and always will be; there are no hard and fast rules.[9]

That said, at Oxford, O'Neill did not shy away from sharing his insights and thinking with his students. In line with his own prior experiences, O'Neill discussed the virtues of light tactics in counter-insurgency: patrolling, gathering intelligence, and working with the people. For Vietnam, he lauded the Marine Corps' combined action platoons that embedded into local forces and lived with them in the village.[10] In contrast, he strongly criticised the conventionally minded US search and destroy operations, and the use of mechanised vehicles in Vietnam. From his point of view, it was tough to substitute for the light infantryman. (While at Oxford, O'Neill was also Honorary Colonel of the 5th Battalion, Royal Green Jackets, a descendant of the 60th Royal American Regiment, one of the first light infantry units in the British Army; designed specially to fight in another irregular war — the French and Indian War, 1754–1763.) And he was deeply critical of heavy-handed behaviour on the part of Western troops. For him, indiscriminate use of firepower — as demonstrated in the My Lai massacre, the killings of the Phoenix program, and other tragic events — oppressed the local people and turned them against the government. Publics would not accept such behaviour, especially in the media age.

With 30 years of contemplation behind him, O'Neill did not merely talk about tactics. On the controversial question of whether the United States could have won the Vietnam War, he was pessimistic. In his assessment, the best chance would have been for the South Vietnamese government (with US support) to have adopted better counter-insurgency tactics pre-1965, before the main force war. Doing so might have given politicians the breathing space to support a long war. Nevertheless, for O'Neill, the key factor was the South Vietnamese Government. It would have had to improve its policies and solidify for success to have been possible. Overlooking the possibility that the South Vietnamese Government was illegitimate in the eyes of the common

---

9   Discussion between Daniel Marston and Robert O'Neill, 2005.
10 See Hennessey, Michael (1997) *Strategy in Vietnam: The Marines and Revolutionary Warfare in I Corps*, Westport, CT: Praeger.

people was one of the fundamental flaws of the Vietnam campaign.[11] In correspondence with Carter, O'Neill explained: 'Westmoreland's plan of mid-1965 ignored the domestic political struggle in Vietnam. It would not have mattered how effective his military operations were if the South Vietnamese Government continued to be ineffective in addressing the state of popular welfare, and failed to compete more strongly with the Communists in this area.'[12]

Above all, in his teachings at Oxford, O'Neill offered a strategic viewpoint on insurgency and counter-insurgency that has strongly influenced us and his other students, specifically three larger points that had not appeared in *Vietnam Task*. They are harshly realistic and sober.

First, successful counter-insurgency may demand a long commitment and possibly also a large number of troops.

Second, such a commitment must be politically sustainable, which means that early successes are essential. The foreign forces 'must be able to win at an acceptable cost in a reasonable amount of time', he said in a 2000 lecture. 'Lives of the intervening forces and time are the two most precious commodities.'[13] A democratic politician may not be able to gather the necessary support if under political fire over setbacks or atrocities in the field. For this reason, a military insufficiently sensitive to the local population can torpedo the whole effort.

Third, the host government needs political cohesion. A government that is too divided or broken by sectarianism, feuds, or cycles of revenge is unlikely to defeat an insurgency, no matter how many troops are poured in. He told his students: 'wars for other people's futures require their support. Security of all states rests ultimately on their own shoulders.'[14] Ultimately, even if the interventionist power could clear enough space to permit a host nation to attempt to restore governance, the host nation still needs to decide how this government should look — and govern. The interventionist can provide support in terms of advisors, but must accept the possibility that the solution may not look anything like our own governance structures in the

---

11 Discussion between Daniel Marston and Robert O'Neill, 2005.
12 Correspondence between Robert O'Neill and Carter Malkasian, 26 May 2003.
13 O'Neill, Robert (2000) lecture on 'Vietnam, 1968–1975', Oxford University, 4 March.
14 Ibid.

West. We cannot make a host nation into little America or Britain, yet we must remember and maintain the idea that without a cohesive government, counter-insurgency is likely to fail.[15] This strategic realism would later define his assessment of the chances for success in Iraq and Afghanistan.

Beyond his lectures, O'Neill pressured his graduate students to understand the dynamics of insurgencies and how to address them. He directed graduate students writing on general strategy or land war in the twentieth century to be familiar with relevant history in insurgency and counter-insurgency. John Hillen, a US Army officer, wrote a dissertation on peacekeeping and the United Nations that captured O'Neill's cautious guidance, that intervention is often long and difficult, but is also an unavoidable feature of the international system. Carter's dissertation on wars of attrition contained material on counter-insurgency and Vietnam because O'Neill felt he needed to compare attrition and counter-insurgency. Dan's dissertation on the Indian Army in the Burma campaign focused on how fostering a culture of learning and adaptation is a key aspect of both developing professionalism within the military and improving performance in combat.

O'Neill's most important student in this field was John Nagl, a US Army officer who was convinced that the United States would face more insurgencies than conventional wars in its future. Nagl first came to Oxford in 1988 as a master's student. He returned in 1995 to earn his doctorate under O'Neill's tutelage.[16] His dissertation compared the British effort in Malaya to the United States' effort in Vietnam. His argument strongly mirrored O'Neill's own emphasis on adaptation. Nagl found that organisational culture had prevented the United States from adopting good counter-insurgency tactics. The dissertation was eventually published as *Learning to Eat Soup with a Knife*,[17] one of the most widely read books on counter-insurgency. O'Neill was pleased, both with the dissertation and with Nagl's courage in questioning the doctrines of the army in which he was a serving officer. As graduate

---

15 Discussion between Daniel Marston and Robert O'Neill, 2005.
16 Nagl, John (2014) *Knife Fights: A Memoir of Modern War in Theory and Practice*, New York: Penguin, pp. 38–9.
17 Nagl, John (2005) *Learning to Eat Soup with a Knife: Counterinsurgency Lessons from Malaya and Vietnam*, Chicago: Chicago University Press.

students, we were assigned Nagl's dissertation right off O'Neill's All Souls office shelf, long before the published version ever hit the bookstores.

Iraq and Afghanistan

When 11 September 2001 struck, O'Neill was completing his tenure at Oxford, soon to move back to Australia. As the wars in Afghanistan and Iraq unfolded, O'Neill's own thoughts were characteristically sober. He advocated good counter-insurgency tactics, but was circumspect about how much could actually be achieved.

Students at War

O'Neill found his students heavily involved in the war effort. John Hillen became Assistant Secretary of State for Political–Military Affairs. Dan started teaching at Sandhurst, made repeated trips to Iraq and Afghanistan, and later took a chair at the US Army Command and Staff College. He brought O'Neill's emphasis on learning and adaptation into the strategic discussions in which he was involved with British and American commanders in the UK, the US, Iraq, and Afghanistan. Carter spent 18 months as a civilian advisor to the Marines in Al Anbar province, and then nearly four years in Afghanistan, two in a district of Helmand and another two as the political advisor to the top US commander, General Joseph Dunford. Nagl was perhaps the most involved of all. He served as the operations officer of a battalion in Iraq and then became one of the leading and most well-known reformers calling for a new, better approach.

At a time when most US officers and policy-makers found themselves ill-prepared to deal with the problem of insurgency, O'Neill's students were ready to make recommendations from a solid academic grounding. He had given them a framework to examine the problem. He continued to be a mentor and sounding board for us as we worked to address various tactical, operational, and strategic aspects of the wars.

Unlike Vietnam, the US military instituted a dramatic attempt to adapt itself to fight an insurgency in Iraq and Afghanistan. Within the military, General David Petraeus, General James Mattis, Dr David

Kilcullen, and John Nagl spearheaded the creation of a new counter-insurgency doctrine and its implementation. Nagl's *Learning to Eat Soup with a Knife* was standard fare for officers. The reform effort culminated in the publication of the *Counterinsurgency Field Manual*, for which Nagl wrote the introduction. O'Neill's influence can be seen in the introduction's emphasis on knowledge of history, the length and difficulty of counter-insurgency campaigns, the limited utility of massed operational manoeuvre and heavy firepower, and the dominance of insurgency in modern warfare. The passage 'most enemies either do not try to defeat the United States with conventional operations or do not limit themselves to purely military means' especially echoes O'Neill's views.[18]

The counter-insurgency manual eventually came under heavy criticism for two things. First, critics on the right claimed the manual de-emphasised killing and had soldiers and marines concern themselves too much with building relations with local population. Second, critics on the left claimed that the manual was overly optimistic about the ability of a heavy, lengthy, and expensive troop commitment to defeat an insurgency. O'Neill never directly weighed in on these debates, but we can guess at his thoughts. He would have outright rejected the first criticism. For him, building relationships lessens resistance and gives democratic politicians political space to support a war effort. For the second criticism, he would have been partly sympathetic about the dangers of over-optimism, especially given his own emphasis on the precedence of politics and a cohesive government. Yet he would not have backed away from a long and possibly substantial commitment as a necessary condition for success. In O'Neill's opinion, if a democratic state wants to defeat an insurgency, it may have to confront that burden.

O'Neill's other students have also contributed to US and allied strategy. Now Assistant Secretary of State for Political–Military Affairs within the US Department of State, John Hillen worked to coordinate guidelines for counter insurgency across the entire US Government.

---

18 (2007) *The U.S. Army/Marine Corps Counterinsurgency Field Manual*, Chicago: Chicago University Press, pp. li–liv.

He shared O'Neill's idea that dealing with insurgent and terrorist adversaries is as much political as military, and that therefore diplomats and development experts had to be involved.[19]

On the more academic side of things, in 2008 we put together *Counterinsurgency in Modern Warfare*, an edited collection of case studies of the major counter-insurgency campaigns. Though far less influential than the counter-insurgency manual, it followed O'Neill's model of using historical cases to inform understanding. We asked a range of academics and practitioners to write specific chapters to provide a variety of perspectives, and avoided listing any specific lessons for people to walk away with. We hewed closely to O'Neill's thoughts on the key role of context and how it inhibits drawing out specific lessons for future campaigns.[20] We considered that the proper role of the book was to act as a catalyst for debate and discussion; it would be left to the reader to draw their own conclusions. Consequently, the book has no conclusion and foreswears any general theory — for which we were sometimes criticised in reviews. A few points in the introduction show O'Neill's influence, particularly where it highlights the dangers of overly militarised strategies and the role of politics and society, stating 'tactical brilliance at counter-insurgency translates into very little when political and social context is ignored or misinterpreted'.[21] As usual, O'Neill was involved in developing the book; he read several chapters and provided important critical feedback.

Carter later wrote *War Comes to Garmser*. Published in 2013, the book is a 30-year history of conflict in one district of war-torn Helmand province. The book's commentary on the need to build relationships with local leaders and do no harm owes something to O'Neill's teachings a decade before. Carter and O'Neill corresponded heavily during the book's revision process, especially about how local dynamics can shape the course of a conflict as much as foreign intervention, which is a theme of the book. In correspondence, O'Neill noted: 'Armies come,

---

19 Hodge, Nathan (2011) *Armed Humanitarians: The Rise of the Nation Builders*, New York: Bloomsbury Publishing, pp. 155–60.
20 Malkasian, Carter and Daniel Marston (eds) (2008) *Counterinsurgency in Modern Warfare*, Oxford: Osprey Publishing.
21 Ibid., p. 16.

armies go, but the people of Afghanistan continue to move along their own path through the history of the region in which they live. What more can one say?'[22]

Wisdom

Throughout the Iraq and Afghan wars, O'Neill developed his own assessment of the situation, which he delivered in lectures and talks on Iraq and Afghanistan. He kept his eye firmly on the overall strategic situation. When Dan sent in reports from his various trips, highlighting the reform and apparent progress that he was witnessing on the battlefields, O'Neill would always ask the same question: 'To what end?' He had been right to ask. At times, all of us students had been guilty of losing sight of the bigger picture, focusing on tactical progress and assuming larger strategic problems could be fixed later.

On Iraq, O'Neill always doubted the odds of success. He never bought into the idea of a short, quick war. Unlike many other experts, including ourselves, O'Neill expected an insurgency to break out after the 2003 US invasion. Though no fan of the invasion, he believed the United States and its allies needed to be ready to face an insurgency.[23]

As the Iraqi insurgency gained speed, O'Neill criticised US tactics as overly conventional. In 2006, he told IISS: 'Although some US and allied soldiers have by now developed good ideas on what to do to win the support of the civilian population, the Coalition lacks the strength to put them into effect.'[24]

For O'Neill, the central problem in Iraq was not tactics, but the absence of a government that could control the country. He thought it would be impossible to build one: 'I cannot see the Iraqi government retaining the political cohesion and authority which is necessary for an army to function well in counter insurgency … [T]he only way to keep the country together is by dictatorial rule and massive occasional applications of force.'[25] On the face of it, O'Neill appears overly

---

22 Correspondence between Robert O'Neill and Carter Malkasian, 17 February 2012.
23 O'Neill, Robert (2006) 'World Order and the War on Terror: Prospects and Perspectives', lecture at International Institute for Strategic Studies, 29 November.
24 Ibid.
25 Correspondence between Robert O'Neill and Carter Malkasian, 13 December 2006.

pessimistic, given that within a year the surge would win dramatic successes. Over the longer term, he appears prescient. He wrote to Carter in early 2004:

> The insurgency in Iraq is much more complex than that in Vietnam, and much more difficult to handle. I shall be very surprised if, a few years after the US pulls out of Iraq, there is a stable, democratic government there. The society is just too divided—so many factions, so many different loyalties, so much history, so little trust, so much vengeance to be taken — both on rival factions and on the US.[26]

This, it seems, is exactly what has come to pass. The United States indeed was not interested in a protracted commitment, and in June 2014 the Iraqi Government suffered a devastating defeat at the hands of the Islamic State, the progeny of the original Iraqi insurgents.

O'Neill was similarly pessimistic about Afghanistan. Although he supported the US and allied commitment, he found Afghanistan to be just as complex as Iraq: 'the whole country is deeply marked by very complex historical experience—the waves of migration, the proximity of India, the Durand line, the Pashtun problem, and the five or six wars that the region was been through in the past thirty odd years ... these are peculiarly difficult people for intervention forces to control and work with.'[27] Even more than Iraq, O'Neill doubted that his critical component of counter-insurgency — a cohesive government — could be built. He wrote to Carter in 2012:

> The final outcome ... will depend on the leadership capacities of the men in Kabul ... Of course there is a deeper question here: can foreigners ever hope to implant a government in Afghanistan and then watch it take root successfully? We have an awful lot of history which says that the answer to this question is No. There is too much history of foreign attempts at domination, local resistance of many kinds and at many levels, offered with such perseverance so that it was ultimately successful.[28]

---

26   Ibid., 17 January 2004.
27   Ibid., 8 February 2012.
28   Ibid., 12 March 2012.

Because of the stakes, O'Neill never called for abandoning Afghanistan. He also never thought that the West could solve the country's problems. There was almost a sense of inevitability in his view of the West's intervention and then defeat, a tragedy bound to play itself out.

For O'Neill, Iraq and Afghanistan epitomised the difficulties and tragedies of facing insurgencies — wars that cannot be wished away. Often, in his opinion, the United States and its allies would have to get involved. In 2015, he advised that, strategically, there are two choices:

> [E]ither stay out or (and preferably in my view) intervene very judiciously, building support for the local good guys, not undercutting them. It takes years, but so be it ... The US armed forces are not going to be able to avoid this kind of intervention — but I stress the word 'judiciously'. And here is the mission for the new generation of leading military thinkers and practitioners.[29]

Conclusion

We have tried to trace an evolution in Professor O'Neill's thoughts from Vietnam to the present. As a young officer in Vietnam, his experiences gave him a framework for what he believed counter-insurgency should look like on the ground. His experiences highlighted for him the dangers of certain approaches, especially mistreating the people, or using too much firepower. As a professor, tactics gave way to strategy. A long commitment, early successes, and a cohesive government were necessary conditions for success, if a Western democracy chose to intervene. By the time of Iraq and Afghanistan, this final point — placed within the surrounding political and cultural context — became a critical factor in his thinking. Throughout, he asserted that insurgency is now the dominant form of war and, in spite of its difficulties, cannot always be avoided.

Today, counter-insurgency has fallen into ill repute because of America's difficulties in Iraq and Afghanistan. After 2011, US policy-makers deemed its successes too small to be worth the cost. Meanwhile, new counter-terrorist tactics that offer a different way to

---

29 Ibid., 4 January 2015.

15. LESSONS FOR IRAQ AND AFGHANISTAN

fight have gained credence, and the United States has tried to work through partners in order to avoid a substantial deployment of troops. These methods may succeed. If so, a substantial troop deployment may be less important than O'Neill believed. Nevertheless, these new approaches are only under consideration because O'Neill's points on a long commitment, a cohesive government, and the inevitability of insurgency have proven all too true.

Ultimately, more than a decade into both the Afghanistan and Iraq campaigns, we must acknowledge that we have not put these points into practice to the extent required. As a Western coalition we can rightly claim that we have undertaken tactical reform, and grown to understand the changing character of the war, but we have not truly integrated these points, especially regarding a cohesive government, sufficiently to articulate and seek a realistic end state that would constitute a true victory for the host nation.

For us, Professor O'Neill is a realistic and far-thinking scholar who shaped the modern understanding of insurgency and counter-insurgency through teaching and mentoring. He put in place a cadre of scholar-practitioners with a solid grounding in insurgency. He forced his students to learn about insurgency and counter-insurgency during more peaceful times, when their study was too often deemed unnecessary. We would have lacked the wisdom to study them on our own. Whatever successes we have had over this past 15 years of small wars begin with his teachings.

16

Robert O'Neill and the Birth of ASPI

Hugh White

On 29 August 2001, a group of people gathered in a pleasant but nondescript conference room in a pleasant but nondescript office building in the inner Canberra suburb of Barton to launch the operations of a new, government-funded but independent think tank, the Australian Strategic Policy Institute (ASPI). This was the first meeting of ASPI's Board of Directors, or Council as it was decided they should be called. They were a moderately diverse and distinctly talented group of people, including several former cabinet ministers and other senior politicians, two currently serving heads of major Commonwealth departments, a former senior public servant, a retired major general, and a distinguished senior international businessman. At the head of the table sat Professor Robert J. O'Neill AO, who thus began his time as Chairman of the ASPI Council and guiding hand for this new venture, a position in which he was to serve until 2005.

For some people, the duties of a position like that might be taken rather lightly, as an agreeable and not too onerous way to keep busy in retirement. Bob O'Neill is not one of those people. As chairman, Bob brought all the energy, acumen, tact and organising ability that he has shown throughout his remarkable career. These capacities were certainly needed, because the task of establishing ASPI was, in its own small way, quite formidable, and one to which Bob's capacities and experience were ideally matched. Indeed, Bob's engagement with this task began several years before that first council meeting. To understand the nature of the challenge — and Bob's contribution to it — we need to go back to the origins of the idea that became ASPI and see how it developed.

Those origins can be traced to late March 1996, a few weeks after the installation of the first Howard Government following the general election that month. Howard's first defence minister was Ian McLachlan, who came to the portfolio with strong ideas about the importance of contestability in policy advice. He had been influenced especially by the quite radical experiments in contestability that had been undertaken in New Zealand by both Labour and National governments over the preceding decade, which he had got to know well in his earlier roles as a leader of farmer's organisations. These views were shared by many of his ministerial colleagues, but McLachlan, as a committed activist and Canberra outsider, was more inclined than most to push to see them implemented.

Thus it was that during one of the many introductory discussions on policy questions with senior military and civilian defence officials — conducted in this case on a government VIP plane over central Australia — McLachlan taxed his advisers to suggest alternative sources of advice on the big defence policy questions he was going to face as minister. It was explained to him that defence remained one of the dwindling number of bastions of non-contestability in public policy in Australia. While many individuals and institutions studied international relations and the diplomatic aspects of strategic policy — especially in relation to alliances — very few did detailed or authoritative work on core questions of defence and strategic policy in ways that could contribute to informing and contesting official policy advice. 'Well', said the minister, 'we will have to fix that. Prepare me some advice about how that can be done.'

It would take a careful study of defence records not yet open to the public to track the progress of this task over the years that followed, but by the time McLachlan left the portfolio following the 1998 election he had decided that the best way to enhance defence policy contestability was to establish a small, stand-alone institute. This body was to be funded from the defence budget while operating quite independently of it, with the mission to provide ministers with

16. ROBERT O'NEILL AND THE BIRTH OF ASPI

alternative advice on the full range of high-level defence and strategic policy decisions. He was succeeded as minister by John Moore, who shared McLachlan's interest in policy contestability and enthusiastically took up the task of establishing the new institute. Work on establishing the new institute proceeded over the next couple of years, though perhaps inevitably it had to jostle for high level attention with major issues like the unfolding East Timor crisis of 1999 and the preparation of the Defence White Paper in 2000. A series of decisions by the minister based on submissions from defence began to lay out the broad outlines of the proposed institute.

Perhaps most importantly, the institute's roles and functions were established and, flowing from that, the basic organisational structure was determined. At a fairly early stage it was decided that the institute would have four main functions. The first three of these were clearly set out in 2001 in the charter letter sent by the then minister to council members on the occasion of that first council meeting in 2001. He wrote:

> The Government has three key underlying purposes in setting up an independent strategic policy institute.
>
> - First, to provide alternative sources of input to Government decision-making processes on major strategic and defence policy issues. The Government believes that contestability of advice is an important contributor to good public policy, and is concerned that in the strategic and defence policy arena the range of alternative views on which the government can draw is not well developed. ASPI is intended to help remedy this, both directly through its own work and indirectly by encouraging others into the field. An independent policy institute structured along the lines envisaged has the potential to be a valuable source of alternative views on a wide range of issues. By doing so it should also encourage other organisations and individuals to seek to contribute in more concrete and realistic ways to addressing our strategic and defence challenges.
> - Second, ASPI is intended to help nourish public debate and understanding. The Government believes that improved public understanding of strategic and defence issues is an important long-term investment in Australia's security. Good policy must be informed by a well-informed public debate, and be supported by a sophisticated public understanding of the choices that need to be made.

- Third, the Government believes that Australia needs to invest in nurturing a body of men and women, working both inside and outside Government, who are expert in the strategic policy issues faced by Government. The Government therefore hopes that ASPI, in fulfilling the first two objectives outlined above, will also contribute to the development of professional strategic policy expertise in Australia.[1]

The fourth purpose was reflected in the words the minister quoted from ASPI's corporate constitution, which cast additional light on the other roles, as follows:

> The company's object is to function as a strategic policy research centre, independent of Government, providing policy-relevant research and analysis to better inform Government decisions and public understanding of strategic and defence issues, by:

- Conducting and publishing research on issues related to Australia's strategic and defence policy choices.
- Preparing policy inputs on strategic and defence issues to Government, as requested by Government, subject to funding.
- Conducting a program of activities to increase understanding of strategic and defence policy issues among Australians, and to encourage the development of expertise in topics relevant to Australia's strategic and defence policy choices.
- Promoting international understanding of Australia's strategic and defence policy perspectives.[2]

The differences in these formulations are intriguing, but the key elements are very plain. Most importantly, it is very clear that the government's original key aim in establishing ASPI was to provide alternative sources of policy advice to the government itself on specific defence policy decisions. This reflected not just the somewhat doctrinaire commitment to policy contestability which McLachlan, Moore, and others had brought into government in 1996, but their experience of dealing with defence policy questions since then. For reasons that would be hard to pin down, and although relations between ministers, individual officers, and officials were professional, respectful, and even at times warm, it might be said that the Howard Government never established an easy relationship with the defence

---

1 ASPI (2001) 'ASPI Charter'. Available at: www.aspi.org.au/about-aspi/charter.
2 Ibid.

organisation. A few specific issues, especially on questions of defence material and acquisition, and most particularly the troubles of the Collins-class submarine, led ministers to be impatient and even suspicious of defence advice, and thus increasingly eager to find alternative ideas and arguments to test that advice against.

The second major role — very important, but clearly subordinate to the first — was to 'nourish public debate and understanding' of defence issues. Ministers clearly felt that building and sustaining support for good defence policy was made harder by the relatively unsophisticated way that defence issues were seen and debated by the public. The contrast was drawn here with the way public understanding of and debate about economic policy issues had evolved over recent decades, and how important that has been to building public support for major economic reforms of the kind that had been carried out in the 1980s. It was intended that ASPI would provide a source of well-informed, professional, impartial, and non-partisan commentary that would help Australians understand the real nature of defence policy choices facing the country.

The third major role was to help build professional strategic policy expertise, both in government and in the wider community. Ministers had become aware that the pool of such expertise seemed to be shrinking as the group of people who had lived and worked through the major defence policy revolutions of the 1960s, 1970s, and early 1980s began to retire. Shifts in attitudes and expectations after the Cold War especially seemed to reduce interest in the rather demanding and often arcane disciples of defence policy, especially those related to the complex interconnections between high strategy on the one hand and specific choices about capability and operations on the other. It was never intended that ASPI should run educational courses of its own, but it was expected that its work would support and contribute to courses run by others, and that it would provide career development opportunities for people committed to working in the field.

The fourth role was to help promote international understanding of Australian strategic and defence policies. This reflected ministers' awareness that the 1990s had seen something of a boom in the development of non-official and semi-official — 'Second Track' and 'One and a Half Track' — security dialogues in Asia. They had become a key element of the slow, tentative, but nonetheless important process of development of regional multilateral security institutions and architectures in the post-Cold War Asia; such exchanges were favoured in a region still very wary of anything that smacked of formal alliances or defence groupings. They had also become important in the development of a number of key bilateral security relationships between Australia and Asian countries — especially those major powers beyond Southeast Asia, with which we had previously had little contact on strategic and defence questions. When the end of the Cold War began to raise new questions about the future strategic order in Asia and the roles of these major powers in it, Canberra was keen to build these relations and dialogues in a low-key way. Second Track and One and a Half Track exchanges were seen as a very effective way of doing so. Australia had already taken a big part in these exchanges and dialogues through institutions such as ANU Strategic and Defence Studies Centre, but the ministers saw merit in broadening and deepening the range of participants available from Australia. In particular, it was thought that the new institute might evolve into a fitting counterpart for the government-funded institutes of strategic studies that had been established in most ASEAN countries, and which played a central role in these dialogues.

Once these functions had been broadly agreed, attention turned to the structure and organisation of the institute intended to fulfil them. Clearly this was something that had to be approached very carefully. To achieve the first of its goals — independent policy advice to government — the new institute would need to be independent of defence, and some consideration was given to it being established within or attached to another department, such as finance. But to achieve its second goal — to contribute to public debate — it was clearly essential that it should be, and be seen to be, independent of government as a whole. At the same time, the government needed to be sure that the institute would fulfil the functions for which it was being established and funded. Some initial consideration was given to the idea of establishing it within an existing university, but preliminary exchanges with potential hosts clearly indicated that it would be hard to strike the right balance between independence of output and fulfilment of broad purposes under that kind of arrangement.

An extensive survey was undertaken by defence into different organisational models for the institute. It examined the institutional structures of government-funded but independent policy research institutes and think tanks in the strategic and defence policy field and more broadly in Australia and overseas. The conclusion was reached that the best approach would be to establish the institute as a company limited by guarantee under the *Corporations Act*. The key features of this model were that the Commonwealth would be the sole member — shareholder and owner — of the company with the right to appoint members of the board or council, while the council would be independently responsible for fulfilling the purposes for which it had been established. The government could fund the institute via a straightforward contract between itself (in this case, defence) and the company. In order to absolutely clarify the government's intentions to the council, a charter letter could be issued from the minister, as shareholder, setting out these intentions — including its intentions in regard to independence. The key passage on this issue in the charter letter addressing this issue is as follows:

> [T]he Government places high priority on the development of ASPI as a centre of excellence in strategic thinking which both is, and is seen to be, independent of Government. At the same time, the Government will want to ensure that its significant investment in the establishment of ASPI is being used effectively to achieve the aims outlined in this letter. The Government will therefore seek, through the mechanisms outlined earlier in this letter, to have a regular input into the setting of ASPI's research agenda.
>
> The Government's aim through those mechanisms will be to ensure that the Institute's research program generally addresses the kinds of strategic issues that confront Australian policymakers, and that specific issues of high interest are addressed. It will not seek to exercise a veto over the study of any particular topic, nor will it seek to direct the conclusions that might be published on any topic.[3]

Though this could hardly have been expressed more clearly, it was nonetheless very evident, as it had been from the time the idea for the institute had first been put forward, that the job of leading and steering the institute would fall very heavily on the chairman of the council. The chairman would have to be able both to guide the work of the institute in the fulfilment of its roles, and to steer it through the inherent complexities of its relationships with government and a wide range of key stakeholders. This was going to demand a rare

---

3   Ibid.

combination of skills and attributes. First, the chair would need to have real expertise and standing in Australian defence and strategic policy issues. Second, the chair would need experience in the leadership and management of centres of research and think tanks working in the strategic and defence fields. Third, the chair would need a strong public reputation, both in Australia and internationally, and a network of contacts around the world to establish the new institute's standing and help it build connections within Australia and beyond. And, finally, the chair would need high order political and diplomatic skills to manage the delicate balancing of the institute's unusual position and status.

It is immediately clear from this list of attributes why Bob O'Neill was not just the most obvious and best possible candidate for the role of chairman, but in a very real sense was the only possible candidate. There is no need here to elaborate on just how perfectly Bob met the demands of the position. His credentials as an army officer, an official historian, a major contributor to debates on defence policy, and a noted pubic intellectual; his leadership of SDSC, and later of IISS, both as director and chairman; his contribution to international strategic debates in these roles and at Oxford; his phenomenal international standing and network; and his renowned skill in the delicate and principled management of complex personal relations and organisational politics — all of these made him the ideal person to become Chairman of the ASPI Council. By great good fortune the timing worked well with Bob's plans to return to Australia after his retirement from the chair at Oxford.

All this was clear long before the final arrangements for the establishment of ASPI had taken shape. Bob was first approached about taking on the chair over dinner in the Berkeley Hotel, London, by John Moore during a visit to the UK in November 1999, and a public announcement was made about his willingness to take up the position soon after. The ensuing delays in getting the institute up and running were a little frustrating, but they did mean that by the time of the first council meeting, Bob had finished at Oxford and had returned to Australia, having in the meantime built his remarkable house at Long Gully. The final cabinet considerations regarding the structure, organisation, and funding of ASPI were concluded in August 2000, and it remained only for the defence minister — now Peter Reith, following Moore's resignation in January 2001 — to nominate and

16. ROBERT O'NEILL AND THE BIRTH OF ASPI

appoint the remaining council members before the work of creating the institute could commence. This final step took far longer than anyone expected, and it was not until the middle of 2001 that the minister, in close consultation with the prime minister, settled on a list of names.

The group that assembled for the first council meeting were, as we have seen, an interesting and impressive body. The Deputy Chairman was Major General (Retd) Adrian Clunies-Ross, former Deputy Chief of Army. The prime minister's nominee was former senior minister Jim Carlton, and the leader of the opposition's nominee was former Senator Stephen Loosely. Alan Hawke and Ashton Calvert were members *ex officio* as secretaries of defence and foreign affairs. Other members included former cabinet minister and shadow defence spokesperson, Jocelyn Newman; Roland Williams, a leading businessman and former senior Shell executive; and former Treasury Deputy Secretary and prominent economics commentator, Des Moore. Over the next few years this proved to be a capable and generally harmonious group, though the task of chairing it was not always a simple one, and there were occasions in which Bob's formidable skills as chairman were needed to keep things moving forward.

At that first meeting, the council confirmed the appointment of ASPI's first director — that was me — and approved initial plans, which had been developed under Bob's guidance, for the establishment of the institute, including its organisational structure, staffing, recruitment, premises, and financing. Following that meeting, a contract was signed with defence for funding of around $2.7 million per year over seven years. The institute was to consist of three major research programs — strategic and international, capability and operations, and resources and management — reflecting ASPI's remit to work across the whole range of defence policy questions. Each program would be headed by a program director. The permanent staff would be kept quite small, with a lot of research work to be contracted out. Total staff would number about 12, and recruitment would get underway immediately, with a view to the office opening for business and commencing work in early 2002. After some consideration of whether the institute should be located somewhere other than Canberra, it was confirmed that it would operate from the office suite which defence had leased in Arts House, Braddon. This location was chosen because it was close to Parliament House, the Press Gallery, and major departments, and it was convenient to, but symbolically across the lake from the Department of Defence on Russell Hill.

While all this work was underway, of course, the world moved on. Within a few weeks of the first council meeting, and before ASPI had begun operations, the terrorist attacks of 11 September 2001 transformed many aspects of strategic and defence debates in Australia and around the world. Moreover, a federal election in November 2001 returned the Howard Government, and immediately thereafter Robert Hill replaced Peter Reith as defence minister. These changes had complex implications for ASPI's early years, and for Bob's role at the helm. On the one hand, the 9/11 attacks and all that followed ensured that defence and security questions would loom large in public and policy debates over the following years, and thus provided a very receptive environment for ASPI's launch and early work. On the other hand, the highly contested nature of some of those debates made the task of locating ASPI's role, and navigating bureaucratic, political, and ideological currents, more demanding than it might otherwise have been. Minister Robert Hill in many ways proved less receptive to ASPI's role and potential then his predecessors. While not in any sense hostile to the new institute, it would be fair to say that he was less interested in policy contestability and alternative sources of advice than his predecessors. This did nothing to prevent ASPI from flourishing, but it did mean that the nature of its role soon diverged somewhat from that envisaged at its original conception.

By the end of 2001, almost all the staff had been appointed. The three program directors were Dr Ellie Wainwright in the Strategic and International Program, Mr Aldo Borgu in the Capability and Operations Program, and Dr Mark Thomson in the Budget and Management Program. Mr Brendan McRandle, who had laid the organisational foundations for the institute as project manager for the establishment of ASPI in defence, became company secretary and outreach manager. Janis Johnston, recruited as librarian and publications officer, took on the major task of developing the look and feel of ASPI's publications and the creation of its website. From mid-January 2002, the staff began to assemble at the Arts House office, and ASPI was officially launched at a gala dinner, hosted by Bob, held at the Australian War Memorial on 13 March 2002. The keynote speech was delivered by the new Defence Minister, Robert Hill, who spoke warmly of ASPI's role.

'ASPI's success will depend on its ability to make a real contribution to the Government's thinking and to public understanding on the questions and choices that confront Australia in the defence and strategic area', Senator Hill said. 'It is an important and exciting task. I wish Chairman Bob O'Neill and his council and Hugh White and his staff success with their mission.'[4]

Well before this formal launch, the staff had begun work on ASPI's first publications. The first was released on 20 May 2002, the day East Timor's independence from Indonesia was formalised after the crisis of 1999. The report, *New Neighbour, New Challenge: Australia and the Security of East Timor*, was prepared by Ellie Wainwright.[5] It explored the security challenges that East Timor would face as an independent state, and the role Australia might have to play in supporting it, including specific recommendations. It was launched by the Deputy Prime Minister Tim Fischer, and was very positively received in Canberra, Dili, and elsewhere. ASPI's second publication was released just a few days later. It was a highly ambitious attempt to analyse and explain the government's annual defence budget as it was presented on budget night in terms that laypersons could understand.[6] The official presentation of the defence budget had always been notoriously opaque and incomprehensible, even to people within government and defence. ASPI believed that it would be impossible to foster a more rational and better-informed debate on defence priorities without a clear understanding of how the money was being spent and what things cost. Moreover, it was decided that, for maximum impact and benefit, this analysis should be published in time to help inform the senate committee budget hearings which begin just a few weeks after the budget is brought down in early May. After an astonishing marathon effort, Mark Thomson duly produced the first of what has become an annual series of ASPI defence budget briefs, which was launched in Parliament House in late May. This laid out in clear terms just what the defence budget was being spent on, and how well the

---

4   Hill, Robert, Minister for Defence (2002) 'Launch of the Australia Strategic Policy Institute', Media Release, 13 March. Available at: pandora.nla.gov.au/pan/33784/20030619-0000/www.minister.defence.gov.au/Hilltpl73be.html?CurrentId=1322.
5   Wainwright, Elsina (2002) *New Neighbour, New Challenge: Australia and the Security of East Timor*, Canberra: ASPI. Available at: www.aspi.org.au/publications/new-neighbour,-new-challenge-australia-and-the-security-of-east-timor/aspi-east-timor-book.pdf.
6   ASPI (2002) *The Cost of Defence: ASPI Defence Budget Brief 2002–2003*, Canberra: Australian Strategic Policy Institute.

numbers added up, as well as including clear recommendations for what could be done better. This immediately established ASPI as the authoritative source of information on and analysis of the hard nuts and bolts of defence policy.

Many more reports were to follow, each reflecting some basic principles that Bob had helped establish: that ASPI would only write on issues that had a clear *Australian* dimension, that it would focus on issues which were predominantly *strategic* in nature — in the narrower sense of that word — and that it would aim always to engage directly in policy debates by addressing questions on which Australia was facing clear choices and would not shy away from giving a well-reasoned, evidence-based view of what choice should be made. In these exciting early days, Bob played a crucial role in shaping the broad direction and tone of our research and publication program, and in scrutinising each publication as it evolved. He read everything in draft and offered invaluable guidance on matters large and small. More broadly, he was closely engaged in every aspect of the setting to work of ASPI as a live operation.

This was not all he had to do in those early days. ASPI quickly found itself drawn into some quite difficult and contentious issues. Over those first few months, while ASPI's first reports were being prepared and launched, Australians — like others around the world — were starting to debate an issue which became unquestionably the most divisive question of national strategic policy since Vietnam — the proposal to invade Iraq. There was no way that ASPI staff could or should have avoided participating in that debate, but it naturally raised serious challenges as the new institute was looking to establish its position and role as a government owned and funded but independent policy player. The potential for ASPI to find itself embroiled in intense and difficult public debates had, of course, been recognised and accepted from the outset, and some important principles had been established and embodied in ASPI's charter: that ASPI as an institution would hold no view, but present the views of staff and others who contributed to its work, and that it would seek to publish a range of views on contentious issues. These principles served ASPI well, but it was nonetheless a stern test to find that, within a few months of its launch, ASPI staff were among those arguing against an invasion of Iraq for which the government was doing all it could to build support. It is worth noting that John Howard never, at least to my knowledge, made any criticism of the role ASPI staff played in the debates over Iraq, which is a telling testament to his commitment to the concept on which it was established. Bob's steadying hand no doubt played a big part in that. Bob played an enormously important role — including within the ASPI Council — in ensuring that these waves did not swamp the little ASPI craft so early in its voyage.

In all this, Bob showed perfect judgment in calibrating his role with mine as director. It helped enormously, of course, that in earlier times he had served on both sides of that line with great distinction, as Director and then Chairman of IISS. He always insisted scrupulously on the director's responsibilities for running the institute day to day, and was quite firm in resisting any attempt by other council members to intrude on the director's role. On the other hand, he was extremely generous with advice, encouragement, and support, and took very seriously his responsibilities, with his council colleagues, to set the parameters within which the institute should operate. No one could have brought as much experience, expertise, gracious generosity, and strength of character to the task of establishing ASPI as Bob. And it perhaps goes without saying that his standing as a major international figure in the world of strategic studies, his high public profile here in Australia, and the respect in which he was held by senior figures in the government did perhaps more than anything to establish ASPI's credibility in those early days, as it did throughout his five years as chairman. We were very lucky indeed to have him.

17

The Rumble of Think Tanks: National Security and Public Policy Contestability in Australia

Allan Gyngell

Introduction

Australia was late in developing a foreign policy separate from British imperial policy. Legislation to implement the Statute of Westminster establishing Australia's full sovereign identity was not passed until 1942. Partly because of this, engaged individuals and institutions outside government have always played a role in shaping ideas about, and public attitudes towards, the way Australia protects and advances its international interests.

This chapter looks at one comparatively recent dimension of that non-government involvement in Australian public policy, the role of think tanks in Australian defence and foreign policy. It examines the reason for their emergence around the turn of the twenty-first century against the background of earlier efforts to shape public policy, assesses the contribution they have made, and explores their future.

From the 1970s onwards, Robert O'Neill played an important part in the development of some of most important of these institutions. From 1971–1982 he was head of the Strategic and Defence Studies Centre (SDSC) at The Australian National University. Then, after his return from London and Oxford, he was involved in the formation of the Australian Strategic Policy Institute (ASPI) in Canberra, the Lowy Institute for International Policy in Sydney, and the United States Studies Centre at the University of Sydney.

In his 2006 Lowy Lecture, 'Problems and Perspectives on International Security', O'Neill described the qualities Australian think tanks needed to bring to the task of assisting policy-makers deal with contemporary security challenges:

> [W]e need good ideas, dialogue with government and a relationship which tolerates free expression of views, especially on differences with existing policies. None of these essentials comes easily. We, the analysts, need experience in practical work — diplomacy, war, business and politics — as well as intellectual quality before we have any notion as to what is a good idea. Once we develop some ideas we need to be able to discuss them with senior people in government so that our views are taken into account in the mix that goes into decision-making. Our colleagues in government will not bother to listen to us if they do not respect the relevance and quality of our work. It is up to us to win their attention and hold it.[1]

What is a Think Tank?

The concept of a think tank is, as Thomas Medvetz writes, 'fuzzy, mutable and contentious'.[2] A broadly accepted definition used in the development of the most prominent think tank rating system is that they are

> public-policy research, analysis and engagement organizations that generate policy-oriented research, analysis, and advice on domestic and international issues, thereby enabling policymakers and the public to make informed decisions about public policy. Think tanks may be affiliated or independent institutions that are structured as permanent bodies, not ad hoc commissions. These institutions often act as a bridge between the academic and policymaking communities and between states and civil society, serving in the public interest.[3]

---

1   O'Neill, Robert (2006) 'Problems and Perspectives on International Security', *The Lowy Lecture on Australia in the World*, 27 November, Sydney: Lowy Institute for International Policy.
2   Medvetz, Thomas (2012) *Think Tanks in America*, Chicago: University of Chicago Press.
3   McGann, James G. (2013) *2013 Global Go To Think Tank Index Report*, Philadelphia: University of Pennsylvania.

Think tanks differ from the much larger group of non-government organisations (NGOs), advocacy groups, industry associations, online communities, and university research centres which are also trying to influence public debate and the direction of public policy, in that think tanks:

- exist for the primary purpose of undertaking applied research in public policy and shaping policy outcomes;
- are not-for-profit institutions;
- have a breadth of focus which can be broader or more limited, but which extends beyond a single narrow cause — oceans, for example, but not highly migratory tuna; and
- contribute to the public debate; that is, they conduct their principal work in the public realm.

Some think tanks look across many dimensions of public policy (e.g. Brookings). Others, look more narrowly at a particular area (e.g. Peterson Institute for International Economics, the Center for Strategic and International Studies).

Some emphasise the independence of view of individual researchers and their broad and non-partisan approach (e.g. Brookings, the International Institute for Strategic Studies). Others, such as Heritage, Cato, or the Center for American Progress in Washington bring to the job a particular philosophical approach. In Australia, the Centre for Independent Studies describes itself as 'engaged in support of a free enterprise economy and a free society under limited government',[4] while the Australia Institute pursues what it terms a progressive agenda.

The term 'think tank' is now used to describe institutions ranging in size from the RAND Corporation, with its 1800 staff and revenue of US$269 million, to a couple of part-time bloggers with some strong views. An estimated 6,828 think tanks operate internationally, with nearly 400 of them in Washington DC.[5] Australian numbers are much

---

4   www.cis.org.au/app/uploads/2015/06/precis2012-web.pdf.
5   Ibid.

smaller and depend on definitions. One recent estimate puts the number of 'main think tanks' in Australia at 12, but acknowledges that definitions are fluid and the number is always in flux.[6]

Some scholars adopt a more theoretical approach to think tanks. Medvetz defines them as occupying 'a distinct subspace of knowledge production which has arisen over time at the point of intersection between the academic, political, economic and media fields'.[7] They have emerged, he argues, through the very process of practically differentiating themselves from their surrounding fields of universities, lobby groups, and media outlets, increasingly orientating themselves towards each other, until they have come to constitute 'a semi distinct social universe with its own logic, history, and interior structures, not to mention its own agents'.[8]

It is certainly true that strict typologies of think tanks fail to account for the regular changes and adaptations to new pressures and demands which we see even in the much smaller field of Australian think tanks. Nor do they adequately represent the fluid spectrum between university-based centres such as SDSC which undertake some public policy research and outreach and the work of stand-alone institutions undertaking applied research in public policy. (One clear difference in Australia is that Australian Research Council funding is available only to researchers within the university system.)

Even the origin of think tanks is disputed. Some scholars point to the Duke of Wellington's establishment of the forerunner of the Royal United Services in 1831; others to the formation of the Royal Institute of International Affairs (Chatham House) in 1920.[9] But in the broad sense in which think tanks are currently defined, a critical step came in 1916 when Robert S. Brookings and others formed the Institute for Government Research in Washington DC, the first private institute devoted to the 'fact-based study of national public policy issues'.[10] Eleven years later, this became the Brookings Institution.

---

6   Milliken, Robert (2105) 'An Incisive Guide to Australia's Think Tanks', *Anne Summers Reports* 11, pp. 35–45.
7   Medvetz, Thomas (2012) *Think Tanks in America*, Chicago: University of Chicago Press.
8   Ibid.
9   For an excellent contemporary survey of this history, see Roberts, Priscilla (2015) 'A Century of International Affairs Think Tanks in Historical Perspective', *International Journal* 70(4).
10   www.brookings.edu/about/history.

After the Second World War, as governments faced new strategic and economic challenges which demanded fresh technocratic solutions, the growth of think tanks blossomed and their forms multiplied. The term came into wider use with its current meaning during the 1970s.[11]

However they are defined, think tanks help structure the public debate, shaping public understanding of the world by providing an alternative source of views about it. The views from think tanks are typically different from those generated in other areas of the public debate: less cautious than from the public service; less short-term than most media commentary; but more immediate than most academic work.

Because the coinage of think tanks is the production of new ideas, think tanks need to be alert to developments in the world. Successful think tank staff demonstrate a combination of attributes which are often very different from those required in the fields from which many of them come, such as the public service or academia. In addition to subject knowledge, they need to know how governments and businesses operate in the real world, to understand and utilise the link between knowledge and power, and to be skilful advocates.

Think tanks can float ideas that are too risky for governments. They can more easily bring together groups with different interests to work through problems and they can facilitate second track diplomacy — more informal and indirect channels of communication between countries.

The Role of Non-government Institutions in the Development of Australian International Policy

Efforts by members of the public to define and deepen the debate in Australia about international policy began early in the life of the new Commonwealth. Groups such as the Round Table and Chatham House,

---

[11] Medvetz, Thomas (2012) *Think Tanks in America*, Chicago: University of Chicago Press.

and later the Australian Institute of International Affairs (AIIA), began the process of arguing for the development of an Australian role in the formulation of imperial policy.

If the establishment of Chatham House marks one step in the appearance of the modern think tank, it is important to note that Australians were present at the inaugural meetings in May 1919 in Paris — John Latham was charged with preparing the summary of the proceedings. John Latham, Frederic Eggleston and Robert Garran returned from Paris as members of the emerging institution; local branches of Chatham House were established in 1924–1925 and the Australian Institute of International Affairs was reorganised as a national body in 1933. Meanwhile, a local manifestation of the Institute of Pacific Relations — the first genuinely regional (in this case, trans-Pacific) think tank — was established in 1925, eventually working as part of the AIIA. From the first, the individuals concerned (scholars, practitioners, and commentators were all participants) were devoted to promoting public enlightenment on issues of foreign affairs, to sponsoring and authoring studies of contemporary international issues of particular relevance to Australia (the first in 1928), and in particular to exploring options for policy. Membership of the Chatham House, the Institute of Pacific Relations, and the International Institute of Intellectual Cooperation (established in 1926) networks brought Australian commentators and scholars into contact with advanced analysis in the new discipline of international relations, while also opening the way to the first funding of work in Australia by international foundations, notably Rockefeller and Carnegie. The first time the phrase 'Australian Foreign Policy' was used as a book title was in an AIIA symposium volume, *Australian Foreign Policy 1934*;[12] the most comprehensive study of Australia's perceptions of regional security to that date was in the AIIA work *Security Problems in the Pacific Region*.[13] Until the 1960s, the AIIA, especially through its journal *Australian Outlook* (founded in 1947), was unrivalled as a focus for analysis and debate in the fields of foreign and security policy.[14]

---

12 Dinner, Hector and J. G. Holmes (eds) (1935) *Australian Foreign Policy 1934*, Queensland: Australian Institute for International Affairs.
13 Buesst, Tristan, W. Macmahon Ball and Gerald Packer (1949) *Security Problems in the Pacific Region*, Melbourne: Robertson & Mullens.
14 I am indebted to James Cotton for his contribution to this section.

The establishment of The Australian National University in 1946 was linked to ideas of national development and to the requirements of public policy. In 1966, the Strategic and Defence Studies Centre was established under Dr T. B. Millar, separate from the work of the International Relations Department, to advance the study of Australian, regional and global strategic and defence issues as the country came to terms with dramatic changes in Asia and the beginning of the Vietnam War. The centre was also seen as a way of attracting external funding to the university, first from the Ford Foundation and later from the Australian Defence Department.[15] O'Neill became the centre's second director in 1971 and stayed until 1982, strengthening its position within the university, securing its finances, and cementing its role as a proto-think tank, engaging directly with the policy-advising and policy-making community.

Outside the university system, the AIIA continued its essentially educational role, its constitution preventing it from expressing particular opinions on any aspect of international affairs, although its precise objectives continued to be the subject of debate within the organisation.[16] A private, not-for-profit Pacific Security Research Institute focused on foreign and defence policy was established in Sydney in April 1989, with Owen Harries as president, and former diplomat, David Anderson, as executive director. It was short-lived, but published several papers and held two conferences.[17]

At the same time, groups such the Institute for Public Affairs in Melbourne and the Sydney-based Centre for Independent Studies were pursuing free-market, liberal, and libertarian philosophies largely in the areas of economic and social policy.

---

15 Thatcher, Meredith and Desmond Ball (2006) *A National Asset: Essays Commemorating the 40th Anniversary of the Strategic and Defence Studies Centre*, Canberra: Strategic and Defence Studies Centre, The Australian National University.
16 Legge, John D. (1999) *Australian Outlook: A History of the Australian Institute of International Affairs*, Sydney: Allen & Unwin.
17 Thatcher, Meredith and Desmond Ball (2006) *A National Asset: Essays Commemorating the 40th Anniversary of the Strategic and Defence Studies Centre*, Canberra: Strategic and Defence Studies Centre, The Australian National University.

The Turn of the Century Expansion of Think Tanks

It was not until the beginning of the twenty-first century, however, that think tanks became a more established feature of policy development in Australia. This section examines the reasons for this sudden expansion. Elements of chance were involved (the 50th anniversary of the arrival in Australia of a prominent businessman), but more important were the changes taking place in each of the three domains within which think tanks operated — government, research, and media.

Government

From the mid-1990s onwards, but most notably between the Asian financial crisis of 1997–1998 and the Al Qaeda attacks on the World Trade Centre in 2001, the implications of the revolution in information technology — digital communications, personal computing, and mobile telephony — which underpinned economic globalisation became fully apparent to policy-makers.

As the cost of transferring information around the world was reduced to near zero, the relative power in the international system of state and non-state actors shifted. Groups ranging from transnational corporations, through internationally networked NGOs, to terrorists and transnational criminals, were empowered and found new and more effective ways of acting together.

One consequence for Australian governments, as for others, was to erode the barriers between domestic and international policy. By 1997, the Howard Government's foreign and trade policy White Paper, *In the National Interest*, was calling for a 'whole-of-nation approach which emphasises the linkages between domestic policies and foreign and trade policies'.[18] New transnational issues on the international agenda, such as climate change, involved many different departments and agencies.

---

18   Department of Foreign Affairs and Trade (1997) *In the National Interest*, Canberra: Australian Government Public Service.

In particular, ideas about national security — what it was, who was responsible for it, and how it was delivered — changed fundamentally after 9/11. Governments faced a range of difficult new questions. Were the intelligence agencies, the defence forces, and the police adequate to deal with the new challenges of terrorism and asymmetric warfare? How should they work together? How could non-state actors be deterred? More aspects of public policy, from transport to social policy, were becoming securitised. Just as the earlier generation of think tanks, notably the International Institute for Strategic Studies (IISS), which O'Neill had led, had been a response to the complex strategic challenges thrown up by the arrival of the nuclear age, so new thinking was now required about these difficult questions.

In a parallel process, the expansion of neoliberal thinking through the 1980s and 1990s had led to a normative change in public administration in favour of contestable policy advice and competitive project delivery.[19] Think tanks and commercial consultancies were beneficiaries as governments began deliberately to seek advice outside the regular channels of the public service.

Research

Universities were also changing, driven by a more demanding and competitive market for students, and the need to prove their relevance to governments. One response was the establishment of new centres, such as SDSC, which combined teaching, research and public outreach. The Centre for International Security Studies at Sydney University (established in 2006) and the National Security Institute at the University of Canberra (founded in 2007) were examples. At the same time, however, the academic reward system — based on student numbers and driven by publication in peer-reviewed academic journals — was fundamentally different from that required to succeed as a think tank, where the key measurements of success were entrepreneurial skills, and access to and influence upon policy-makers. Universities struggled as think tanks.

---

19 Keating, M. (2000) 'The Pressures for Change', in G. Davis and M. Keating (eds), *The Future of Governance: Policy Choices,* Sydney: Allen & Unwin.

Media

It was becoming clear from the early years of the century that the business model for newspapers in Australia, especially broadsheet newspapers, which depended heavily on classified advertising, was being fundamentally threatened by the rise of the internet. Circulation fell, advertising dropped, and the number of specialist correspondents in areas such as defence and foreign affairs was reduced. As senior Australian journalist, Laura Tingle, reflected: 'forced to generate 24-hour-a-day news, and under intense financial pressure, the media struggle to retain their own memory of what has gone before, and — if they do to keep it — the capacity to tell a story in any longer-term context.'[20] Meanwhile, online access, first through desktop computers, then tablets and smart phones, was changing the way the Australian public received information about the world. Opportunities were opened up for think tanks, with electronic publications, blogs, and later social media in a market which had escaped from the traditional editorial gatekeepers of the mainstream media and the 800-word op-ed.

All these changes were important in preparing the ground for the arrival, at the beginning of the 2000s, of three new internationally-focused institutions, each with the characteristics of think tanks, to varying degrees, and each well-funded enough to make a contribution from its inception. O'Neill had a founding role in all of them. On his retirement from Oxford in 2001, he returned to Australia to chair the Council of the Australian Strategic Policy Institute, Canberra, until 2005. He joined the board of the Lowy Institute for International Policy and in 2006–2007, and became Planning Director for the new United States Studies Centre at the University of Sydney.

ASPI

John Howard had come to office as prime minister in 1996 with no great background or focus on defence and foreign policy. By 1999, however, following the successful intervention in East Timor, he had

---

20 Tingle, Laura (2015) *Political Amnesia: How We Forgot to Govern*, Quarterly Essay 60, Melbourne: Black Inc.

begun to think of himself as a national security leader. The National Security Committee of Cabinet, a Howard Government innovation, had become a central part of the machinery of government.

Howard's first Defence Minister, Ian McLaughlin, brought to the job a strong belief that policy advice needed to be contestable. Public policy reforms in New Zealand had had an impact on his thinking. At his request, the Defence Department began examining the role of think tanks and what might be done in Australia. McLaughlin's successor as minister after the 1998 election, John Moore, shared that interest.

It took until 2000 for Howard to agree formally with the idea that the government should fund, initially at least, a think tank to be called the Australian Strategic Policy Institute which would encourage and inform public debate and understanding of Australia's strategic and defence policy choices; provide an alternative source of policy ideas to government; nurture expertise in defence and strategic policy across and outside government; and promote international understanding of Australia's strategic and defence policy perspectives.[21] O'Neill had already been approached to chair such a body.

The third of Howard's five defence ministers, Peter Reith, oversaw the relevant legislation and signed the charter letter establishing the principle of independence. By the time ASPI became operational under Robert Hill, however, the terrorist attacks of September 2001 had brought about fundamental changes to the debate about national security policy.

ASPI was funded largely by the government which appointed its council, but it was to be independent in its views. By 2015, ASPI had 32 staff and a $6 million budget. Most of the core budget still came from the Department of Defence, but as the institute's role expanded into other areas of national security policy, including border security and cyber security, other departments and agencies, as well as industry sponsors, made growing contributions to its budget.

---

21 Australian Security Policy Institute (2015) *Annual Report 2014–15*, Canberra: Australian Strategic Policy Institute.

Lowy Institute for International Policy

In 2002, the founder of the Westfield retail and property business, Frank Lowy, was looking for a way of marking the 50th anniversary of his arrival in Australia with a gift to the nation. An early interest in establishing an institute to look at immigration issues gradually widened, partly at the instigation of his son, Peter Lowy, who had been resident in the United States for 15 years, into the idea of an international policy think tank based in Australia.

A member of the Holocaust generation, Lowy was deeply conscious of the importance of paying alert attention to changes in the international system. As a businessman with global interests, he also believed that Australia's successes needed to be projected better onto the international stage.[22]

Lowy commissioned a scoping study from Michael Fullilove, who would later become executive director of the institute, and began discussing the idea with a number of people, including Ian McFarlane, the Governor of the Reserve Bank of Australia (on the board of which Lowy sat), and Robert O'Neill.[23] Another prominent former Australian, Dr Martin Indyk, a think tank entrepreneur in his own right, and by then at Brookings, also provided advice.

The institute which — after some initial caution on Lowy's part — carried the family name, was formally announced in September 2002, and opened in April 2003 in a heritage building close to the centre of the Sydney business district. Lowy pledged $30 million in funding. The decision to base it in Sydney rather than Canberra was never in doubt: Lowy intended to be a hands-on chairman. But the Sydney base also had an important effect in shifting and expanding the specialist international policy debate in Australia outside Canberra.

The institute had a broad mandate, covering economic as well as political and strategic issues. Its mission was to:

- produce distinctive research and fresh policy options for Australia's international policy and to contribute to the wider international debate; and

---

22   Margo, Jill (2015) *Frank Lowy: A Second Life*, Sydney: HarperCollins.
23   Ibid.

- promote discussion of Australia's role in the world by providing an accessible and high quality forum for discussion of Australian international relations through debates, seminars, lectures, dialogues and conferences.

The institute was to be independent, non-partisan, and empirically driven. There would be no Lowy Institute view of the world — apart from a general disposition to support an open Australia which was internationally engaged. This was an important commitment in the light of Lowy's own deep support for Israel, where he had first arrived from Europe after the war, and in whose war of independence he had fought.

The board brought together a group of people with formidable experience. It included O'Neill; McFarlane; the former senior banker, Rob Ferguson; the distinguished Australian economist and former ambassador to China, Ross Garnaut; the former Ambassador to the United States, Michael Thawley; and Peter and Stephen Lowy.

The writer was appointed as executive director, from a background largely in government policy advising and intelligence analysis. That appointment itself signalled that the institute would seek to influence practical public policy.

United States Studies Centre

One of the first major initiatives of the Lowy Institute was to commission an annual poll of Australian views of international affairs. The initial survey had revealed considerable concern about the role of the United States in the world. This helped to generate momentum from business and government supporters of the alliance for the establishment of a new centre to support understanding of the United States.

A number of earlier attempts to promote American studies in Australia had foundered through lack of resources, but in 2006 Prime Minister Howard announced the creation of a $25 million endowment to establish a United States Studies Centre. A national competition was held, and O'Neill was asked to be the strategic advisor for the University of Sydney's bid. Sydney was successful and the centre was established there in partnership with the New York-based American Australian Association (AAA), with funding coming from the federal and state governments, the AAA, and various individuals, foundations and corporate sponsors. O'Neill was the first CEO until a permanent appointment was made.

The centre was a hybrid academic and research centre, although it described itself as a think tank. Its mission was 'to increase awareness and understanding about the United States in Australia'.[24]

During this period, established institutions responded to the same external demands. The venerable community-based AIIA strengthened its think tank dimensions, while the well-established Centre for Independent Studies expanded the range of its work in the international area.

A second round of internationally focused think tanks emerged a few years later in response to the growing policy focus on China. As with the first group, a parallel set of university centres — ANU Centre for China in the World, established in 2010, and Sydney University's China Studies Centre, which started operations in 2011 — also appeared.

The Australia–China Relations Institute (ACRI), headed by former Foreign Minister Bob Carr, was established in December 2013 at the University of Technology, Sydney, with financial assistance from a prominent Chinese Australian businessman, Xiangmo Huang. In some ways an analogue of the United States Studies Centre, ACRI defined its role, in the words of its Director, the former Foreign Minister Bob Carr, as 'leading and shaping the public debate in Australia through accessible and interactive public engagement, real time insights and a research agenda with impact'.[25]

Another China focused think tank, the not-for-profit China Matters, followed in 2014 as a personal initiative of a leading China scholar, Linda Jakobson, formerly at the Lowy Institute, and in Beijing with the China and Global Security Programme of the Stockholm International Peace Research Institute (SIPRI). China Matters was a new model in its independence from existing institutional ties. Its role

---

24 ussc.edu.au/about.
25 www.australiachinarelations.org/content/acri-launch-hon-julie-bishop.

was to 'stimulate a realistic and nuanced discussion of China among Australian business, government and the security establishment, and advance sound policy'.[26]

Of course, the expansion of international political and security think tanks was replicated in other areas. The Climate Institute (founded in 2005), the Mitchell Institute (established in 2013) and, most notably in terms of size and influence, the Grattan Institute, in Melbourne (which began in 2008), were established in the fields of economic and social policy.

What Differences Have Think Tanks Made?

All think tanks collect metrics to demonstrate the extent of their influence and reach to funders and supporters. Some of these metrics are simple: records of the number of events held and people present, research papers published, media coverage (including quotes from and appearances by scholars), and measures of the audience reach of websites, blogs, and social media feeds.

Another important measurement of success is finance: fund-raising in all its forms — endowments, philanthropic donations, foundation funding, corporate or individual membership, and sponsorship for specific purposes, whether from government or industry. The dependence on funding has generated increasing pressure in recent years for greater transparency in think tanks' declaration of their financial support.[27]

It is more difficult to measure the convening power of think tanks, that is, the quality and reputation that draws the public, policy-makers and the media to think tanks and in order to introduce their ideas and research. This depends in part on their capacity to attract and maintain the interest and loyalty of a diverse group of high calibre supporters and partners, and to recruit the best scholars and researchers. In recent years, as with universities, international rankings have become another way for think tanks to define success.[28]

---

26 chinamatters.org.au.
27 www.transparify.org.
28 McGann, James G. (2015) *2014 Global Go To Think Tank Index Report*, Philadelphia: University of Pennsylvania Press.

Hardest of all to evaluate, however, is whether a think tank has made a difference; whether decision-makers were influenced by its ideas. Ideas are intangible and infinitely fungible. It is very difficult to ascribe a single cause to a policy change. In any case, one of the larger roles of think tanks is not simply to propose actions but to reframe the way in which issues are seen.

Over the past 15 years, think tanks have changed Australian national security policy in five particular ways: by injecting new data into the public debate; by reframing some of the ways in which Australians think about the world; by suggesting specific policy ideas; by amplifying Australian voices in the international debate, including through second track processes; and by providing a new career path for Australians interested in working on international policy.

New Data

The annual Lowy Institute poll, described by the former Prime Minister, John Howard, as 'invaluable',[29] has provided a deeper and more consistent set of empirical data on the changing views of Australians about international policy questions. It has helped change the terms of the public debate on issues such as climate change, the United States alliance, and attitudes of young Australians towards democracy, and has provided a much more solid foundation for debate about community views and a way of tracing changes in them.

Similarly, ASPI's work through Mark Thomson in clarifying, analysing, and parsing the defence budget[30] has helped transform the way in which the Australian defence budget is debated, and even the way in which it is publicly presented.

Framing Ideas

A second way in which think tanks have influenced Australian policy has been by helping to reframe familiar debates in new ways. For example, Rory Medcalf's work at the Lowy Institute encouraged

---

29   Howard, John (2015), speech at launch of Jill Margo's *Frank Lowy: A Second Life*, Art Gallery of NSW, 7 October.
30   Thomson, Mark (2015) *The Cost of Defence: ASPI Defence Budget Brief 2015–2016*, Canberra: ASPI.

policy-makers from Labor and the Coalition to reconceptualise the country's strategic environment in Indo-Pacific rather than Asia-Pacific terms.[31] Alan Dupont's and Graeme Pearman's research on climate change and international security for the Lowy Institute[32] helped reframe the debate about what constituted international security in Australia. Hugh White's extensive writing on Australia's 'China choice' from SDSC and the Lowy Institute[33] has been another influential example of framing.

Policy Proposals

It is often hard to point to specific policy changes implemented as a result of recommendations by think tanks. Nevertheless, several examples from Australian policy in the Pacific are clear. The 2003 ASPI report by Elsina Wainwright on Solomon Islands, *Our Failing Neighbour*,[34] provided a background to and argument for a change in government policy to support Australia's military and police intervention in Solomon Islands. Jenny Hayward-Jones's work on the role of labour mobility in Pacific development,[35] and later on the need for Australia to reengage with Fiji[36] was acknowledged to have been influential.

In a different area, Linda Jakobson's 2012 Lowy Institute paper on the need for a strategic dialogue with China[37] played a direct role in the eventual creation of that dialogue according to government sources.

---

31 Medcalf, Rory (2013) 'The Indo-Pacific: What's in a Name?', *The American Interest* 9(2). Available at: www.the-american-interest.com/2013/10/10/the-indo-pacific-whats-in-a-name/.
32 Dupont, Alan and Graham Pearman (2006) *Heating up the Planet: Climate Change and Security*, Canberra: Lowy Institute for International Policy.
33 White, Hugh (2012) *The China Choice: Why America Should Share Power*, Melbourne: Black Inc.
34 Wainwright, Elsina (2003) *Our Failing Neighbour: Australia and the Future of Solomon Islands*, Canberra: Australian Strategic Policy Institute.
35 Hayward-Jones, Jenny (2008) *Labour Mobility: An Australian Seasonal Work Visa Scheme for Pacific Islands Labour*, Canberra: Lowy Institute for International Policy.
36 Hayward-Jones, Jenny (2014) *Fiji's Election and Australia: The Terms of Re-engagement*, Canberra: Lowy Institute for International Policy.
37 Jakobson, Linda (2012) *Australia-China Ties: In Search of Political Trust*, Canberra: Lowy Institute for International Policy.

Projecting Australian Voices

As a result of the shifts in global power noted earlier, governments and diplomats in the early twenty-first century found themselves seeking to influence a much greater range of international actors beyond their familiar interlocutors in other foreign ministries. Issues as diverse as the deterrence of people smuggling and the promotion of an Australian brand abroad required new forms of diplomacy with communities beyond governments. This opened up opportunities for think tanks in areas of second track diplomacy and media exchanges. Leadership dialogues proliferated and the government supported new forms of civil society engagement such as the Lowy Institute's Australia PNG Network.

Career Paths

Given the small number of Australians working on international policy, the reluctance of public servants to engage in public debate, and the speed with which a Canberra consensus develops around most international issues, one significant result of the development of think tanks was the creation of a new career path — outside the public service and universities — for a group of people interested in international policy. This has helped bring new voices, many of them with public service experience, into an otherwise cautious public debate. It has also facilitated greater movement into and out of the national security areas of government. Although Coral Bell (and Bob O'Neill) were early pioneers of this route, by 2015, policy analysts such as Hugh White, Peter Jennings, Michael Wesley, and Rory Medcalf had operated effectively across the three distinct areas of academia, government, and think tanks. Strong internship programs also developed at the key think tanks, offering students and new graduates a taste of the work.

In weighing up the influence of Australian international security think tanks, it is less clear that they have offered fundamental challenges to existing defence, foreign, and national security policies. Indeed, they seem to have been less prepared to do so than their counterparts in social and economic policy. The reasons for this are unclear. Nevertheless, the intrinsic bipartisanship of Australian foreign policy, the need for think tankers to retain access to decision-makers, the influence of funding sources, including the government, and a common cultural background among participants, all impose a subtle levelling effect on debate. Any deeper or more radical enquiry about international policy is still more likely to come from independent academic research in universities.

Future Outlook

The systemic pressures which favoured the emergence of think tanks in the early twenty-first century — the normative changes which led governments to seek contestable policy advice, and the inscription on the international agenda of issues that demanded fresh strategic approaches — seem unlikely to abate. Most economic observers believe that Australian Government expenditure will be constrained for the foreseeable future, so think tanks will continue to offer potentially cost-effective ways of developing and delivering policy objectives.

Any reader of speeches by Australian defence and foreign policy-makers over the past 80 years soon tires of the repetitious claims that the country is poised to enter new, more fluid and complex times. Still, it is certainly true that the challenges to the regional and global strategic order that Australia faces as a result of the rise of China will be more testing than most. Three responses have been woven through the policies every Australian government since the Second World War has used to address the nation's strategic vulnerabilities: alliance with a more powerful partner, efforts to influence the rules-based international order, and engagement with Asian neighbours to try to shape the regional environment. Each is clearly becoming harder to manage.

Bob O'Neill's 2006 prescription for think tanks: 'good ideas, dialogue with government and a relationship which tolerates free expression of views, especially on differences with existing policies',[38] remains relevant 10 years later.

---

38 O'Neill, Robert (2006) 'Problems and Perspectives on International Security', *The Lowy Lecture on Australia in the World*, 27 November, Sydney: Lowy Institute for International Policy.

18

Australian Thinking About Asia

Michael Wesley

Like some of the other great scholars of the late twentieth century, it was war that introduced Bob O'Neill to Asia.[1] Already a well-credentialed strategist and military historian, Bob was posted to Vietnam with the 5th Battalion, Royal Australian Regiment (5RAR), in May 1966, where from the start he began a diary which would become his second book, *Vietnam Task*.[2] Tellingly, Bob titled the first chapter 'The Problem', and used it to inform the reader (initially his wife, Sally, to whom he posted instalments of his diary) about the terrain, politics, and military situation in South Vietnam. The chapter (like the rest of the book) shows a thorough-going strategist at work. 'The Problem' refers not self-indulgently to the plight of a young academic who has left his bride to enter a war zone, nor ideologically to the scourge of rampant Asian communism, but to a strategic challenge, to be thought about with the cold, dry logic of Liddell-Hart and Clausewitz, and addressed with the attitude that there can be a solution. Never one to think things half through, Bob didn't leave the Vietnam War behind when he shipped out in 1967, or when *Vietnam Task* was published in

---

1 Others who immediately come to mind include Clifford Geertz, Chalmers Johnson, and Stephan Haggard.
2 O'Neill, Robert J. (1968) *Vietnam Task*, Melbourne: Cassell.

1968. In quick succession, Bob published an analysis of the Vietnam conflict[3] and a biography of General Giap,[4] the strategist behind the forces against which Bob had been fighting.

In these early books, along with his monumental official history, *Australia in the Korean War 1950–1953*,[5] Bob studied Vietnam and Korea closely, and thought about the contexts of these two conflicts deeply. His biography of General Giap, and his introductory chapter on the historical antecedents of the Korean War are testament to a scholar who read widely and thought profoundly about the local conditions and dynamics underpinning the two wars. His tenure as Head of ANU Strategic and Defence Studies Centre (SDSC) and then as Director of the International Institute of Strategic Studies (IISS) saw his attention return again and again to the strategic challenges of Asia. The conception of Asia that emerges from his writings is of a complicated and dynamic realm, less stable than any other region with the possible exception of the Middle East, and scantly covered by alliances, institutions, or other stabilising mechanisms. Asia is a region of intense competition within and between four layers of contention: the superpowers, the larger regional powers, the lesser regional powers, and various sub-national and transnational forces.[6] It is a realm where some of the Cold War's strict divisions began to unravel, while others remained stubbornly militarised; a realm that delivers puzzling variations to Bob's enduring strategic interests, including nuclear strategy and insurgency.[7]

Bob's writings on Asia's strategic dynamics are a significant contribution to evolving Australian thinking on the security challenges it faced after the end of the Vietnam War. Although Australians have been pondering and writing about Asia since at least the mid-nineteenth century,[8] the final quarter of the twentieth century became an

---

3   O'Neill, Robert J. (1968) *The Indo China Tragedy*, Melbourne: F. W. Cheshire.
4   O'Neill, Robert J. (1969) *General Giap: Politician and Strategist*, North Melbourne: Cassell
5   O'Neill, Robert J. (1981) *Australia in the Korean War 1950–53*, Volume 1: Strategy and Diplomacy, Canberra: The Australian War Memorial and the Australian Government Publishing Service.
6   O'Neill, Robert J. (ed.) (1984) *Security in East Asia*, Adelphi Library 9, London: International Institute for Strategic Studies, p. vii.
7   O'Neill, Robert J. (ed.) (1987) *East Asia, the West and International Security*, London: Macmillan.
8   Walker, David (1999) *Anxious Nation: Australia and the Rise of Asia, 1850–1939*, St Lucia: University of Queensland Press.

extremely fertile period of intellectual inquiry and policy development about Asia's evolving order and how Australia should relate to and, perhaps help shape, this order. Alongside the strategists were economists charting the beginnings of an era of explosive economic growth and its pervasive gravitational effects on the Australian economy. Political scientists delved into the sources of stability and instability within Australia's neighbours, charting the correlation of stable, if authoritarian, political settlements with sustained and remarkable equitable economic growth. Australian Government policy became closely entwined with these developments; initiatives such as the Pacific Economic Cooperation Council and Australia's initially isolated quest to find peace in Indochina saw academics and officials working closely together to address challenges and opportunities identified by both. The burst of policy innovation (the Defence of Australia) and institution building (Asia-Pacific Economic Cooperation (APEC), Association of Southeast Asian Nations (ASEAN) Regional Forum (ARF)) in the late 1980s and early 1990s was the culmination of Australian academics' and officials' long, entwined intellectual engagement with Asia.

And yet the founding of the ARF in 1994 can be seen as the conclusion of an era of Australian academic and official thinking about Asia. Many of the seeming verities that Australians had studied deeply in Asia seemed to have unravelled. For the strategists, with the end of the Cold War and the war in Indochina, there were new concerns: North Korea's nuclear program, China's assertiveness over the 1996 Taiwanese elections and the South China Sea, India's and Pakistan's breakout nuclear tests, and the fight to dislodge the Taliban and al Qaeda from Afghanistan and Pakistan. The economists were celebrating the arrival of the next rank of Asia's miracle — China, Thailand, and Indonesia — but, troublingly, the original miracle economy, Japan, had hit a wall from which it wouldn't recover. Then, in 1997, a financial crisis rippled across the region, rapidly reversing the miracle trade gains and casting doubt on the viability of state-directed approaches to economic development. The institutions created to great fanfare failed to live up to expectations; not only did they not galvanise in the face of security or financial crises,[9] by the end of the century it was clear

---

9   Wesley, Michael (1999) 'The Asian Crisis and the Adequacy of Regional Institutions', *Contemporary Southeast Asia* 21(1), pp. 54–73; Acharya, Amitav (1999) 'Realism, Institutionalism and the Asian Economic Crisis', *Contemporary Southeast Asia* 21(1), pp. 1–29.

that they had not been able to socialise a rising China to the region's norms and standards of behaviour. The political scientists saw their attention shift from authoritarian stability to democratic transition, instability, and increasing extremism.[10]

The quantum of Australian thinking about Asia did not abate after the mid-1990s; if anything, a greater range and diversity of voices joined the discussion. With the advent of the Howard Government in 1996, the close interaction between academics and officials on Australian policy towards the region frayed and at times became adversarial. Many of the themes and approaches to understanding Asia and Australia's relation to the region pioneered since the end of Vietnam War continued, but, perhaps reflecting the rate of change in the region itself, these were joined by new lines of inquiry and critique. In reviewing Australian thinking on Asia over the past two decades, I am going to separate Australian thinking about Asia from Australian thinking about how to relate to Asia. This is a somewhat artificial distinction, because there is an organic connection between a perspective on the region and a consequent attitude to how Australia should relate to the region. I try to rectify this distinction in the conclusion by identifying some of the continuities between understandings and prescriptions in the Australian conversation on Asia.

What is Asia?

'Asia' is a word heavily used in Australian political discourse, but its meanings are much less stable than those of other continents. Australian definitions of Asia have fluctuated according to the dynamics of wealth and power. In 1946, in mandating that its new national university in Canberra should devote one of four Research Schools to 'Pacific Studies', the Australian Government assumed all would know that this geographic designation was intended to include a large part of the Asian continent, on the verge of independence, and thus presenting a pressing imperative upon Australian government and society to understand the region.[11] Soon after, under the terms of the 1948

---

10 Robison, Richard and Vedi R. Hadiz (2004) *Reorganising Power in Indonesia: The Politics of Oligarchy in an Age of Markets*, London: Routledge Curzon.
11 *Australian National University Act 1946*. Available at: www.comlaw.gov.au/Details/C2004C02218.

UKUSA signals intelligence agreement (between the United States, United Kingdom, Canada, Australia, and New Zealand), Australia was given responsibility for collecting and sharing intelligence on Southeast Asia and the South Pacific — thus drawing much tighter boundaries on Australia's Asian area of interest and expertise.[12] Later, in 1951, Australia was a key player in the development of the Colombo Plan, which focused development assistance efforts on South and Southeast Asia.[13] Also in 1951, Australia signed the ANZUS Treaty with the United States and New Zealand, which returned to a broader geographic scope of alliance obligations:

> Each Party recognizes that an armed attack in the Pacific Area on any of the Parties would be dangerous to its own peace and safety and declares that it would act to meet the common danger in accordance with its constitutional processes.[14]

As we will see, the vagueness of the 'Pacific' definition of Asia — so clear to those who had just lived through the Pacific War — would cause real misunderstandings and tensions in the Australia–US alliance after the turn of the twenty-first century.

Involvement in the Korean War, and the signing of a Commerce Agreement with Japan in 1957 and the subsequent boom in Australian trade with Northeast Asia broadened Australia's Asia interests beyond Southeast Asia and focused them from a diffuse Pacific area.[15] At the same time, the communist victory in China, and Beijing's subsequent sponsorship of militant communist insurgencies throughout Southeast Asia, drew Australia's attention to Northeast and Southeast Asia as regions of primary security concern.[16] This coincidence of Australia's economic and security interests in East Asia would endure past the end of the Vietnam War, the deep enmeshment of the Australian economy with Asia, and the end of the Cold War. The dismantling of the White Australia Policy in the early 1970s, followed by the large-scale

---

12   Ball, Desmond and Jeffery T. Richelson (1990) *The Ties That Bind: Intelligence Cooperation Between the UKUSA Countries*, Boston: Unwin Hyman.
13   Oakman, Daniel (2004) *Facing Asia: A History of the Colombo Plan*, Canberra: Pandanus Books.
14   Commonwealth of Australia (1951) *ANZUS Treaty*. Available at: australianpolitics.com/topics/foreign-policy/anzus-treaty-text.
15   Tweedie, Sandra (1994) *Trading Partners: Australia and Asia 1790–1993*, Sydney: UNSW Press, pp. 154–6.
16   Millar, T. B. (1965) *Australia's Defence*, Melbourne: Melbourne University Press.

acceptance of Vietnamese refugees under the Fraser Government, brought a demographic dimension to Australia's new enmeshment with East Asia. In the Australian vernacular, the term 'Asian' was used to refer to people of East Asian ethnicity, unlike in Britain, where 'Asians' were universally taken to be South Asians. So embedded had East Asia become in Australian definitions of Asia that Foreign Minister Gareth Evans felt comfortable enough to propose an 'East Asian Hemisphere' in 1995, complete with cartographic illustrations showing Australia as part of this hemisphere.[17]

Following the turn of the century, three events combined to disturb this comfortable truncation of Asia in the Australian mind. The first was the September 11 terrorist attacks on the United States, which saw Australian Prime Minister John Howard invoke the ANZUS Treaty for the first time in its history, and commit Australian forces to the invasions of Afghanistan in 2001 and Iraq in 2003. The second was increasing evidence that the post-1991 economic reforms in India were translating into rapid economic growth in the world's other billion-plus people economy — which, in turn, were beginning to manifest in trade, investment and migration flows to Australia. Third was a rediscovery of geopolitical interest in the Indian Ocean, a part of the world that had not evinced much interest since the collapse of Soviet naval ambitions in the mid-1980s.[18] It wasn't long before Australia's commitments in the Middle East and South Asia were causing tensions in its relations with some Southeast Asian countries, while forging new operational military partnerships with countries such as Japan in Northeast Asia. Meanwhile, concerns over China's assertiveness in the South and East China Seas gave rise to hopes that India would soon begin to play a credible balancing role to China's growing power, and a series of growing security relations between New Delhi and countries such as Japan and Vietnam.[19] As a result, Australian commentators began to resurrect an older and largely forgotten term, the 'Indo-Pacific', as an explicit replacement of the term 'Asia Pacific'

---

17 Evans, Gareth (1995) 'Australia, ASEAN and the East Asian Hemisphere', Statement by the Australian Foreign Minister to the ASEAN PMC 7+1, Bandar Seri Bagawan, 2 August. Available at: www.gevans.org/speeches/old/1995/020895_australia_asean_eahemisphere.pdf.
18 Kaplan, Robert D. (2010) *Monsoon: The Indian Ocean and the Battle for Supremacy in the Twenty-First Century*, Melbourne: Black Inc Books.
19 Brewster, David (2012) *India as an Asia Pacific Power*, Abingdon: Routledge.

to define the part of Asia of most relevance to Australia.[20] The terms soon began to be picked up by policy-makers in Australia and the United States.

There is a case to be made that, despite this recent widening, the subdivision of Asia into segments that are of most interest to Australia makes little sense. The growing economic interdependence across Asia's subregions — in energy flows, investment, distributed manufacturing, and increasingly services — means that there is no one sub-region that is important on its own terms and independent of its relations with others. The growth in Asian powers' military capabilities and rivalries, and the recession of American strategic primacy means that drawing geopolitical boundaries around Asia's sub-regions makes little sense. The growth of institutions such as the Shanghai Cooperation Organisation, the One Belt-One Road and Eurasian Union initiatives, and the Asian Infrastructure Investment Banks shows that Asia's powers are not thinking in terms of Asia's subdivisions, but rather in terms of its possibilities and unities. Increasingly, I argue in my recent book, it will only make sense to think of Asia as a geographic whole — from the Pacific to the Mediterranean, from the Arctic to the Indian Ocean.[21]

Quite apart from the geographic definition of Asia, Australians have long discussed Asia as a cultural challenge to a Western society moored a long way from its cultural kin in Europe and North America. Primary among the newly independent Commonwealth's impulses towards the societies to its north west was a desire to assert the superiority of Australia's 'Anglo-Saxon' culture and institutions, and a desire to keep out the polluting influence of what were assumed to be 'lesser' Asian races.[22] The first piece of legislation issued by the Commonwealth Parliament in 1901 was the *Immigration Restriction Act*, which established the White Australia Policy, which would endure for over 70 years. Yet, at the same time as these fearful, exclusionary impulses were dominant, there was a constant sub-theme of Australians

---

20 Wesley, Michael (2011) *There Goes the Neighbourhood: Australia and the Rise of Asia*, Sydney: NewSouth Books; Medcalf, Rory (2013) 'Indo-Pacific: What's in a Name?', in Michael Fullilove and Anthony Bubalo (eds), *Reports From a Turbulent Decade*, Melbourne: Viking.
21 Wesley, Michael (2015) *Restless Continent: Wealth, Rivalry and Asia's New Geopolitics*, Melbourne: Black Inc Books.
22 Reynolds, Henry and Marylin Lake (2008) *Drawing the Global Colour Line: White Men's Countries and the Question of Racial Equality*, Melbourne: Melbourne University Press.

fascinated by the antiquity and sophistication of Asian cultures and religions. The study of Asian thought and society, and increasingly tourism to Asia became a significant current in Australian society from the late nineteenth century.[23]

With the end of the Second World War and the coming of independence to the countries of Asia, Australian writers began to question the compatibility of the White Australia Policy with the imperative of building close relations with the new states to our north.[24] The growing assertiveness of post-colonial states in the United Nations over racial questions during the 1960s saw the Australian Government begin to quietly dismantle the White Australia Policy. And as security and economic trends drew Australia's attention ever more insistently towards Asia, there was a surge in Australian research and writing on the impact of cultural and values differences on international relations and foreign policy.[25] The Australian debates and discussions at the time were affected by two external factors: the worldwide resurgence of regionalism at the end of the Cold War, and the surge of debate around the impact of culture on world politics following the publication of Samuel Huntington's essay, 'The Clash of Civilizations?'.[26] Huntington explicitly drew Australia into his provocative argument, labelling it a 'torn country in reverse' whose 'current leaders are in effect proposing that it defect from the West, redefine itself as an Asian country and cultivate close ties with its neighbours'.[27] Huntington's intervention had the effect of further politicising Australia's policy of enmeshment with the Asian region, with opposition leader John Howard accusing

---

23 Walker, David (1999) *Anxious Nation: Australia and the Rise of Asia, 1850–1939*, St Lucia: University of Queensland Press; Strahan, Lachlan (1996) *Australia's China: Changing Perceptions from the 1930s to the 1990s*, Cambridge: Cambridge University Press; McFarlane, Jenny (2006) *A Sacred Space: Theosophy and Alternative Modernism in Australia, 1890–1934*, PhD Thesis, The Australian National University.
24 Levi, Walter (1947) *American-Australian Relations*, Minneapolis: Minnesota University Press; Borrie, W. D. (1950) 'Australian Population and its Relation to Asia', *Australian Outlook* 4(3), pp. 162–9; Crocker, Walter R. (1956) *The Racial Factor in International Relations*, Canberra: Australian National University Press.
25 Viviani, Nancy (1993) 'The Politics of Nationalism and Regionalism in Australia', *Asian Journal of Political Science* 1(2), pp. 39–56; Milner, Anthony and Mary Quilty (1995) *Comparing Cultures*, Melbourne: Oxford University Press; FitzGerald, Stephen (1997) *Is Australia an Asian Country?* Sydney: Allen & Unwin.
26 Huntington, Samuel P. (1993) 'The Clash of Civilizations?' *Foreign Affairs* 72(3), pp. 22–49.
27 Ibid., p. 45

the government of selling out Australia's identity, and Prime Minister Paul Keating vehemently rejecting Huntington's and Howard's characterisations.[28]

The imperative of post-Cold War regionalism also added intensity to the debate within Australia. Being so dependent on the region for economic and security reasons, Canberra sensed the danger of being left on the outer if an exclusionary bloc were to form in East Asia. This was heightened by Malaysia's combative Prime Minister Mahathir, who championed Asian regionalism in explicitly cultural terms (while conveniently glossing over the differences among Asian societies by promoting the idea of common Asian values). Foreign Minister Gareth Evans argued that cultural differences were becoming less and less relevant in the age of globalisation, while his successor Alexander Downer argued that Australia's cultural differences with Asian societies mattered little given the wide cultural and values differences among Asian societies. In the end, Mahathir's vision of an exclusionary, Asianist regional grouping was rejected in favour of the open regionalism embodied by APEC, the ARF, and eventually the East Asia Summit. The intensity of discussions about Australia's cultural differences with East Asian societies were themselves superseded by a post-9/11 anxiety about asylum seekers from South and West Asia and a growing debate about how Australian society should relate to Muslim communities within and beyond its borders.[29]

A third theme in Australian thinking about Asia has been a repeated return to using Asia as a mirror in which Australian society appraises itself. Australian society's comfortable sense of superiority to the societies to its north began to be unsettled in the 1960s as the Japanese economy boomed, soon to be followed by the economies of South Korea, Taiwan, Hong Kong, and a procession of Asian tigers. The period of Asia's economic boom coincided with the end of Australia's own postwar long boom. After 1974, Australia's economy succumbed to over a decade of sluggish growth, high inflation and unemployment, and collapsing consumer and export demand, while a succession of Asian economies industrialised and grew at the fastest rates ever seen.

---

28   Keating, Paul (2000) *Engagement: Australia Faces the Asia Pacific*, Sydney: Pan Macmillan; Wesley, Michael (2007) *The Howard Paradox: Australian Diplomacy in Asia 1996–2006*, Sydney: ABC Books.
29   Burke, Anthony (2008) *Fear of Security: Australia's Invasion Anxiety*, Melbourne: Cambridge University Press

Australians could no longer look to Europe and America for solutions, because these regions were suffering as severe economic recessions as Australia. Inevitably, comparisons began to be made between a struggling Australian economy and the booming fortunes of its neighbours.[30] These anxieties were only stoked by Asian leaders, such as Singapore's Lee Kwan Yew, who warned Australians that unless they changed they would become the 'poor white trash of Asia'. Treasurer Paul Keating seemed to echo Lee's warning when he famously said in 1986 that Australia risked becoming a 'banana republic' if it did not deregulate and diversify its economy.

Partly against the background of Australia's lagging performance compared to Asia's, a broad suite of liberalising economic reforms were undertaken in the 1980s and 1990s.[31] By the mid-1990s, the Australian economy had entered a period of expansion and prosperity that was to survive three global and regional slowdowns, coming to be seen as a miracle economy. It was in this state of economic buoyancy that Australia watched the tiger economies to its north stumble — first Japan's long recession, then the collapse of the Thai, Korean, Philippines, Malaysian, and Indonesian economies in the 1997–1998 Asian Financial Crisis. Suddenly the logic of comparison had flipped. Foreign Minister Downer couldn't resist providing some helpful inspiration to the struggling economies in Asia: 'we have through our own strong [economic] performance shown the region … what commitment to openness and transparency in economic and political affairs can achieve'.[32]

Asia also provided a mirror to those Australians who worried about the country's alliance relationship with the United States. The alliance has been controversial for decades among those who worry that it makes Australia vulnerable as collateral damage in a possible nuclear exchange[33] or that Australia risks being dragged into American strategic mistakes.[34] For many commentators of this view, the countries

---

30 Castles, Francis G. (1988) *Australian Public Policy and Economic Vulnerability*, Sydney: Allen & Unwin; Drysdale, Peter (1988) *International Economic Pluralism: Economic Policy in East Asia and the Pacific*, Canberra: Australian National University Press.
31 Kelly, Paul (1992) *The End of Certainty*, Sydney: Allen & Unwin.
32 Quoted in Wesley, Michael (2011) *There Goes the Neighbourhood: Australia and the Rise of Asia*, Sydney: NewSouth Books, p. 310.
33 Camilleri, Joseph A. (1987) *ANZUS: Australia's Predicament in the Nuclear Age*, Melbourne: Macmillan.
34 Wilkie, Andrew (2004) *Axis of Deceit*, Melbourne: Black Inc Agenda.

of Asia that refused to align with either side of the Cold War divide, or those that did ally but in a low key, ambiguous way, provided a clear example of how a country in Australia's neighbourhood could maintain its security without compromising its foreign policy independence.[35] In some iterations of this argument, Australia's close alignment with the United States was a major factor that prevented it from playing a genuine insider's role in Asia.[36] On the other side of this debate were those who argued that rather than diminishing Australia's influence in Asia, the US alliance actually enhances it.[37]

The rise of China as Australia's most important economic partner emerged as a major complication in managing a bifurcation of Australia's economic and security interests. Like many regional countries, Australia has tightened its security relationship with the United States as it has been drawn ever more powerfully into China's economic orbit. The thickening economic relationship with China has repeatedly raised questions over whether, if China and the United States were to come to blows, Australia would support its ally or remain aloof in the interests of preserving its economic relationship with China. Here, the ambiguity of the ANZUS Treaty's wording has not helped. While some Australian leaders, such as Kevin Rudd, have been clear in their intention to side with Washington, others, such as Alexander Downer and Defence Minister David Johnston, have been much more equivocal. The changing structure of forces in the Pacific has led some scholars to argue that the balance of risks within the alliance has shifted, as the United States has moved from being at risk of entrapment to a risk of abandonment by its smaller ally.[38]

Another Asian mirror shed light on Australian values for many commentators. After promising democratic starts, many of Asia's countries lurched towards semi-authoritarian one-party rule in the decades after independence.[39] At times this led to bitter divisions among

---

35 Fraser, Malcolm, (2014) *Dangerous Allies*, Melbourne: Melbourne University Press.
36 Broinowski, Alison (2003) *About Face: Asian Accounts of Australia*, Melbourne: Scribe Publications.
37 Sheridan, Greg (2006) *The Partnership: The Inside Story of the US–Australian Alliance Under Bush and Howard*, Sydney: UNSW Press.
38 Green, Michael J., Peter J. Dean, Brendan Taylor and Zack Cooper (2015) *The ANZUS Alliance in an Ascending Asia*, Centre of Gravity Paper, Canberra: Strategic and Defence Studies Centre, The Australian National University.
39 Dressel, Bjeorn and Michael Wesley (2014) 'Asian States in Crisis', *Strategic Analysis* 38(4), pp. 452–3.

Australia's Asianist scholars, some of whom advocated continuing to study and engage with Australia's authoritarian neighbours, while others adopted a much more critical attitude to shortfalls in democracy, the rule of law, and human rights.[40] Writers such as Pierre Ryckmans urged Australians not to be duped by superficial enthusiasm for countries such as the People's Republic of China, where vicious regimes were tearing societies apart.[41] Ryckmans was particularly cutting about Australia jettisoning its moral compass in pursuit of material gains, arguing that admiration for Deng Xiaoping was the result of an eagerness for 'signing fat business deals with China'.[42] Some Indonesianists were highly critical of Canberra's close relationship with the authoritarian, corrupt Suharto regime in Indonesia, directing particular criticism towards the Australian Defence Force's intimate embrace of the Indonesian Armed Forces, the cutting edge of repression and human rights abuses. Others argued that as Australia had become more integrated into Asian regional institutions, it had adopted a more Asian foreign policy stance in its increasing reluctance to criticise the internal practices of its co-members.

Australia and Asia

Of course, these different manifestations of Asia in the Australian imagination have often been related in some way to distinct opinions about how Australia should relate to the huge continent and archipelagos to its north. Perhaps the longest running theme on how Asia affects Australia centres around the several iterations of 'Asiapessimism' versus 'Asiaphoria'. Asiapessimists have come in several varieties. At the end of the Second World War, there were many Australians who were fearful of the prospect of a region of newly independent countries, believing that the new nations of the region would soon become prey to resurgent Japanese militarism or the march of Asian communism.[43] The response was to pursue an alliance with the United States, push for a development assistance plan

---

40   See Kelly, David and Anthony Reid (eds) (1998) *Asian Freedoms*, Melbourne: Cambridge University Press.
41   Leys, Simon (1977) *Chinese Shadows*, New York: Viking Press.
42   Quoted in Strahan, Lachlan (1996) *Australia's China: Changing Perceptions from the 1930s to the 1990s*, Cambridge: Cambridge University Press, p. 302.
43   Fitzgerald, C. P. (1957) 'Australia in Asia', in Gordon Greenwood and Norman Harper (eds), *Australia in World Affairs 1950–1955*, Melbourne: F. W. Cheshire, p. 201.

at Colombo to bolster resilience in new states, and adopt a forward defence strategy.[44] More recent forms of Asiapessimism focus on the persistent or new causes of instability in Asia, from corruption and crime to environmental degradation, with several scholars pointing out the role of Australia's energy exports in Asia's mounting challenge to the global environment.[45]

On the other side were the Asiaphoric commentators who tended to see Asia's future as bright and therefore viewed Australia's future as clearly wedded to the booming countries to the north. Many saw the economic rise of Asia as a re-emergence of Asian societies to a place of global pre-eminence after the long night of colonialism, and celebrated the political and cultural decolonisation that was occurring as a consequence as Asian societies gained the confidence to stand up to Western dominance.[46] Some could see the dawn of a new age in Asia's rise, a post-Western economic and security order to which Australia would have to adjust in order to secure its future.[47] The logic was that Asia's rise was an opportunity for Australia, if only Australia could prove itself nimble and protean enough to make the most of this millennial activity.[48] Others, particularly on the conservative side of politics, rejected the notion that Australia had to adjust to succeed in Asia; in Prime Minister John Howard's terms, Australia could make its way just by being ourselves.[49]

One interesting aspect of this debate is the extent to which the Asiapessimists are speaking a different language — that of strategy — to that of the Asiaphorists — who speak the language of economics. This is particularly stark in relation to the rise of China and its likely impact on Australia. Strategists tend to see in China's rise the prospects of deepening rivalry with the United States and other Asian powers,

---

44 Lowe, David (1999) *Menzies and the 'Great World Struggle': Australia's Cold War 1948–54*, Sydney: UNSW Press; Edwards, Peter (2014) *Australia and the Vietnam War*, Sydney: NewSouth Books.
45 Dupont, Alan (1999) *East Asia Imperilled*, Melbourne: Cambridge University Press; Beeson, Mark (2011) 'Can Australia Save the World?: The Limits and Possibilities of Middle Power Diplomacy', *Australian Journal of International Affairs* 65 (5), pp. 563–77.
46 FitzGerald, Stephen (1997) *Is Australia an Asian Country?* Sydney: Allen & Unwin, p. 42.
47 Garnaut, Ross (1989) *Australia and the Northeast Asian Ascendancy*, Canberra: Australian Government Public Service.
48 Australian Government (2012) *Australia and the Asian Century*, White Paper, Canberra: Commonwealth of Australia.
49 Wesley, Michael (2007) *The Howard Paradox: Australian Diplomacy in Asia 1996–2006*, Sydney: ABC Books.

leading to the realistic prospect of war, including nuclear exchange.[50] The prescription for Australia is, then, greater independence and activism, playing a role in coaxing the great powers towards some sort of mutual accommodation. The Asiaphorists see in China's rise a new phase of the global economy, in which Australia is particularly well placed to benefit from the remarkable complementarities between its own economy and the soon to be world's largest economy. The imperative of this school of thought is that Australia should get over its suspicions of China's different political and cultural system, and make the most of the demand and investment generated by its giant economy.

Another strand of thinking on Australia and its relation to Asia is the Engagement Project. Believers in the Engagement Project detected in the 1970s and 1980s that one consequence of the rise of Asia would be a challenge to the dominance of Western orders and norms as they applied to Australia's region. The end of the Vietnam War and the announcement of the Nixon Doctrine quickened Australia's search for an alternative defence doctrine to Forward Defence, and a decisive move towards the Defence of Australia Doctrine.[51] Key government messaging around the new doctrine was that in the future, Australia would seek its security '*in* Asia, not *from* Asia'. This new mantra coincided with the rise of the new regionalism around the world, as the Cold War came to an end. Eager to secure a founding membership of any Asian institutions that emerged, Australia became an active regionalist, promoting what were eventually to become APEC and the ARF, and campaigning against exclusivist cultural bloc proposals such as Dr Mahathir's East Asia Economic Caucus. Asian engagement became a defining foreign policy project for Australia and a significant issue in the country's domestic politics. The rhetoric of engagement was redolent with the implications of an apprenticeship: while other countries in the region were automatically assumed to be members, Australia needed to demonstrate its credentials and commitment to

---

50   White, Hugh (2012) *The China Choice: Why America Should Share Power*, Melbourne: Black Inc Books.
51   Dibb, Paul (1986) *Review of Australia's Defence Capabilities*, Canberra: Australian Government Public Service. Available at: www.defence.gov.au/se/publications/defreview/1986/Review-of-Australias-Defence-Capabilities-1986.pdf.

the Asian project — whatever that was. This attracted great attention among Australian scholars and policy-makers to the bounds and rules of the club that we were seeking to join.[52]

The engagement project became a significant issue in domestic politics. Whether Australia was a member of regional groupings (such as APEC and the ARF) or not (such as the Asia–Europe Meeting) became an issue of some controversy. Australian foreign policy actions, and even domestic political developments such as the rise of the xenophobic One Nation party, were appraised according to whether they advanced or hindered the engagement project. For some commentators, participation in the Iraq War or the failure to condemn racism in Australia meant that the 'dowry price just keeps rising'.[53] On the other hand, Australian Foreign Minister Alexander Downer argued that Australia wasn't interested in joining all regional clubs — it was interested in 'practical regionalism', not 'emotional regionalism'.[54] The engagement project seemed to lose cache after Australia signed ASEAN's Treaty of Amity and Cooperation and joined the East Asia Summit in 2005. One scholar challenged Australia's foreign policy community to move on from the engagement era and find a new paradigm for dealing with the region as an acknowledged insider.[55]

Conclusion

Reviews of one nation's thinking about a particular subject are inevitably partial and reflective of the author's experiences and interests. I am aware also that the thinking about Asia I have set out seems very logically and clearly divided into different approaches and streams. The reality is that the Australian conversation about Asia has been ongoing and varied for close to two centuries. Themes merge and coincide; debates rage and die; and what appear to be

---

52   FitzGerald, Stephen (1997) *Is Australia an Asian Country?* Sydney: Allen & Unwin; Ravenhill, John (2001) *APEC and the Construction of Pacific Rim Regionalism*, Cambridge: Cambridge University Press; Wesley, Michael (1997) 'The Politics of Exclusion: Australia, Turkey, and Definitions of Regionalism', *The Pacific Review* 10(4), pp. 523–55.
53   Broinowski, Alison (2003) *About Face: Asian Accounts of Australia*, Melbourne: Scribe Publications.
54   Wesley, Michael (2007) *The Howard Paradox: Australian Diplomacy in Asia 1996–2006*, Sydney: ABC Books, p. 155.
55   Carr, Andrew (2015) *Winning the Peace: Australia's Campaign to Change the Asia Pacific*, Melbourne: Melbourne University Press.

new ideas turn out to have long historical antecedents. There have always been important connections between Australians' geographic definition of Asia and their thinking about the quest for membership and belonging. The irony is, of course, that in defining themselves into the region, the East Asian Hemispherists are at the same time defining out most of the societies that occupy that continent. Another intimate connection has been between currents of Asiaphoria and Asiapessimism, and discussions of whether the rise of Asia represents a challenge or alternative to Australia's Western identity. As observers have sometimes noted, Australian debates about the meaning of Asia's rise often say more about the people engaging in debate than the region they are debating. The same can be said about the various discussions that use Asia as a mirror to reflect on Australia's worth and values.

All of this was grist to Bob O'Neill's mill as he reflected on and wrote about the strategic dynamics of his time. When one reads Bob's writings, one can see the impact of Australia's rich debates about how it defines and relates to the culturally and developmentally different countries to its north. Even while Bob was in the UK, he kept abreast of the developments and debates in his native country, and his own intellectual projects returned regularly to the security dynamics of Asia.[56] Bob's writings are and will remain part of the deep and dynamic conversation in Australia about Asia.

---

56   O'Neill, Robert J. (ed.) (1984) *Security in East Asia*, Adelphi Library 9, London: International Institute for Strategic Studies; O'Neill, Robert J. (1992) *Security Challenges for Southeast Asia After the Cold War*, Singapore: Institute of Southeast Asian Studies.

Contributors

Desmond Ball is Professor at the Strategic and Defence Studies Centre (SDSC), The Australian National University. He was Head of SDSC from 1984–1991, was awarded a personal chair in the Research School of Pacific and Asian Studies in 1987; was a member of the Council of the International Institute for Strategic Studies (IISS) from 1995–2001; and was co-chairman of the Steering Committee of the Council for Security Cooperation in Asia-Pacific from 2000–2002. He was made a Fellow the Academy of the Social Sciences in Australia in 1986, and an Officer of the Order of Australia in 2014. He is the author of over 100 books, articles and chapters on defence and security.

Mats Berdal is Professor of Security and Development in the Department of War Studies at King's College London. Between 2000 and 2003 he was the Director of Studies at the International Institute for Strategic Studies. He received his PhD from Oxford University, which he completed under Robert O'Neill's supervision in 1992.

Paul Dibb is Emeritus Professor of Strategic Studies and Chairman of SDSC. He was Head of SDSC from 1991–2003. His previous positions include Deputy Secretary of the Department of Defence, Director of the Defence Intelligence Organisation, and Head of the National Assessments Staff (National Intelligence Committee). As Deputy Secretary, he chaired the Force Structure Committee with the Vice Chief of the Defence Force as his deputy, and the service chiefs as the other senior committee members. He is the author of five books and four reports to government, as well as more than 150 academic articles and monographs about the security of the Asia-Pacific region, the US alliance, and Australia's defence policy. He wrote the 1986 *Review of Australia's Defence Capabilities* (the Dibb Report) and was the primary author of the 1987 Defence White Paper. His book *The Soviet Union: the Incomplete Superpower* was published by IISS London in 1986, reprinted in 1987, with a second edition in 1988. On behalf of the Department of Foreign and Affairs and Trade, he has represented Australia at 10 meetings of the ASEAN Regional Forum's Expert and Eminent Persons group, most recently in Singapore in March 2016. He was made a Member of the Order of Australia in 1989.

Peter Edwards, currently an Adjunct Professor at SDSC, was the Official Historian of Australia's involvement in Southeast Asian conflicts 1948–1975 (the Malayan Emergency, the Indonesian Confrontation, and the Vietnam War). He was general editor of the nine-volume series and author of the volumes dealing with strategy and diplomacy, *Crises and Commitments* (1992), and *A Nation at War* (1997). He is also the author of *Australia and the Vietnam War* (2014), a single-volume distillation of the nine-volume series, and of *Robert Marsden Hope and Australian Public Policy* (2011), *Arthur Tange: Last of the Mandarins* (2006), *Permanent Friends?: Historical Reflections on the Australian-American Alliance* (2005), and *Prime Ministers and Diplomats: The Making of Australian Foreign Policy 1901–49* (1983); co-author of *A School with a View* (2010); co-editor of *Facing North* (vol. 2, 2003); and editor of *Australia Through American Eyes* (1977). He played a major role in establishing the series of *Documents on Australian Foreign Policy*. A Rhodes Scholar, Dr Edwards is a Member of the Order of Australia (AM), a Fellow of the Australian Institute for International Affairs, a former Trustee of Melbourne's Shrine of Remembrance, and the winner of several literary awards.

Ashley Ekins is head of the Military History Section at the Australian War Memorial, Canberra. A graduate of the University of Adelaide, he specialises in the history of the First World War and the Vietnam War. He wrote two volumes on Australian ground operations in Vietnam for the 'Official History of Australian Involvement in Southeast Asian Conflicts 1948–1975': *On the Offensive: The Australian Army in the Vietnam War, 1967–1968*, co-authored with Ian McNeill (2003); and *Fighting to the Finish: The Australian Army and the Vietnam War 1968–1975* (2012). His publications also include *1918 Year of Victory: The End of the Great War and the Shaping of History* (edited, shortlisted for the Templer Medal, 2010); *War Wounds: Medicine and the Trauma of Conflict* (edited with Elizabeth Stewart, 2011); and *Gallipoli: A Ridge too far* (edited, 2013, second revised edition, 2015).

CONTRIBUTORS

Lawrence Freedman was Professor of War Studies at King's College London from 1982–2014, and was Vice Principal from 2003 to 2013. He was educated at Whitley Bay Grammar School and the universities of Manchester, York, and Oxford. Before joining King's he held research appointments at Nuffield College Oxford, IISS, and the Royal Institute of International Affairs. In 1996, he was appointed Official Historian of the Falklands Campaign in 1997, and in June 2009 he was appointed to serve as a member of the official inquiry into Britain and the 2003 Iraq War. Lawrence Freedman has written extensively on nuclear strategy and the Cold War, as well as commentating regularly on contemporary security issues. His most recent book, *Strategy: A History* (2013), was awarded the W. J. McKenzie Book Prize by the Political Studies Association.

Allan Gyngell is Adjunct Professor in the Crawford School of Public Policy at ANU and a Visiting Fellow at the National Security College. From 2009–2013 he was Director-General of the Office of National Assessments, and from 2003–2009 was the inaugural Executive Director of the Lowy Institute for International Policy. He earlier worked as a senior officer in the Department of Foreign Affairs and Trade, the Office of National Assessments, and the Department of the Prime Minister and Cabinet. He was Senior Adviser (International) to Prime Minister Paul Keating. He has written extensively on Australian foreign policy, Asian regional relations, and the development of global and regional institutions. He is co-author with Michael Wesley of *Making Australian Foreign Policy*. He was appointed as an Officer in the Order of Australia in 2009 and is a Fellow of the Australian Institute of International Affairs.

Marianne Hanson is Associate Professor of International Relations at the University of Queensland. She was fortunate to complete her studies under the guidance of Robert O'Neill at Oxford University. Marianne's main area of focus is international security, especially nuclear arms control, international humanitarian law, and the role of international organisations. She has published widely in these fields.

Beatrice Heuser holds the Chair in International Relations at the University of Reading. She has degrees from the Universities of London (BA, MA) and Oxford (PhD), and a Habilitation from the University of Marburg. She has taught at the Department of War Studies, King's College London, at four French universities/higher education institutions, at two German universities, and has briefly worked at NATO headquarters. Her publications include *The Evolution of Strategy* (2010), *Reading Clausewitz* (2002), and many works on nuclear strategy, NATO, and transatlantic relations.

John Hillen is a former US Assistant Secretary of State and former chief executive officer of a number of US technology services companies, both public and privately held. A decorated combat veteran, he is the author of several books and numerous articles on international security affairs. He served as both a trustee and a member of the Council of IISS for a number of years, and did his PhD under Robert O'Neill's supervision at the University of Oxford in the mid-1990s.

David Horner is Emeritus Professor of Australian Defence History at SDSC, where he has worked since 1990. A graduate of the Royal Military College, Duntroon, in 1969, he saw active service in Vietnam and served for 25 years in the Australian Regular Army. Later, as a colonel in the Army Reserve, he was the first Head of the Australian Army's Land Warfare Studies Centre. He is the author/editor of some 32 books and numerous articles on military history, strategy, and defence. In 2004, he was appointed Official Historian of Australian Peacekeeping, Humanitarian and Post-Cold War Operations and is the general editor of this six-volume series. In 2009 he was appointed Official Historian for the Australian Security Intelligence Organisation (ASIO) and general editor of this three-volume series. The first volume of the ASIO series, *The Spy Catchers*, won the 2015 UK Intelligence Book of the Year prize and was joint winner of the Prime Minister's Literary Award for history in 2015.

Sir Michael Eliot Howard OM, CH, CBE, MC, FBA (born 29 November 1922) is a British military historian, formerly Chichele Professor of the History of War, Emeritus Fellow of All Souls College, Regius Professor of Modern History at Oxford University, Robert A. Lovett Professor of Military and Naval History at Yale University and founder of the Department of War Studies, King's College London.

Catherine McArdle Kelleher is Professor at the University of Maryland's School of Public Policy, and Professor (Emerita) of Strategy at the US Naval War College. In addition to high-level government service under the Carter and Clinton administrations, Kelleher has held fellowships at the Watson Institute at Brown University, the Center for Naval Analysis in Washington, the Institute of Strategic Studies in London, All Souls College at Oxford, and the American Academy of Arts and Sciences. She has received individual research grants from NATO, the Council on Foreign Relations, the MacArthur foundation, the German Marshall Fund, the Carnegie Corporation, and the Ford Foundation. She is graduate of Mount Holyoke College, and MIT, and the recipient of the Medal for Distinguished Public Service of the Department of Defense, the Director's Medal from the Defense Intelligence Agency, the Cross of Honor in Gold of the Federal Armed Forces of Germany, and the Manfred Woerner Medal by the German Ministry of Defense. She was honoured by the German President with the Bundesverdienstkreuz in 2014. She is the author of more than 70 books, monographs, and articles

Carter Malkasian is the special assistant to the Chairman of the Joint Chiefs of Staff, General Joseph Dunford. He has extensive experience working in conflict zones and has published several books. The highlight of his work in conflict zones was nearly two years in Garmser district, Helmand province, Afghanistan, as a State Department Political Officer. Before that, Dr Malkasian deployed as a civilian advisor with the Marines twice to Iraq, for a total of 18 months, in Al Anbar in 2004 and 2006. Other field assignments have been to Honduras, Kuwait (OIF-1), Kunar (2007–2008), and Kabul as Political Advisor to General Dunford (2013–2014), the Commander of all US and Allied forces in Afghanistan. From May 2012 to May 2013, Dr Malkasian directed the office of overseas operations within the US State Department's Bureau of Conflict and Stabilization Operations. From October 2006 to July 2009, he directed the Stability and Development Program at the Center for Naval Analyses, the think tank for the US Navy and Marine Corps. His most recent book is *War Comes to Garmser* (2013), which won the silver medal for the Council on Foreign Relations Arthur Ross Book Award for 2014. Other publications include *A History of Modern Wars of Attrition* (2002), *The Korean War, 1950–1953* (2001), and 'War Downsized: How to Accomplish More with Less' in *Foreign Affairs*. Dr Malkasian completed his doctorate in history at Oxford University. He speaks Pashto.

Octavian Manea, a contributor to *Small Wars Journal*, was a Fulbright Junior Scholar at Maxwell School of Citizenship and Public Affairs at Syracuse University where he completed an MA in International Relations with a focus on security studies.

Daniel Marston is Professor of Military Studies at The Australian National University, and Principal of the Military and Defence Studies Program at the Australian Command and Staff College in Canberra. He has been a Visiting Fellow with the Oxford Leverhulme Programme on the Changing Character of War. He has been working with the USA, United States Marine Corps, British Army in Iraq and Afghanistan since 2006. He completed his doctorate in the history of war at Balliol College, Oxford University, under the supervision of Professor Robert O'Neill.

John Nagl is the ninth Headmaster of the Haverford School in Philadelphia. A veteran of both Iraq Wars, he earned his MA and PhD at Oxford under the supervision of Professor O'Neill.

Gaines Post is Professor Emeritus of History, Claremont McKenna College. A graduate of Cornell University, he served as a lieutenant in the US Army in Germany, and attended Oxford University before obtaining his PhD in modern European history at Stanford University. He taught at the University of Texas (Austin), then became Dean of Faculty at Claremont McKenna College. A specialist on modern Germany and the origins of the Second World War, his major scholarly publications are *The Civil-Military Fabric of Weimar Foreign Policy* (1973), and *Dilemmas of Appeasement: British Deterrence and Defense, 1934–1937* (1993).

Michael Wesley is Professor of International Affairs and Director of the Coral Bell School of Asia Pacific Affairs at The Australian National University. His career has spanned academia, with previous appointments at the University of New South Wales, Griffith University, the University of Hong Kong, Sun Yat-sen University, and the University of Sydney; government, where he worked as Assistant Director General for Transnational Issues at the Office of National Assessments; and think tanks, as Executive Director of the Lowy Institute for International Policy and a Non-Resident Senior Fellow at the Brookings Institution. Professor Wesley has also served as the editor-in-chief of the *Australian Journal of International Affairs*.

He is a Non-Executive Member of the Senior Leadership Group of the Australian Federal Police and a Member of the NSW/ACT Advisory Board for the Committee for Economic Development of Australia. His book, *There Goes the Neighbourhood: Australia and the Rise of Asia* (2011), won the 2011 John Button Prize for the best writing on Australian public policy. His most recent book is *Restless Continent: Wealth, Power and Asia's New Geopolitics* (2015).

Hugh White has been Professor of Strategic Studies at SDSC since 2004. Before that he was a senior official of the Australian Government, and the first director of the Australian Strategic Policy Institute. His recent publications include *Power Shift: Australia's Future Between Washington and Beijing* (2010), and *The China Choice: Why America Should Share Power* (2012).

Tony White was born in Australia but grew up in Kenya. He studied medicine at Cambridge and Sydney universities then took up a short service commission in the Australian Army. He served in Vietnam alongside Robert O'Neill for 12 months (1966–1967) as the Regimental Medical Officer in the 5th Battalion, Royal Australian Regiment, and was awarded a mention-in-despatches. Returning to civilian life, he specialised as a dermatologist, practising in Sydney. He did an annual stint in the outback with the Royal Flying Doctor Service and was involved in dermatology clinics and workshops in the Pacific Islands and Aboriginal communities in the Northern Territory. In 2009, he was appointed a Member of the Order of Australia for contributions to remote area dermatological practice and education. Following his retirement in 2010, he completed a Master of Medical Humanities degree at Sydney University.

Index

Afghanistan War, 155–78, 235–49
    Australian military presence, 87–8
    official history, 88–9
    Operation Enduring Freedom (US), 160–1
American military operations, 127–53. *see also* Operation Desert Storm; Powell doctrine; Reagan doctrine
American–Soviet relations, 219–21, 219–27, 232
    Strategic Defense Initiative (SDI), 227–9
Australia New Zealand and United States Treaty (ANZUS Treaty), 68–9, 289–90
Australian Strategic Policy Institute (ASPI), 251–63, 274–5
Australian War Memorial, 64, 65–6, 78
Australian–American relations. *see* Australia New Zealand and United States Treaty (ANZUS Treaty)
Australian–Asian relations, 285–300
Australian–Soviet relations, 51–3

Balkans War. *see* Yugoslav Wars
bin Laden, Osama, 108, 141–2
Bosnian conflict. *see* Yugoslav Wars
British–Soviet relations, 123–4

Clinton presidency (US), 130–42
Cold War, 18–19, 57, 107–26, 198–203
    post-Cold War period, 127–53
counter-insurgency, 239–46, 248–9. *see also* counter-terrorism
    in Afghanistan, 166–7, 173–4
    in Kosovo conflict, 152
    in Vietnam, 22–7
counter-terrorism, 160–78
Croatian War. *see* Yugoslav Wars

East Timor independence movement, 261

Falklands conflict, 119–20
First World War, 61–3, 73–4

guerilla warfare, 17, 21–5, 133, 152. *see also* Vietnam War, Viet Cong

Hitler, Adolf, 7–8
Hussein, Sadaam, 108, 141

International Institute for Strategic Studies (IISS), 44–5, 51–3, 96–7, 217–33
international relations. *see* strategic studies

International Security Assistance
  Force (ISAF). *see* NATO
Iraq Wars, 141–2, 164–5, 235–49,
  262–3
  Australian military presence,
    87–8
  official history, 88–9

Kissinger, Henry, 25, 198
Korean War, 66, 68–71, 77–80
Kosovo conflict. *see* Yugoslav Wars

military history, 179–96. *see also*
  war historiography
MOOTWs (Military Operations
  Other Than War), 147–53.
  see also peacekeeping

national security policy, 44, 53–6,
  252–8, 265–83
NATO, 135–41, 143–6, 155–78
  International Security
    Assistance Force (ISAF),
    157–76
Nazism in Germany, 1–4, 7–10
nuclear weapons, 43–4, 197–217
  anti-nuclear movement, 119–20,
    205–16
  Canberra Commission on the
    Elimination of Nuclear
    Weapons, 43–4, 205–12
  Cold War, 198–203
  Joint Australia–Japan
    International Commission on
    Nuclear Non-proliferation
    and Disarmament, 212–14
  mutually assured destruction
    (MAD), 200
  nuclear deterrence, 43, 199–201,
    207
  nuclear Non-Proliferation Treaty
    (NPT), 201–3, 209–16
  post-Cold War, 203–5
  Tokyo Forum on Facing Nuclear
    Dangers, 209–12

O'Neill, Robert (Bob) (b. 1936)
  anti-nuclear strategist, 197–216
  author, 34–5, 40–1, 286–7
  bibliography
    *Australia in the Korean
      War 1950–53,
      Volume I: Strategy and
      Diplomacy*, 41
    *Australia in the Korean War
      1950–53, Volume II:
      Combat Operations*, 41
    *Australia's Defence Resources:
      a Compendium of Data*, 54
    *The Conduct of East–West
      Relations in the 1980s*, 201
    *Controlling Australia's
      Threat Environment: a
      Methodology for Planning
      Australia's Defence Force
      Development*, 55
    *The Defence of Australia:
      Fundamental New
      Aspects*, 43, 56
    *The Future of Tactical Air
      Power in the Defence of
      Australia*, 54
    *General Giap: Politician and
      Strategist*, 40–2
    *The German Army and the
      Nazi Party, 1933–1939*,
      3–7, 10, 40
    Hedley Bull on Arms Control,
      201
    *New Directions in Strategic
      Thinking*, 42, 55, 201
    *Options for an Australian
      Defence Technological
      Strategy*, 55

Power and Policy: Doctrine, the Alliance and Arms Control, 201
Problems of Mobilisation in Defence of Australia, 55
Rethinking Australia's Defence, 55
The Strategic Environment in the 1980s, 42
The Strategic Nuclear Balance: An Australian Perspective, 42, 201
Strategy and Defence: Australian Essays, 55
Vietnam Task, 34–5, 40, 236–9, 285–6
Chairman of the Australian Strategic Policy Institute (ASPI), 251–63
Chichele Professor of the History of War, Oxford, 45–6, 144–5, 206, 239–43
Director of International Institute for Strategic Studies (IISS), 44–5, 51–3, 96–7, 217–33
Head of Strategic and Defence Studies Centre (SDSC), 40–2, 49–50, 53–4, 56–8
official Australian war historian, 41, 61–71, 73–89
as PhD supervisor, 41–2, 45–6
research, 3–13
strategist, 285–7
student at Oxford, 1, 3–4, 6–13
in Vietnam, 15–18, 25–7, 31–8, 236–9, 285–6
Operation Desert Storm, 127–53

peacekeeping, 83–7, 149–52, 178
Pine Gap, 49
policy advice, 252–63

political–military relations, 1–13, 67, 79, 150, 244–5
Powell doctrine, 132–3

Reagan doctrine, 217–29
research, 1–13, 41–3, 91–105, 107–26
Responsibility to Protect (R2P) doctrine, 141–2

Second World War, 3–13, 74–5, 149
September 11 Attacks (9/11), 87, 159–63, 260
post-9/11 era, 146–53
Soviet Union, 50–2, 57
strategic studies, 39–46, 68–70, 91–105, 107–26, 265–83
etymology, 179–96
international relations, 100, 121–3, 155–6, 252, 270–1
science in warfare, 183–5, 190–5
strategy vs tactics, 190–5
war studies in academia, 107–11
warfare as art, 185–95

think tanks, 100, 111–14, 217, 265–83. *see also* Australian Strategic Policy Institute (ASPI)
contribution, 279–83
Lowy Institute for International Policy, 276–7
peace studies, 116–17
in policy development, 269–71, 281
RAND, 97–8, 113–4
Royal United Services Institute (RSUI), 112
United States Studies Centre, 277–9

United States (US). *see* entries under America
USSR. *see* Soviet Union

Vietnam War, 15–30, 31–8, 236–9
   American military presence, 20–2, 27–9, 240–1
   Australian military presence, 15–17, 19–29, 30, 31–8
   conscription, 23
   differences in American and Australian military approach, 26–30, 36
   land mines, 24
   official history, 80–2
   Viet Cong, 17, 25–7

war historiography, 1–3, 34–5, 40–1, 61–71, 73–89, 285–6
   Bean, Charles, 61–5, 73–5
   Long, Gavin, 64–5
   official histories
      Afghanistan War, 88–9
      Iraq Wars, 88–9
      Korean War, 41, 66–71, 76–80
      Vietnam War, 80–2
   peacekeeping, 83–7
Weimar Republic, 2–7, 11–12
World War I. *see* First World War
World War II. *see* Second World War

Yugoslav Wars, 129, 133–41, 151–3
   Kosovo conflict, 138–40, 151–3
   Milosevic, Slobodan, 108, 128, 138–40

www.ingramcontent.com/pod-product-compliance
Lightning Source LLC
Chambersburg PA
CBHW041924220426
43670CB00032B/2952